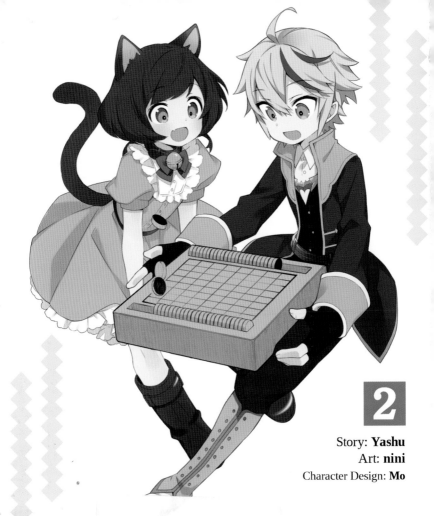

2

Story: **Yashu**
Art: **nini**
Character Design: **Mo**

CHRON… ARISTOCRAT REBORN IN ANOTHER WORLD

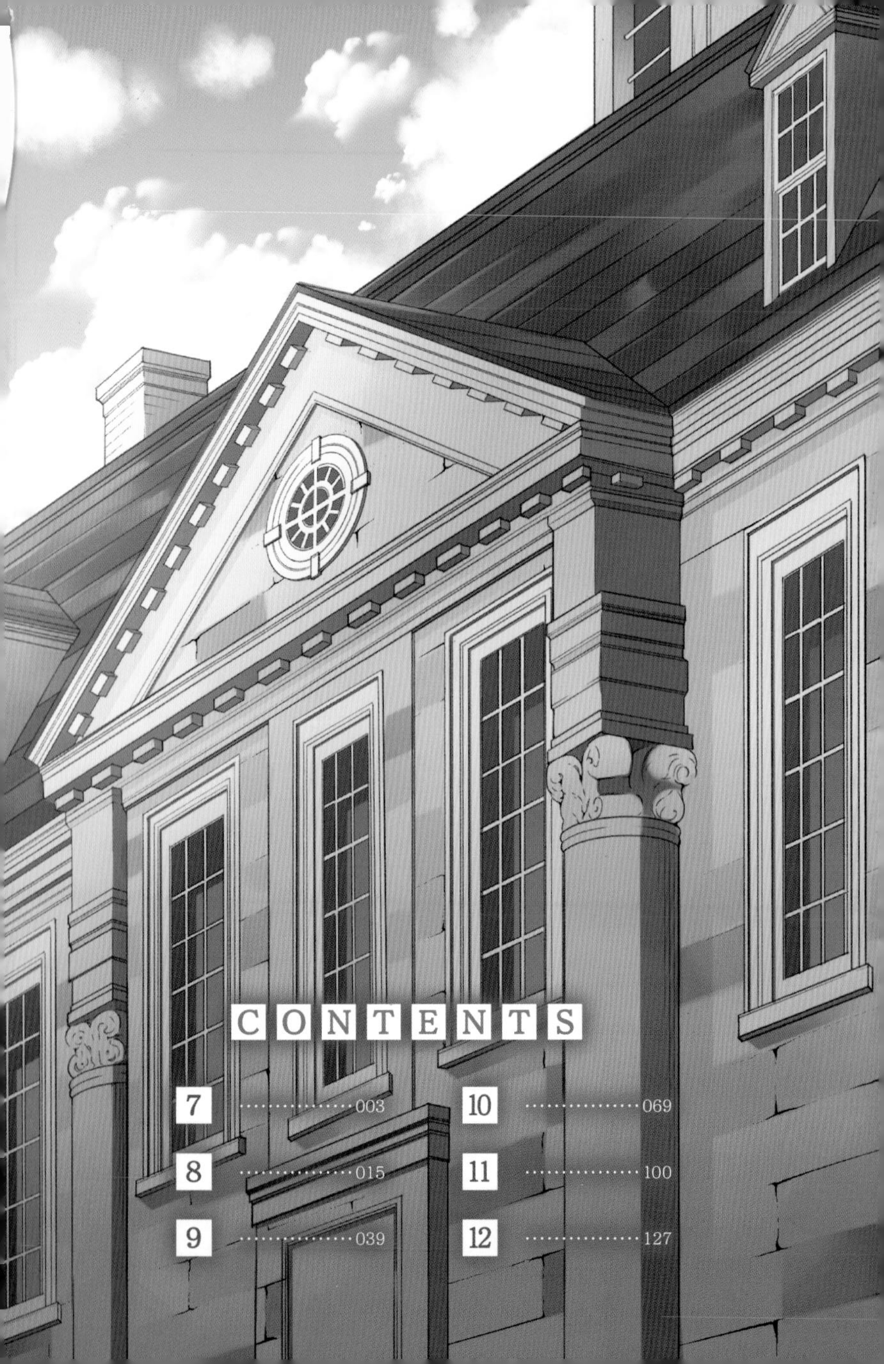

CONTENTS

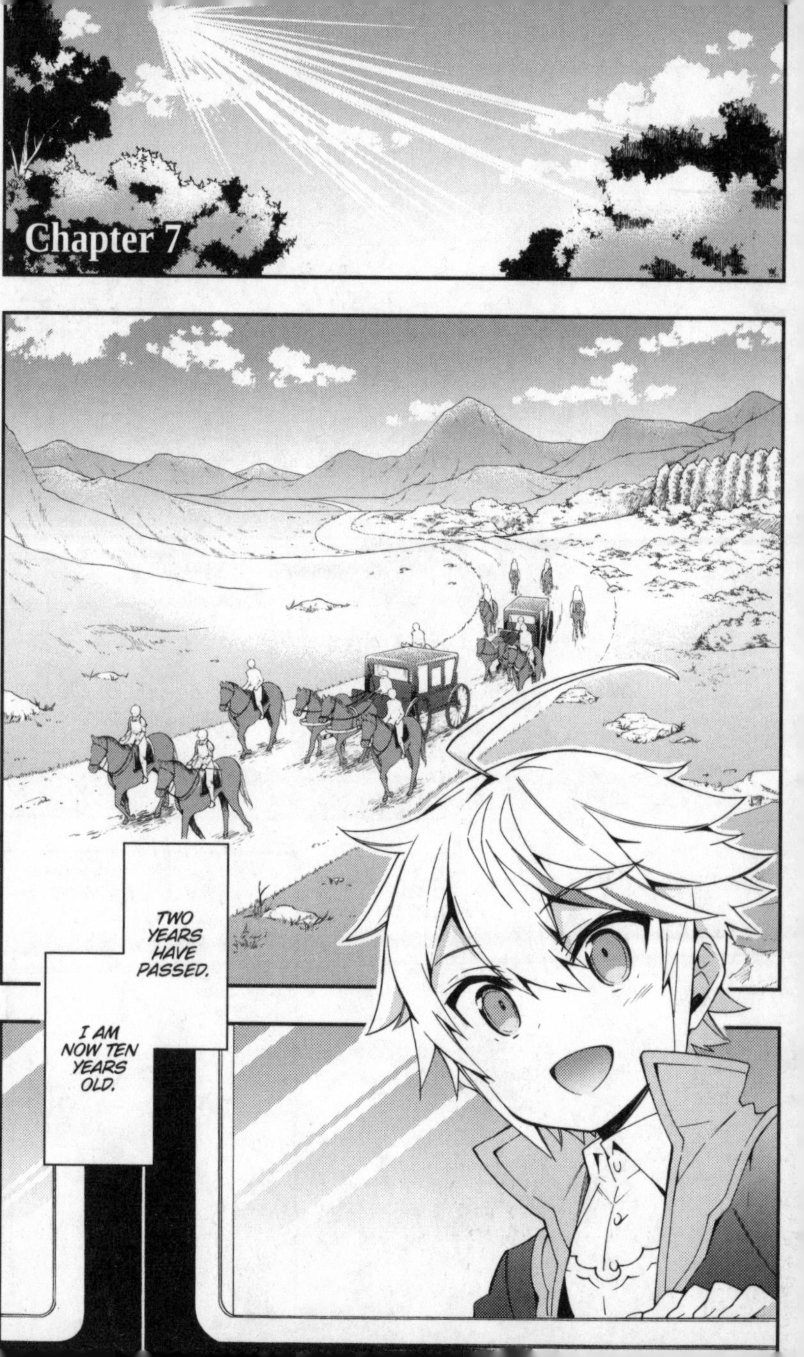
Chapter 7
TWO YEARS HAVE PASSED.
I AM NOW TEN YEARS OLD.

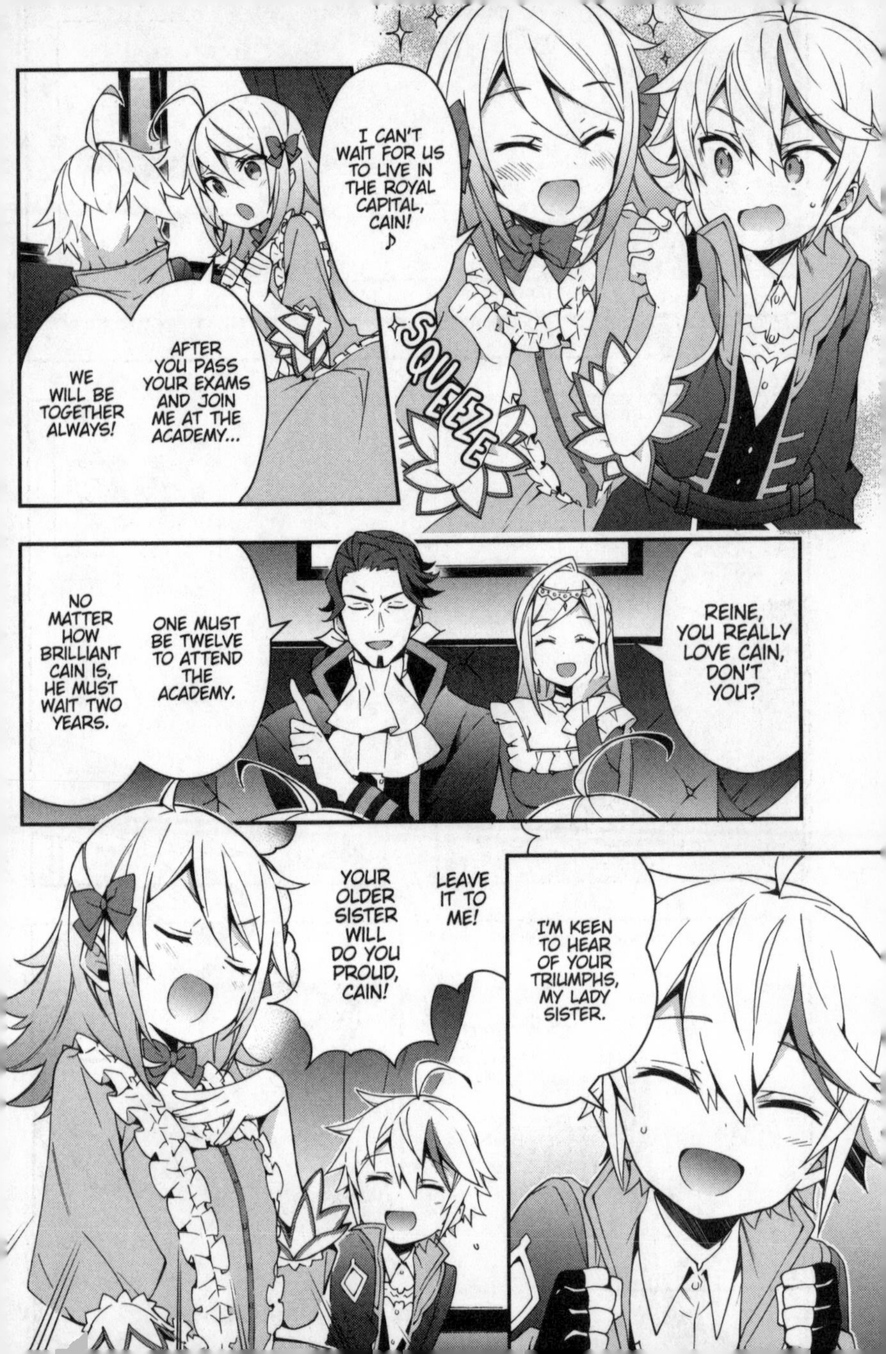
I CAN'T WAIT FOR US TO LIVE IN THE ROYAL CAPITAL, CAIN! ♪
SQUEEZE
AFTER YOU PASS YOUR EXAMS AND JOIN ME AT THE ACADEMY...
WE WILL BE TOGETHER ALWAYS!
REINE, YOU REALLY LOVE CAIN, DON'T YOU?
ONE MUST BE TWELVE TO ATTEND THE ACADEMY.
NO MATTER HOW BRILLIANT CAIN IS, HE MUST WAIT TWO YEARS.
I'M KEEN TO HEAR OF YOUR TRIUMPHS, MY LADY SISTER.
LEAVE IT TO ME!
YOUR OLDER SISTER WILL DO YOU PROUD, CAIN!

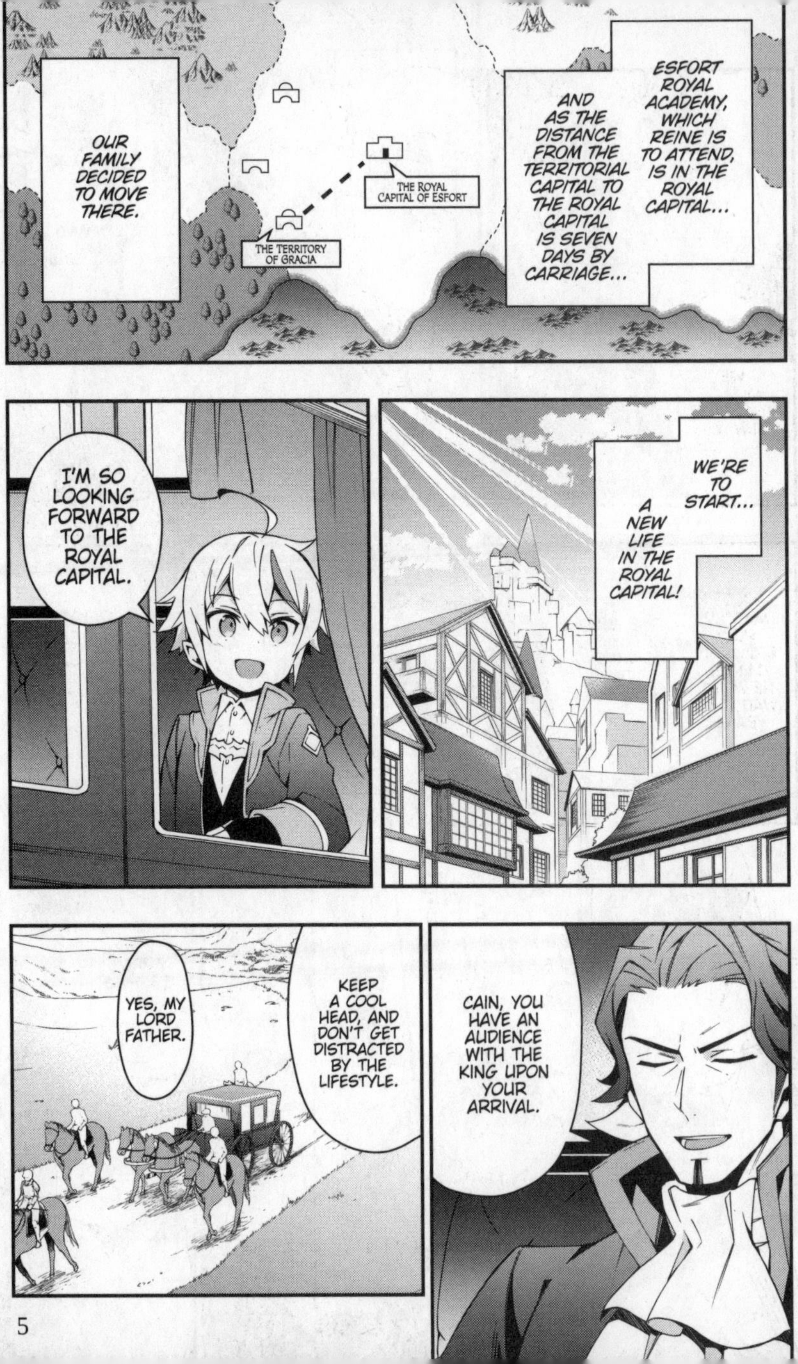
ESFORT ROYAL ACADEMY, WHICH REINE IS TO ATTEND, IS IN THE ROYAL CAPITAL...
AND AS THE DISTANCE FROM THE TERRITORIAL CAPITAL TO THE ROYAL CAPITAL IS SEVEN DAYS BY CARRIAGE...
THE ROYAL CAPITAL OF ESFORT
THE TERRITORY OF GRACIA
OUR FAMILY DECIDED TO MOVE THERE.
WE'RE TO START...
A NEW LIFE IN THE ROYAL CAPITAL!
I'M SO LOOKING FORWARD TO THE ROYAL CAPITAL.
CAIN, YOU HAVE AN AUDIENCE WITH THE KING UPON YOUR ARRIVAL.
KEEP A COOL HEAD, AND DON'T GET DISTRACTED BY THE LIFESTYLE.
YES, MY LORD FATHER.

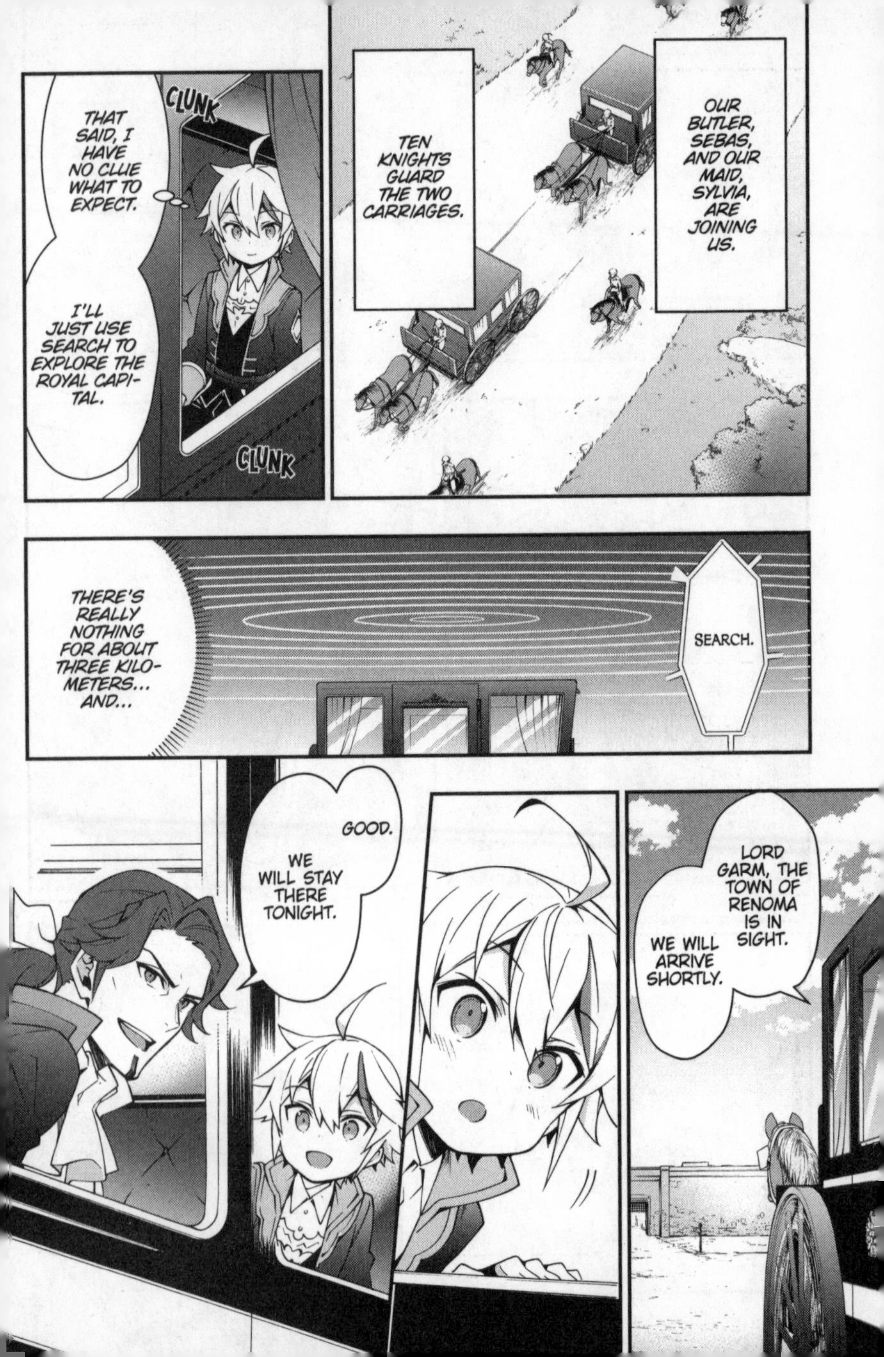
OUR BUTLER, SEBAS, AND OUR MAID, SYLVIA, ARE JOINING US.
TEN KNIGHTS GUARD THE TWO CARRIAGES.
CLUNK
THAT SAID, I HAVE NO CLUE WHAT TO EXPECT.
I'LL JUST USE SEARCH TO EXPLORE THE ROYAL CAPITAL.
CLUNK
SEARCH.
THERE'S REALLY NOTHING FOR ABOUT THREE KILOMETERS... AND...
LORD GARM, THE TOWN OF RENOMA IS IN SIGHT.
WE WILL ARRIVE SHORTLY.
GOOD.
WE WILL STAY THERE TONIGHT.

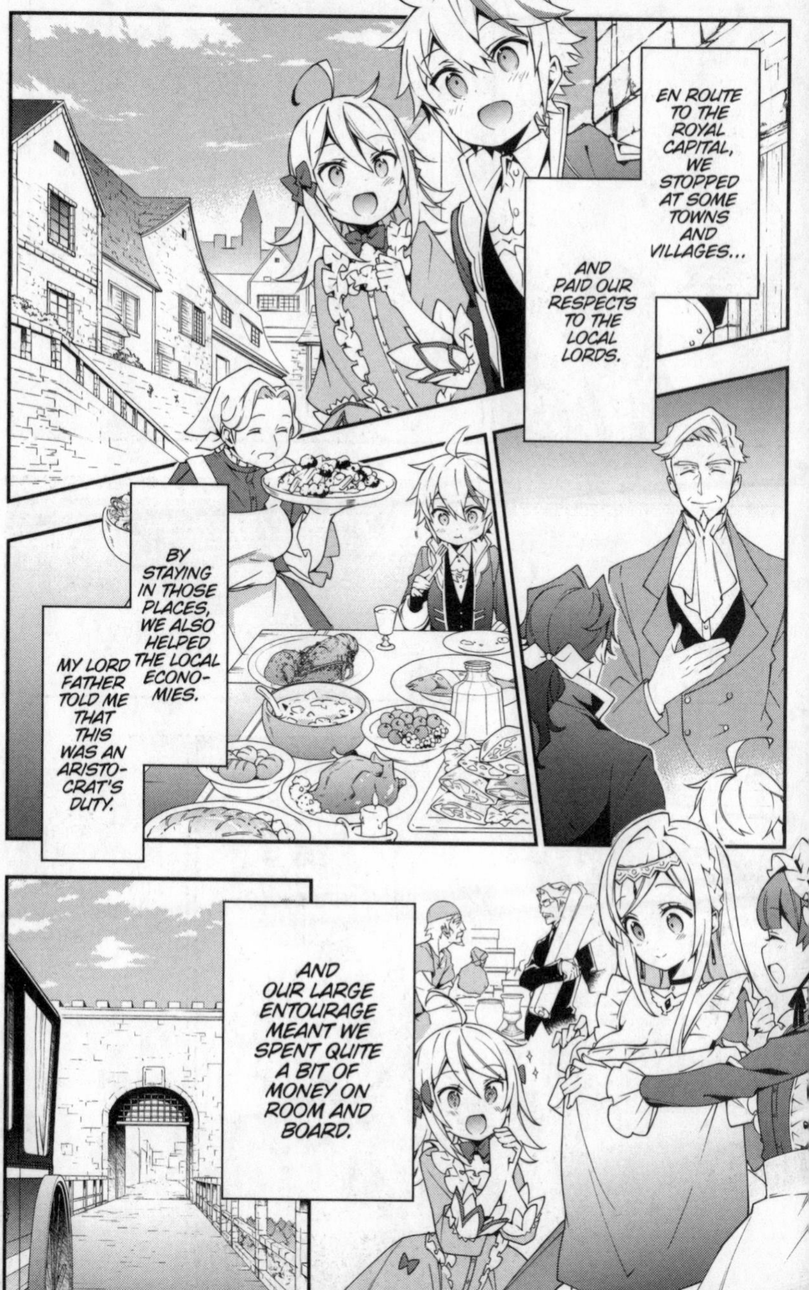
EN ROUTE TO THE ROYAL CAPITAL, WE STOPPED AT SOME TOWNS AND VILLAGES...
AND PAID OUR RESPECTS TO THE LOCAL LORDS.
BY STAYING IN THOSE PLACES, WE ALSO HELPED THE LOCAL ECONOMIES.
MY LORD FATHER TOLD ME THAT THIS WAS AN ARISTOCRAT'S DUTY.
AND OUR LARGE ENTOURAGE MEANT WE SPENT QUITE A BIT OF MONEY ON ROOM AND BOARD.

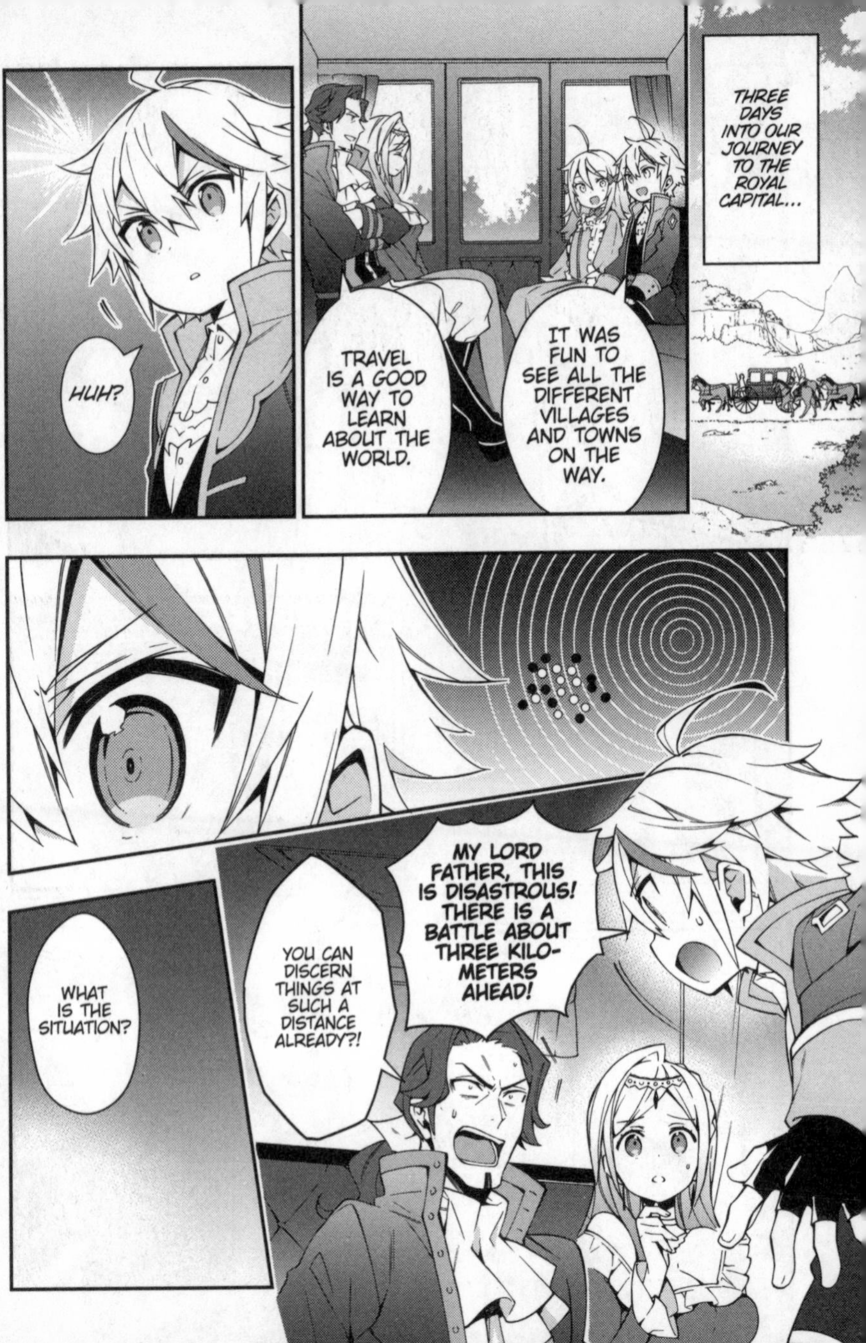
THREE DAYS INTO OUR JOURNEY TO THE ROYAL CAPITAL...
IT WAS FUN TO SEE ALL THE DIFFERENT VILLAGES AND TOWNS ON THE WAY.
TRAVEL IS A GOOD WAY TO LEARN ABOUT THE WORLD.
HUH?
MY LORD FATHER, THIS IS DISASTROUS! THERE IS A BATTLE ABOUT THREE KILO-METERS AHEAD!
YOU CAN DISCERN THINGS AT SUCH A DISTANCE ALREADY?!
WHAT IS THE SITUATION?

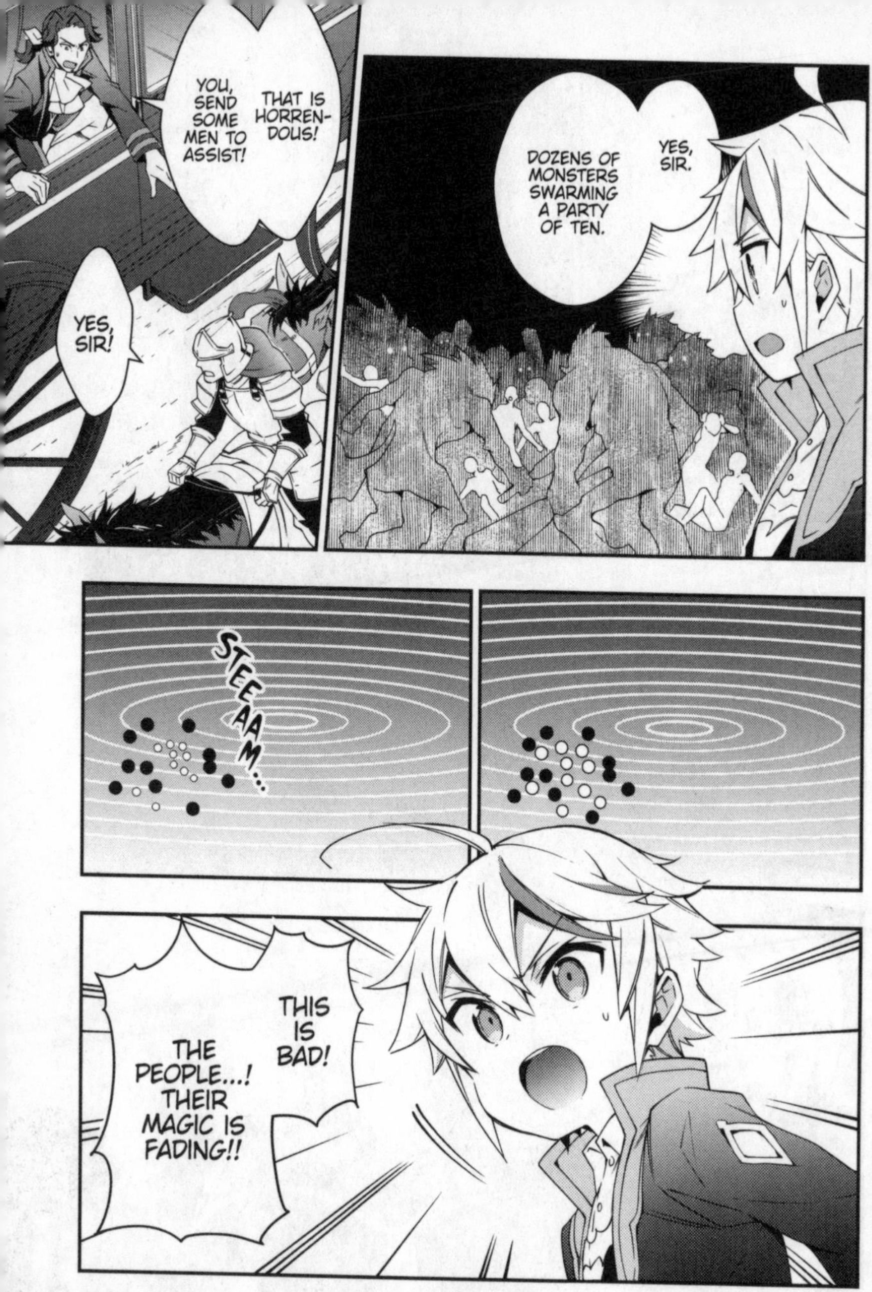
YES, SIR.
DOZENS OF MONSTERS SWARMING A PARTY OF TEN.
THAT IS HORREN-DOUS!
YOU, SEND SOME MEN TO ASSIST!
YES, SIR!
STEEAAAM..
THIS IS BAD!
THE PEOPLE...! THEIR MAGIC IS FADING!!

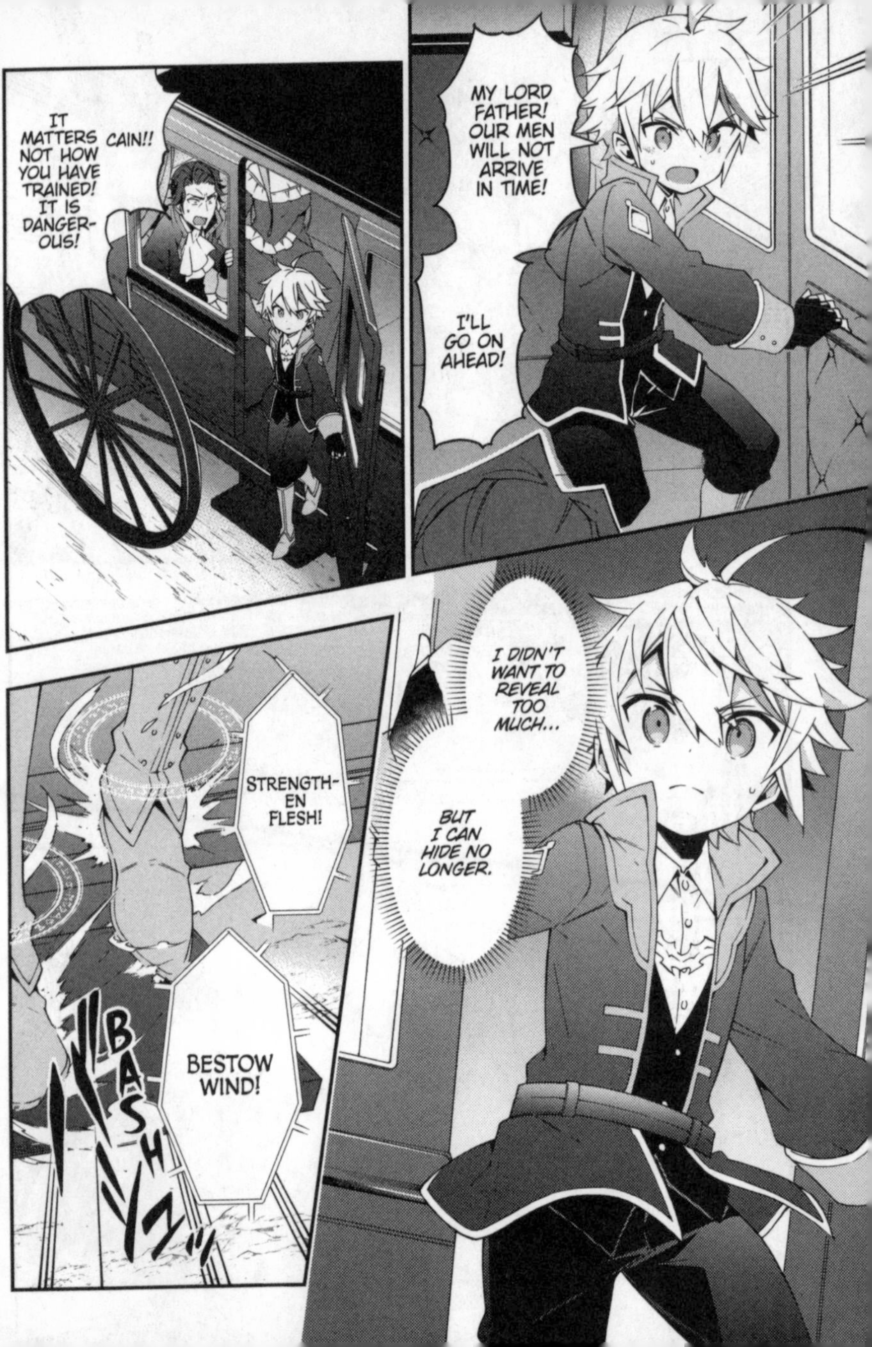
MY LORD FATHER! OUR MEN WILL NOT ARRIVE IN TIME!
I'LL GO ON AHEAD!
CAIN!!
IT MATTERS NOT HOW YOU HAVE TRAINED! IT IS DANGER-OUS!
I DIDN'T WANT TO REVEAL TOO MUCH...
BUT I CAN HIDE NO LONGER.
STRENGTH-EN FLESH!
BESTOW WIND!
BASH

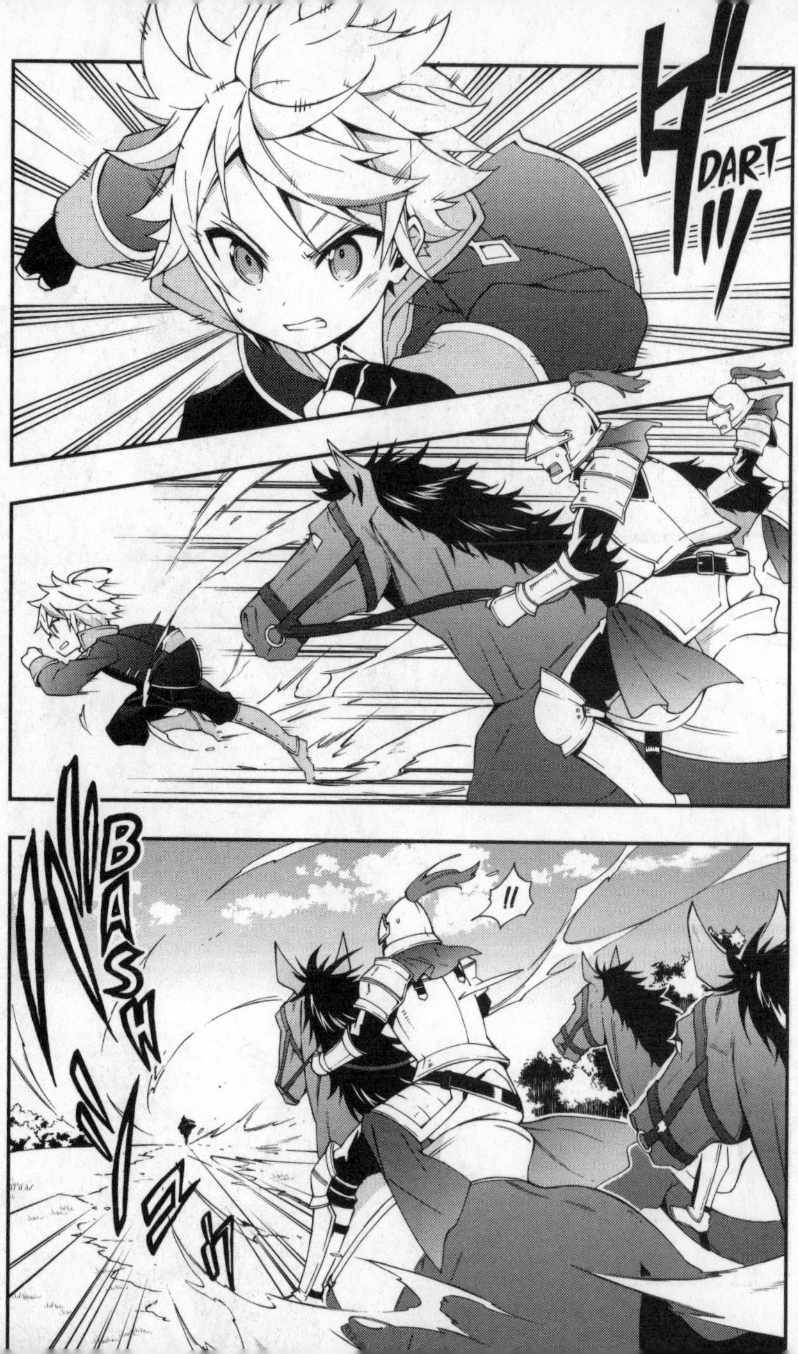
DART
!!
BASH

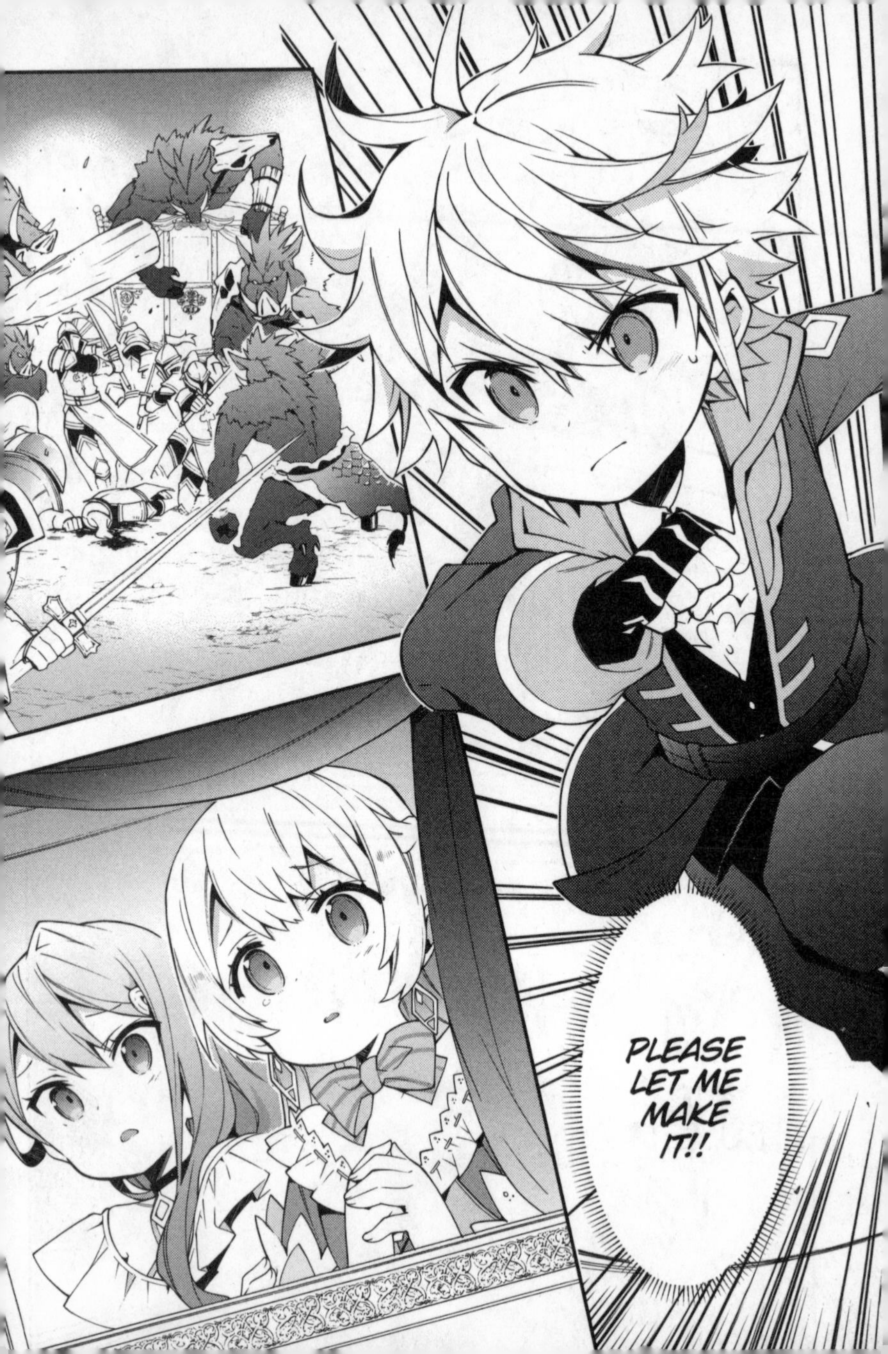
PLEASE LET ME MAKE IT!!

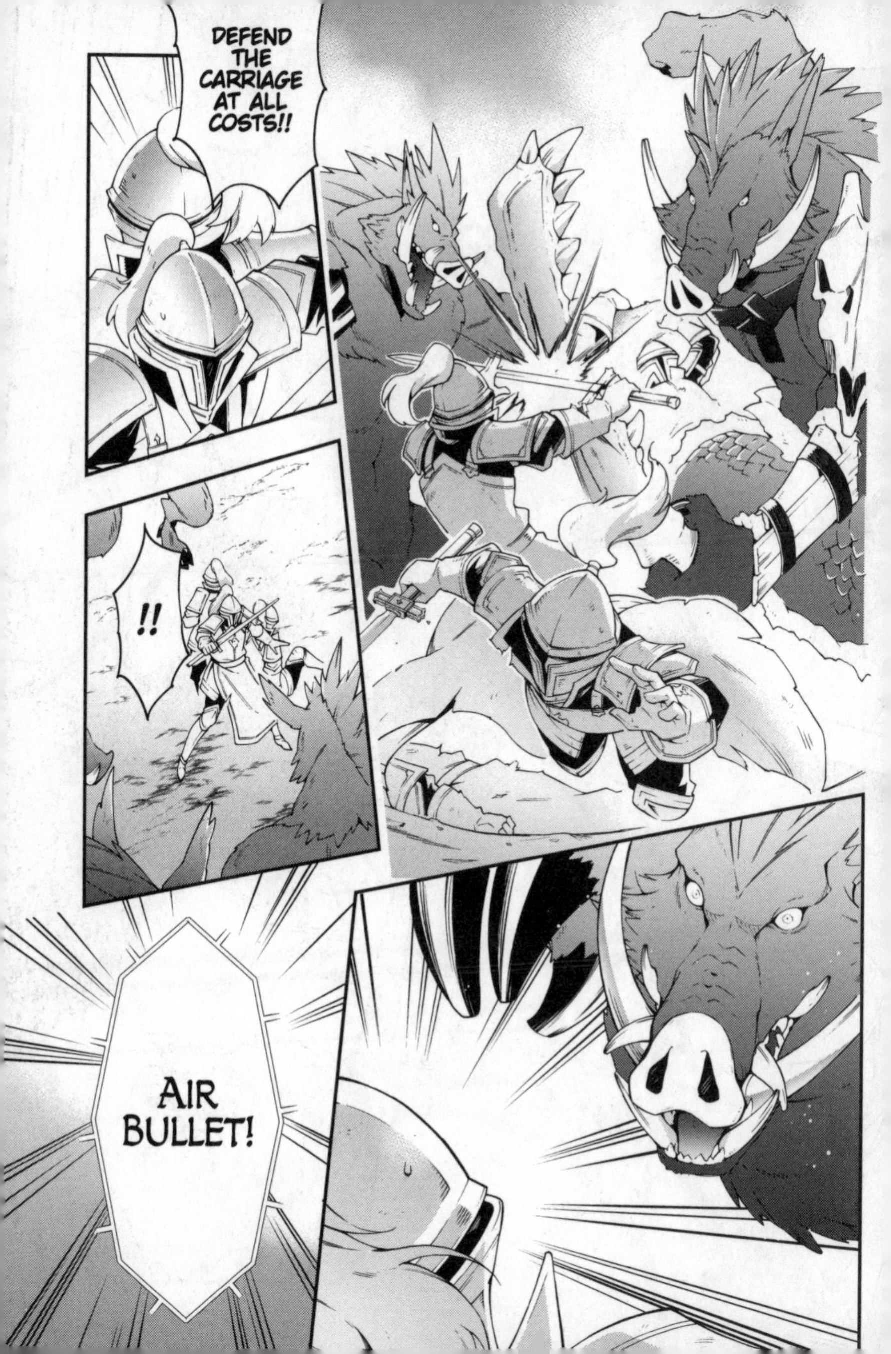
DEFEND THE CARRIAGE AT ALL COSTS!!
!!
AIR BULLET!

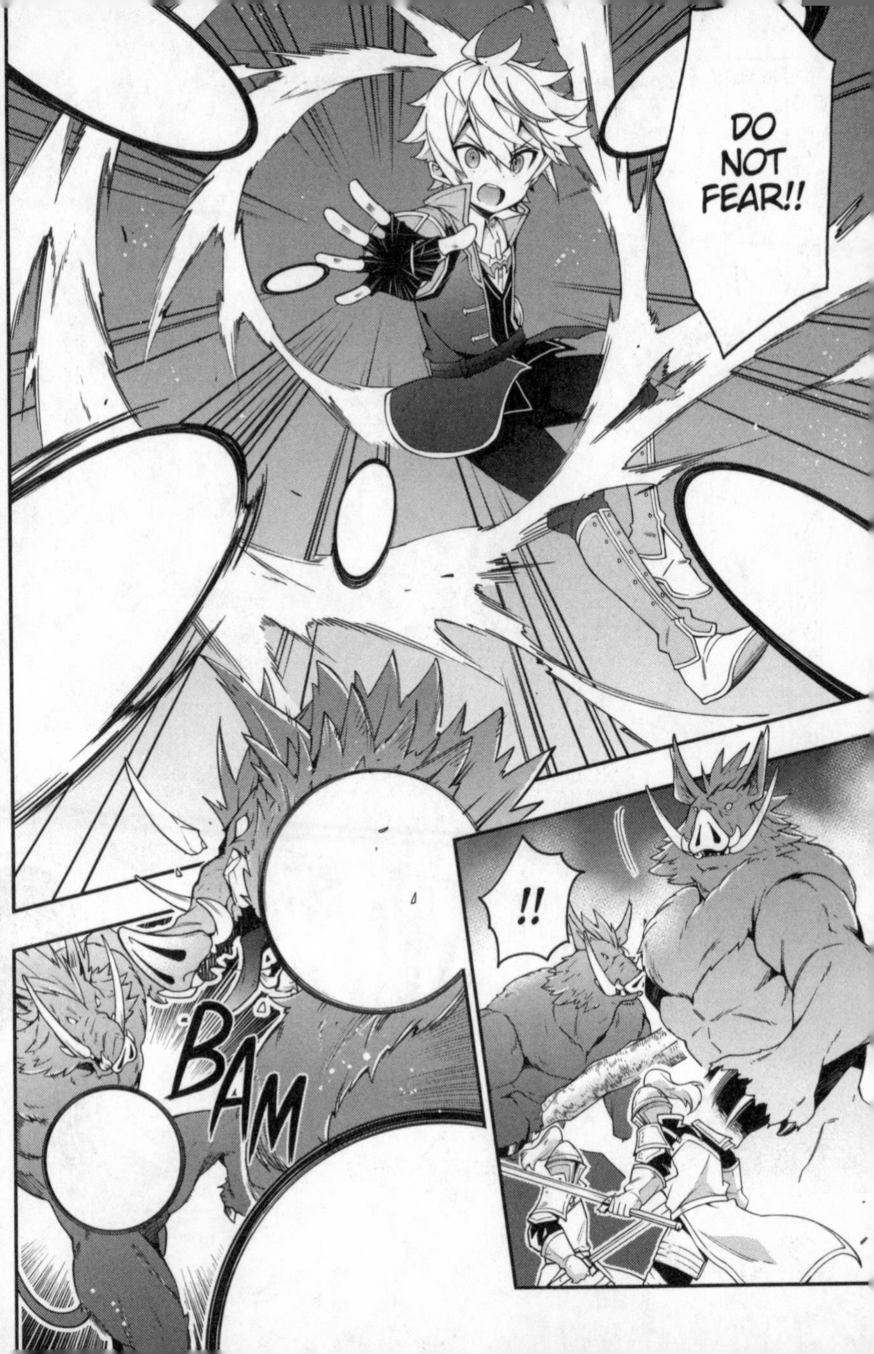
DO NOT FEAR!!
!!
BAM

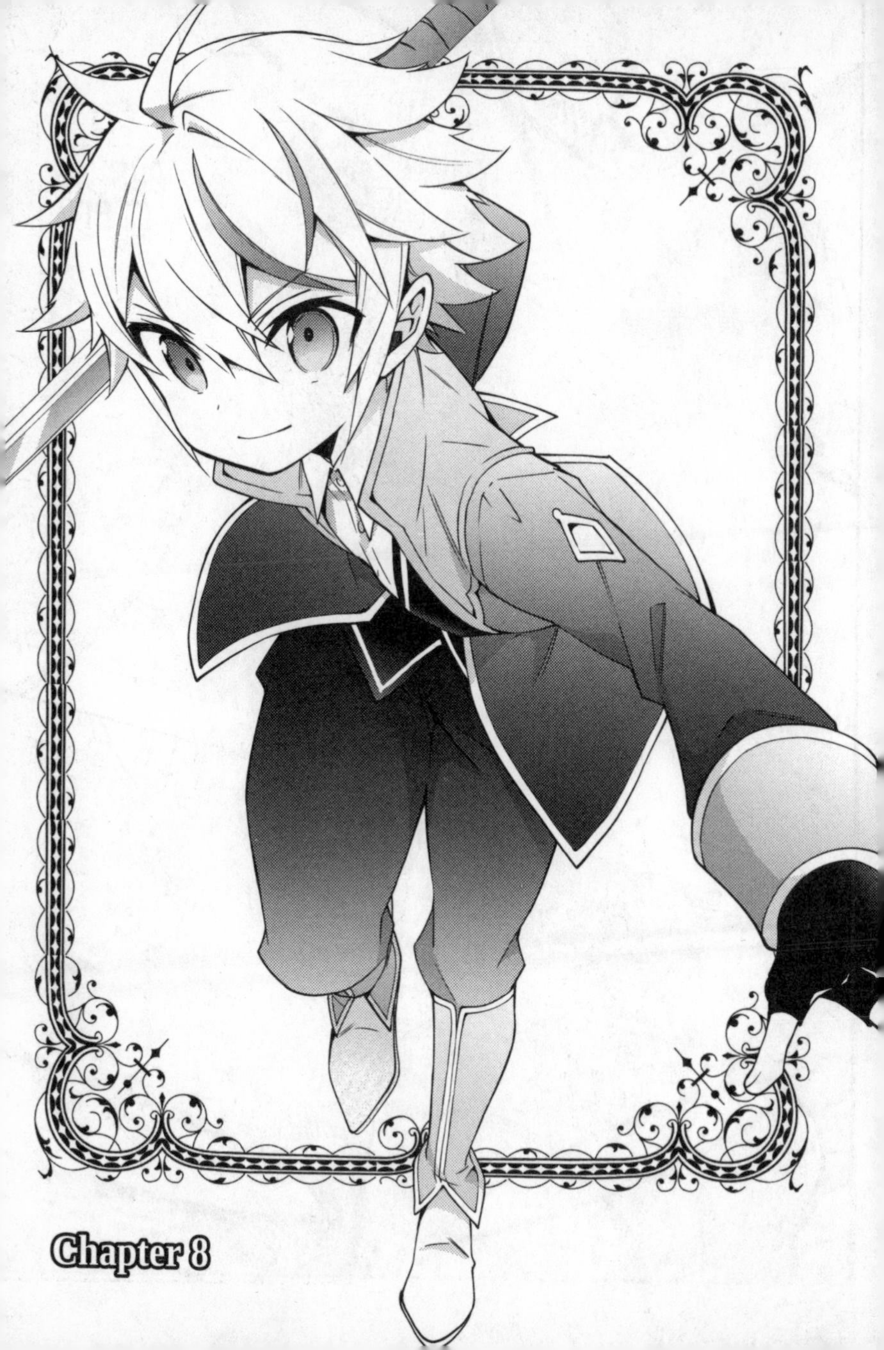

Chapter 8

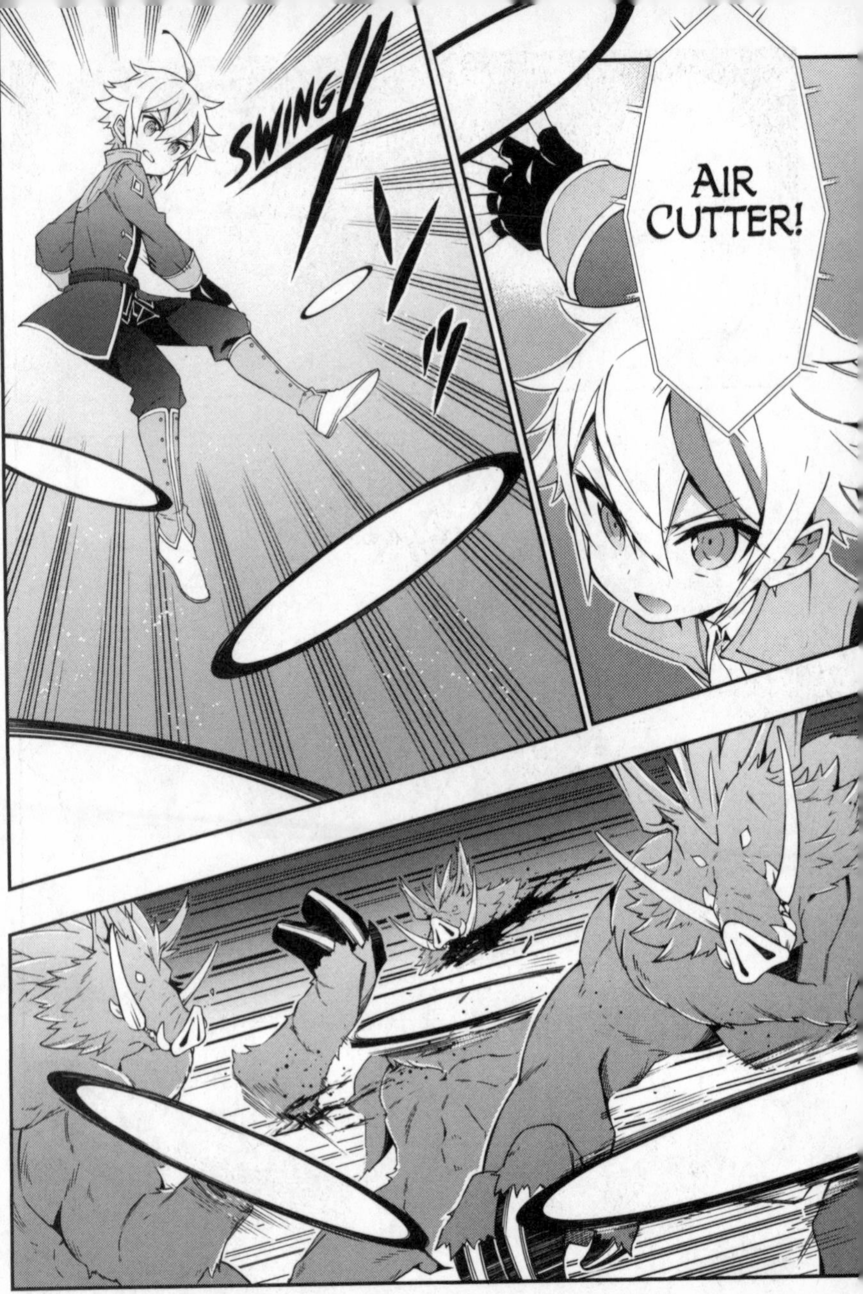
AIR CUTTER!
SWING

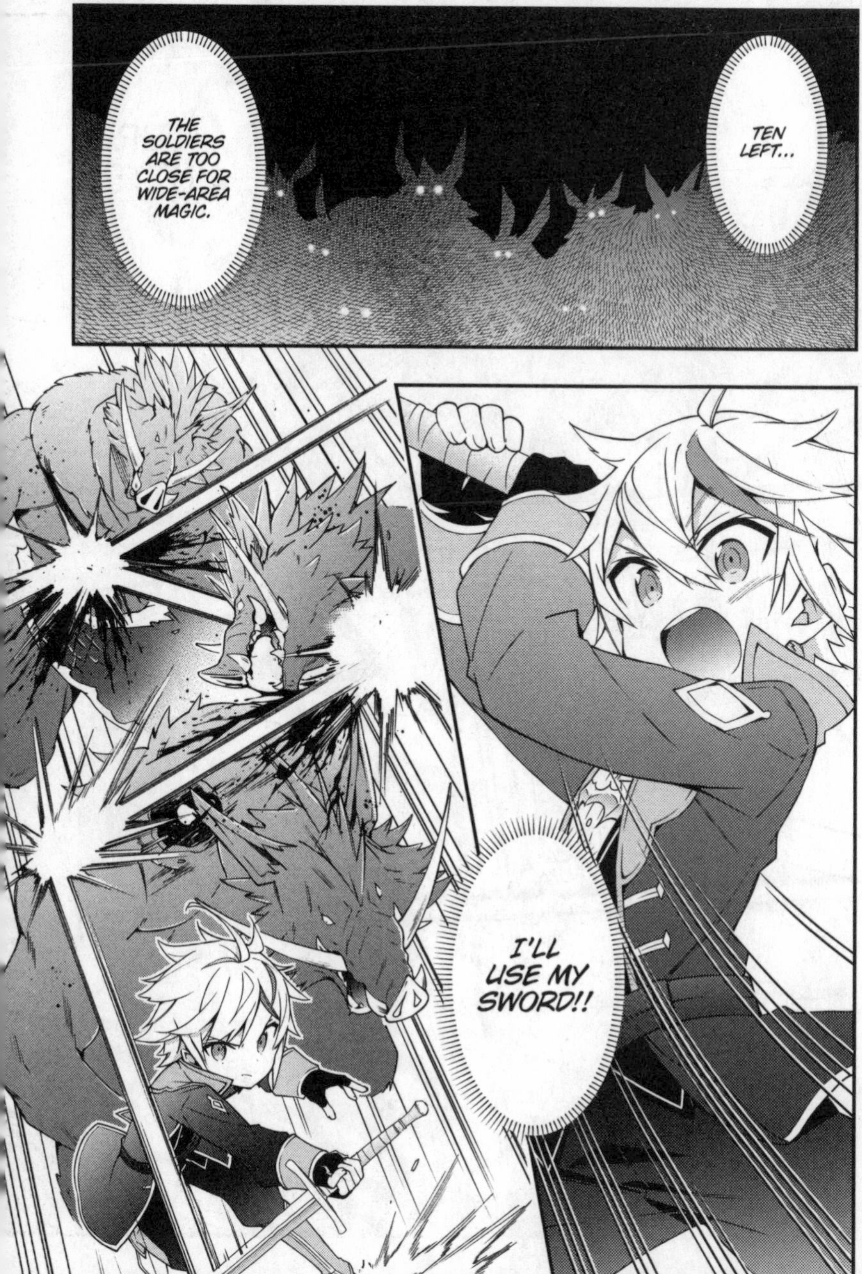
TEN LEFT...
THE SOLDIERS ARE TOO CLOSE FOR WIDE-AREA MAGIC.
I'LL USE MY SWORD!!

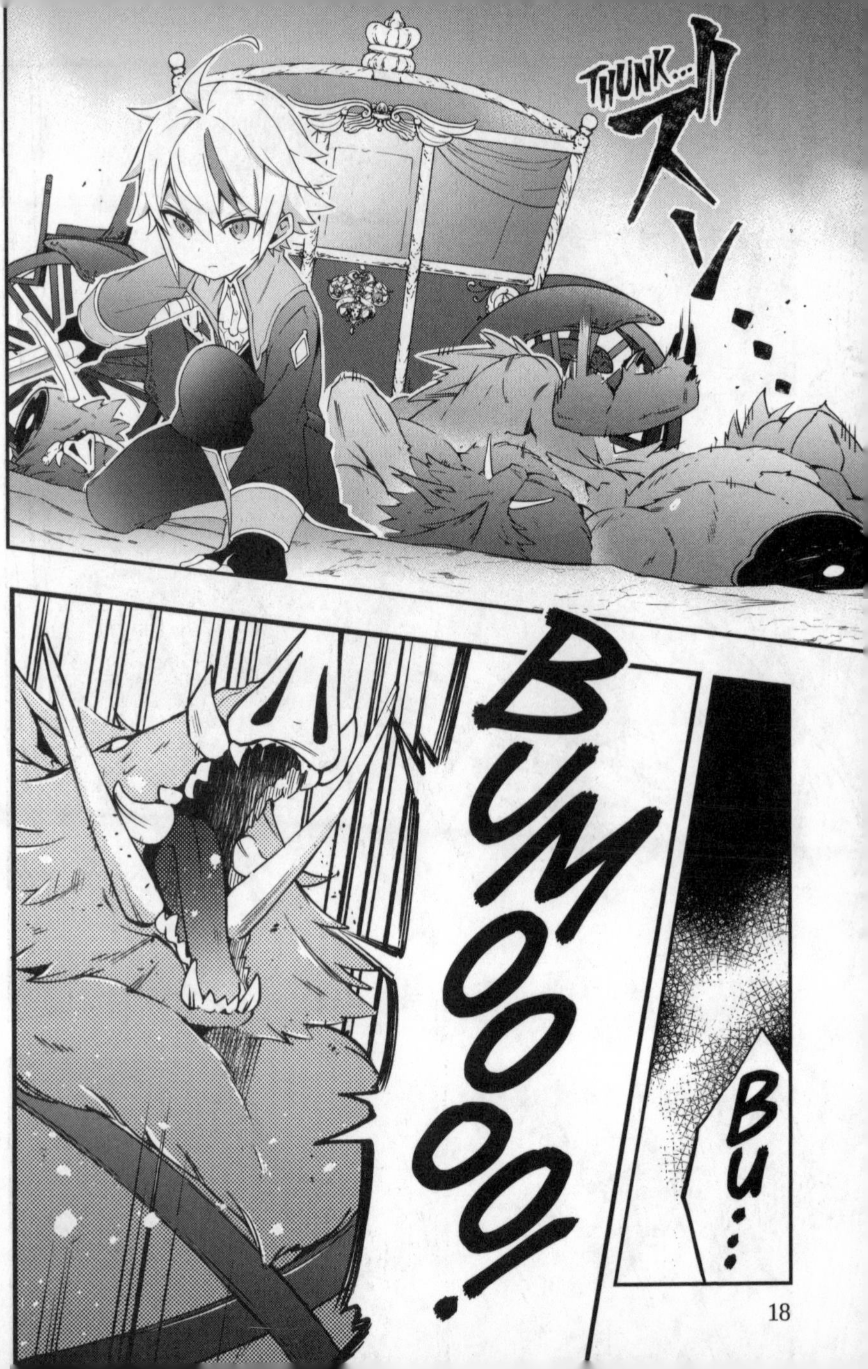
THUNK...
ズン…
BUMOOO!
BU...

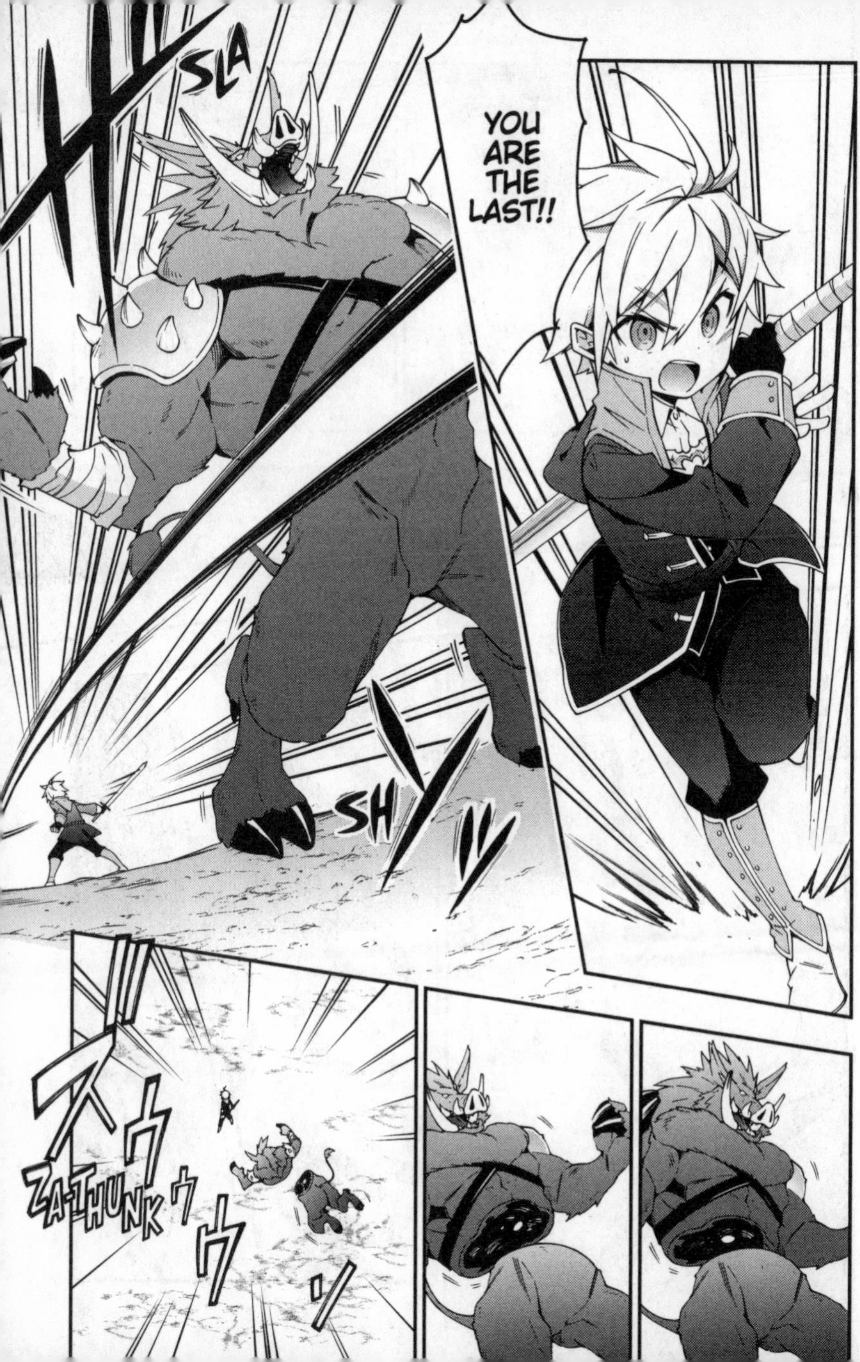
YOU ARE THE LAST!!
SLA
SH
ZA-THUNK

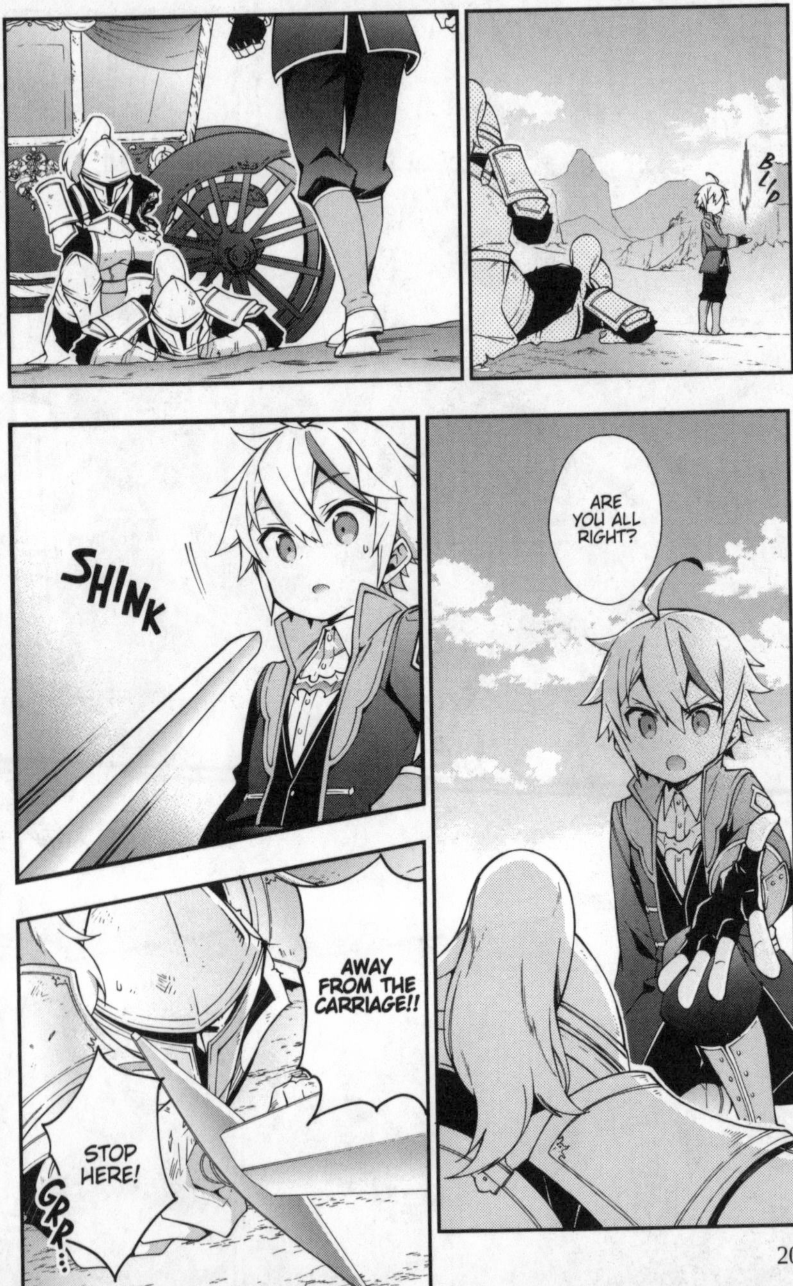
BLIP
ARE YOU ALL RIGHT?
SHINK
AWAY FROM THE CARRIAGE!!
STOP HERE!
GRR...

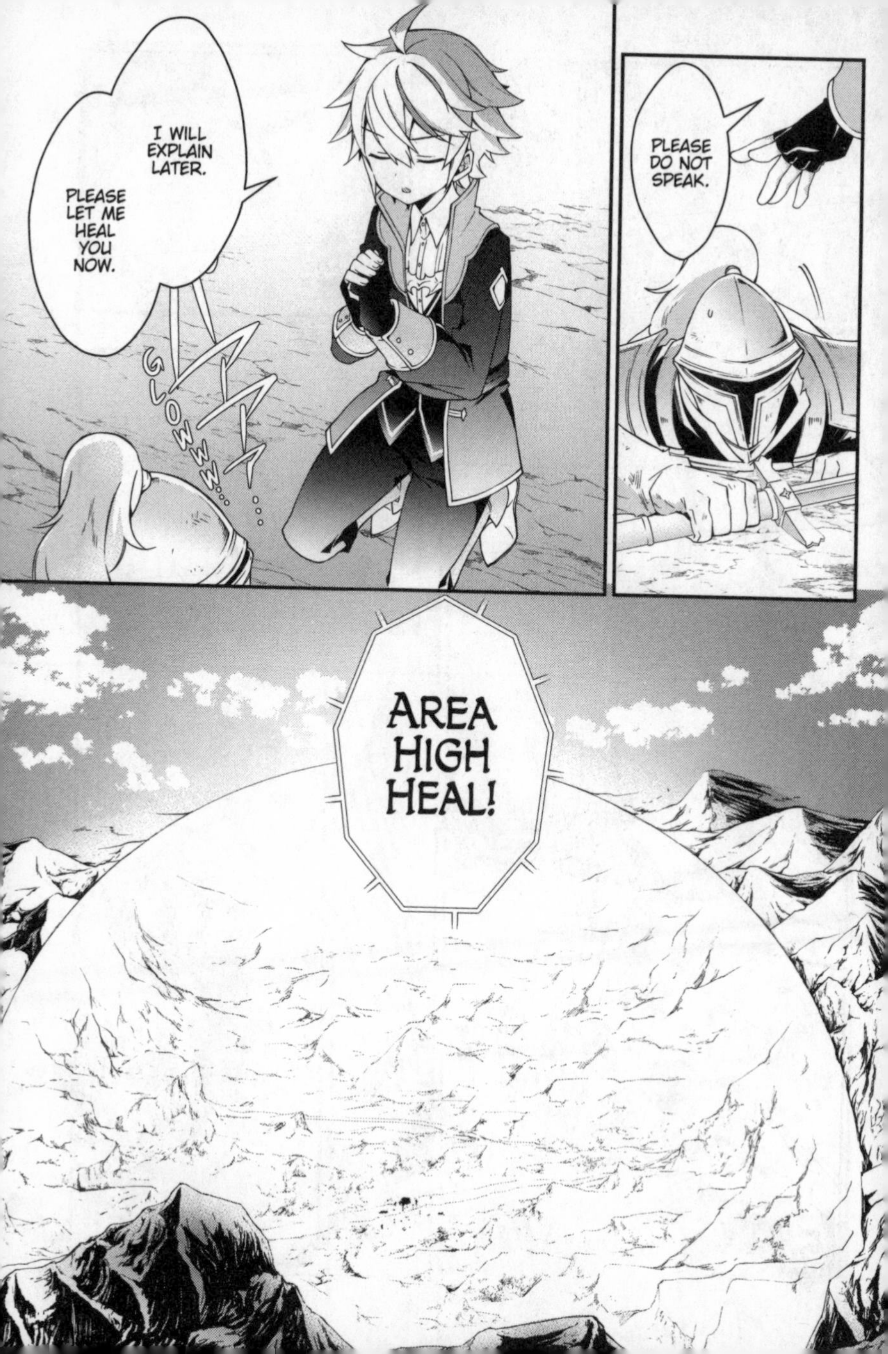
PLEASE DO NOT SPEAK.
I WILL EXPLAIN LATER.
PLEASE LET ME HEAL YOU NOW.
GLOWWW...
AREA HIGH HEAL!

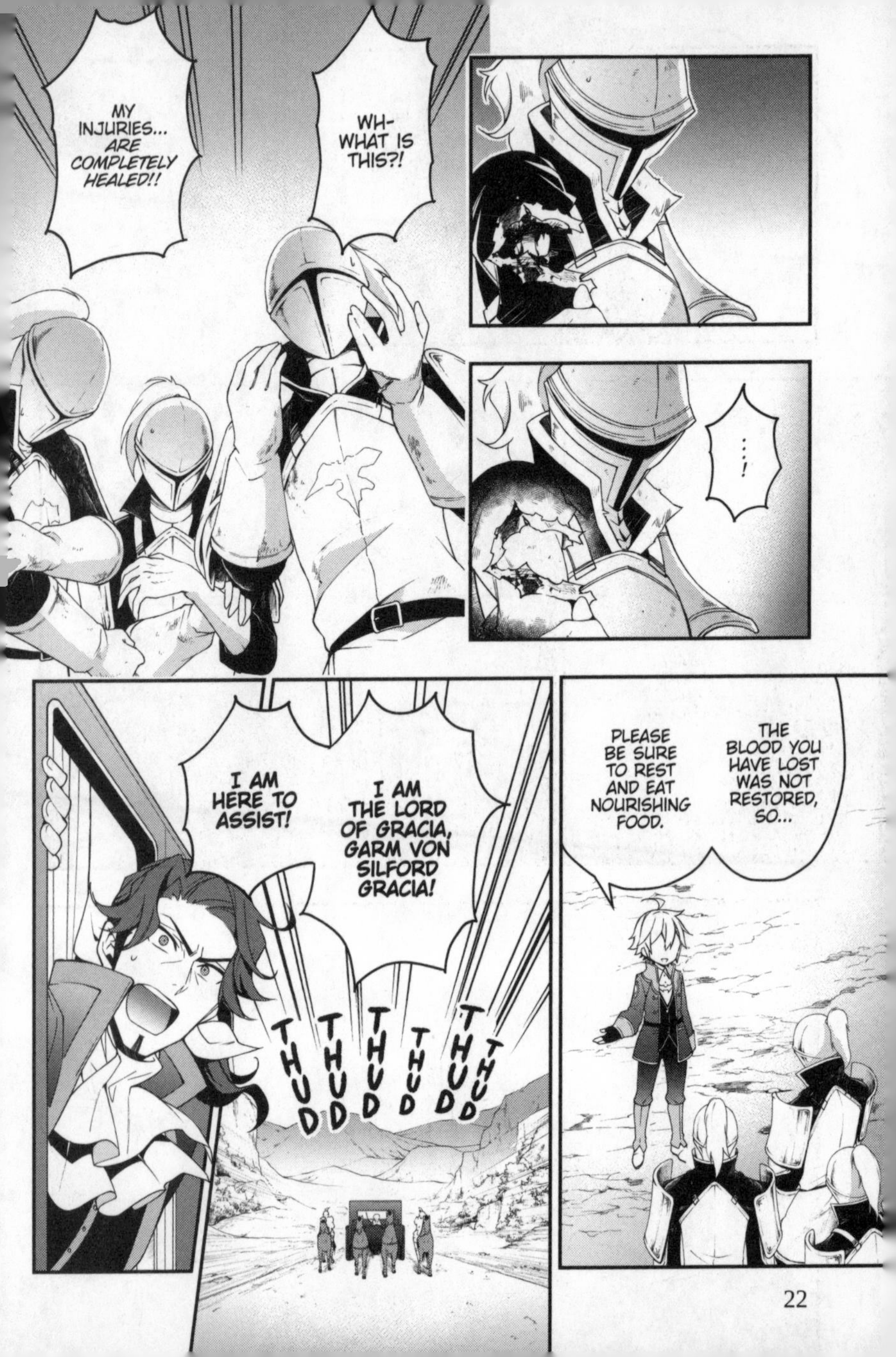
...!
WH-
WHAT IS
THIS?!
MY
INJURIES...
ARE
COMPLETELY
HEALED!!
THE
BLOOD YOU
HAVE LOST
WAS NOT
RESTORED,
SO...
PLEASE
BE SURE
TO REST
AND EAT
NOURISHING
FOOD.
I AM
THE LORD
OF GRACIA,
GARM VON
SILFORD
GRACIA!
I AM
HERE TO
ASSIST!
THUD THUD THUD THUD THUD THUD

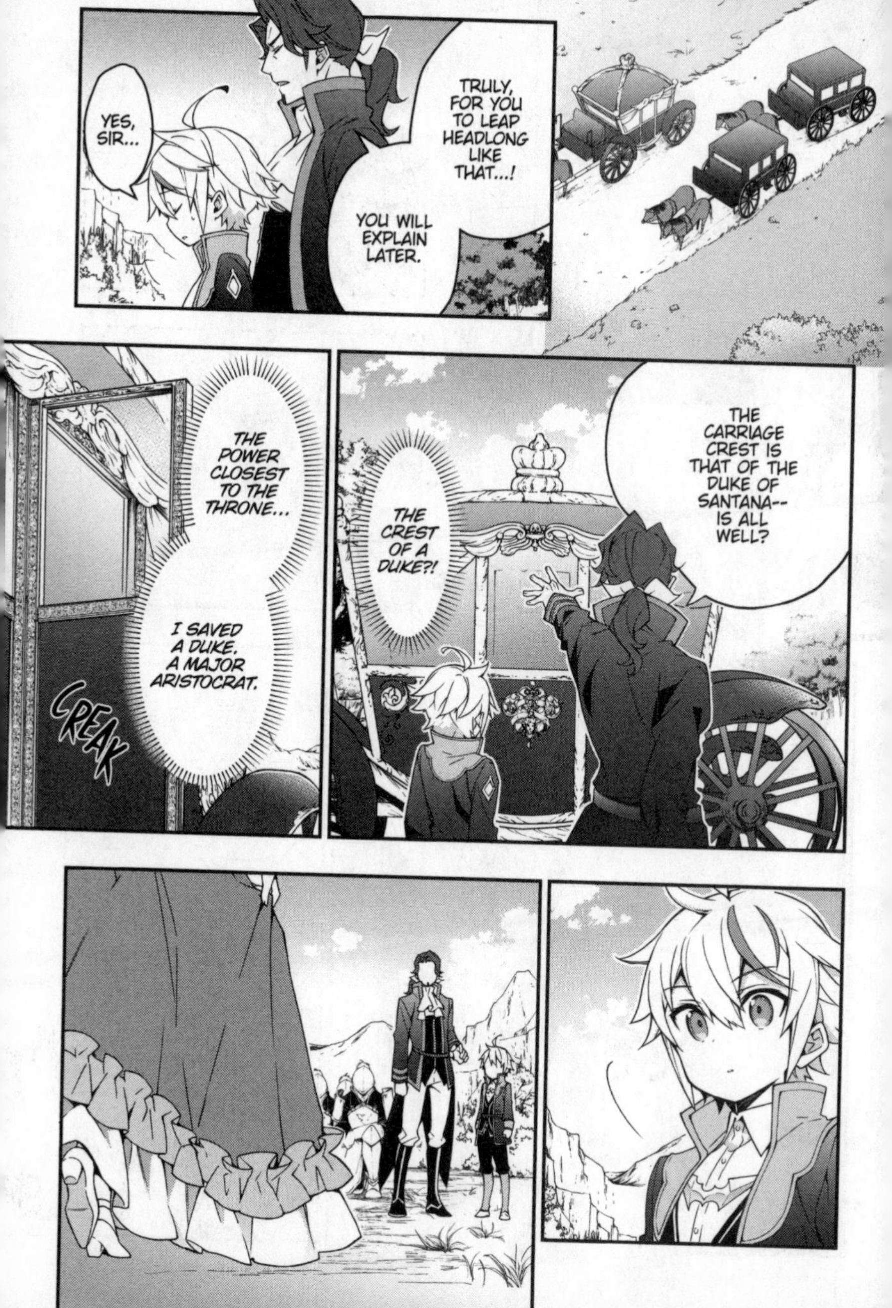
TRULY, FOR YOU TO LEAP HEADLONG LIKE THAT...!
YOU WILL EXPLAIN LATER.
YES, SIR...
THE CARRIAGE CREST IS THAT OF THE DUKE OF SANTANA-- IS ALL WELL?
THE CREST OF A DUKE?!
THE POWER CLOSEST TO THE THRONE...
I SAVED A DUKE. A MAJOR ARISTOCRAT.
CREAK

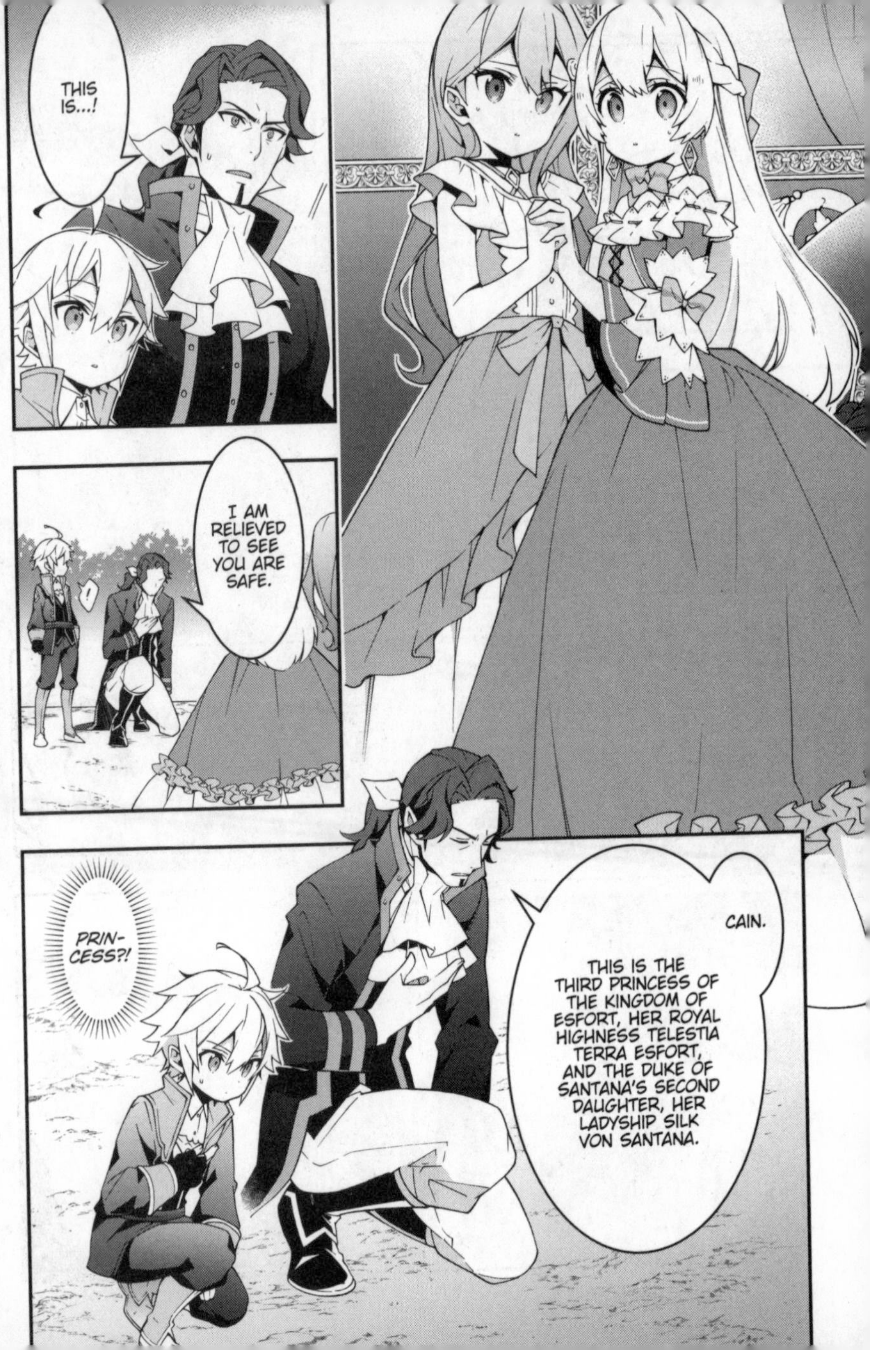
THIS IS...!
I AM RELIEVED TO SEE YOU ARE SAFE.
!
CAIN.
THIS IS THE THIRD PRINCESS OF THE KINGDOM OF ESFORT, HER ROYAL HIGHNESS TELESTIA TERRA ESFORT, AND THE DUKE OF SANTANA'S SECOND DAUGHTER, HER LADYSHIP SILK VON SANTANA.
PRIN-CESS?!

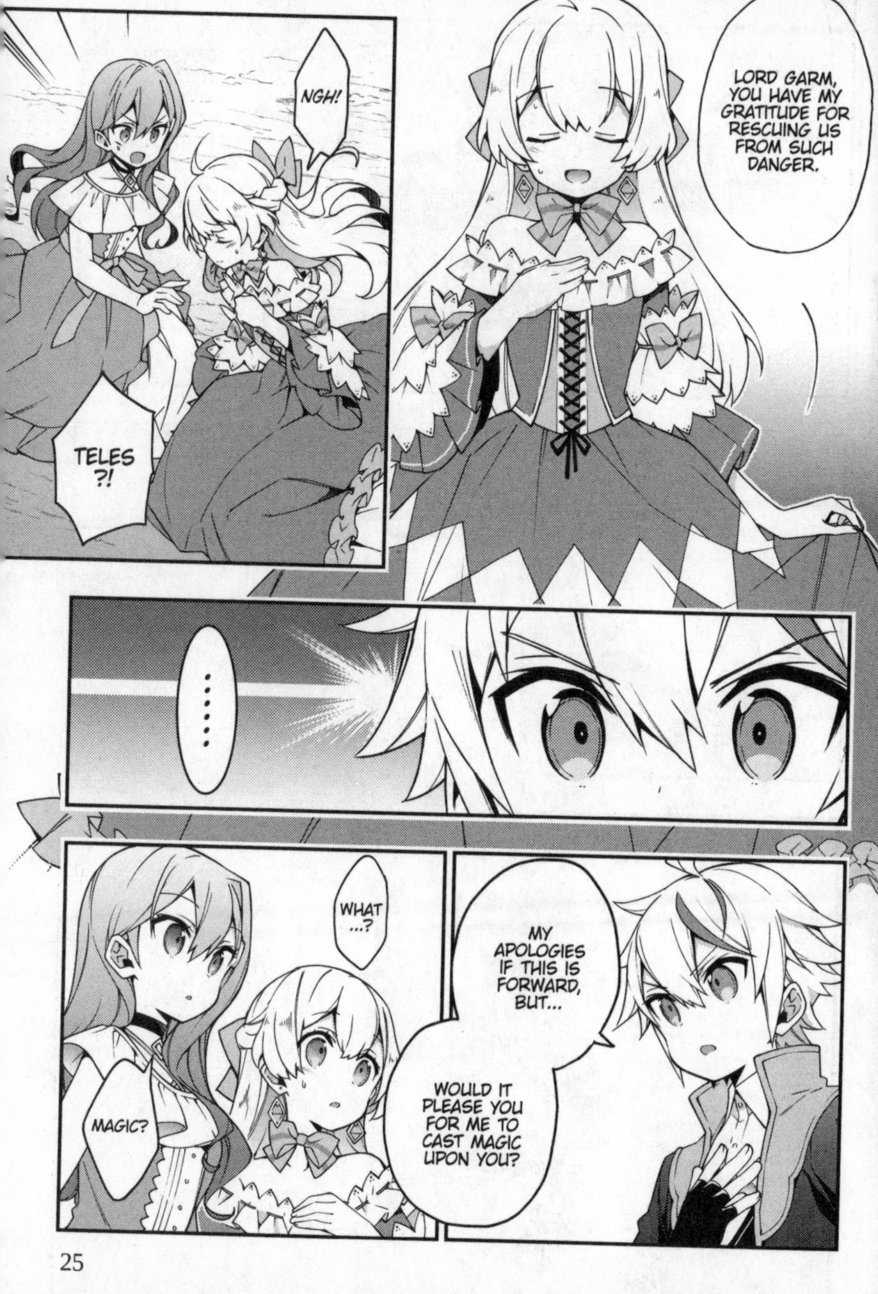
LORD GARM, YOU HAVE MY GRATITUDE FOR RESCUING US FROM SUCH DANGER.
NGH!
TELES ?!
......
MY APOLOGIES IF THIS IS FORWARD, BUT...
WOULD IT PLEASE YOU FOR ME TO CAST MAGIC UPON YOU?
WHAT ...?
MAGIC?

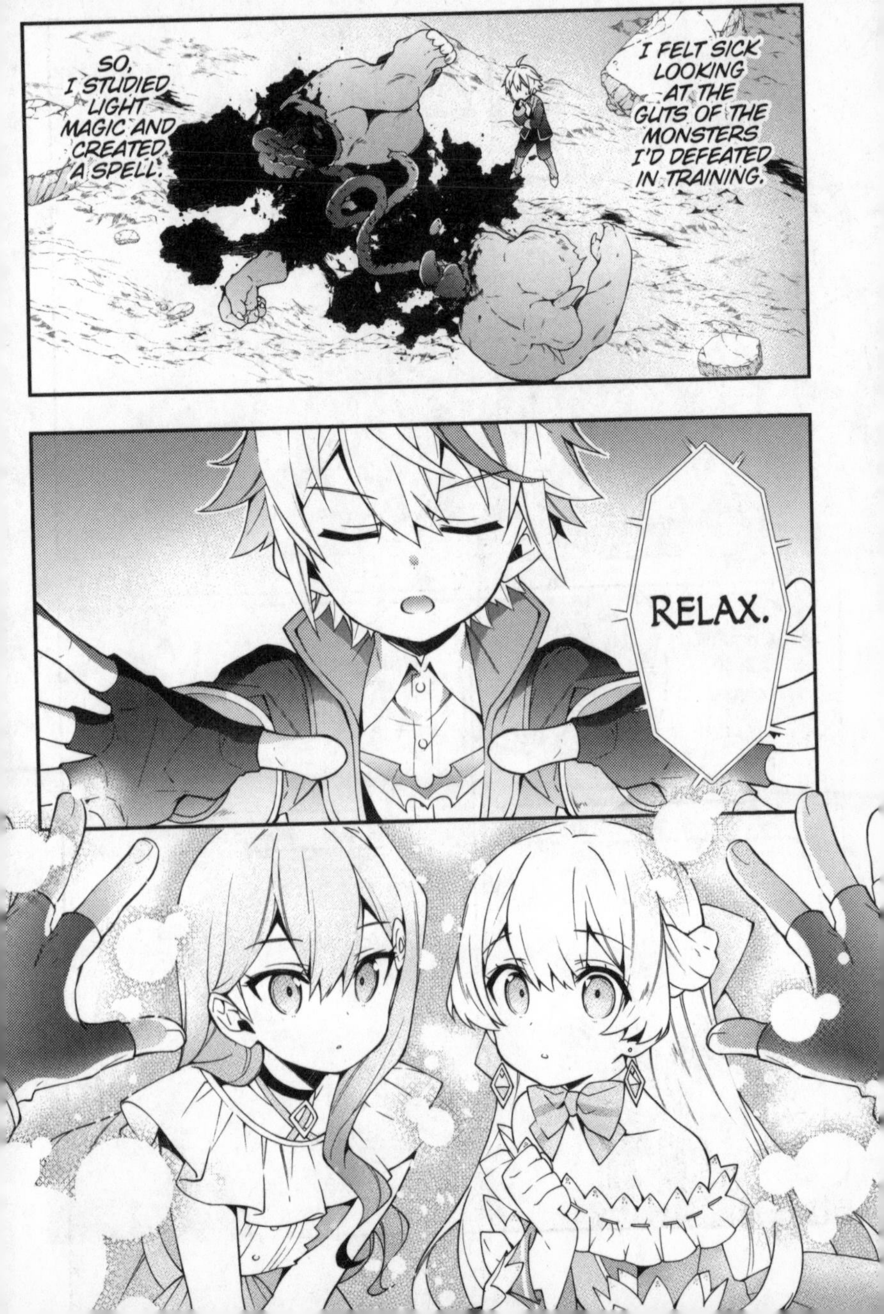
I FELT SICK LOOKING AT THE GUTS OF THE MONSTERS I'D DEFEATED IN TRAINING.
SO, I STUDIED LIGHT MAGIC AND CREATED A SPELL.
RELAX.

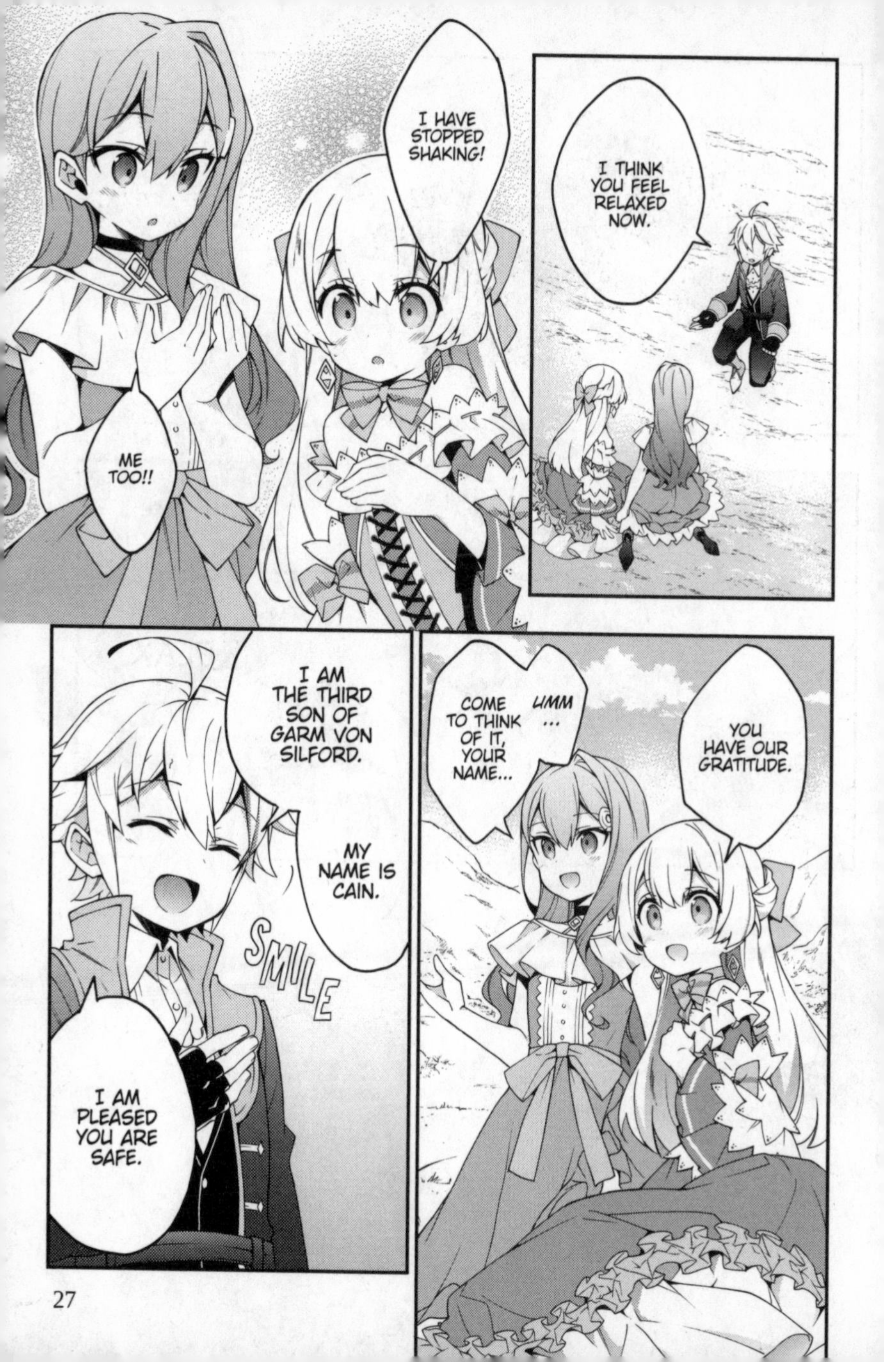
I THINK YOU FEEL RELAXED NOW.
I HAVE STOPPED SHAKING!
ME TOO!!
YOU HAVE OUR GRATITUDE.
UMM ...
COME TO THINK OF IT, YOUR NAME...
I AM THE THIRD SON OF GARM VON SILFORD.
MY NAME IS CAIN.
SMILE
I AM PLEASED YOU ARE SAFE.

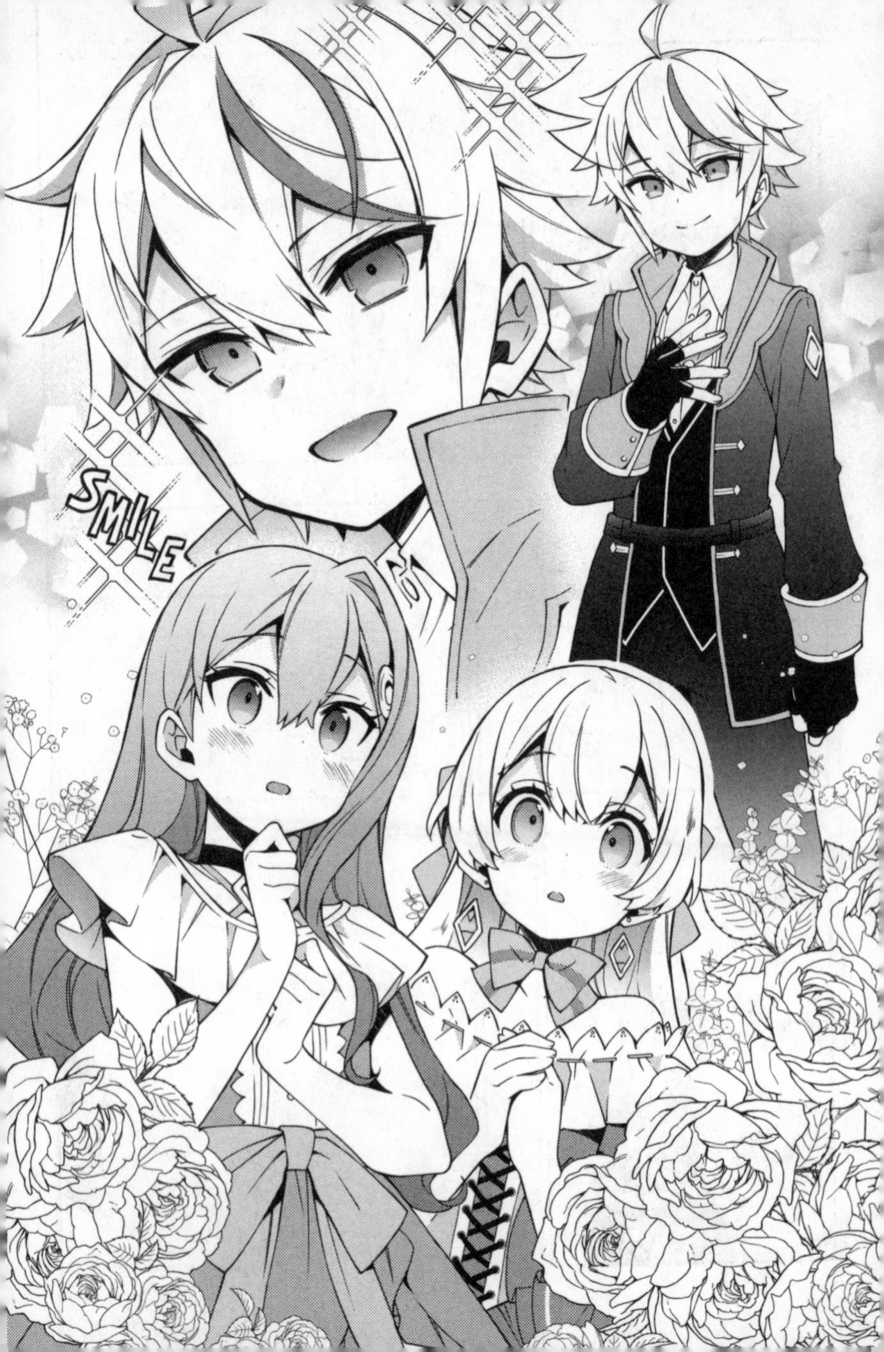
SMILE

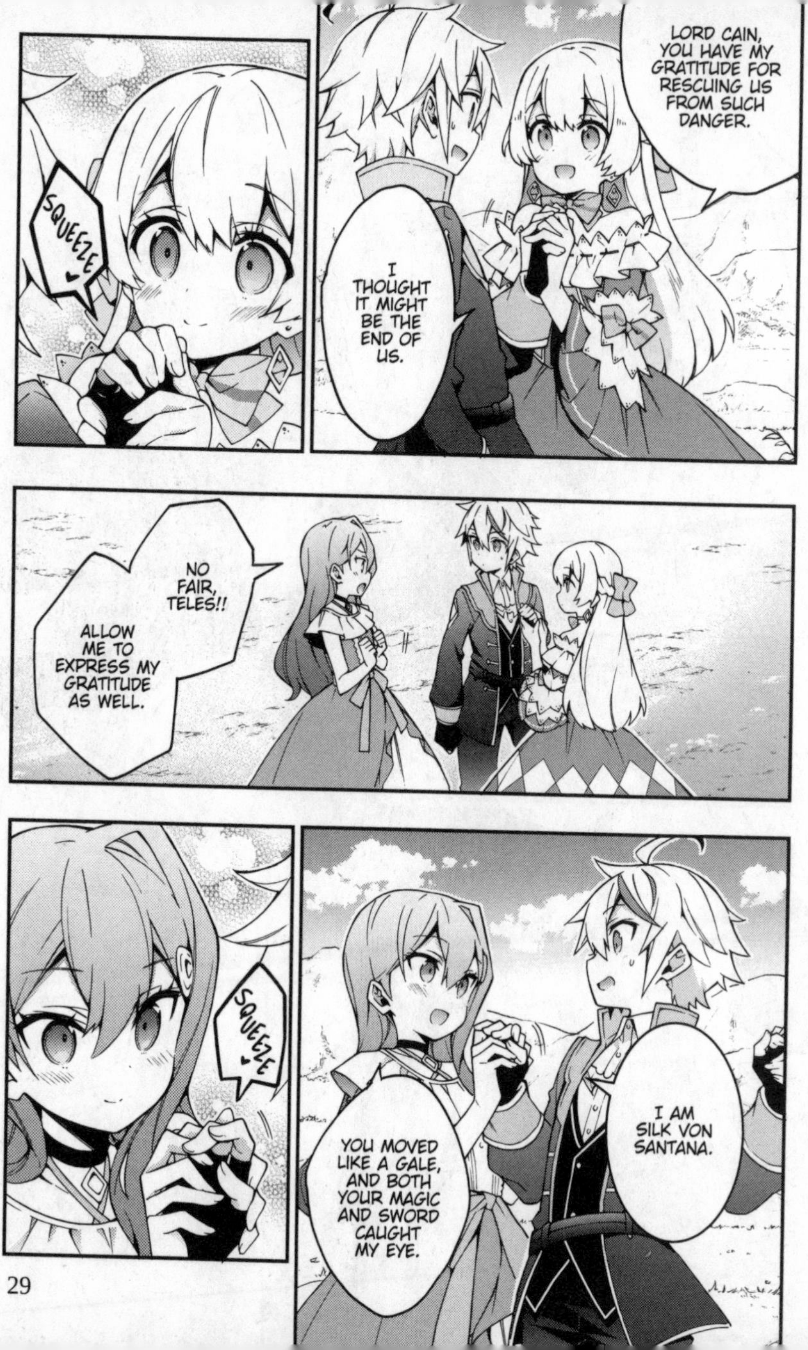
LORD CAIN, YOU HAVE MY GRATITUDE FOR RESCUING US FROM SUCH DANGER.
I THOUGHT IT MIGHT BE THE END OF US.
SQUEEZE
NO FAIR, TELES!!
ALLOW ME TO EXPRESS MY GRATITUDE AS WELL.
I AM SILK VON SANTANA.
YOU MOVED LIKE A GALE, AND BOTH YOUR MAGIC AND SWORD CAUGHT MY EYE.
SQUEEZE

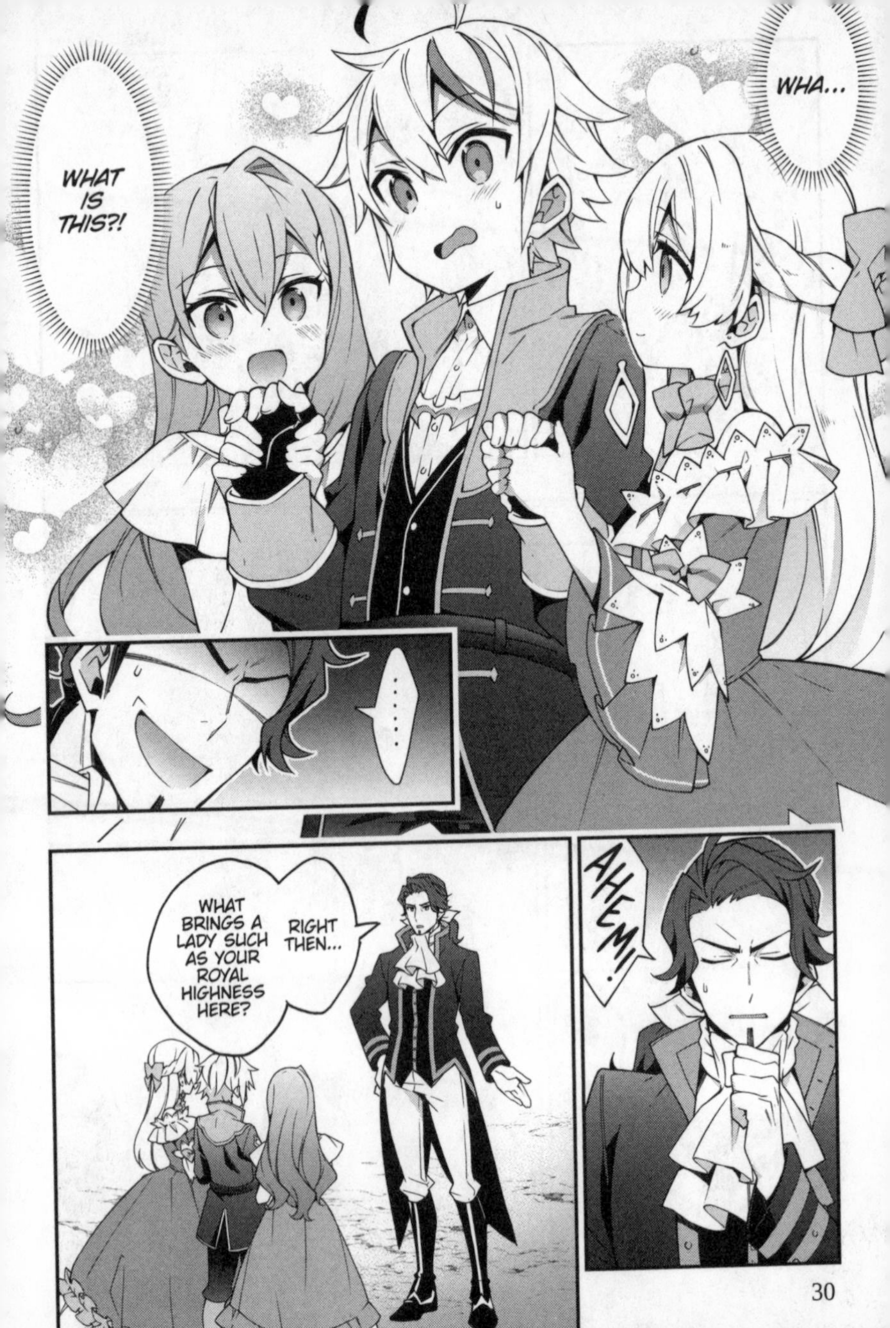
WHA...
WHAT IS THIS?!
......
AHEM!
RIGHT THEN...
WHAT BRINGS A LADY SUCH AS YOUR ROYAL HIGHNESS HERE?

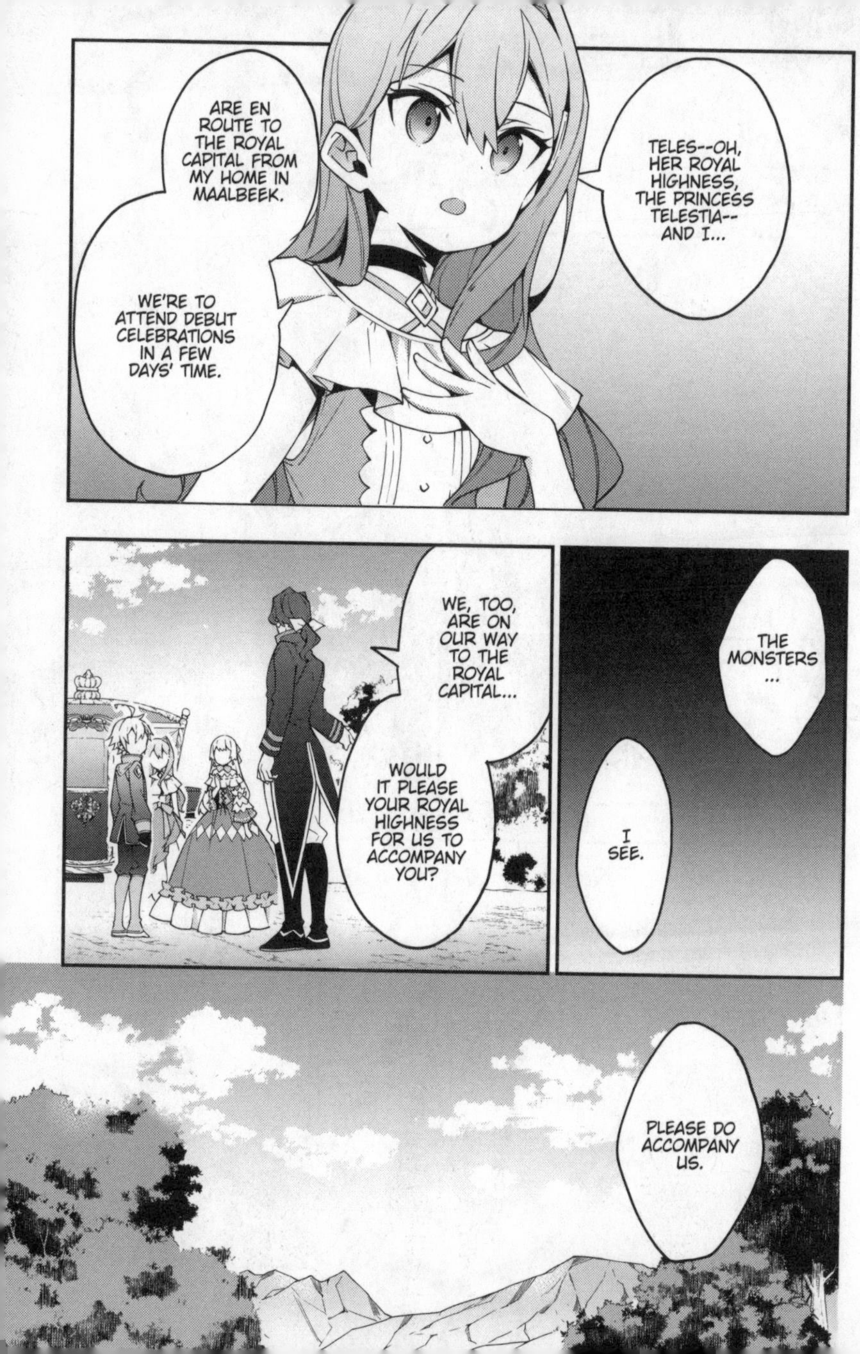
TELES--OH, HER ROYAL HIGHNESS, THE PRINCESS TELESTIA-- AND I...
ARE EN ROUTE TO THE ROYAL CAPITAL FROM MY HOME IN MAALBEEK.
WE'RE TO ATTEND DEBUT CELEBRATIONS IN A FEW DAYS' TIME.
THE MONSTERS...
I SEE.
WE, TOO, ARE ON OUR WAY TO THE ROYAL CAPITAL...
WOULD IT PLEASE YOUR ROYAL HIGHNESS FOR US TO ACCOMPANY YOU?
PLEASE DO ACCOMPANY US.

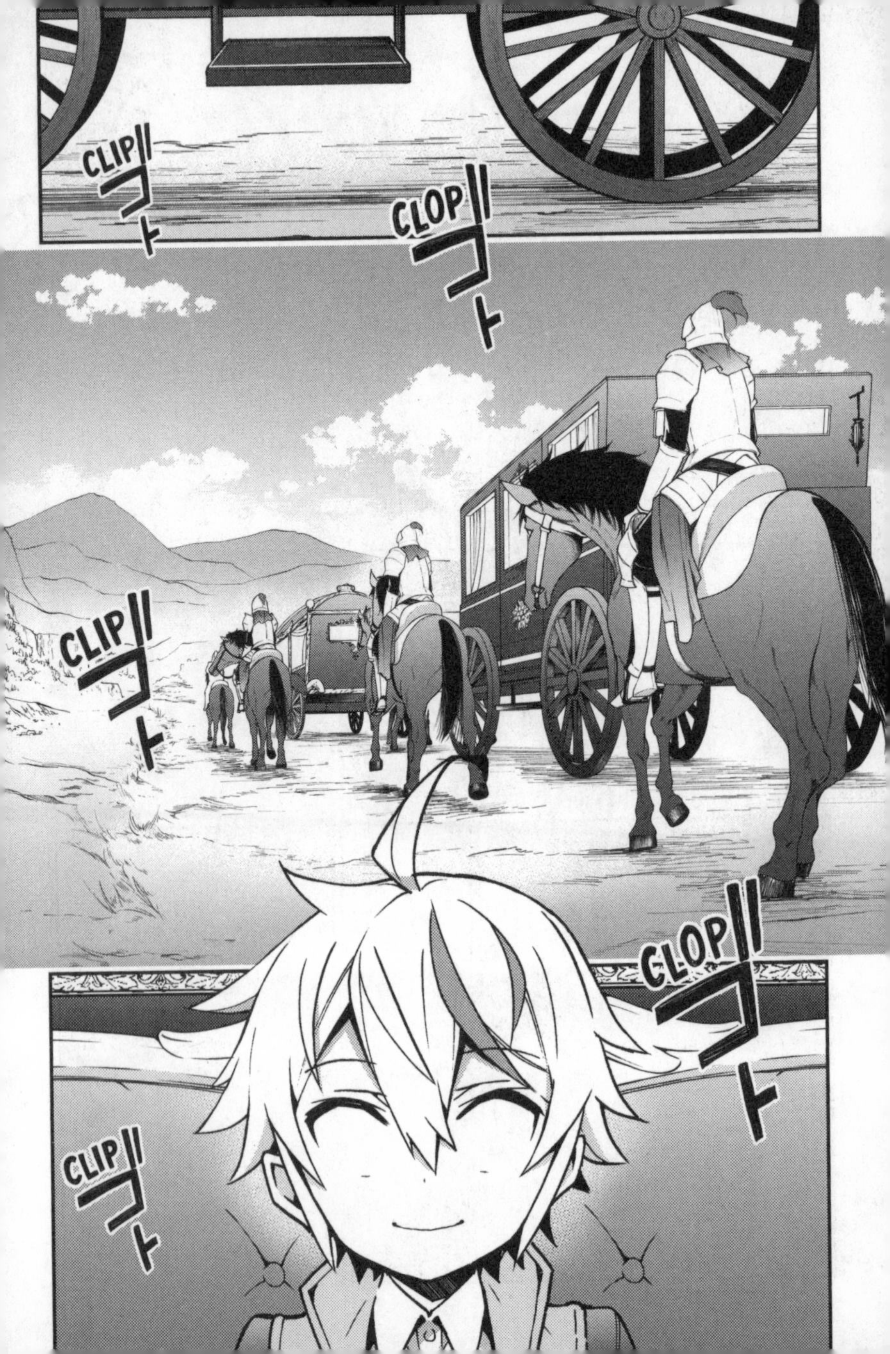
CLIP ゴト
CLOP ゴト
CLIP ゴト
CLOP ゴト
CLIP ゴト

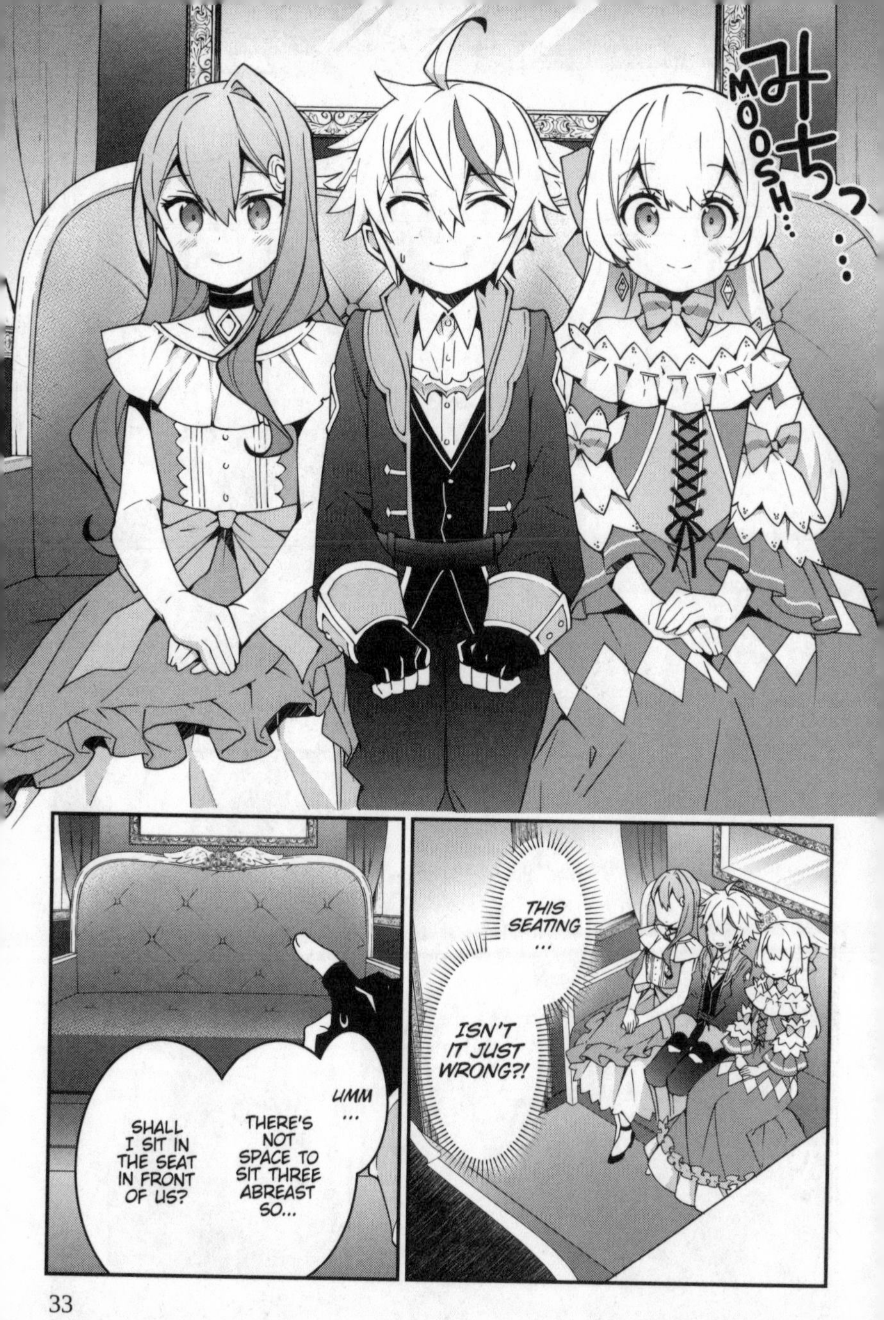
みちっ
MOOSH...
THIS SEATING ...
ISN'T IT JUST WRONG?!
UMM ...
THERE'S NOT SPACE TO SIT THREE ABREAST SO...
SHALL I SIT IN THE SEAT IN FRONT OF US?

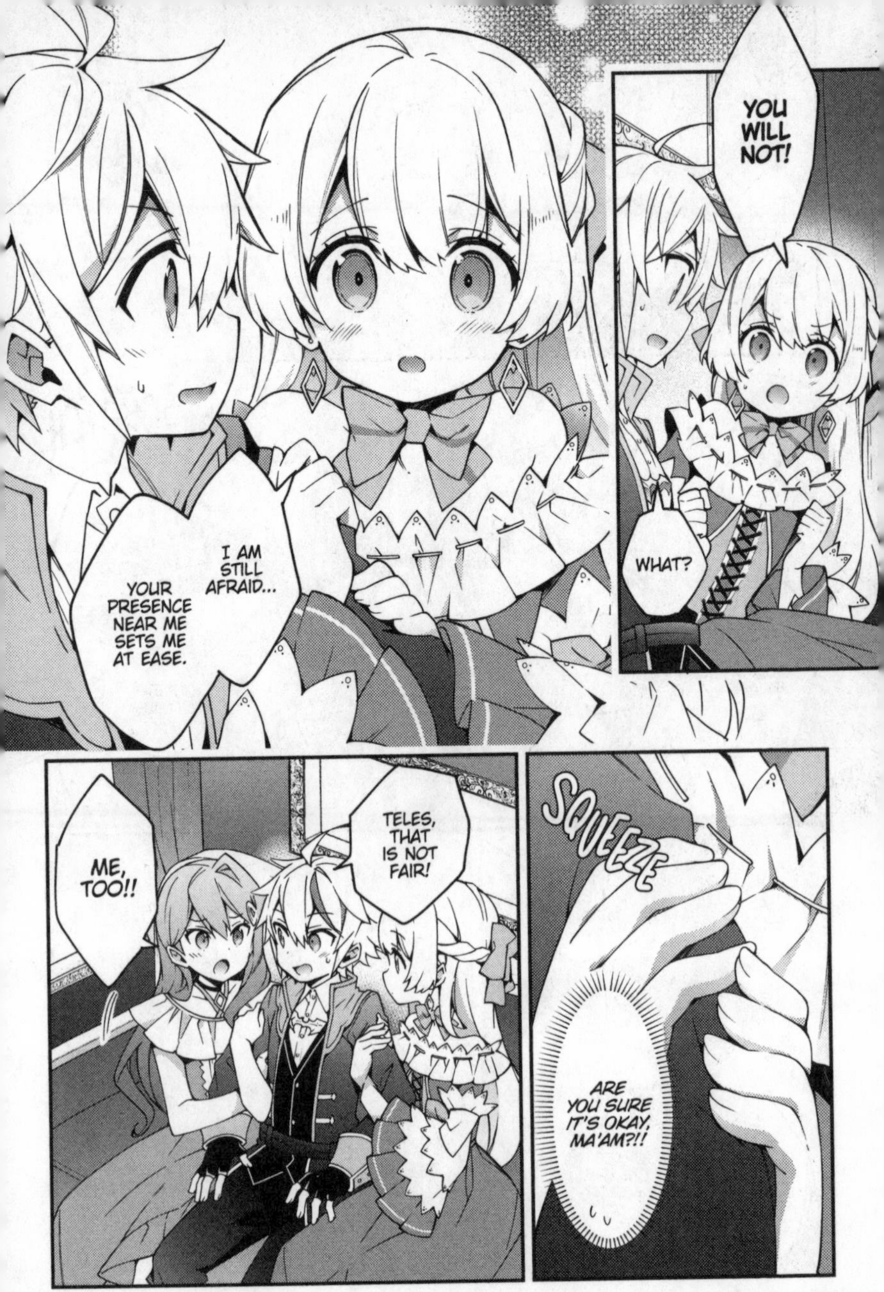
YOU WILL NOT!
WHAT?
I AM STILL AFRAID...
YOUR PRESENCE NEAR ME SETS ME AT EASE.
SQUEEZE
ARE YOU SURE IT'S OKAY, MA'AM?!!
TELES, THAT IS NOT FAIR!
ME, TOO!!

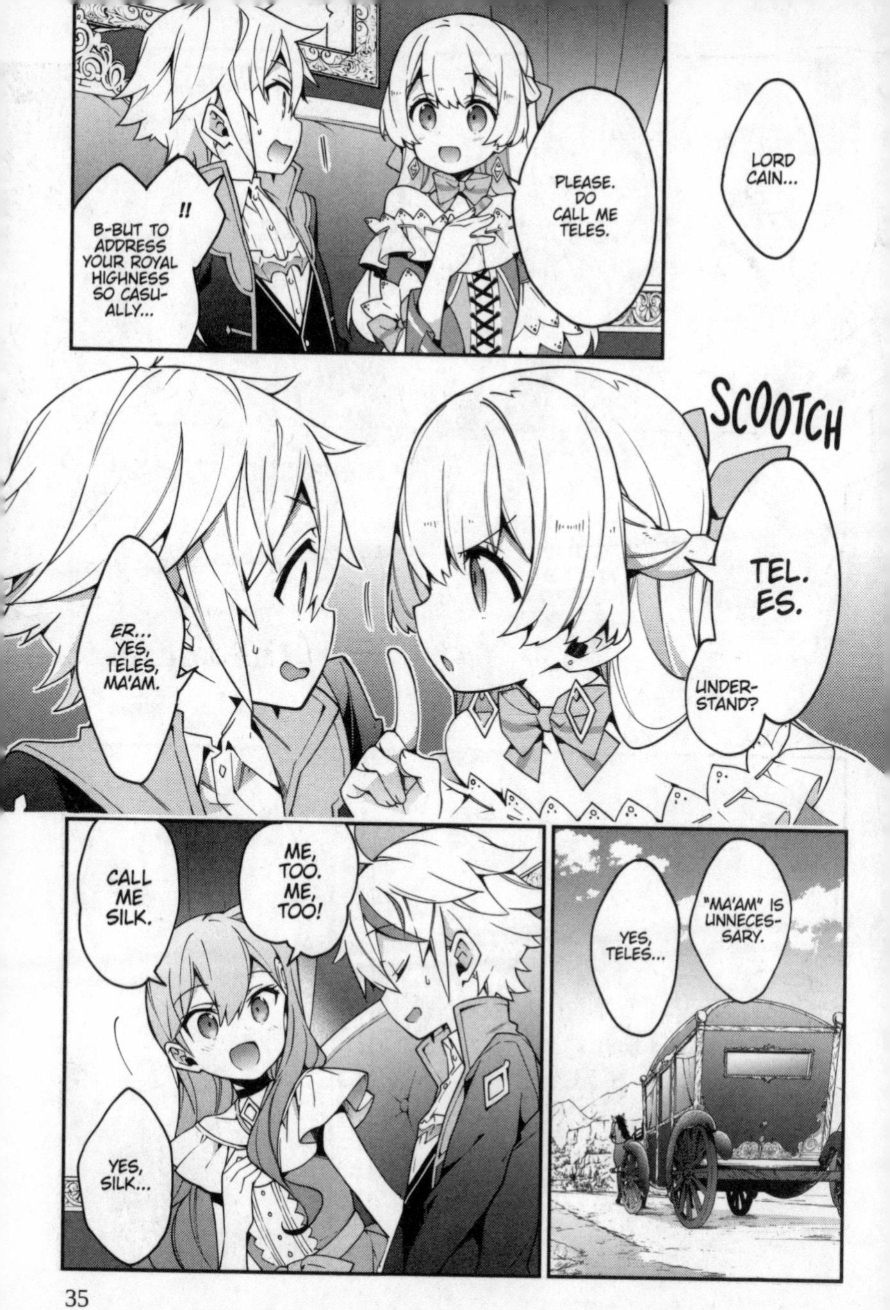
LORD CAIN...
PLEASE. DO CALL ME TELES.
!!
B-BUT TO ADDRESS YOUR ROYAL HIGHNESS SO CASU-ALLY...
SCOOTCH
TEL. ES.
UNDER-STAND?
ER... YES, TELES, MA'AM.
"MA'AM" IS UNNECES-SARY.
YES, TELES...
ME, TOO. ME, TOO!
CALL ME SILK.
YES, SILK...

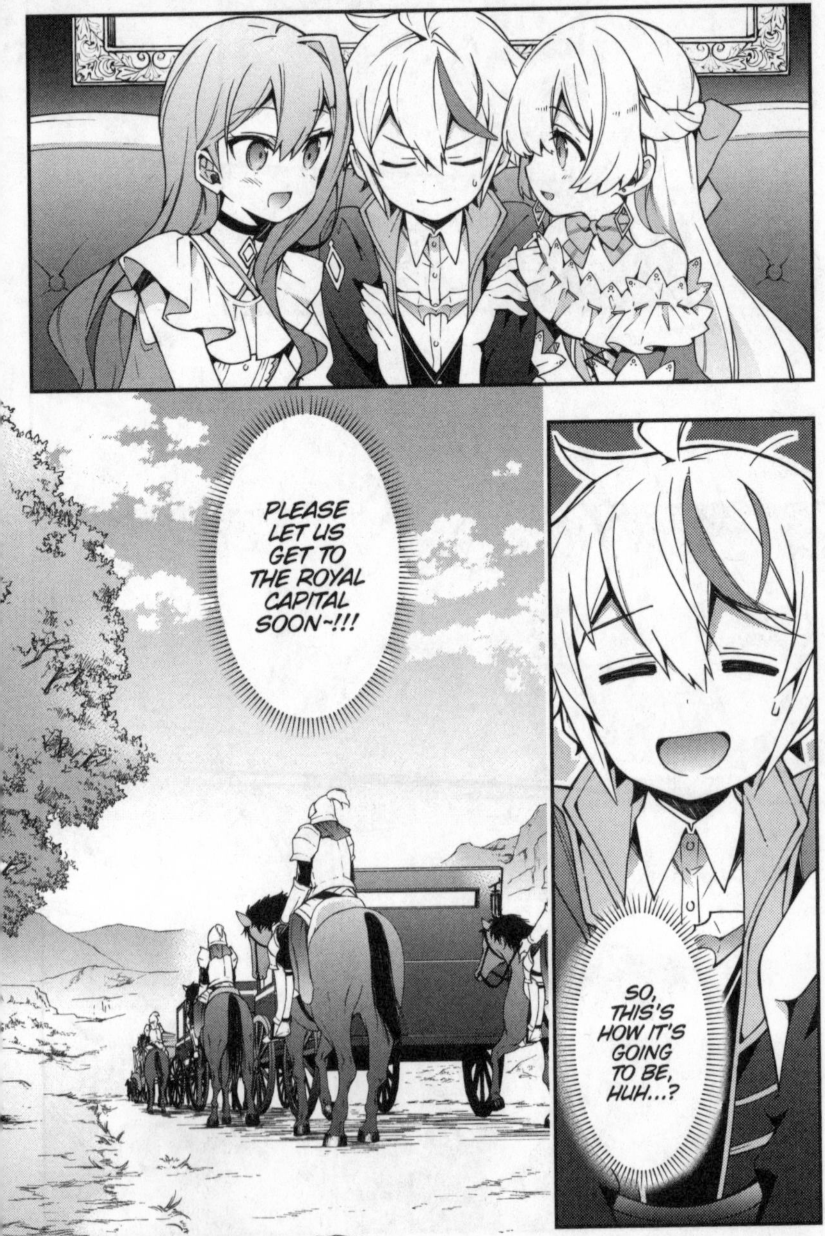
SO, THIS'S HOW IT'S GOING TO BE, HUH...?
PLEASE LET US GET TO THE ROYAL CAPITAL SOON~!!!

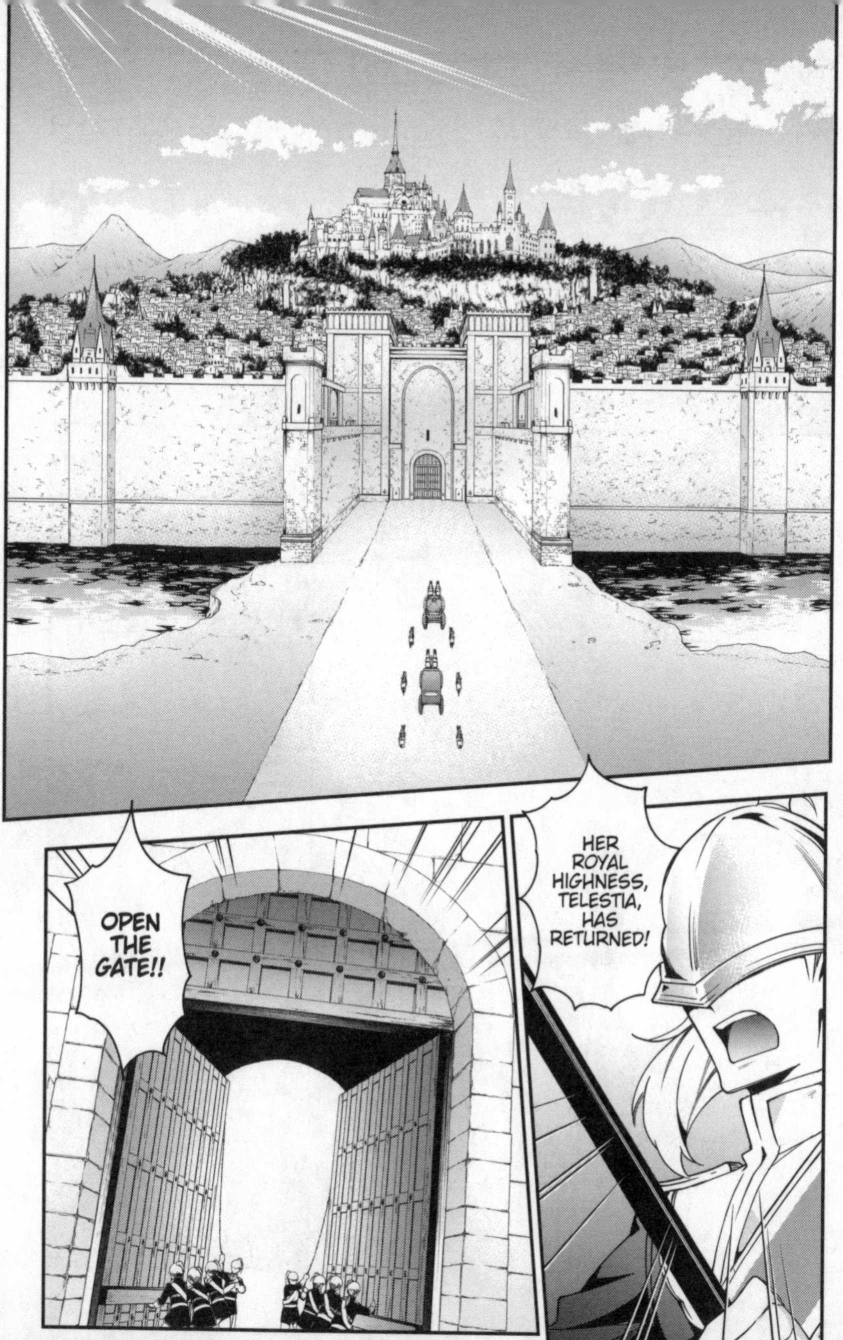
HER ROYAL HIGHNESS, TELESTIA, HAS RETURNED!
OPEN THE GATE!!

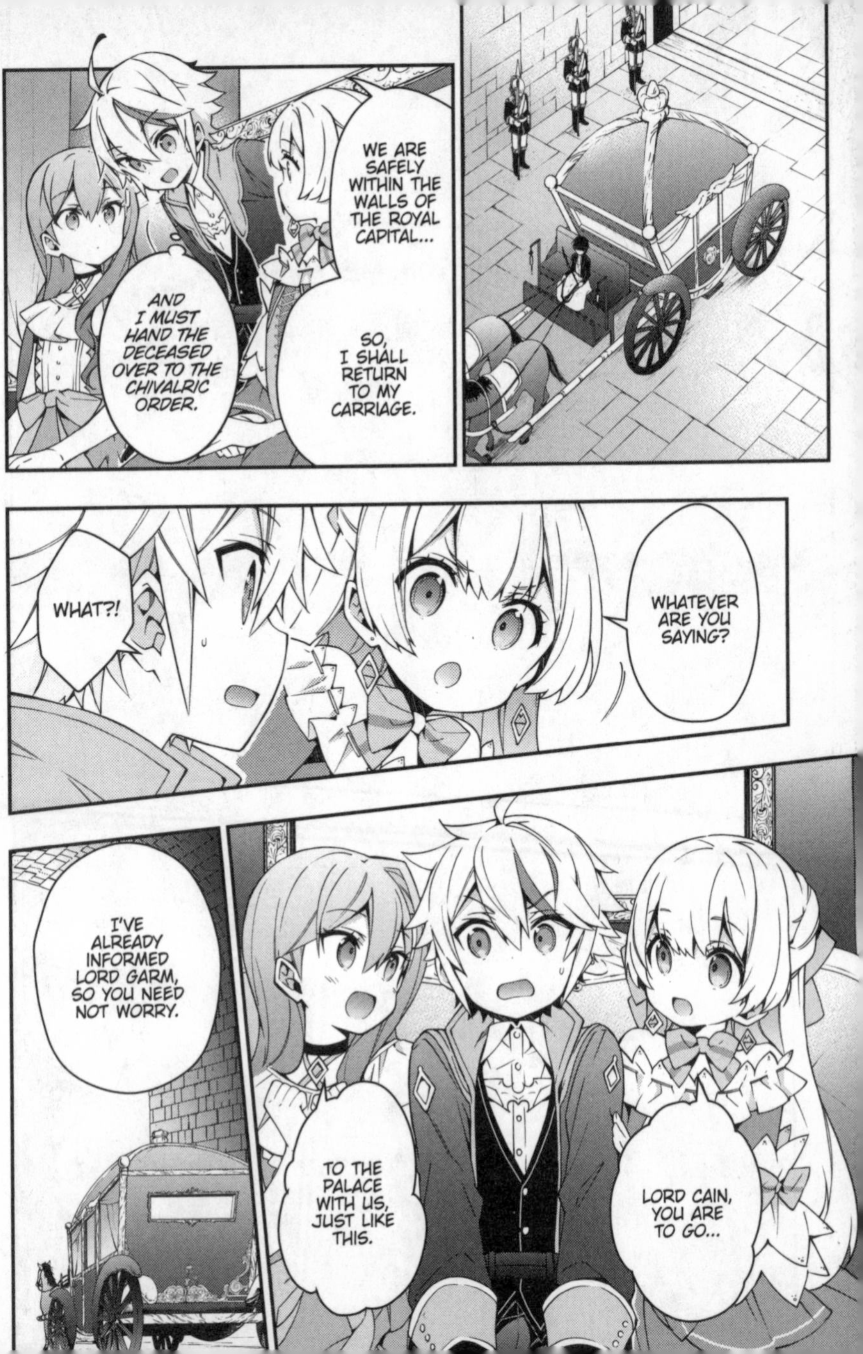
WE ARE SAFELY WITHIN THE WALLS OF THE ROYAL CAPITAL...
SO, I SHALL RETURN TO MY CARRIAGE.
AND I MUST HAND THE DECEASED OVER TO THE CHIVALRIC ORDER.
WHATEVER ARE YOU SAYING?
WHAT?!
LORD CAIN, YOU ARE TO GO...
TO THE PALACE WITH US, JUST LIKE THIS.
I'VE ALREADY INFORMED LORD GARM, SO YOU NEED NOT WORRY.

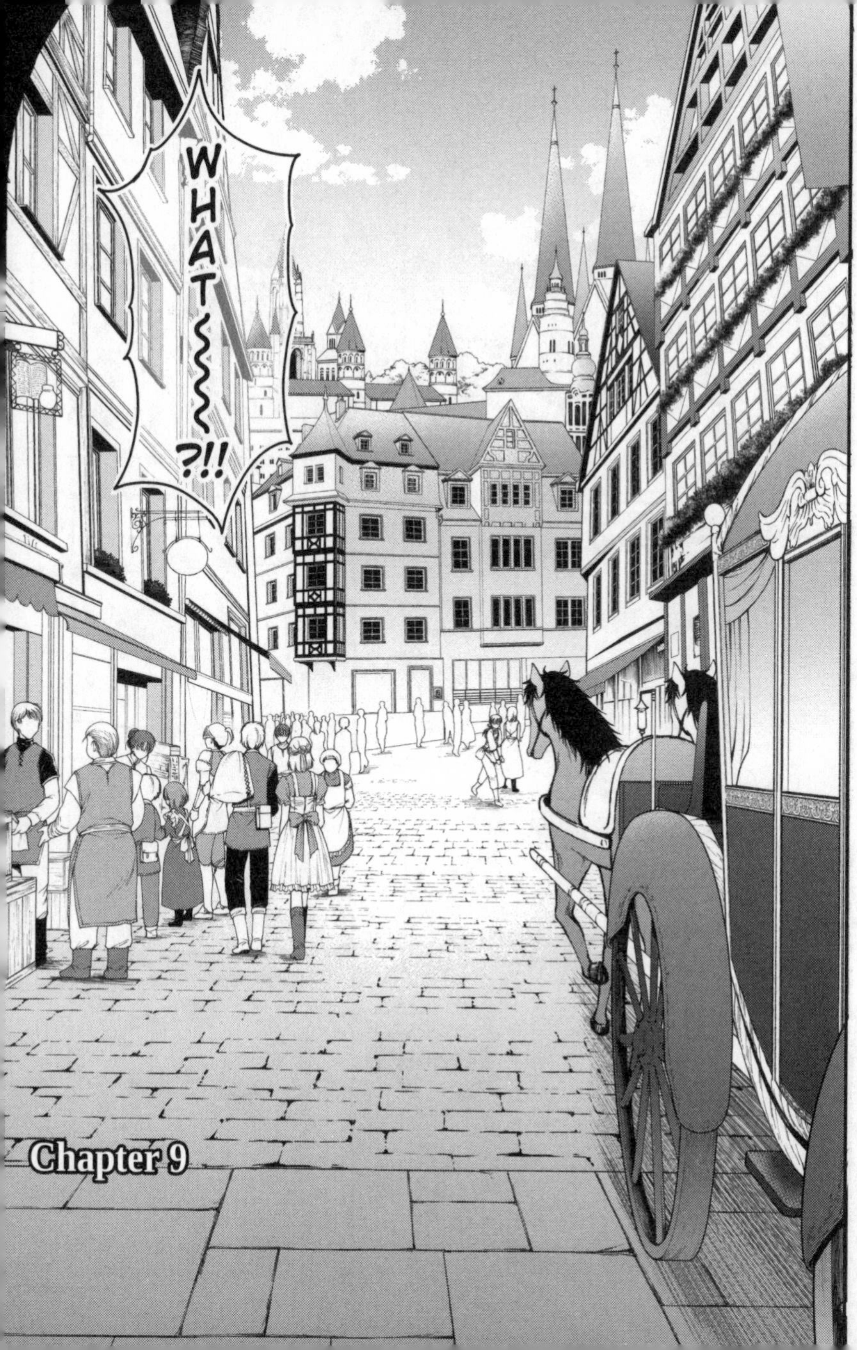
WHAT~~~?!!
Chapter 9

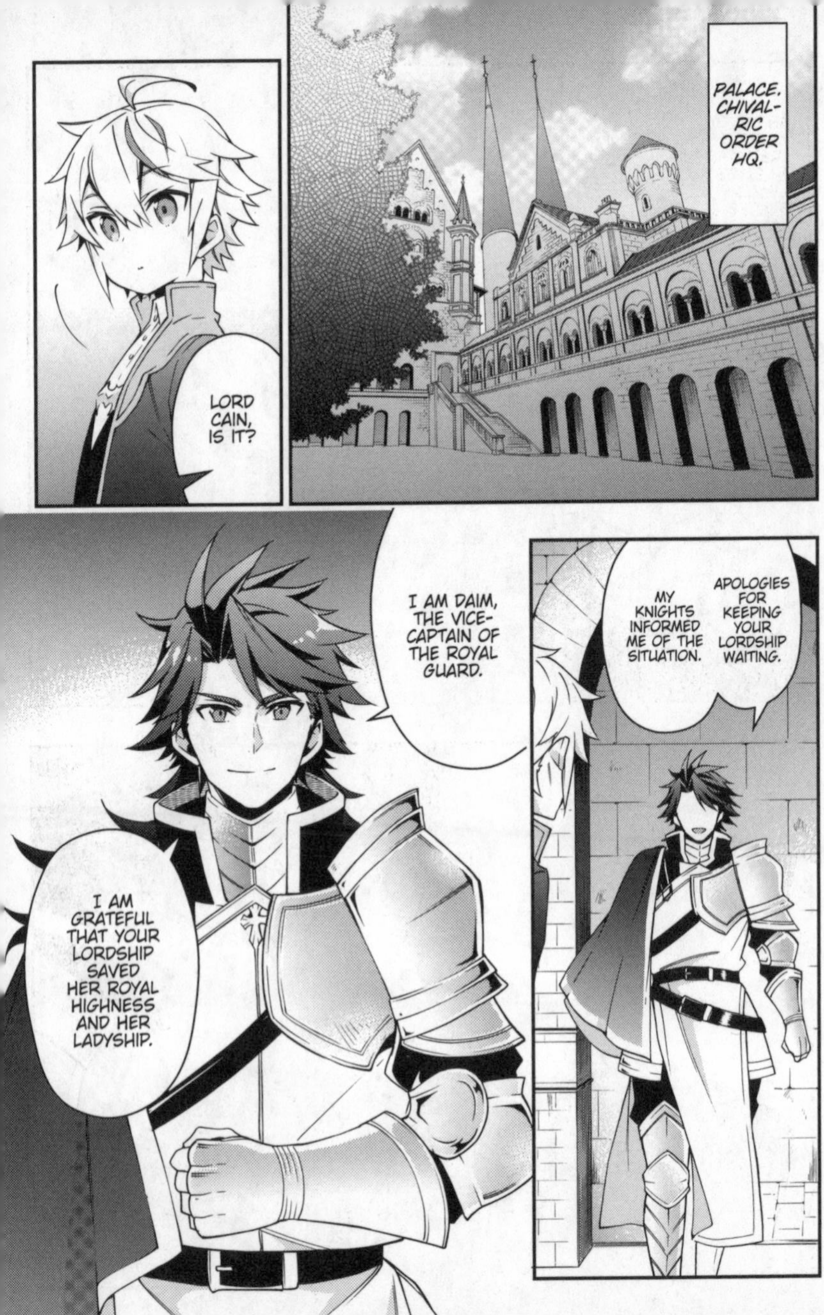
PALACE. CHIVAL-RIC ORDER HQ.
LORD CAIN, IS IT?
APOLOGIES FOR KEEPING YOUR LORDSHIP WAITING.
MY KNIGHTS INFORMED ME OF THE SITUATION.
I AM DAIM, THE VICE-CAPTAIN OF THE ROYAL GUARD.
I AM GRATEFUL THAT YOUR LORDSHIP SAVED HER ROYAL HIGHNESS AND HER LADYSHIP.

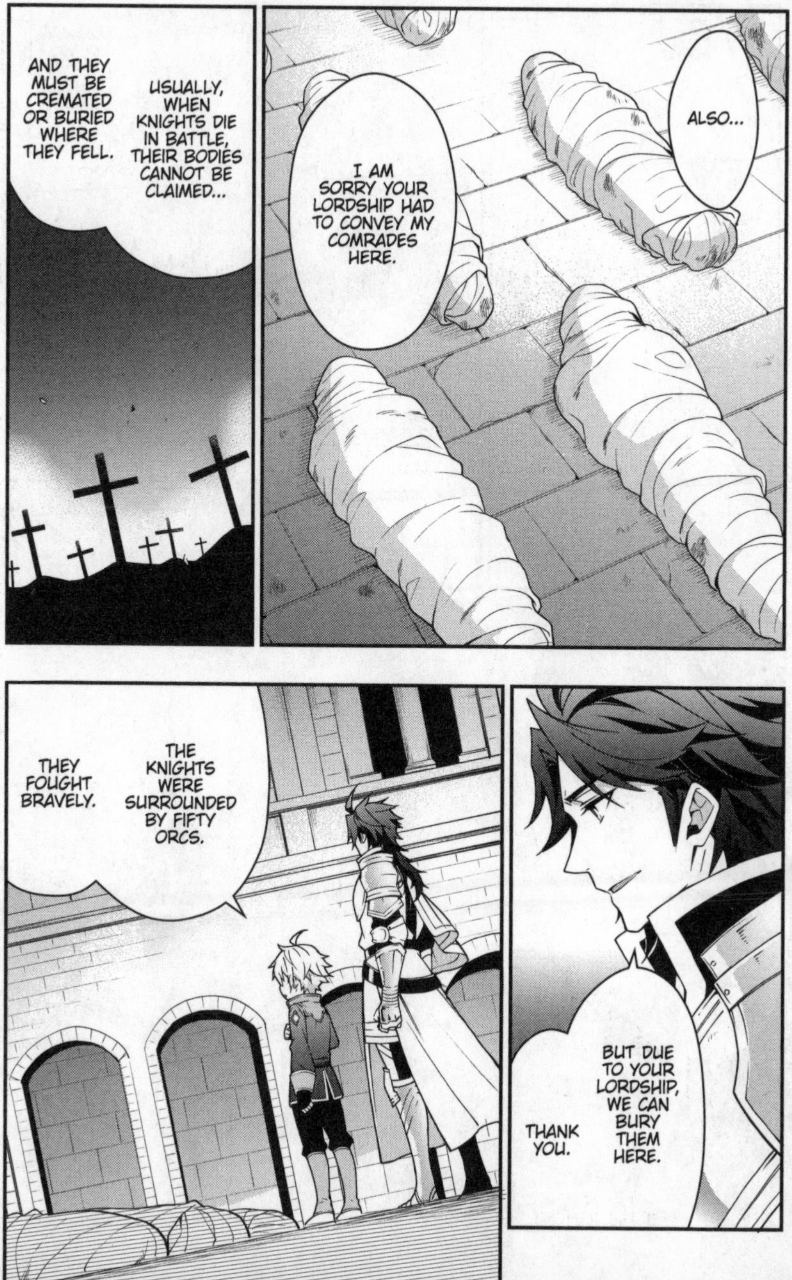
ALSO...
I AM SORRY YOUR LORDSHIP HAD TO CONVEY MY COMRADES HERE.
USUALLY, WHEN KNIGHTS DIE IN BATTLE, THEIR BODIES CANNOT BE CLAIMED...
AND THEY MUST BE CREMATED OR BURIED WHERE THEY FELL.
BUT DUE TO YOUR LORDSHIP, WE CAN BURY THEM HERE.
THANK YOU.
THE KNIGHTS WERE SURROUNDED BY FIFTY ORCS.
THEY FOUGHT BRAVELY.

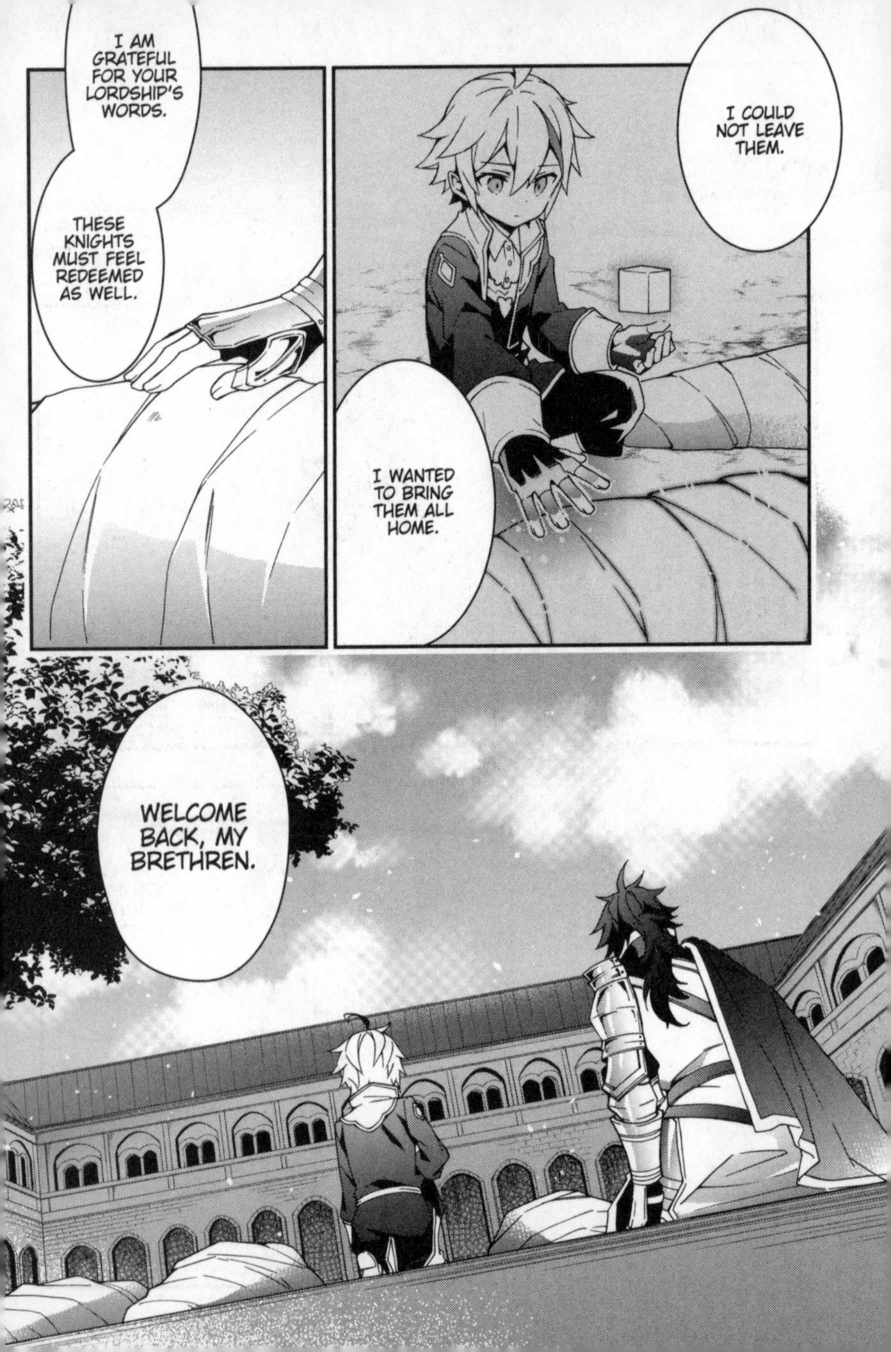
I COULD NOT LEAVE THEM.
I WANTED TO BRING THEM ALL HOME.
I AM GRATEFUL FOR YOUR LORDSHIP'S WORDS.
THESE KNIGHTS MUST FEEL REDEEMED AS WELL.
WELCOME BACK, MY BRETHREN.

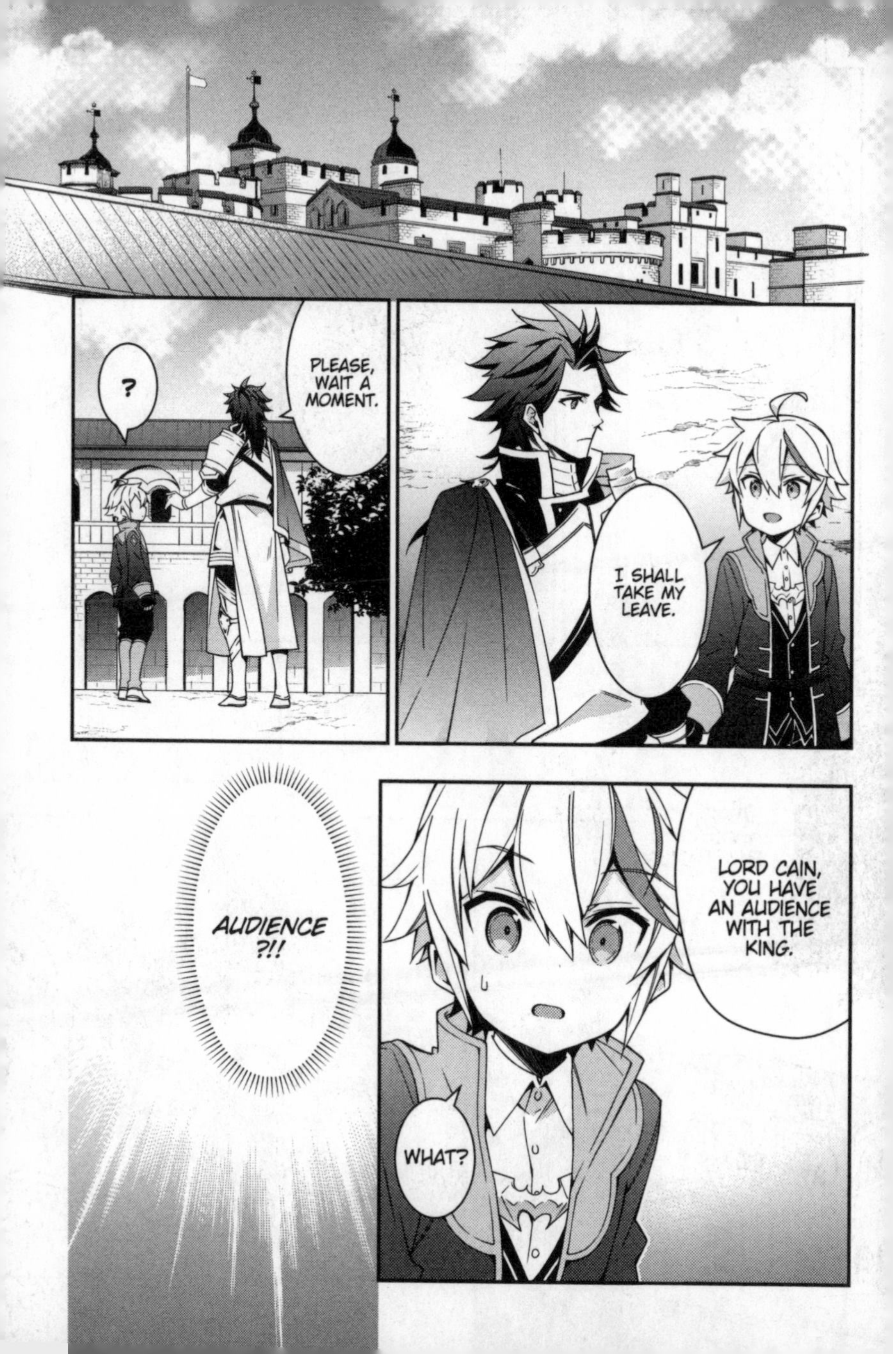
I SHALL TAKE MY LEAVE.
PLEASE, WAIT A MOMENT.
?
LORD CAIN, YOU HAVE AN AUDIENCE WITH THE KING.
WHAT?
AUDIENCE?!!

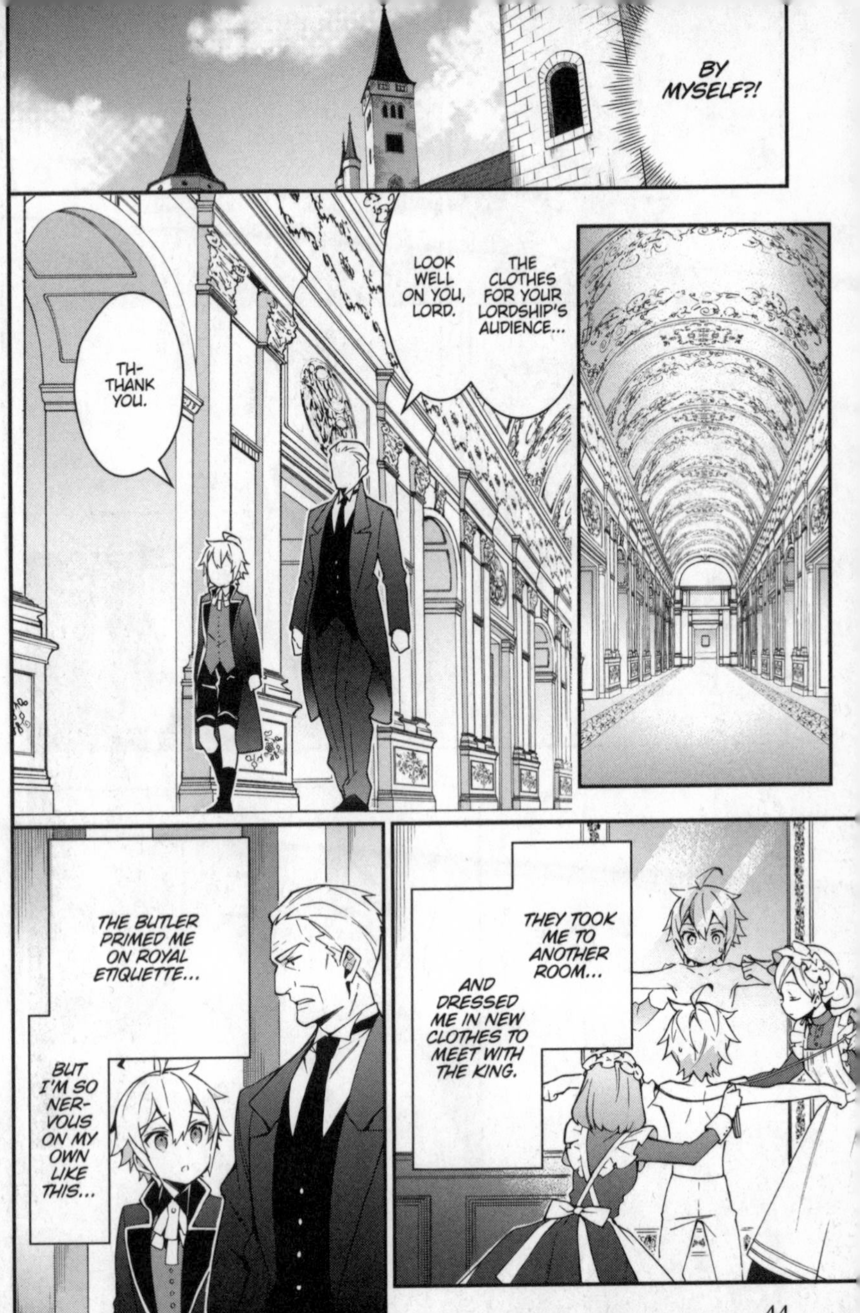
BY MYSELF?!
THE CLOTHES FOR YOUR LORDSHIP'S AUDIENCE...
LOOK WELL ON YOU, LORD.
TH-THANK YOU.
THEY TOOK ME TO ANOTHER ROOM...
AND DRESSED ME IN NEW CLOTHES TO MEET WITH THE KING.
THE BUTLER PRIMED ME ON ROYAL ETIQUETTE...
BUT I'M SO NER-VOUS ON MY OWN LIKE THIS...

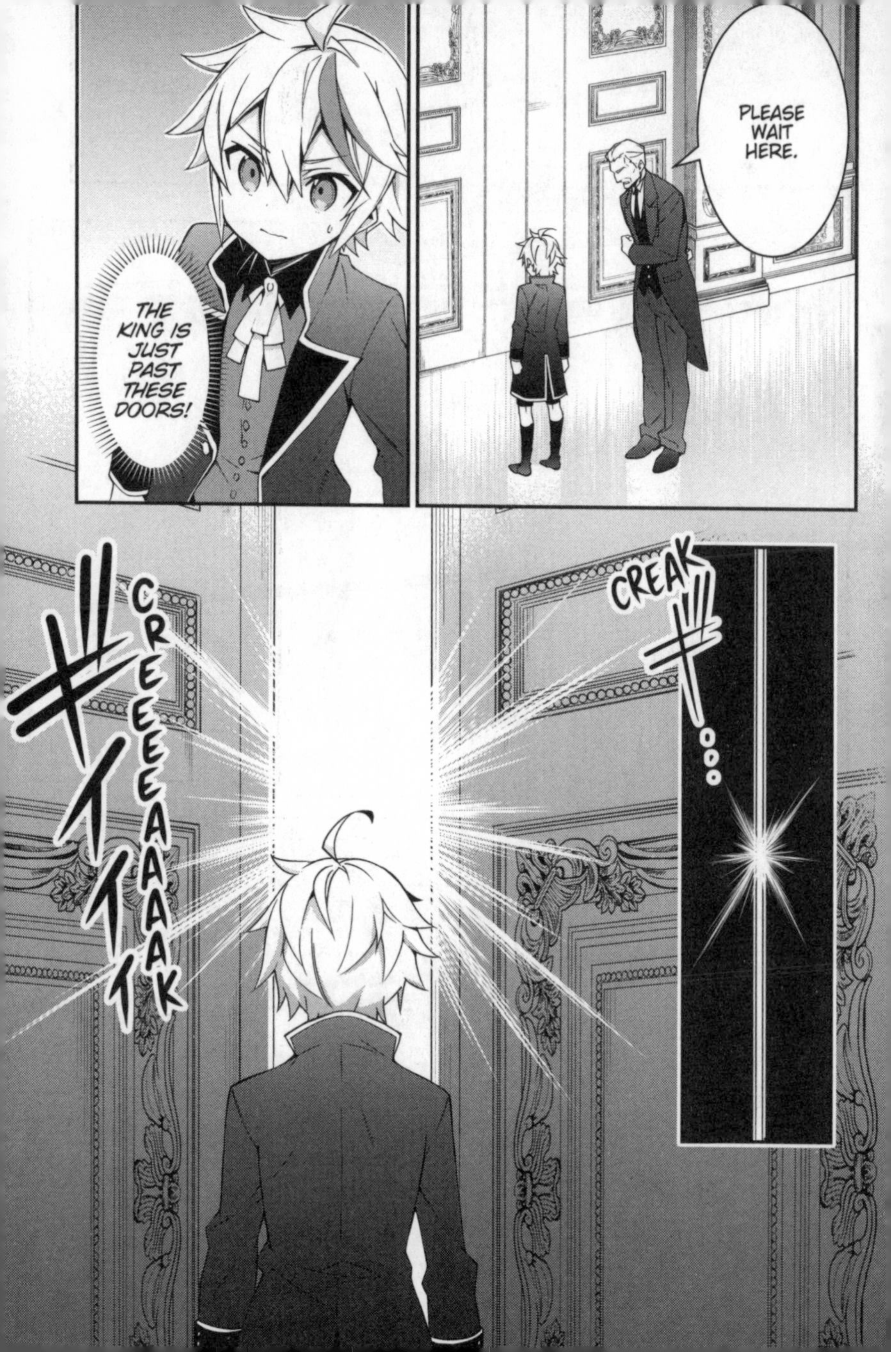
PLEASE WAIT HERE.
THE KING IS JUST PAST THESE DOORS!
CREAK
CREEEEAAAAK

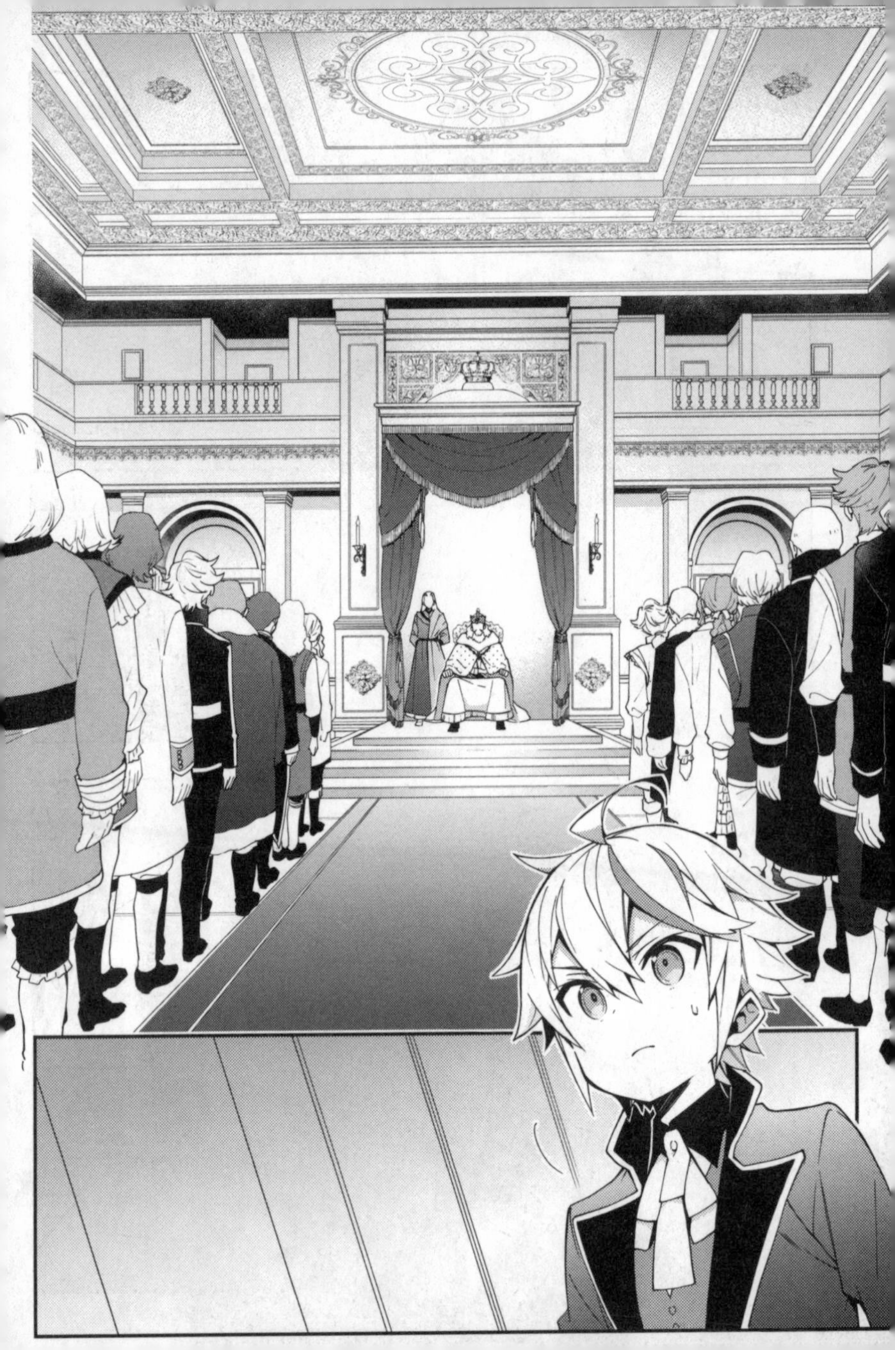

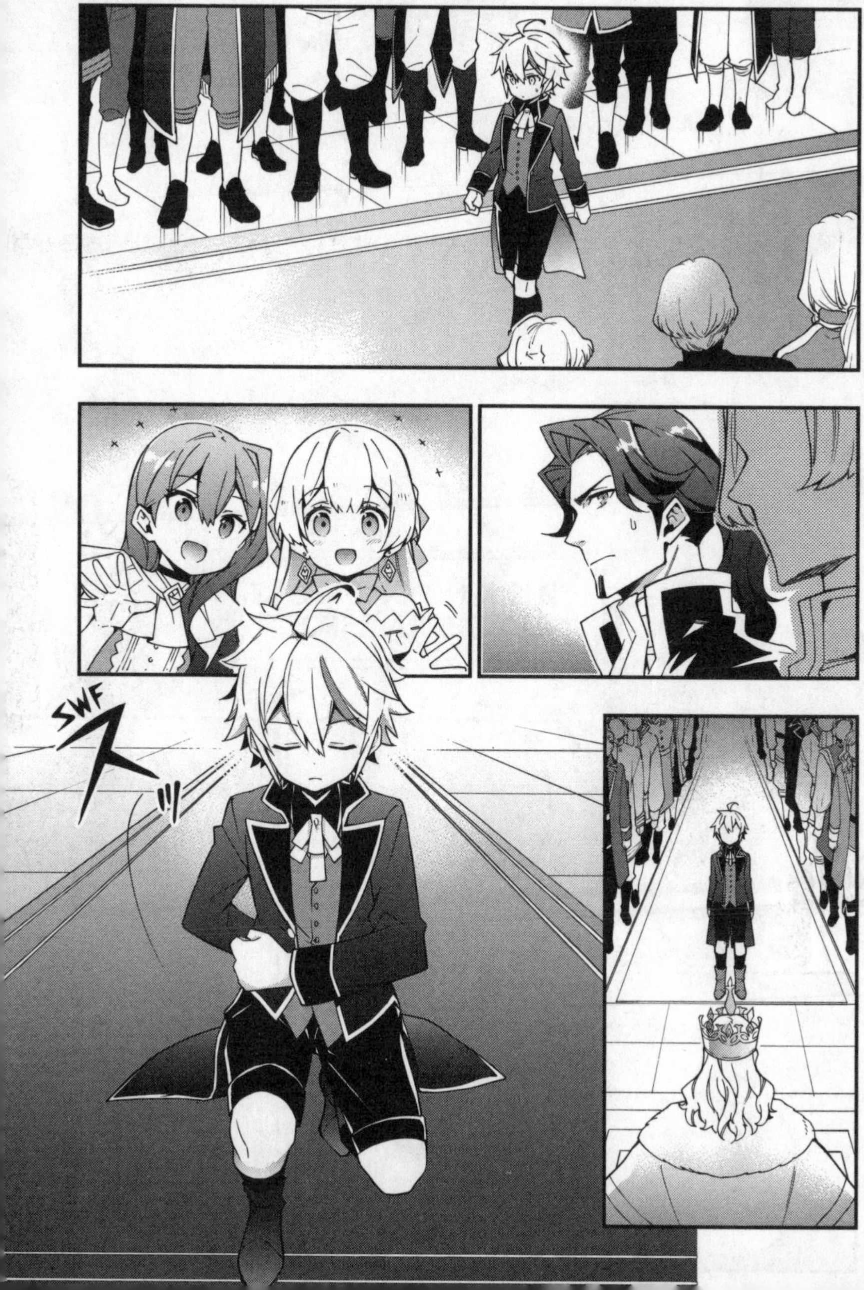
SWF

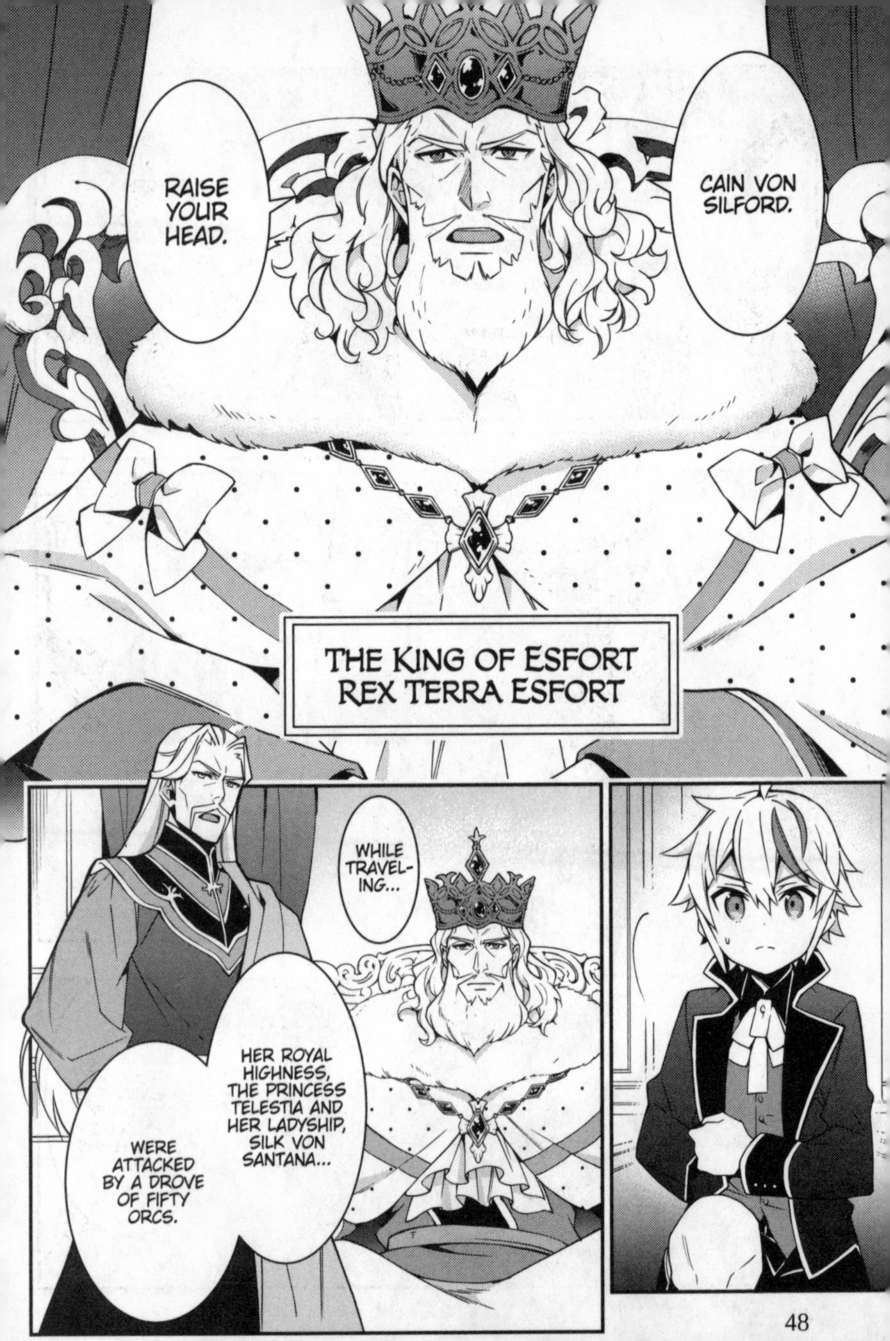
CAIN VON SILFORD.
RAISE YOUR HEAD.
THE KING OF ESFORT
REX TERRA ESFORT
WHILE TRAVEL-ING...
HER ROYAL HIGHNESS, THE PRINCESS TELESTIA AND HER LADYSHIP, SILK VON SANTANA...
WERE ATTACKED BY A DROVE OF FIFTY ORCS.

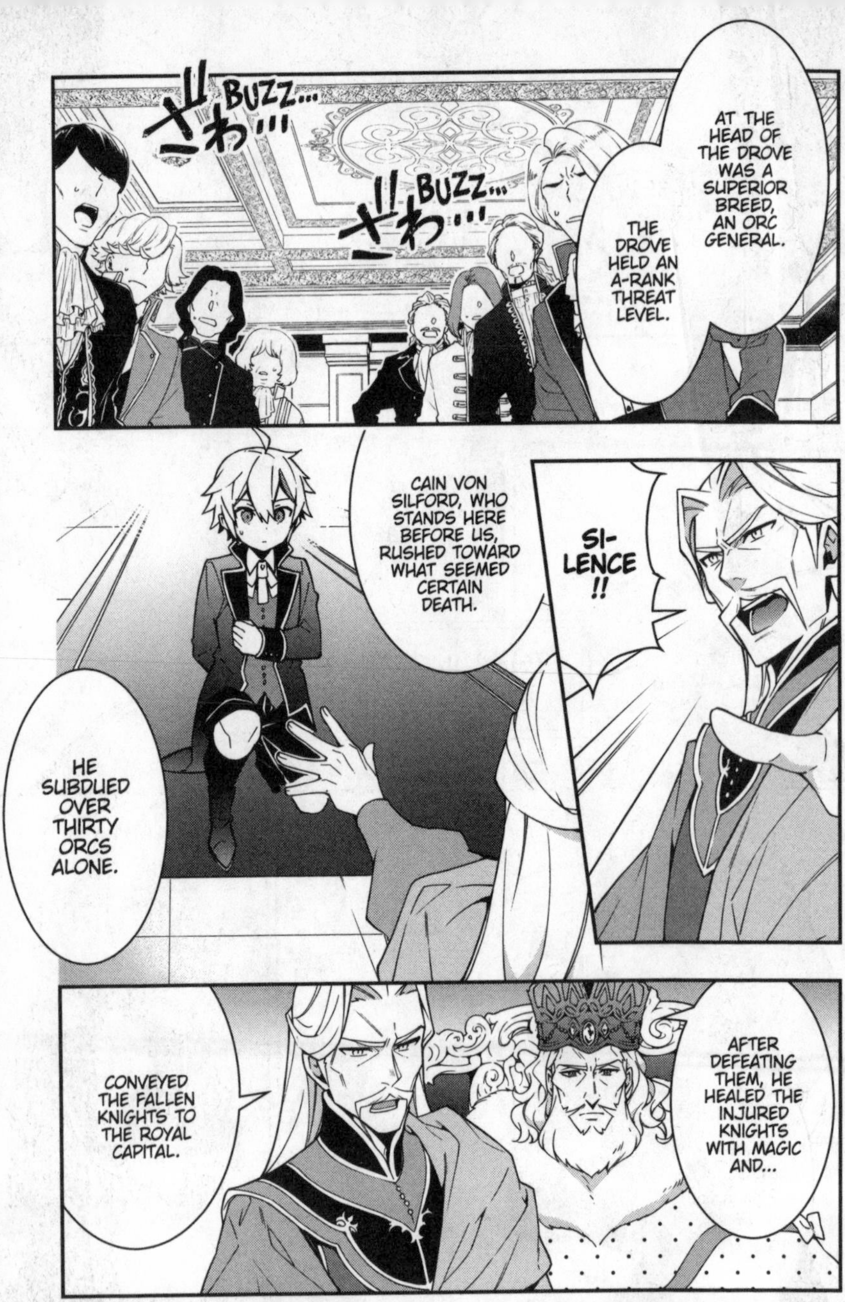
AT THE HEAD OF THE DROVE WAS A SUPERIOR BREED, AN ORC GENERAL.
THE DROVE HELD AN A-RANK THREAT LEVEL.
BUZZ...
BUZZ...
SI-LENCE!!
CAIN VON SILFORD, WHO STANDS HERE BEFORE US, RUSHED TOWARD WHAT SEEMED CERTAIN DEATH.
HE SUBDUED OVER THIRTY ORCS ALONE.
AFTER DEFEATING THEM, HE HEALED THE INJURED KNIGHTS WITH MAGIC AND...
CONVEYED THE FALLEN KNIGHTS TO THE ROYAL CAPITAL.

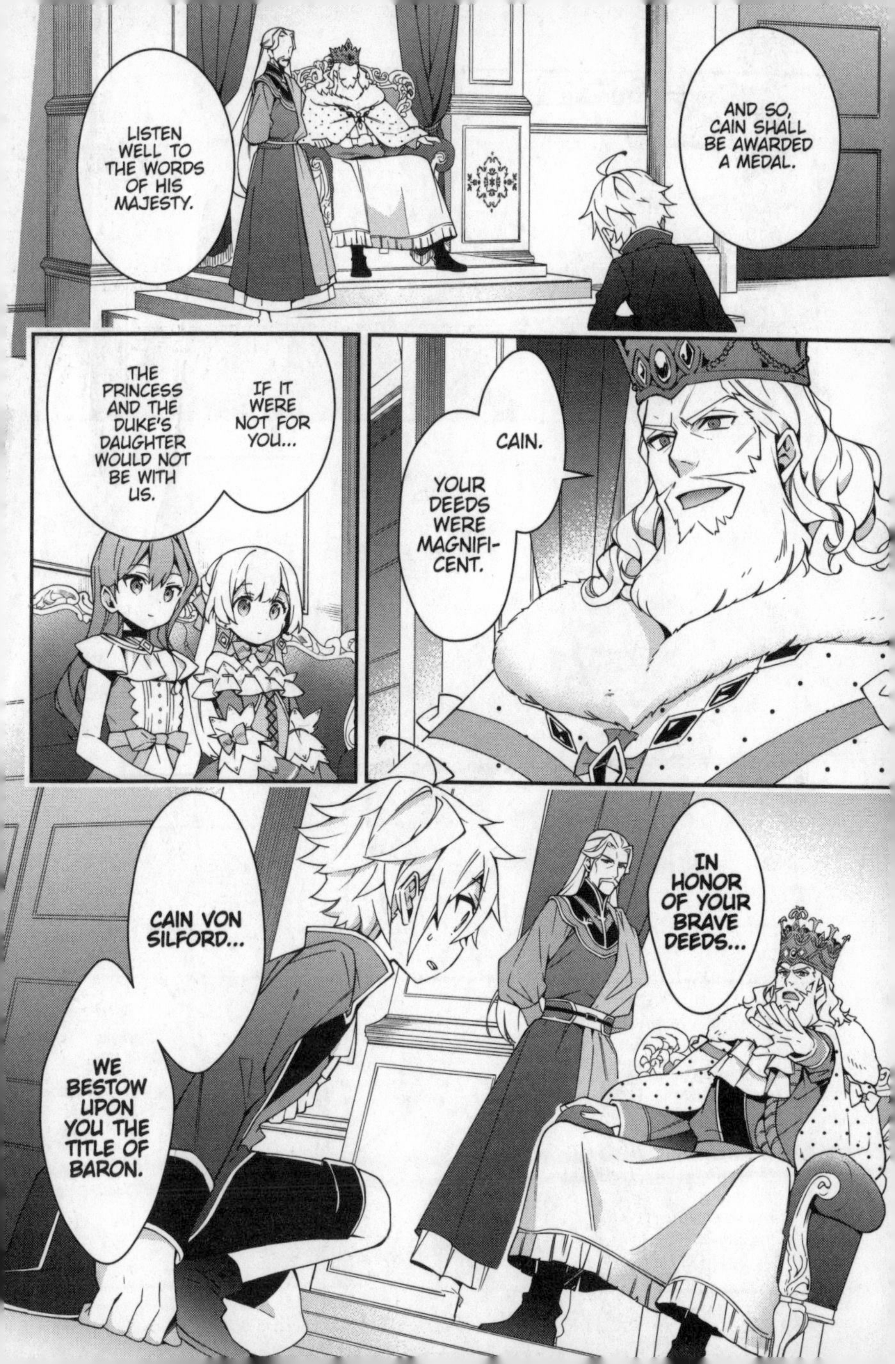
AND SO, CAIN SHALL BE AWARDED A MEDAL.
LISTEN WELL TO THE WORDS OF HIS MAJESTY.
CAIN.
YOUR DEEDS WERE MAGNIFI-CENT.
IF IT WERE NOT FOR YOU...
THE PRINCESS AND THE DUKE'S DAUGHTER WOULD NOT BE WITH US.
IN HONOR OF YOUR BRAVE DEEDS...
CAIN VON SILFORD...
WE BESTOW UPON YOU THE TITLE OF BARON.

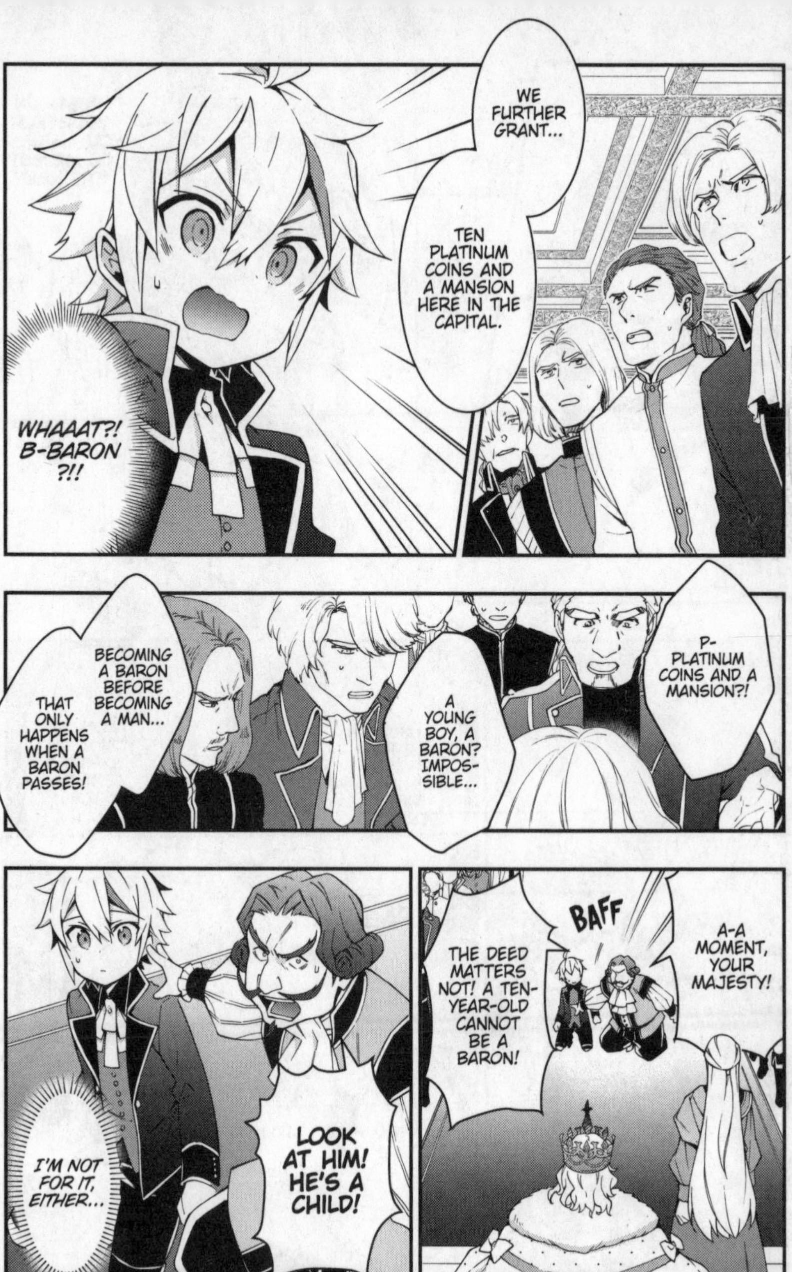
WE FURTHER GRANT...
TEN PLATINUM COINS AND A MANSION HERE IN THE CAPITAL.
WHAAAT?! B-BARON ?!!
P-PLATINUM COINS AND A MANSION?!
A YOUNG BOY, A BARON? IMPOSSIBLE...
BECOMING A BARON BEFORE BECOMING A MAN...
THAT ONLY HAPPENS WHEN A BARON PASSES!
A-A MOMENT, YOUR MAJESTY!
BAFF
THE DEED MATTERS NOT! A TEN-YEAR-OLD CANNOT BE A BARON!
LOOK AT HIM! HE'S A CHILD!
I'M NOT FOR IT, EITHER...

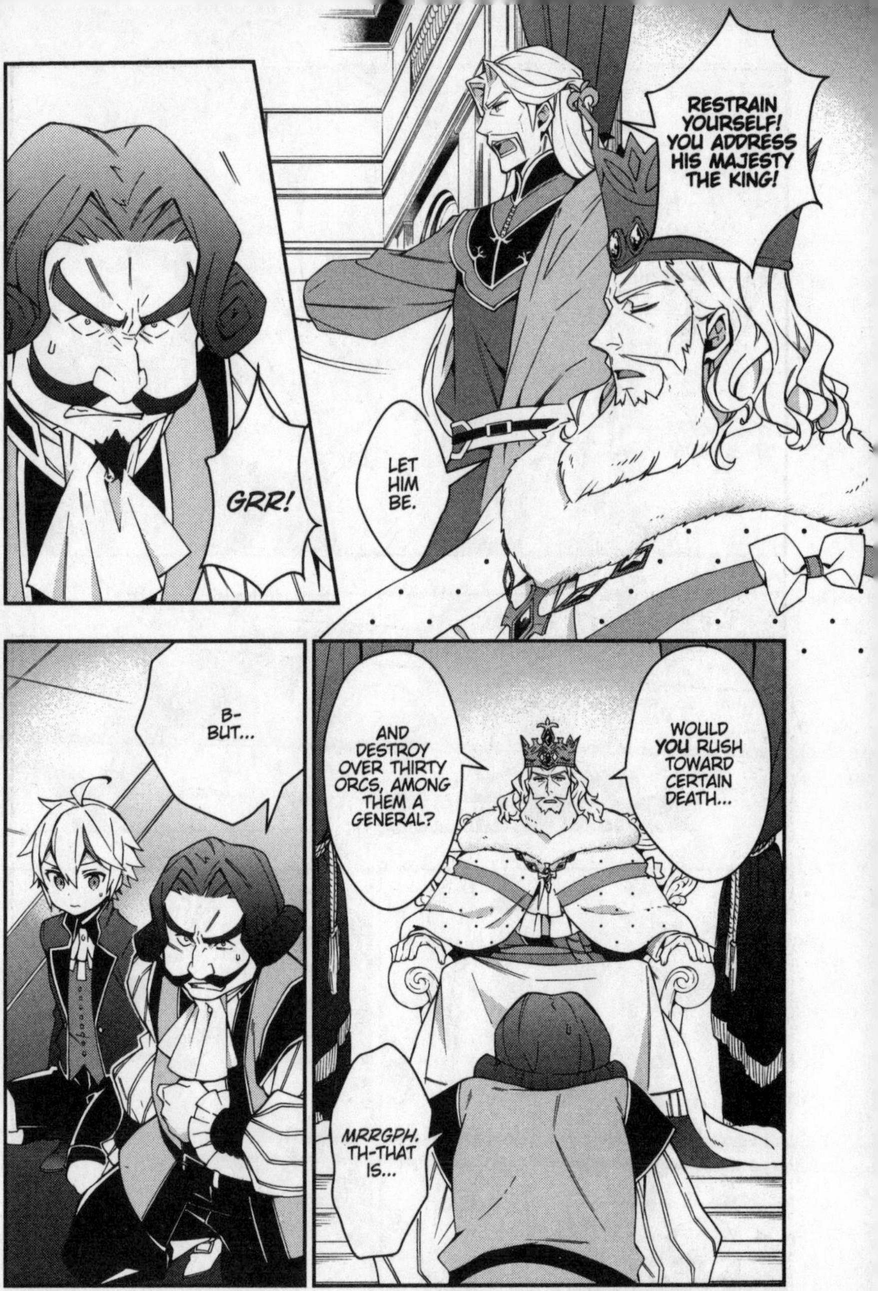
RESTRAIN YOURSELF! YOU ADDRESS HIS MAJESTY THE KING!
LET HIM BE.
GRR!
WOULD YOU RUSH TOWARD CERTAIN DEATH...
AND DESTROY OVER THIRTY ORCS, AMONG THEM A GENERAL?
MRRGPH. TH-THAT IS...
B-BUT...

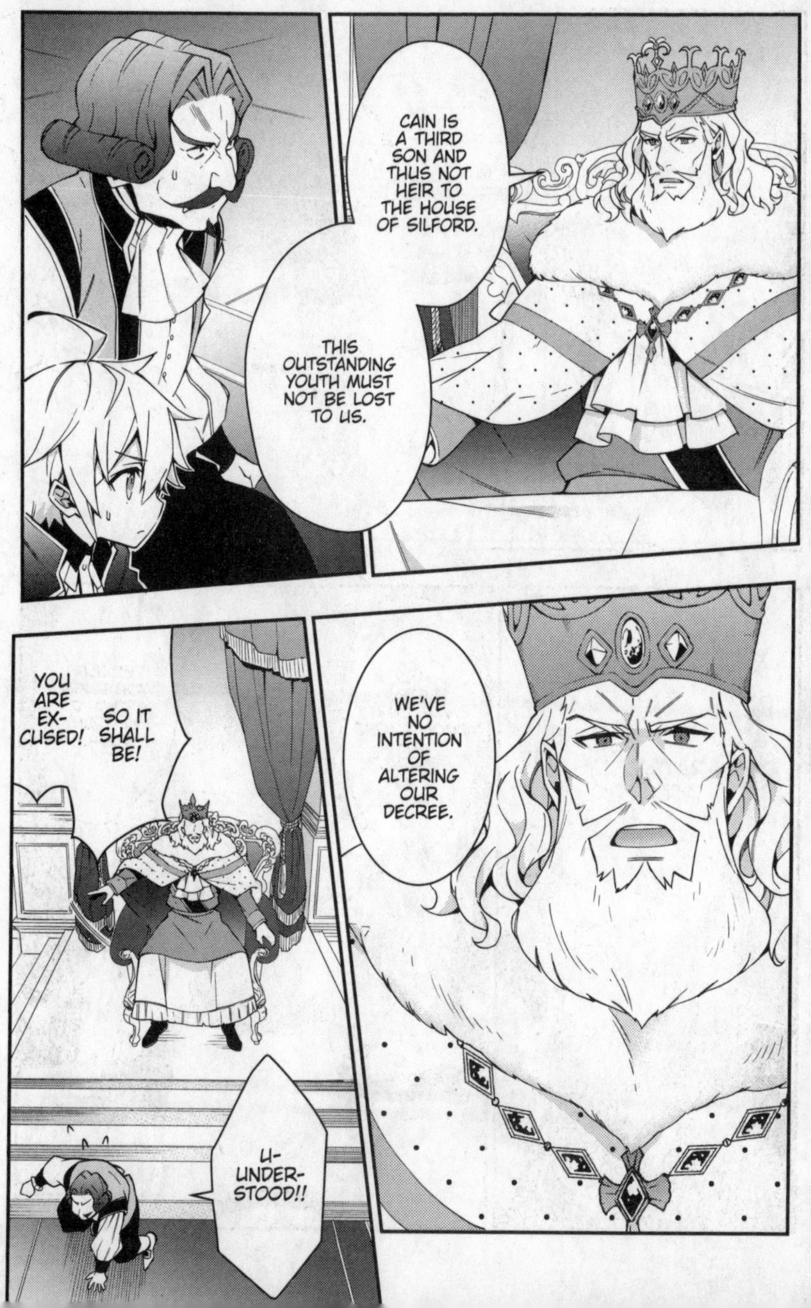
CAIN IS A THIRD SON AND THUS NOT HEIR TO THE HOUSE OF SILFORD.
THIS OUTSTANDING YOUTH MUST NOT BE LOST TO US.
WE'VE NO INTENTION OF ALTERING OUR DECREE.
SO IT SHALL BE!
YOU ARE EX-CUSED!
U-UNDER-STOOD!!

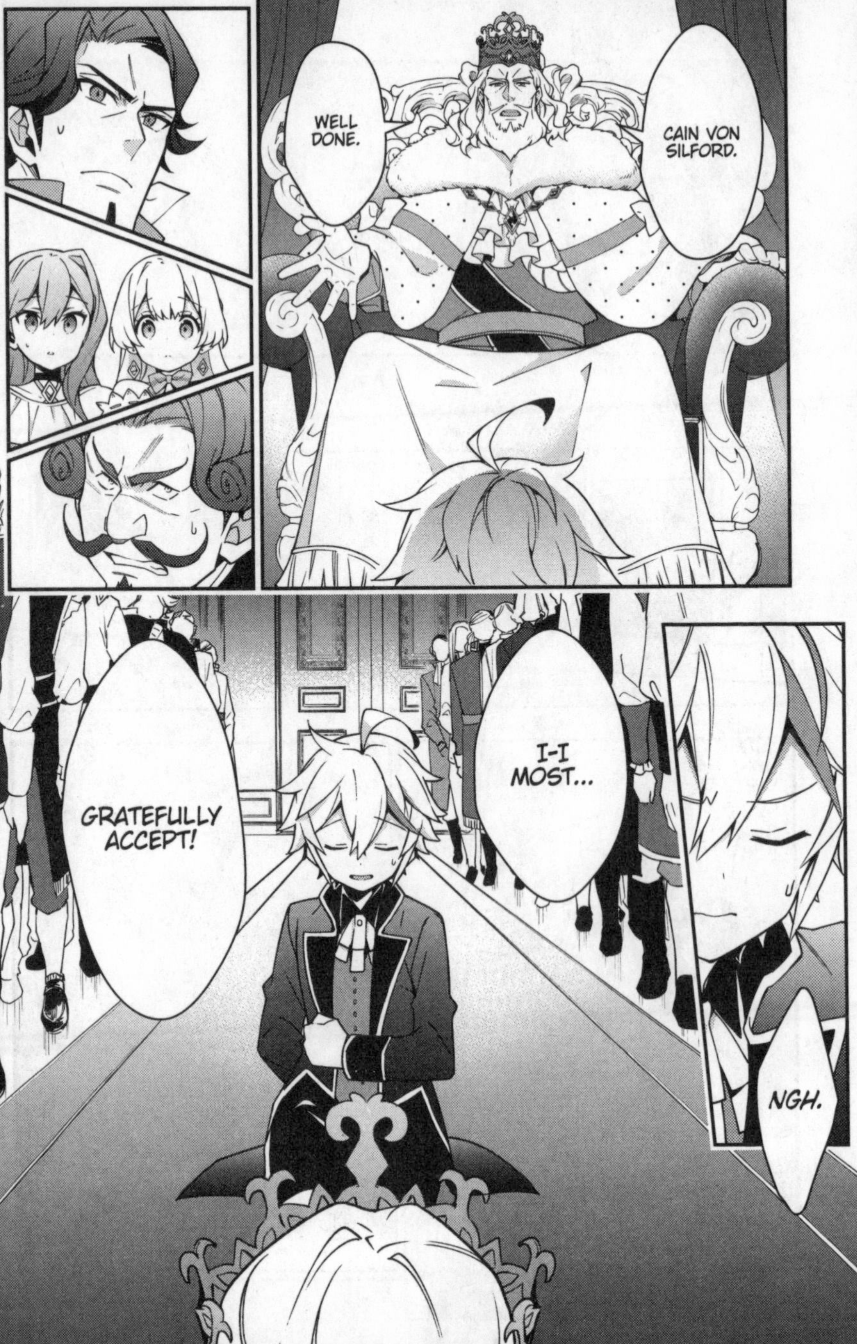
CAIN VON SILFORD.
WELL DONE.
NGH.
I-I MOST...
GRATEFULLY ACCEPT!

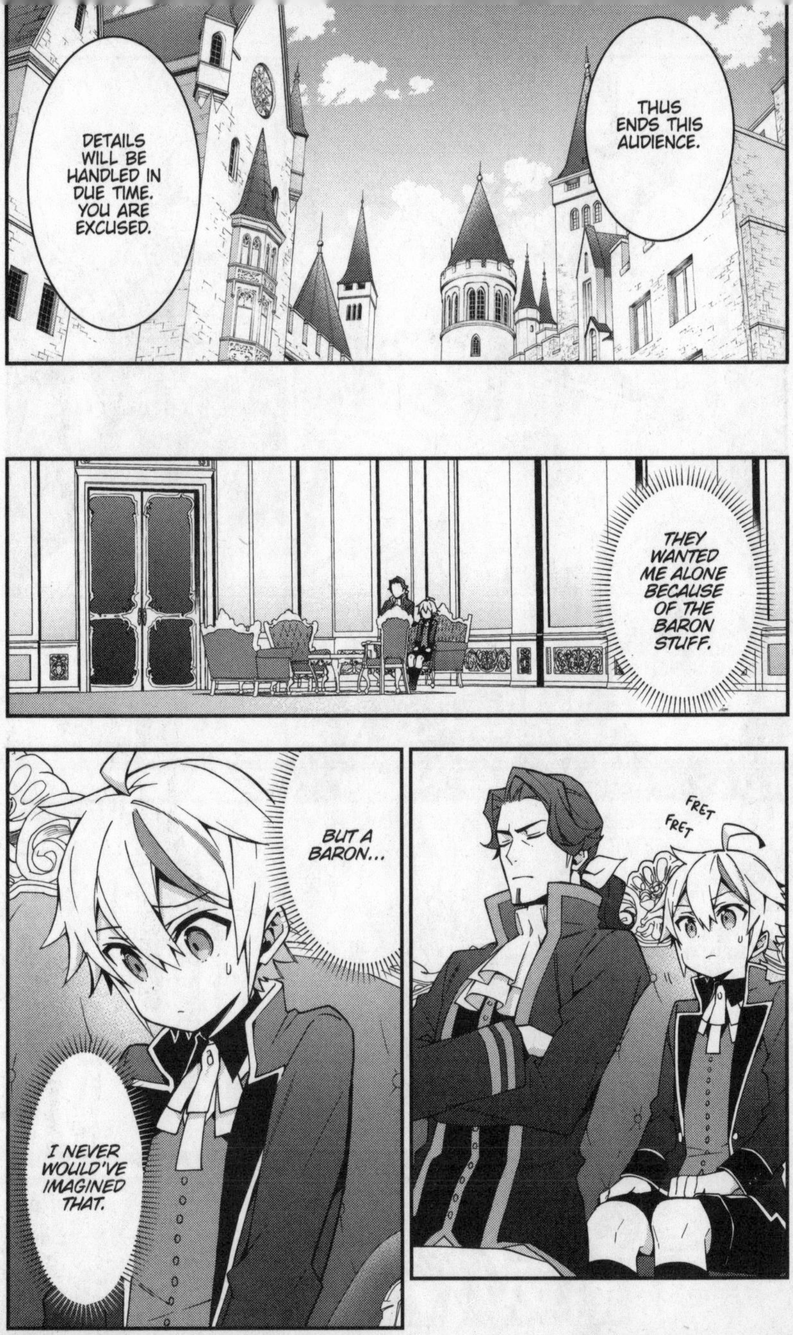
THUS ENDS THIS AUDIENCE.
DETAILS WILL BE HANDLED IN DUE TIME. YOU ARE EXCUSED.
THEY WANTED ME ALONE BECAUSE OF THE BARON STUFF.
FRET FRET
BUT A BARON...
I NEVER WOULD'VE IMAGINED THAT.

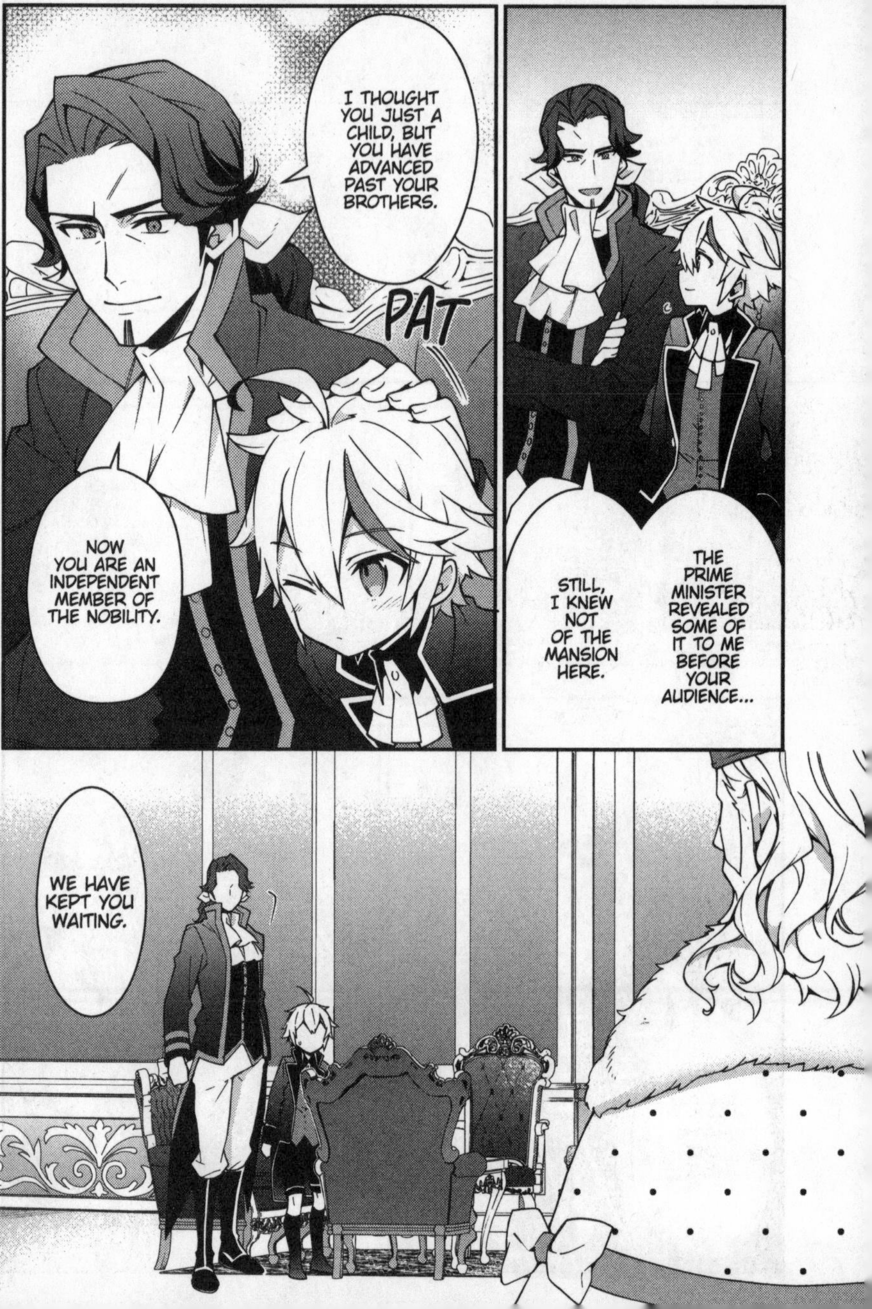
THE PRIME MINISTER REVEALED SOME OF IT TO ME BEFORE YOUR AUDIENCE...
STILL, I KNEW NOT OF THE MANSION HERE.
I THOUGHT YOU JUST A CHILD, BUT YOU HAVE ADVANCED PAST YOUR BROTHERS.
PAT
NOW YOU ARE AN INDEPENDENT MEMBER OF THE NOBILITY.
WE HAVE KEPT YOU WAITING.

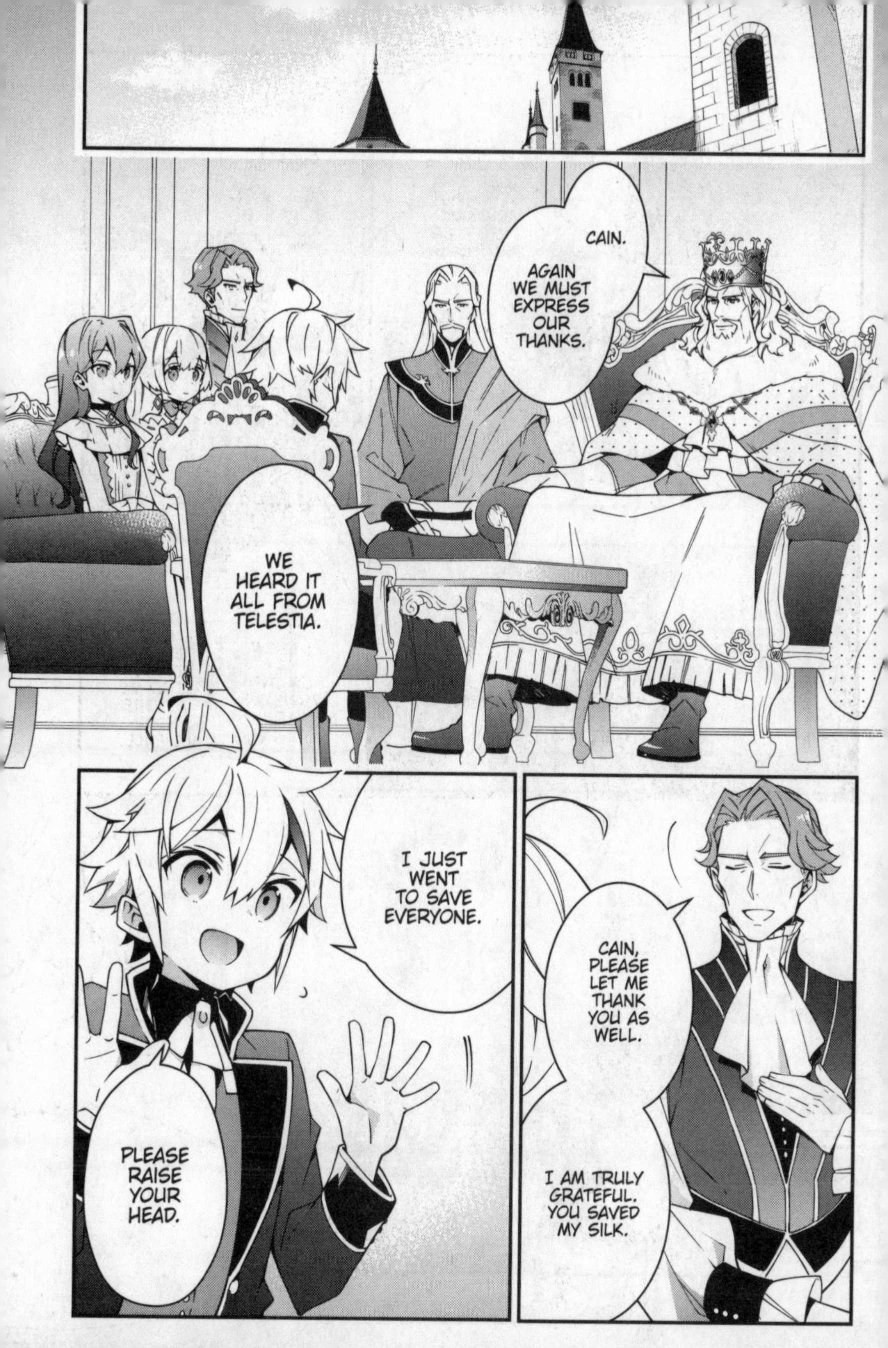
CAIN.
AGAIN WE MUST EXPRESS OUR THANKS.
WE HEARD IT ALL FROM TELESTIA.
CAIN, PLEASE LET ME THANK YOU AS WELL.
I AM TRULY GRATEFUL. YOU SAVED MY SILK.
I JUST WENT TO SAVE EVERYONE.
PLEASE RAISE YOUR HEAD.

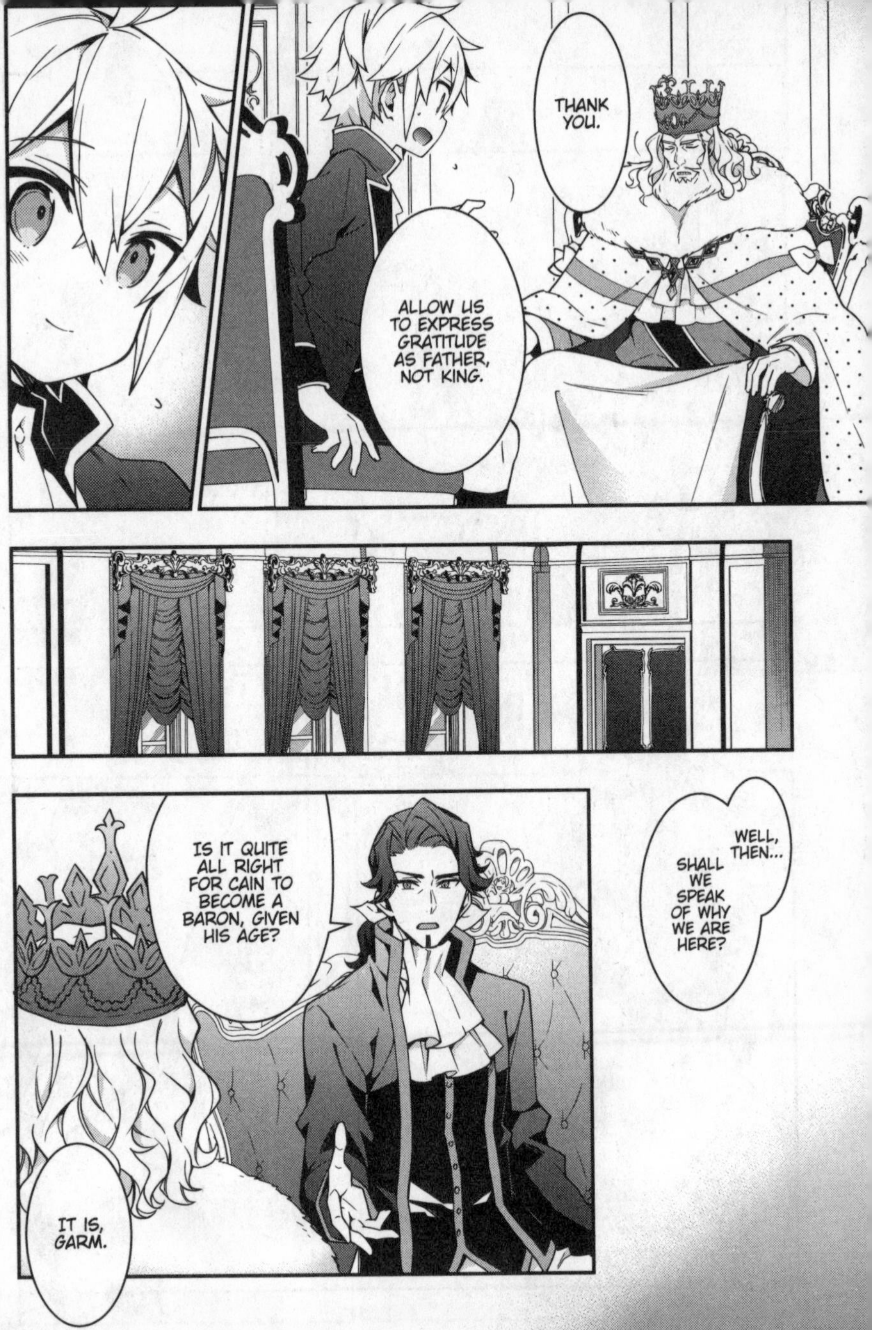
THANK YOU.
ALLOW US TO EXPRESS GRATITUDE AS FATHER, NOT KING.
WELL, THEN... SHALL WE SPEAK OF WHY WE ARE HERE?
IS IT QUITE ALL RIGHT FOR CAIN TO BECOME A BARON, GIVEN HIS AGE?
IT IS, GARM.

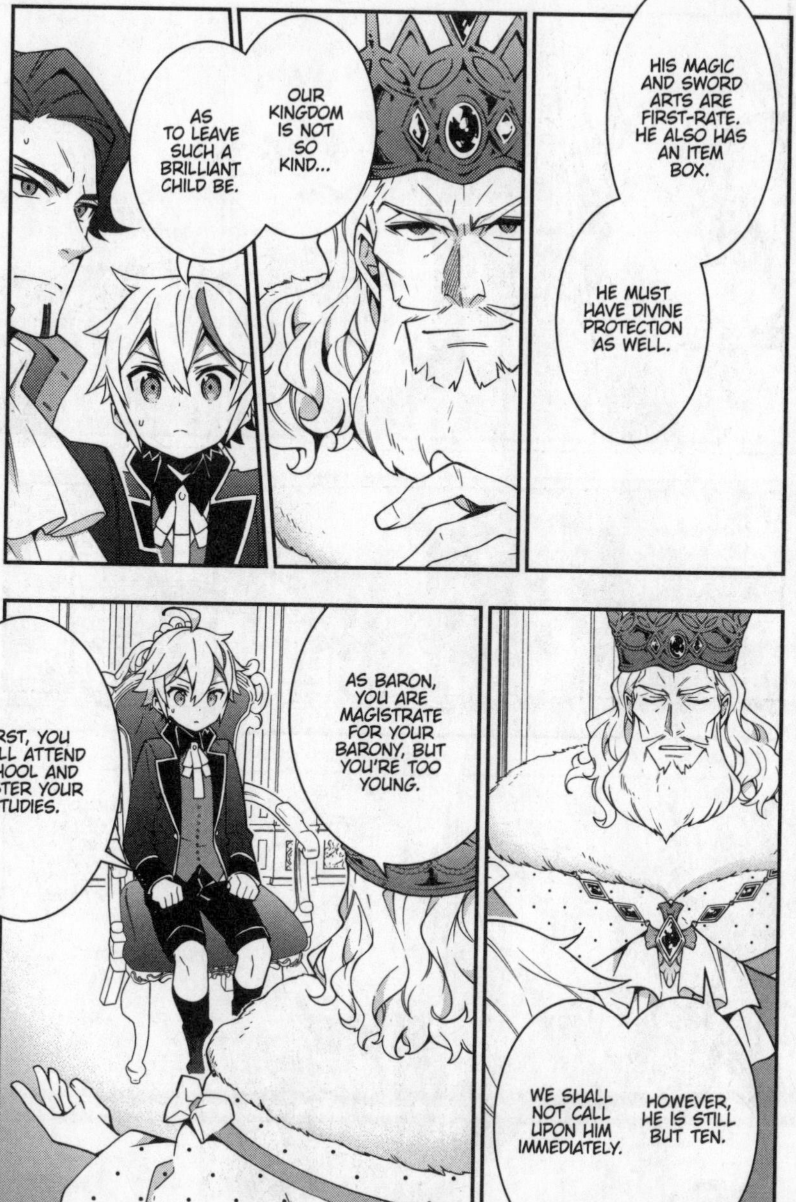
HIS MAGIC AND SWORD ARTS ARE FIRST-RATE. HE ALSO HAS AN ITEM BOX.
HE MUST HAVE DIVINE PROTECTION AS WELL.
OUR KINGDOM IS NOT SO KIND...
AS TO LEAVE SUCH A BRILLIANT CHILD BE.
HOWEVER, HE IS STILL BUT TEN.
WE SHALL NOT CALL UPON HIM IMMEDIATELY.
AS BARON, YOU ARE MAGISTRATE FOR YOUR BARONY, BUT YOU'RE TOO YOUNG.
FIRST, YOU SHALL ATTEND SCHOOL AND MASTER YOUR STUDIES.

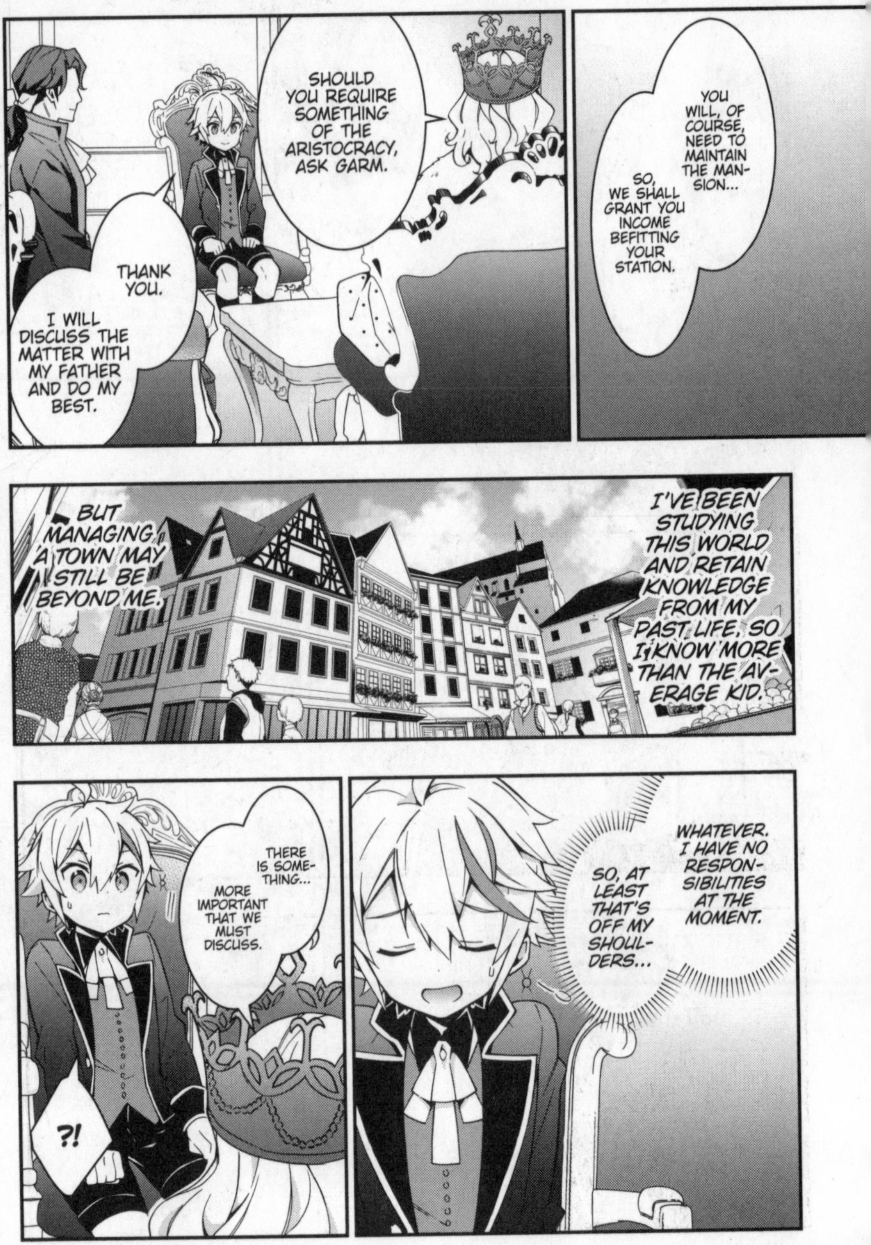
YOU WILL, OF COURSE, NEED TO MAINTAIN THE MAN-SION...
SO, WE SHALL GRANT YOU INCOME BEFITTING YOUR STATION.
SHOULD YOU REQUIRE SOMETHING OF THE ARISTOCRACY, ASK GARM.
THANK YOU.
I WILL DISCUSS THE MATTER WITH MY FATHER AND DO MY BEST.
I'VE BEEN STUDYING THIS WORLD AND RETAIN KNOWLEDGE FROM MY PAST LIFE, SO I KNOW MORE THAN THE AV-ERAGE KID.
BUT MANAGING A TOWN MAY STILL BE BEYOND ME.
WHATEVER. I HAVE NO RESPON-SIBILITIES AT THE MOMENT.
SO, AT LEAST THAT'S OFF MY SHOUL-DERS...
THERE IS SOME-THING...
MORE IMPORTANT THAT WE MUST DISCUSS.
?!

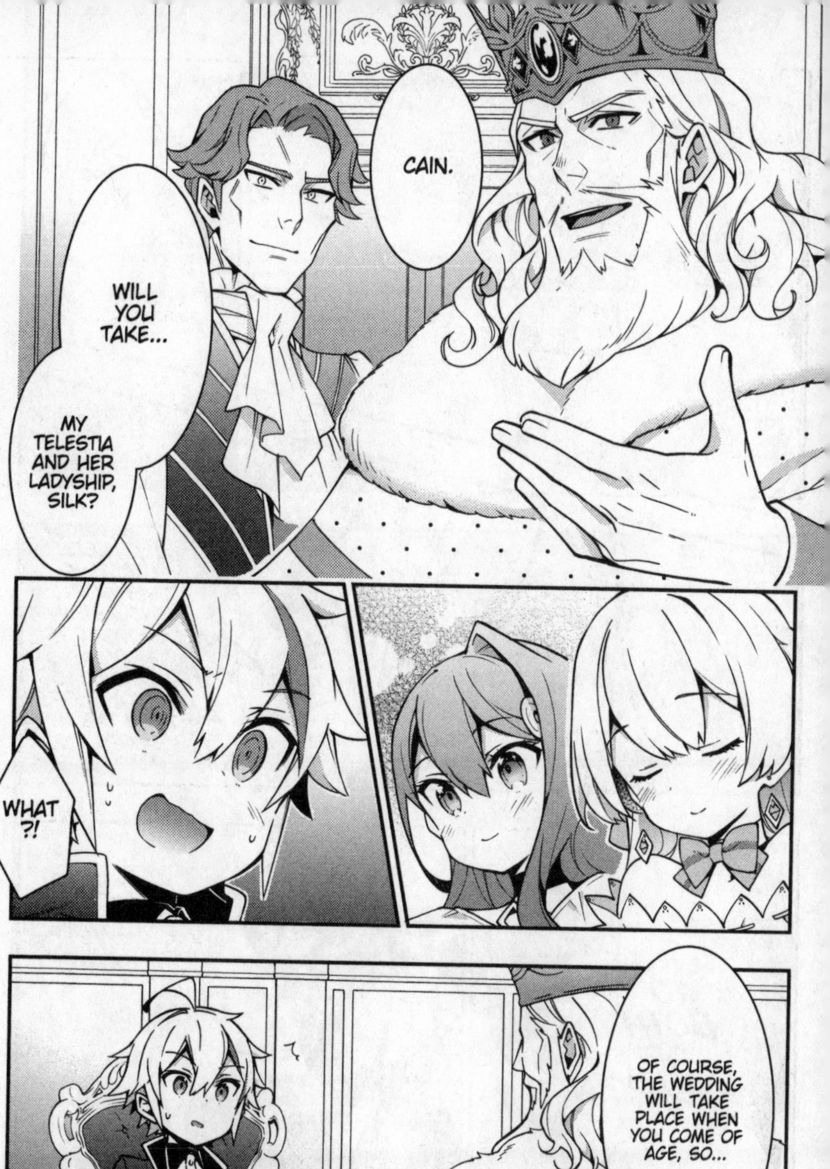
CAIN.
WILL YOU TAKE...
MY TELESTIA AND HER LADYSHIP, SILK?
WHAT?!
OF COURSE, THE WEDDING WILL TAKE PLACE WHEN YOU COME OF AGE, SO...

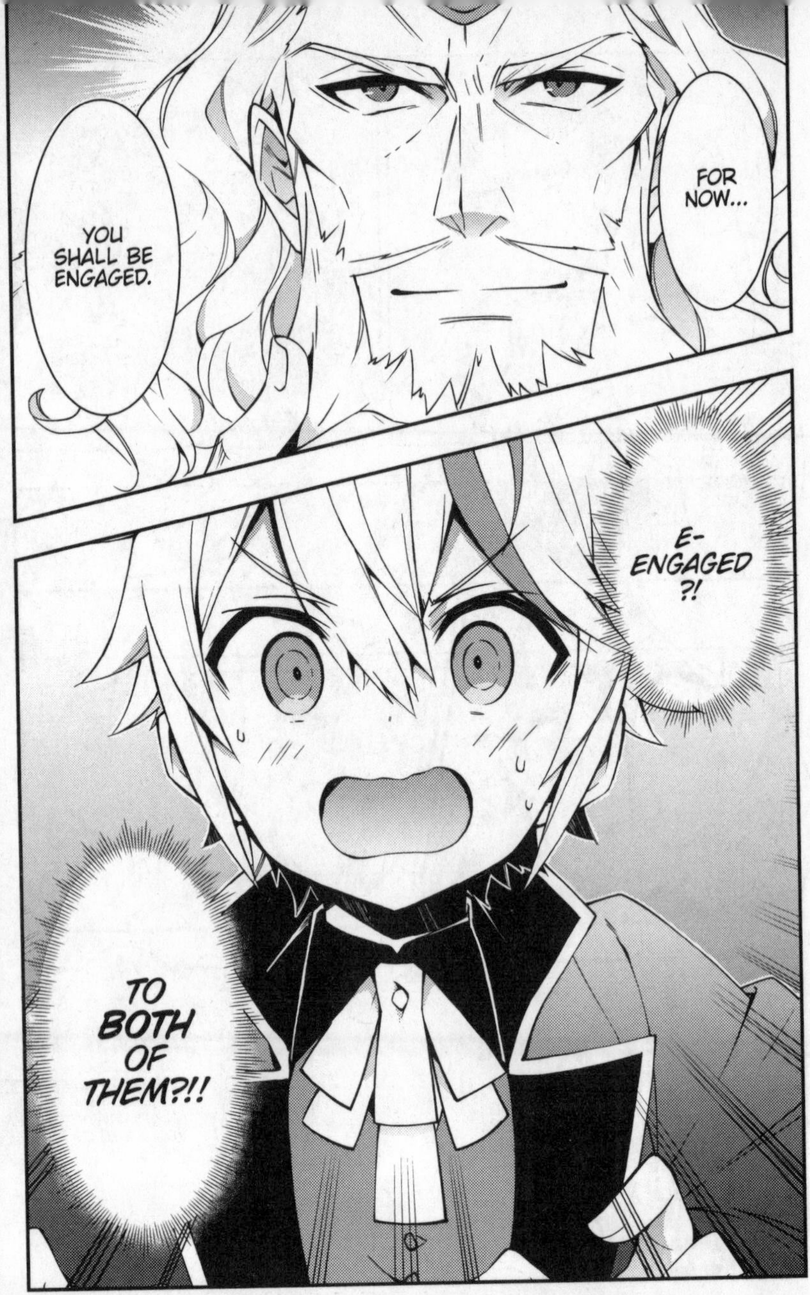
FOR NOW...
YOU SHALL BE ENGAGED.
E-ENGAGED?!
TO BOTH OF THEM?!!

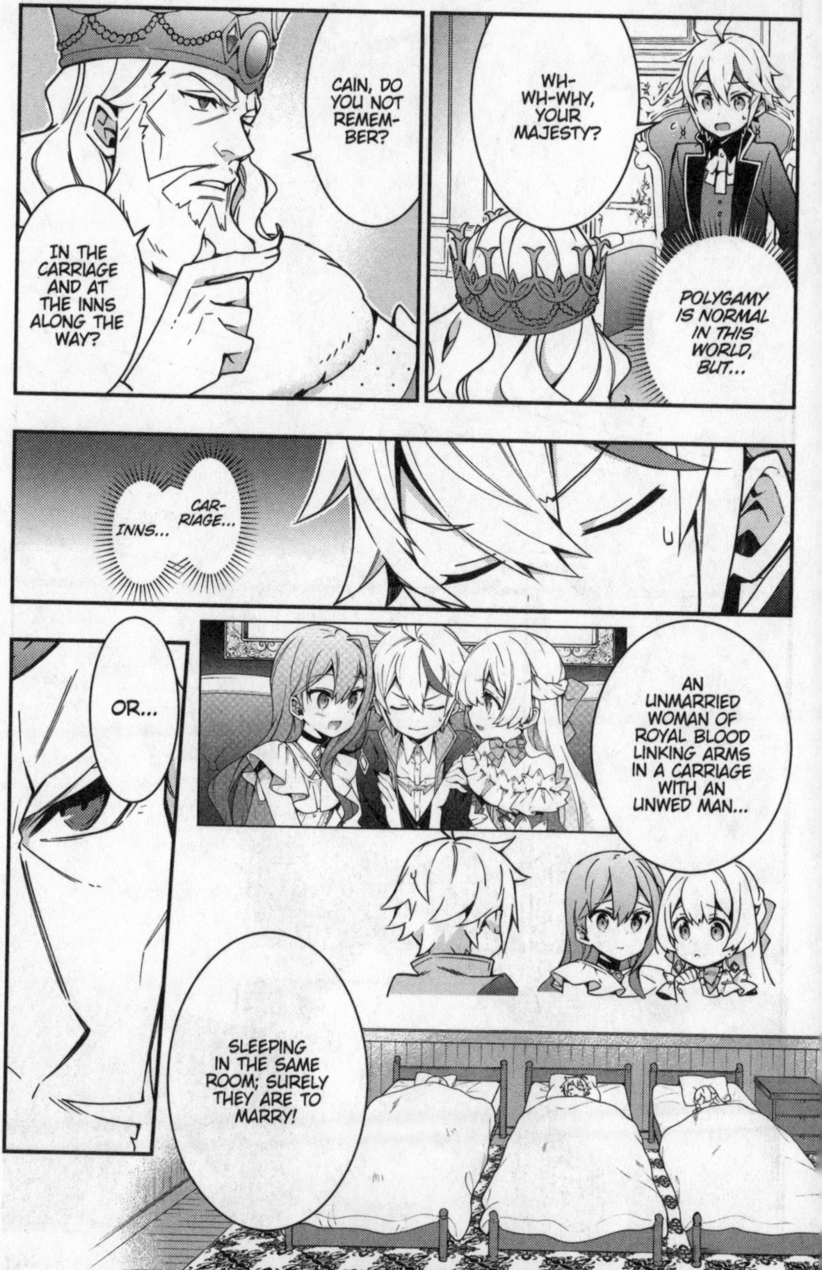
WH-WH-WHY, YOUR MAJESTY?
POLYGAMY IS NORMAL IN THIS WORLD, BUT...
CAIN, DO YOU NOT REMEMBER?
IN THE CARRIAGE AND AT THE INNS ALONG THE WAY?
CARRIAGE...
INNS...
AN UNMARRIED WOMAN OF ROYAL BLOOD LINKING ARMS IN A CARRIAGE WITH AN UNWED MAN...
SLEEPING IN THE SAME ROOM; SURELY THEY ARE TO MARRY!
OR...

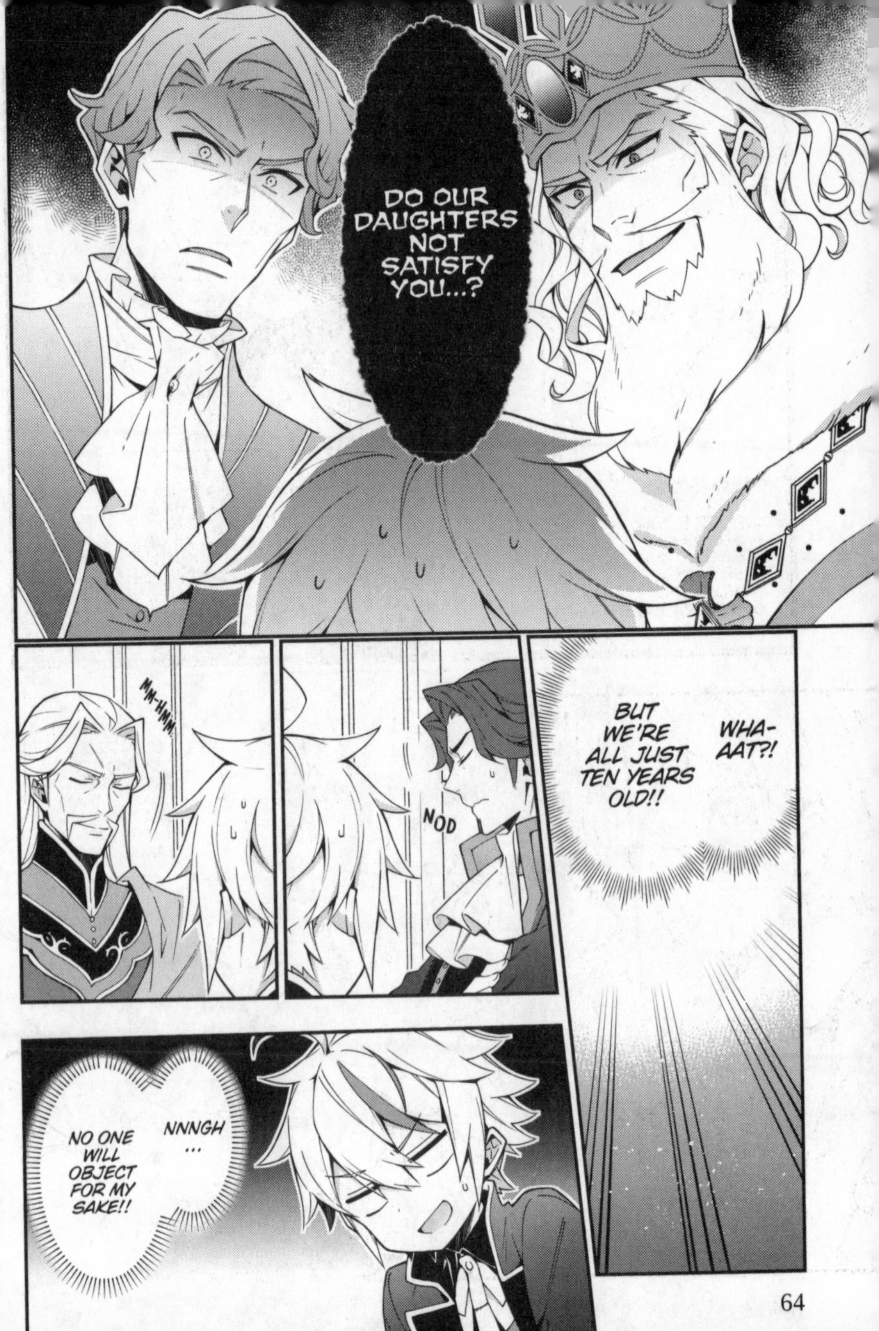
DO OUR DAUGHTERS NOT SATISFY YOU...?
WHA-AAT?!
BUT WE'RE ALL JUST TEN YEARS OLD!!
NOD
MM-HMM
NNNGH...
NO ONE WILL OBJECT FOR MY SAKE!!

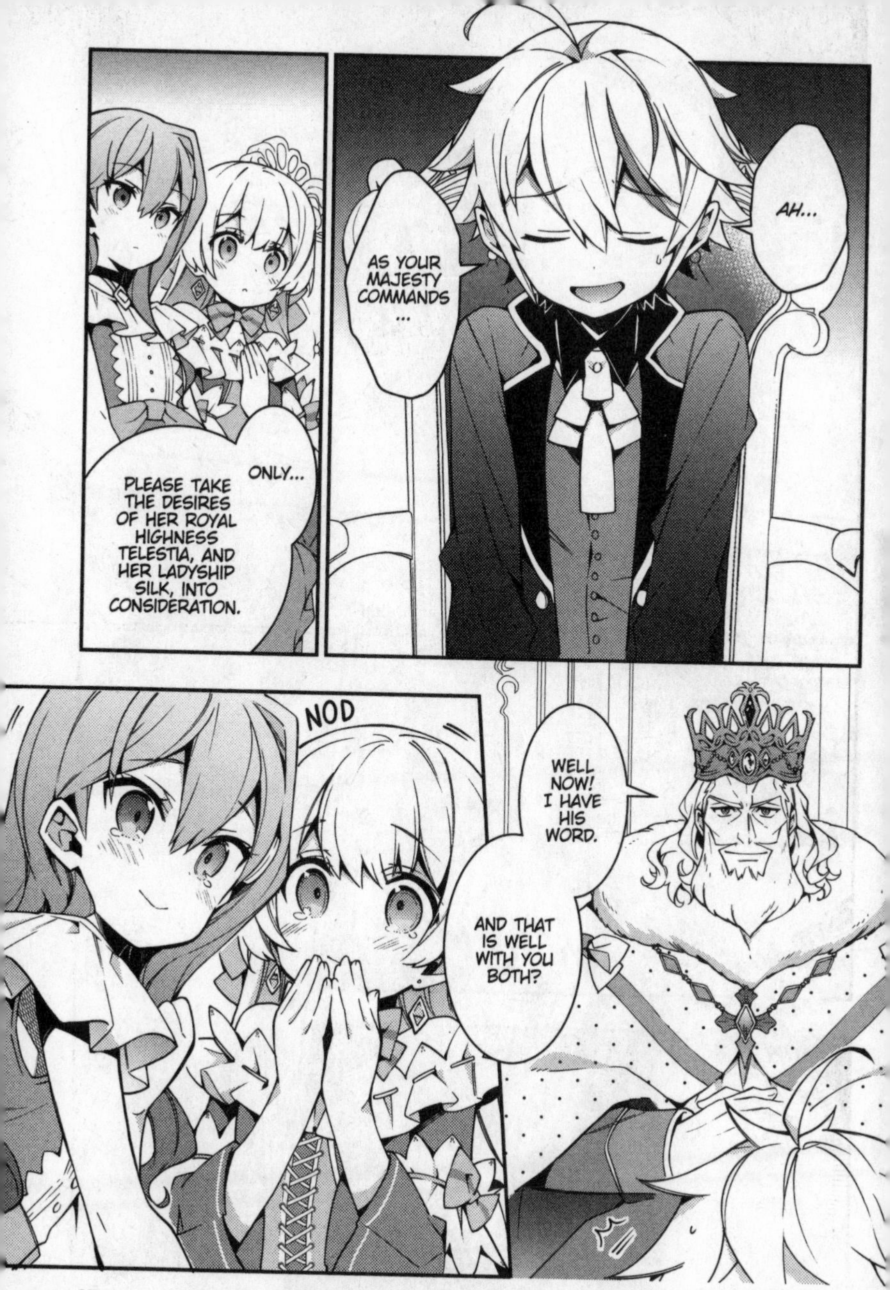
AH...
AS YOUR MAJESTY COMMANDS ...
ONLY...
PLEASE TAKE THE DESIRES OF HER ROYAL HIGHNESS TELESTIA, AND HER LADYSHIP SILK, INTO CONSIDERATION.
WELL NOW! I HAVE HIS WORD.
AND THAT IS WELL WITH YOU BOTH?
NOD

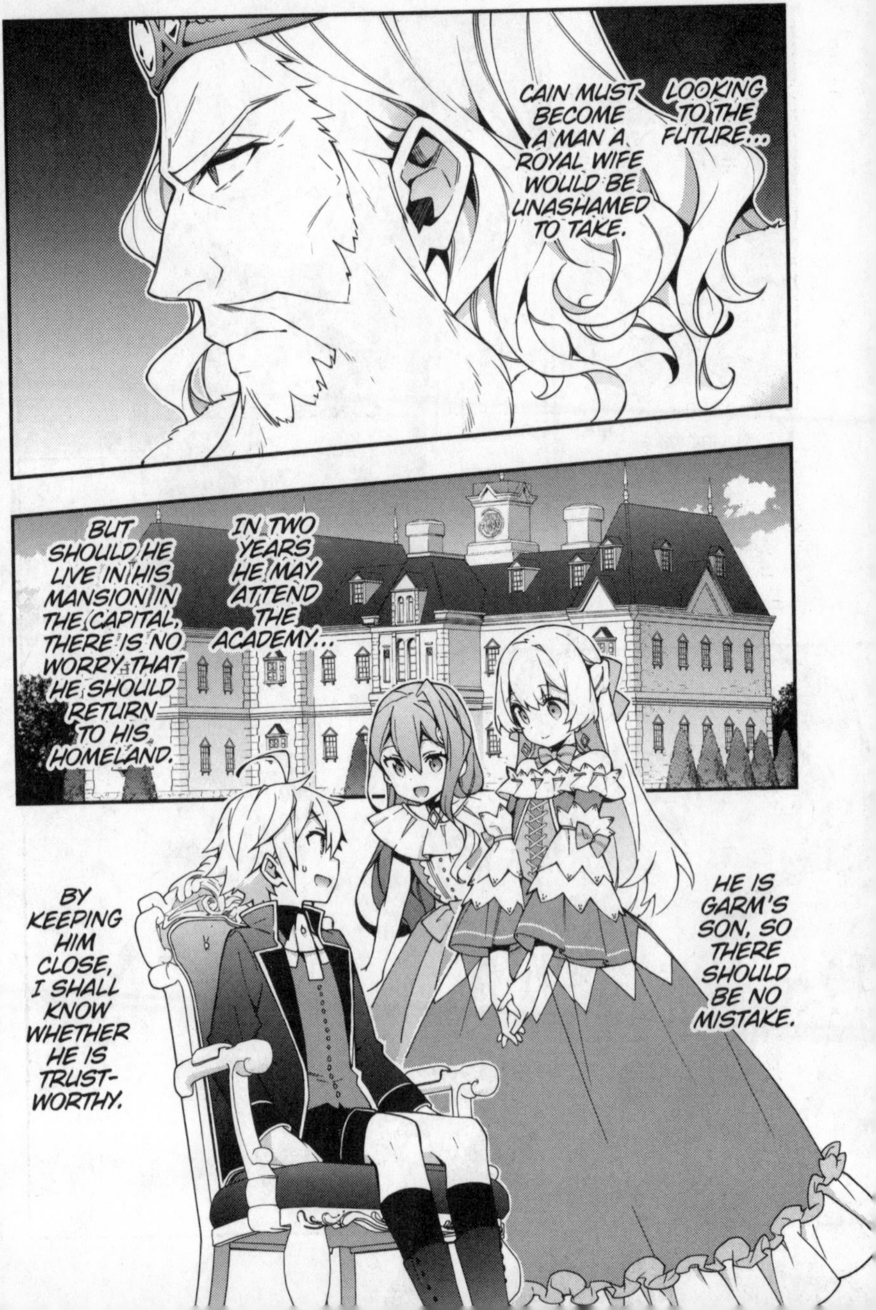
LOOKING TO THE FUTURE...
CAIN MUST BECOME A MAN A ROYAL WIFE WOULD BE UNASHAMED TO TAKE.
IN TWO YEARS HE MAY ATTEND THE ACADEMY...
BUT SHOULD HE LIVE IN HIS MANSION IN THE CAPITAL, THERE IS NO WORRY THAT HE SHOULD RETURN TO HIS HOMELAND.
HE IS GARM'S SON, SO THERE SHOULD BE NO MISTAKE.
BY KEEPING HIM CLOSE, I SHALL KNOW WHETHER HE IS TRUST-WORTHY.

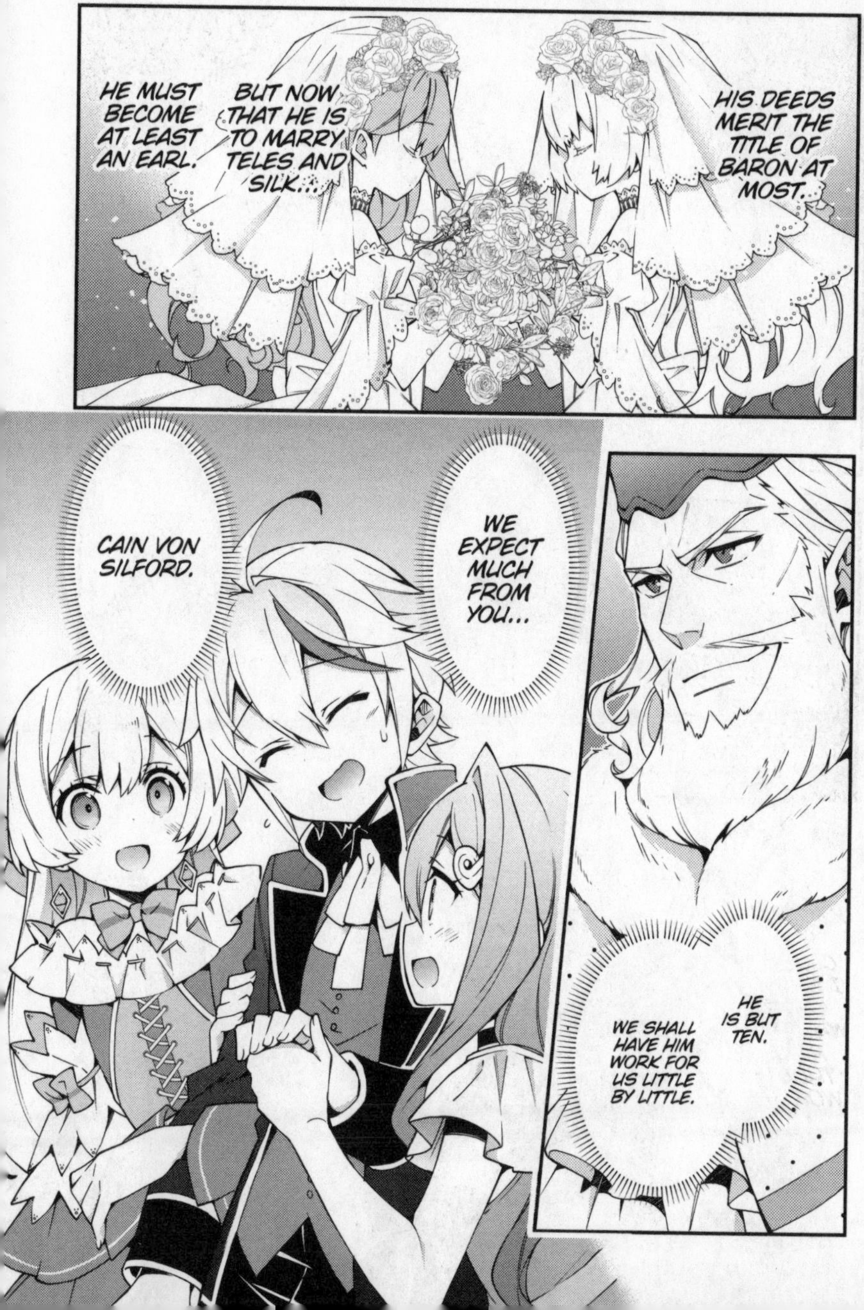
HIS DEEDS MERIT THE TITLE OF BARON AT MOST.
BUT NOW THAT HE IS TO MARRY TELES AND SILK...
HE MUST BECOME AT LEAST AN EARL.
HE IS BUT TEN.
WE SHALL HAVE HIM WORK FOR US LITTLE BY LITTLE.
WE EXPECT MUCH FROM YOU...
CAIN VON SILFORD.

Prime Minister Magna is popular with a faction of maids.

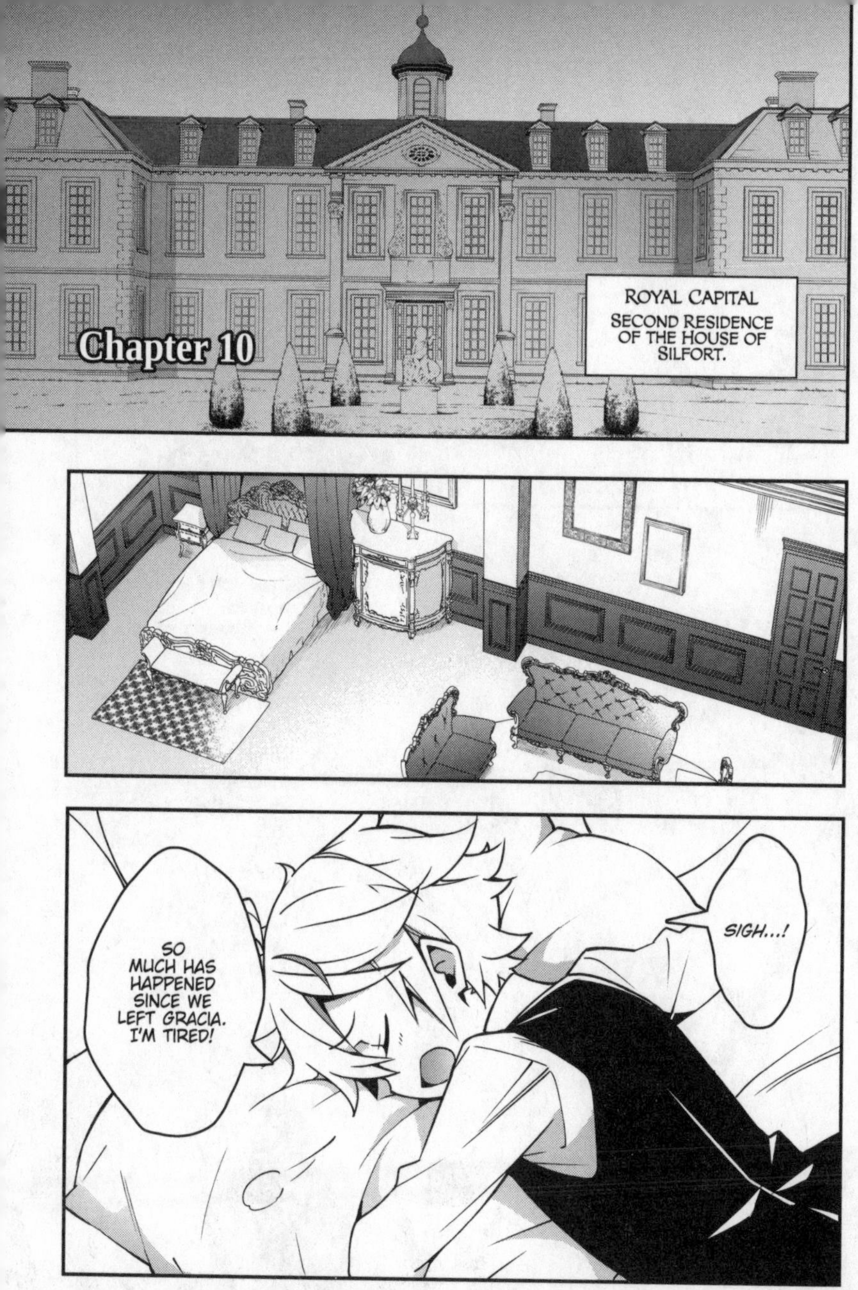
ROYAL CAPITAL SECOND RESIDENCE OF THE HOUSE OF SILFORT.
Chapter 10
SIGH...!
SO MUCH HAS HAPPENED SINCE WE LEFT GRACIA. I'M TIRED!

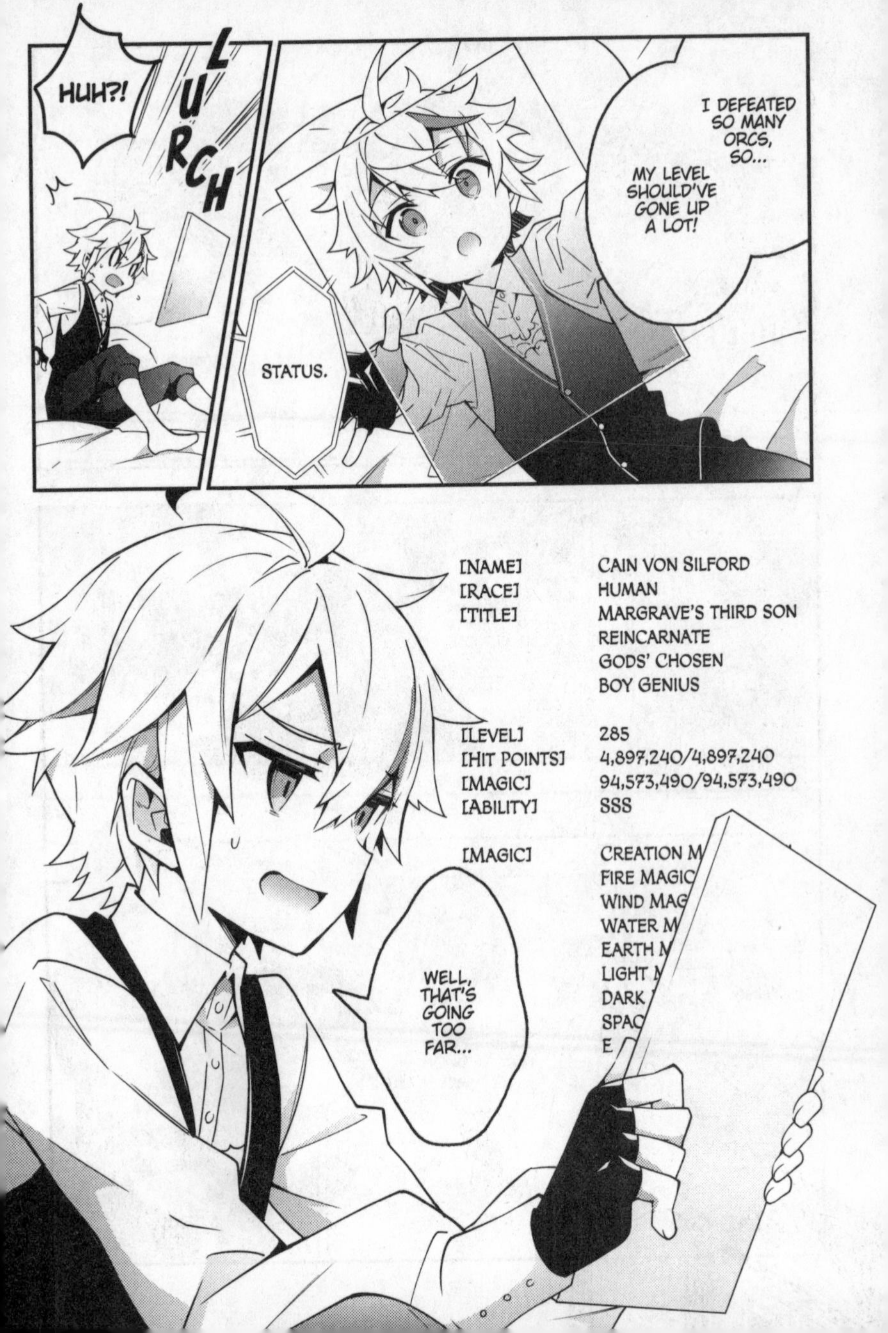

I DEFEATED SO MANY ORCS, SO...
MY LEVEL SHOULD'VE GONE UP A LOT!
STATUS.
LURCH
HUH?!
[NAME] CAIN VON SILFORD
[RACE] HUMAN
[TITLE] MARGRAVE'S THIRD SON
REINCARNATE
GODS' CHOSEN
BOY GENIUS
[LEVEL] 285
[HIT POINTS] 4,897,240/4,897,240
[MAGIC] 94,573,490/94,573,490
[ABILITY] SSS
[MAGIC] CREATION M
FIRE MAGIC
WIND MAG
WATER M
EARTH M
LIGHT M
DARK
SPAC
E
WELL, THAT'S GOING TOO FAR...

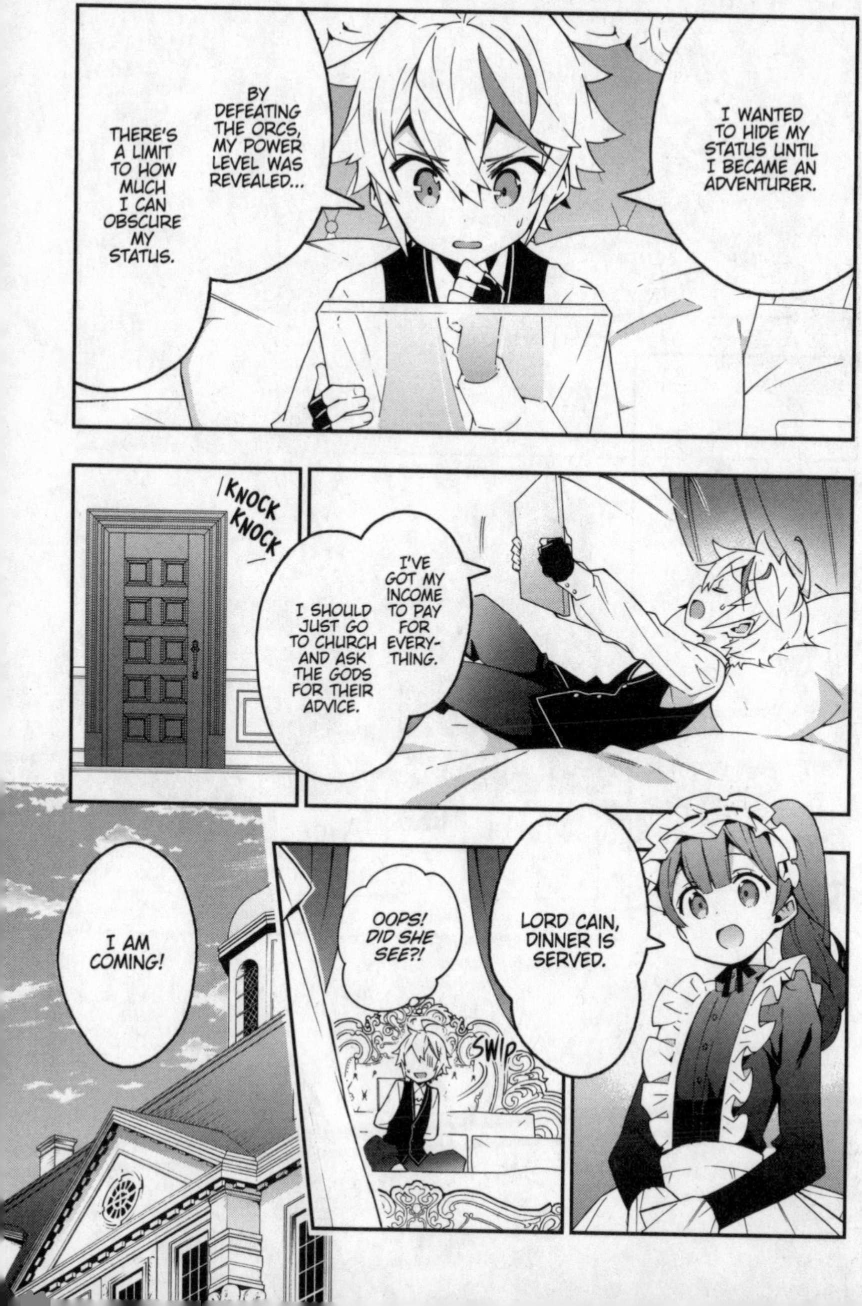
I WANTED TO HIDE MY STATUS UNTIL I BECAME AN ADVENTURER.
BY DEFEATING THE ORCS, MY POWER LEVEL WAS REVEALED...
THERE'S A LIMIT TO HOW MUCH I CAN OBSCURE MY STATUS.
I'VE GOT MY INCOME TO PAY FOR EVERY-THING.
I SHOULD JUST GO TO CHURCH AND ASK THE GODS FOR THEIR ADVICE.
KNOCK KNOCK
LORD CAIN, DINNER IS SERVED.
OOPS! DID SHE SEE?!
SWIP
I AM COMING!

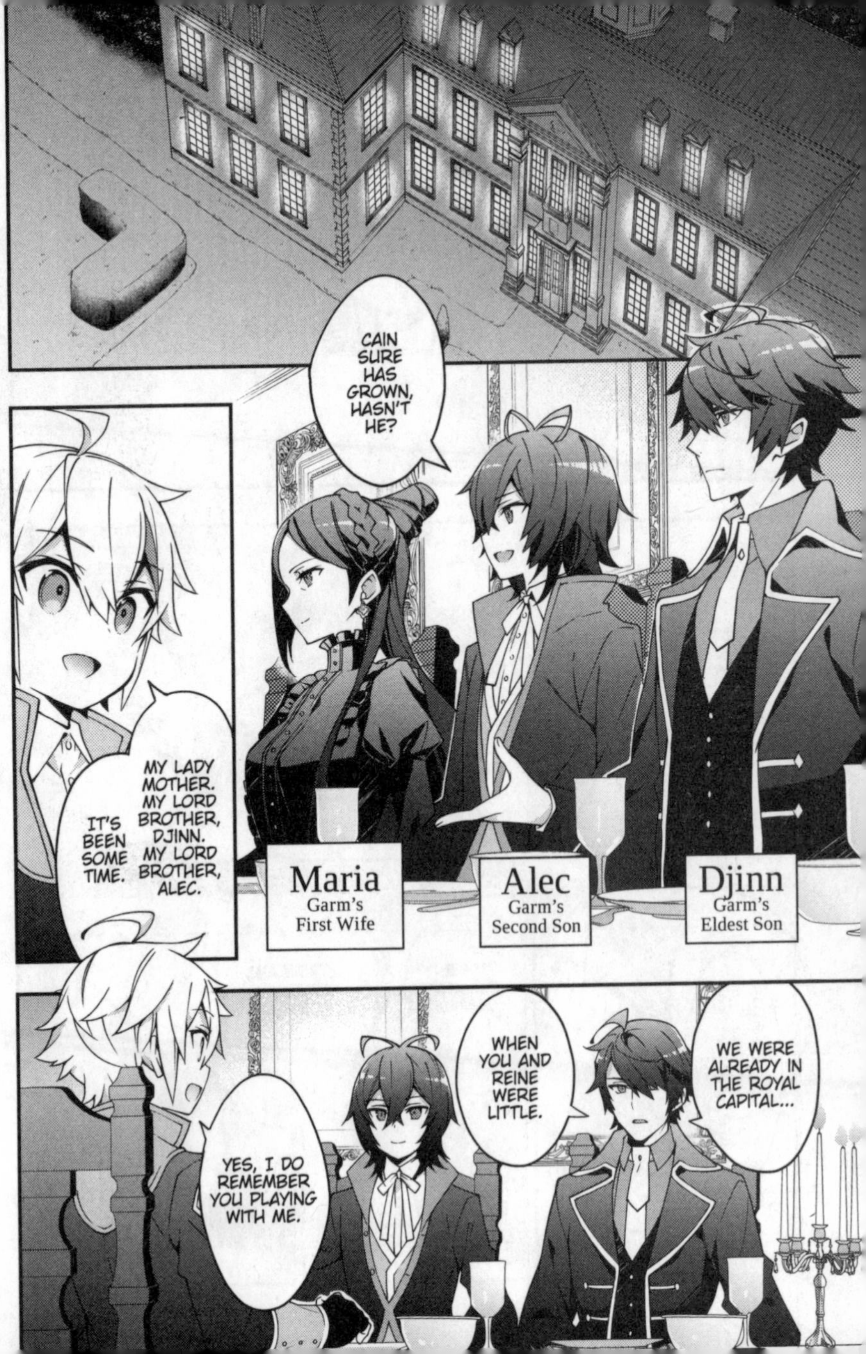
CAIN SURE HAS GROWN, HASN'T HE?
Djinn Garm's Eldest Son
Alec Garm's Second Son
Maria Garm's First Wife
MY LADY MOTHER. MY LORD BROTHER, DJINN. MY LORD BROTHER, ALEC.
IT'S BEEN SOME TIME.
WE WERE ALREADY IN THE ROYAL CAPITAL...
WHEN YOU AND REINE WERE LITTLE.
YES, I DO REMEMBER YOU PLAYING WITH ME.

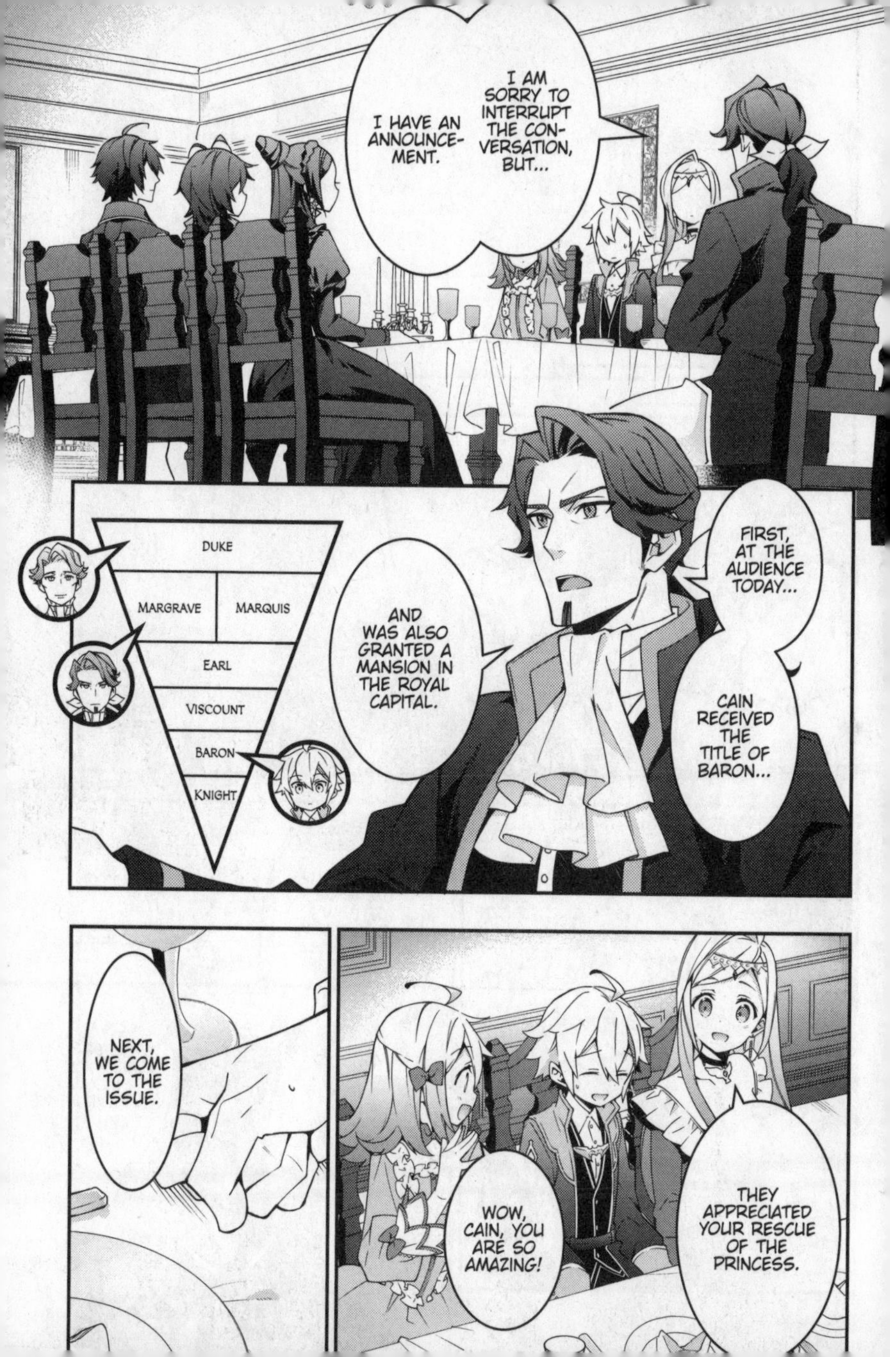

I AM SORRY TO INTERRUPT THE CON-VERSATION, BUT...
I HAVE AN ANNOUNCE-MENT.
FIRST, AT THE AUDIENCE TODAY...
CAIN RECEIVED THE TITLE OF BARON...
AND WAS ALSO GRANTED A MANSION IN THE ROYAL CAPITAL.
DUKE
MARGRAVE
MARQUIS
EARL
VISCOUNT
BARON
KNIGHT
THEY APPRECIATED YOUR RESCUE OF THE PRINCESS.
WOW, CAIN, YOU ARE SO AMAZING!
NEXT, WE COME TO THE ISSUE.

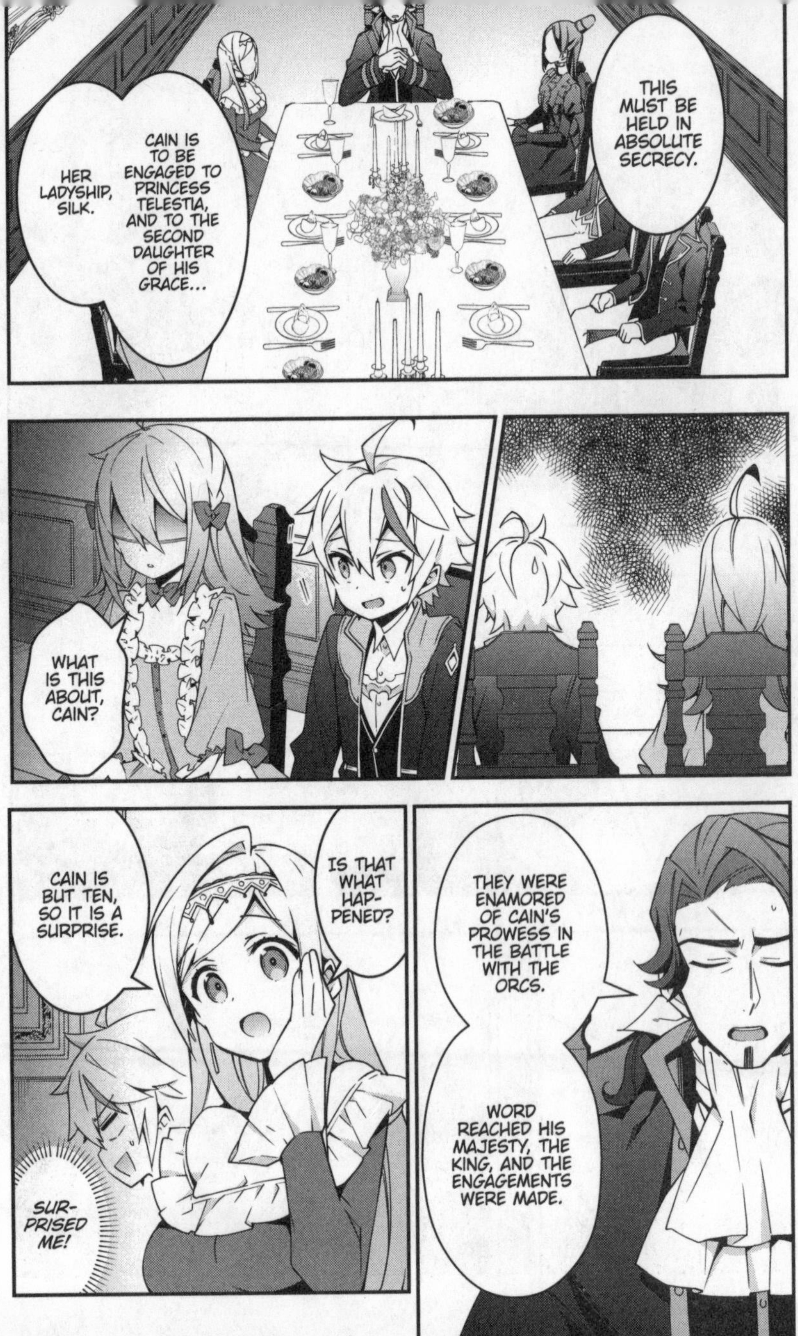
THIS MUST BE HELD IN ABSOLUTE SECRECY.
CAIN IS TO BE ENGAGED TO PRINCESS TELESTIA, AND TO THE SECOND DAUGHTER OF HIS GRACE...
HER LADYSHIP, SILK.
WHAT IS THIS ABOUT, CAIN?
THEY WERE ENAMORED OF CAIN'S PROWESS IN THE BATTLE WITH THE ORCS.
WORD REACHED HIS MAJESTY, THE KING, AND THE ENGAGEMENTS WERE MADE.
IS THAT WHAT HAP-PENED?
CAIN IS BUT TEN, SO IT IS A SURPRISE.
SUR-PRISED ME!

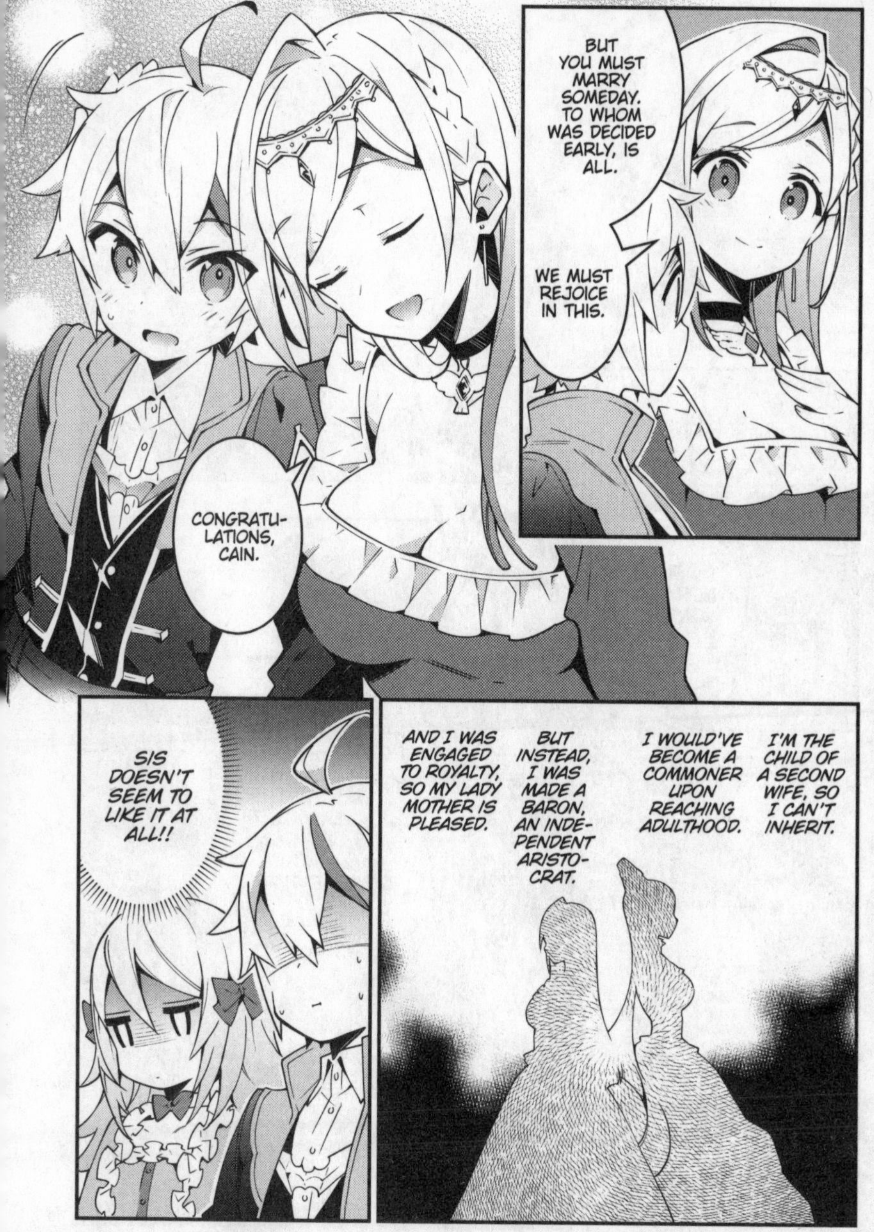
BUT YOU MUST MARRY SOMEDAY. TO WHOM WAS DECIDED EARLY, IS ALL.
WE MUST REJOICE IN THIS.
CONGRATULATIONS, CAIN.
I'M THE CHILD OF A SECOND WIFE, SO I CAN'T INHERIT.
I WOULD'VE BECOME A COMMONER UPON REACHING ADULTHOOD.
BUT INSTEAD, I WAS MADE A BARON, AN INDEPENDENT ARISTOCRAT.
AND I WAS ENGAGED TO ROYALTY, SO MY LADY MOTHER IS PLEASED.
SIS DOESN'T SEEM TO LIKE IT AT ALL!!

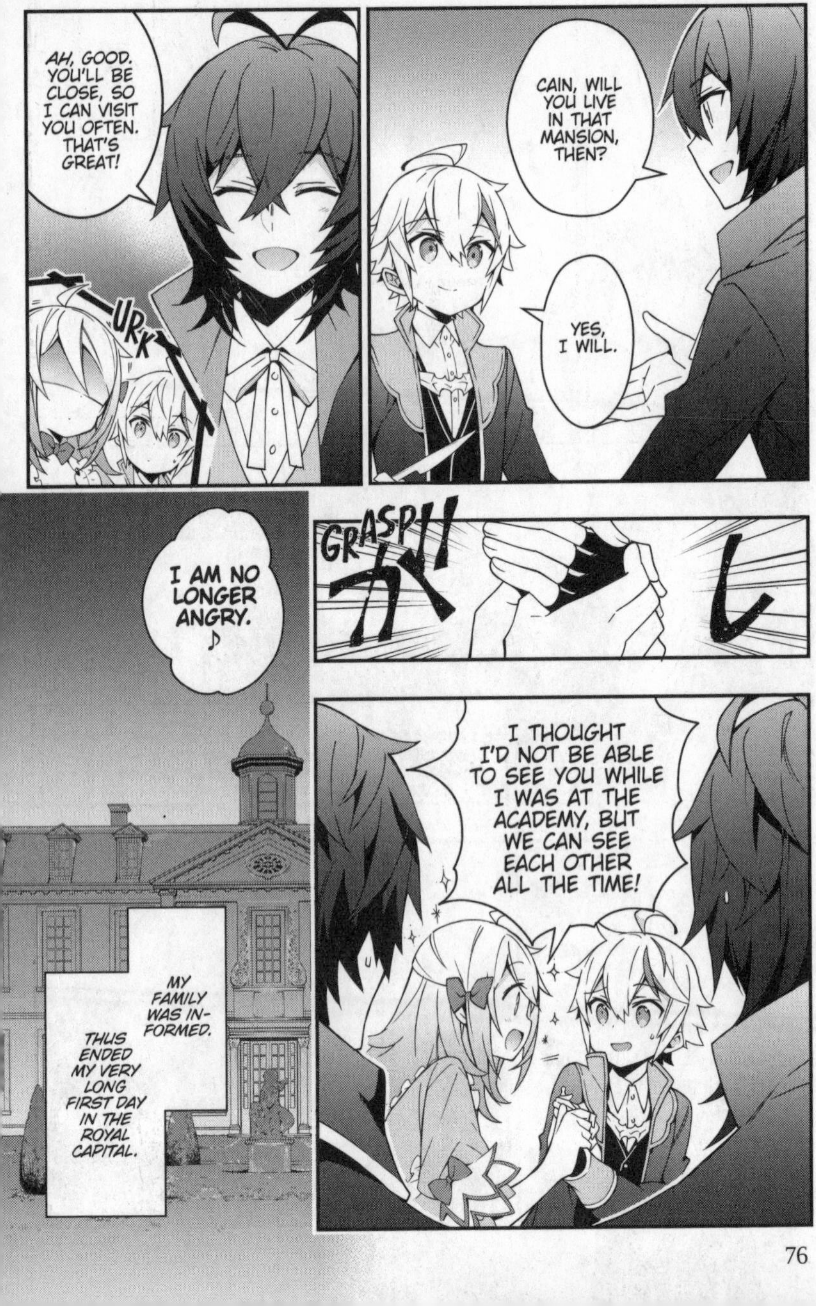
CAIN, WILL YOU LIVE IN THAT MANSION, THEN?
YES, I WILL.
AH, GOOD. YOU'LL BE CLOSE, SO I CAN VISIT YOU OFTEN. THAT'S GREAT!
URK
GRASP!!
ガシ
I THOUGHT I'D NOT BE ABLE TO SEE YOU WHILE I WAS AT THE ACADEMY, BUT WE CAN SEE EACH OTHER ALL THE TIME!
I AM NO LONGER ANGRY. ♪
MY FAMILY WAS IN-FORMED.
THUS ENDED MY VERY LONG FIRST DAY IN THE ROYAL CAPITAL.

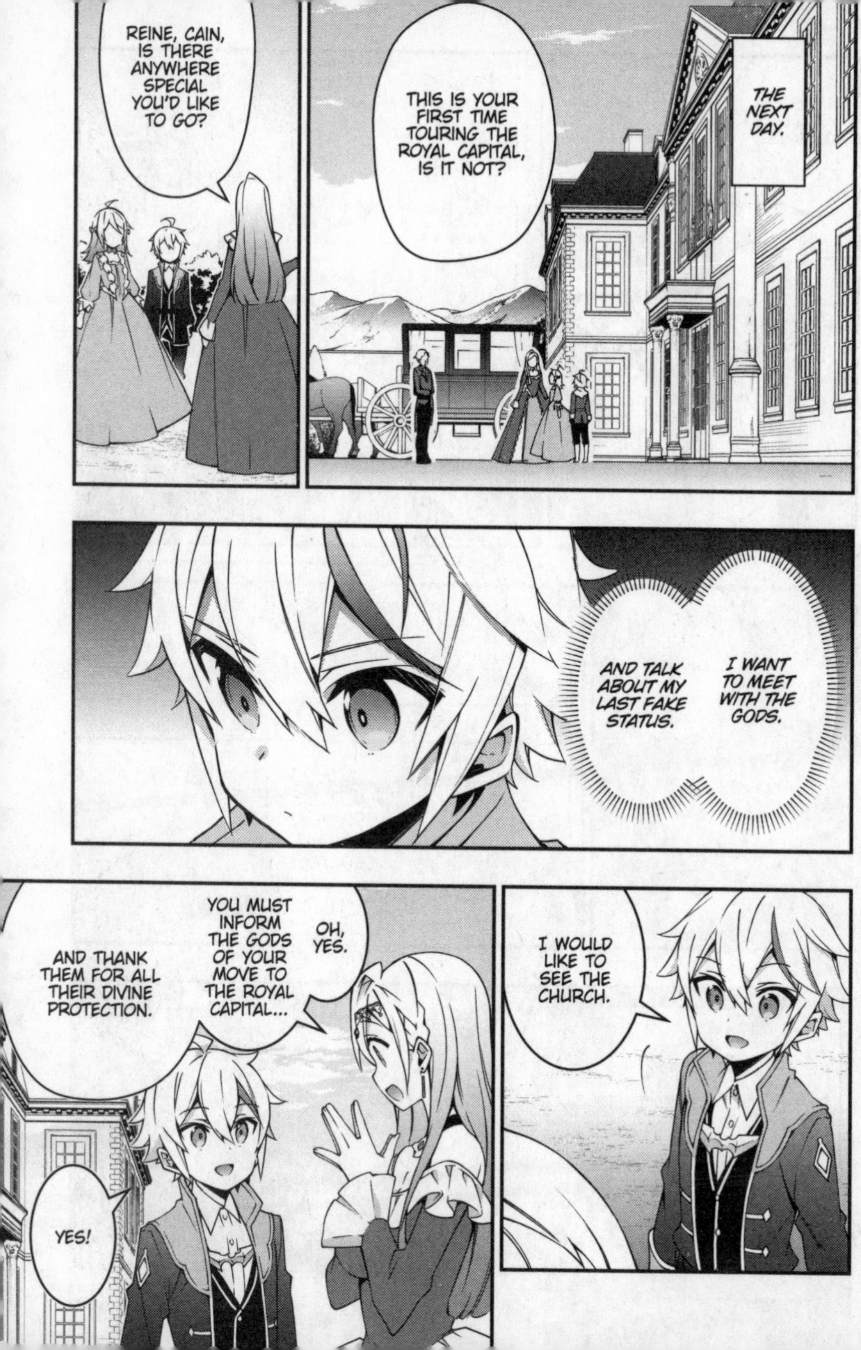
THE NEXT DAY.
THIS IS YOUR FIRST TIME TOURING THE ROYAL CAPITAL, IS IT NOT?
REINE, CAIN, IS THERE ANYWHERE SPECIAL YOU'D LIKE TO GO?
I WANT TO MEET WITH THE GODS.
AND TALK ABOUT MY LAST FAKE STATUS.
I WOULD LIKE TO SEE THE CHURCH.
OH, YES.
YOU MUST INFORM THE GODS OF YOUR MOVE TO THE ROYAL CAPITAL...
AND THANK THEM FOR ALL THEIR DIVINE PROTECTION.
YES!

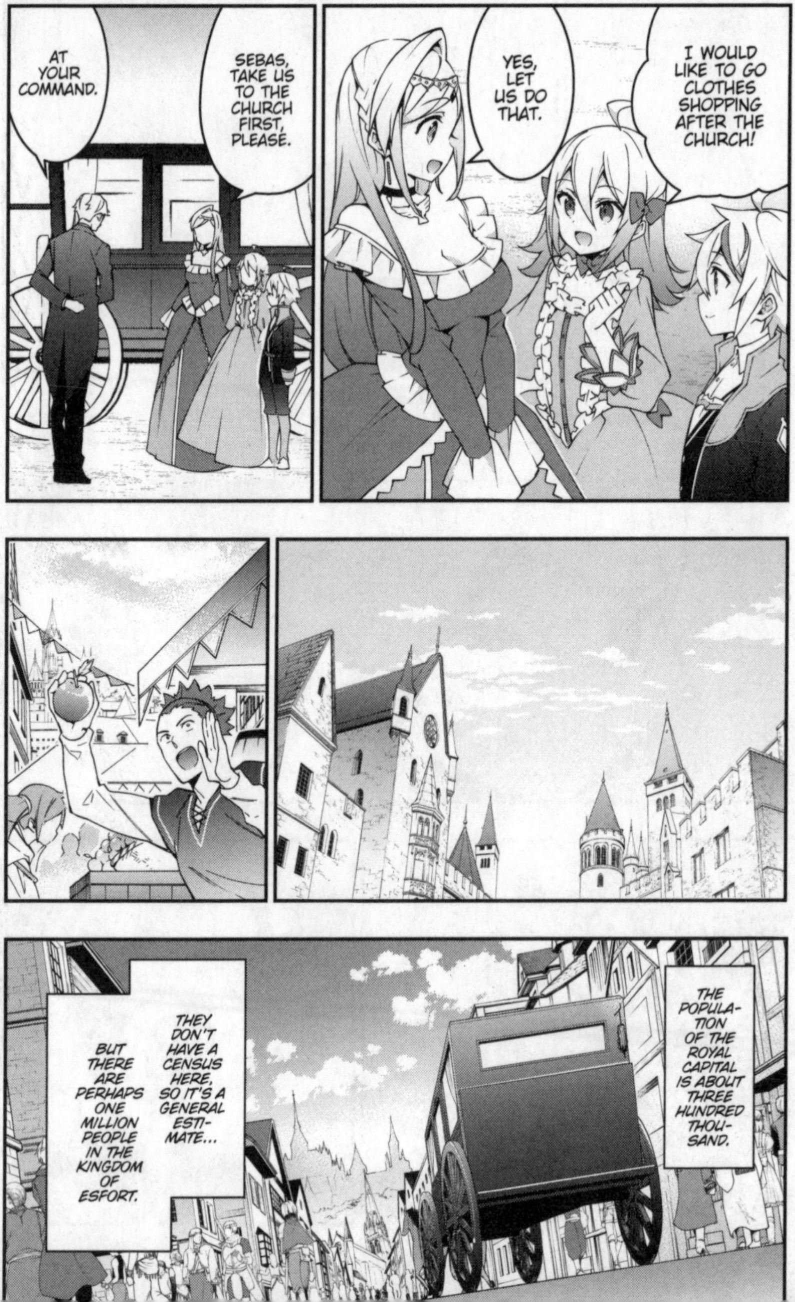
I WOULD LIKE TO GO CLOTHES SHOPPING AFTER THE CHURCH!
YES, LET US DO THAT.
SEBAS, TAKE US TO THE CHURCH FIRST, PLEASE.
AT YOUR COMMAND.
THE POPULATION OF THE ROYAL CAPITAL IS ABOUT THREE HUNDRED THOUSAND.
THEY DON'T HAVE A CENSUS HERE, SO IT'S A GENERAL ESTIMATE...
BUT THERE ARE PERHAPS ONE MILLION PEOPLE IN THE KINGDOM OF ESFORT.

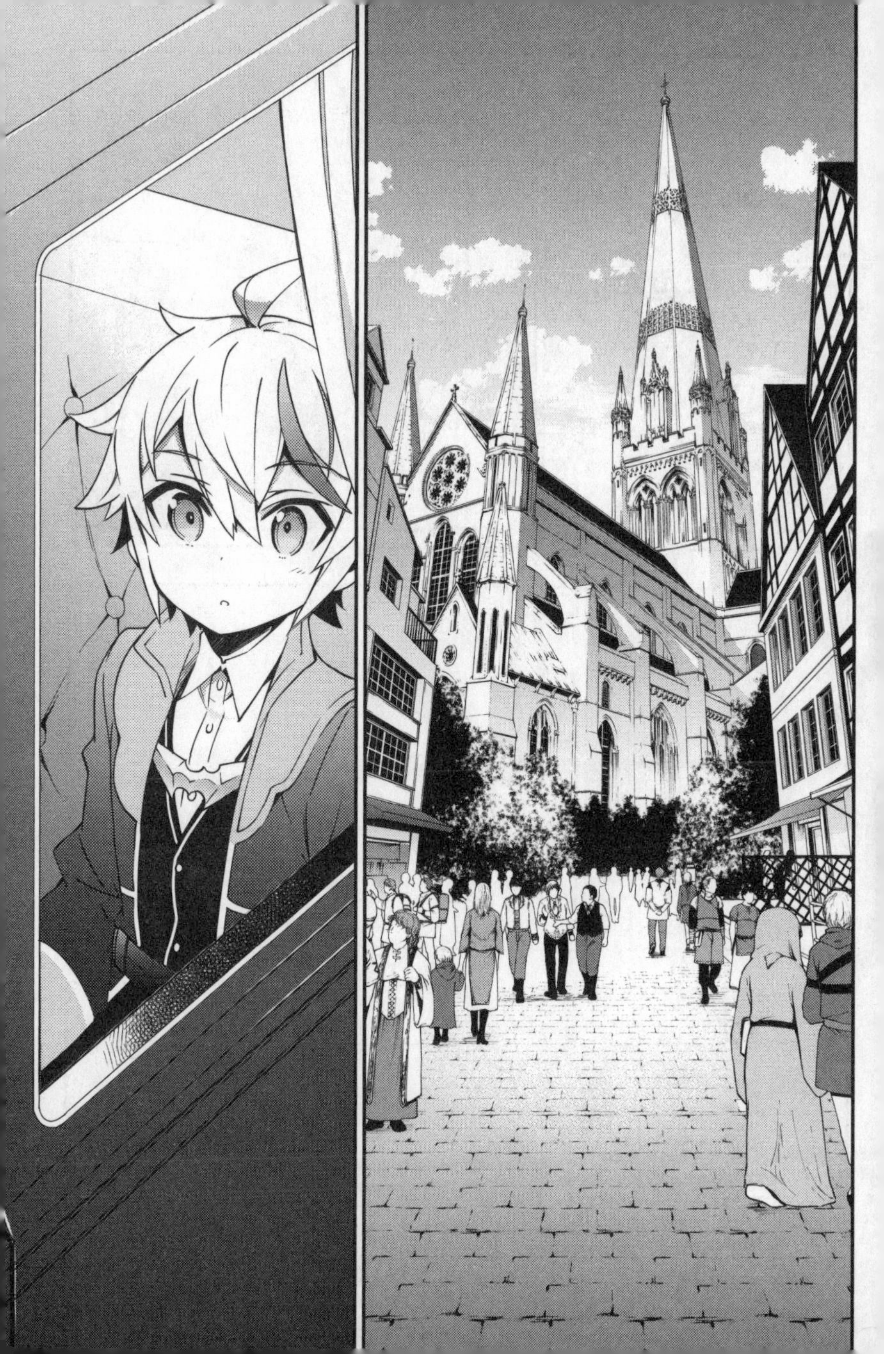

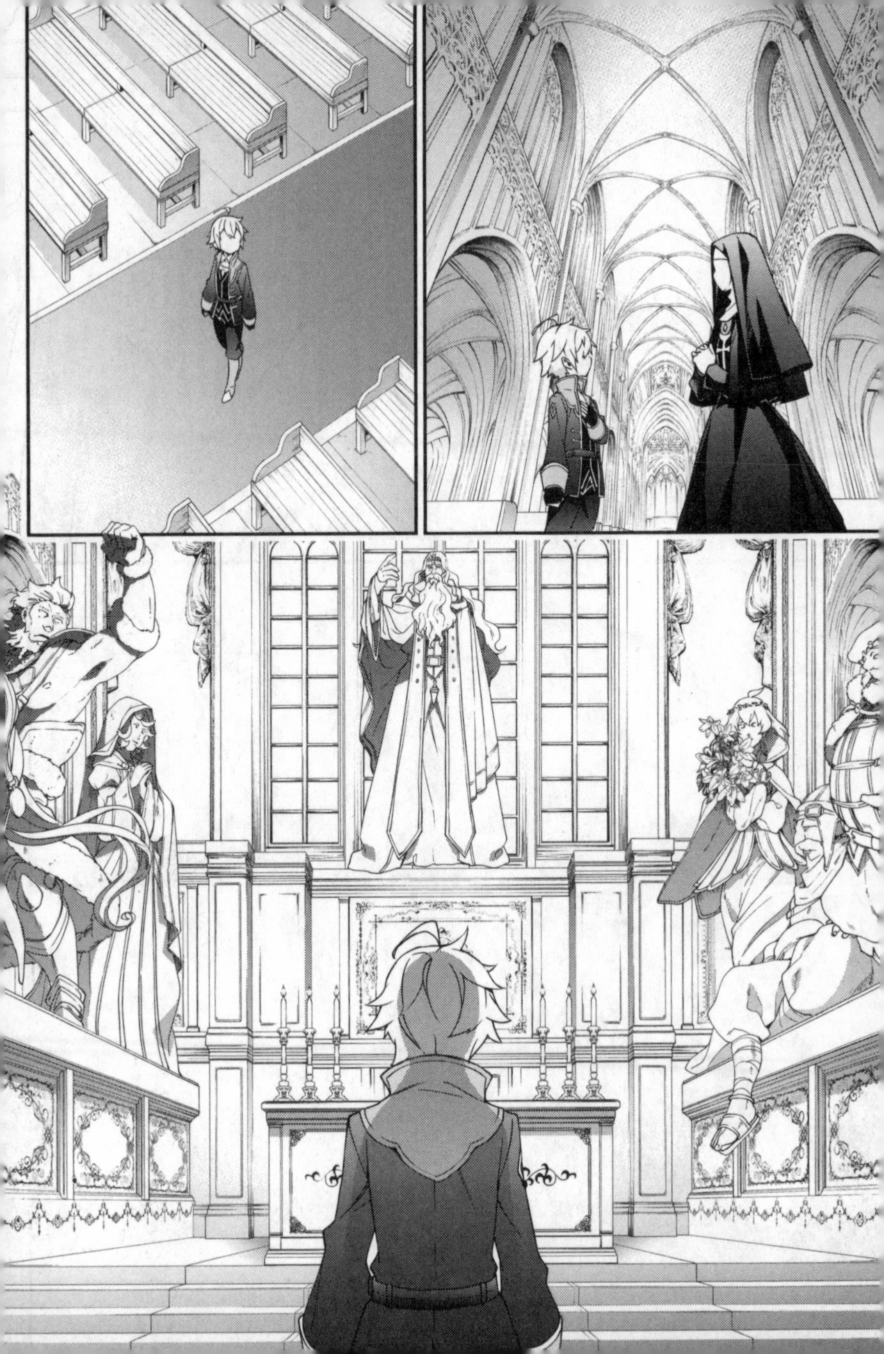

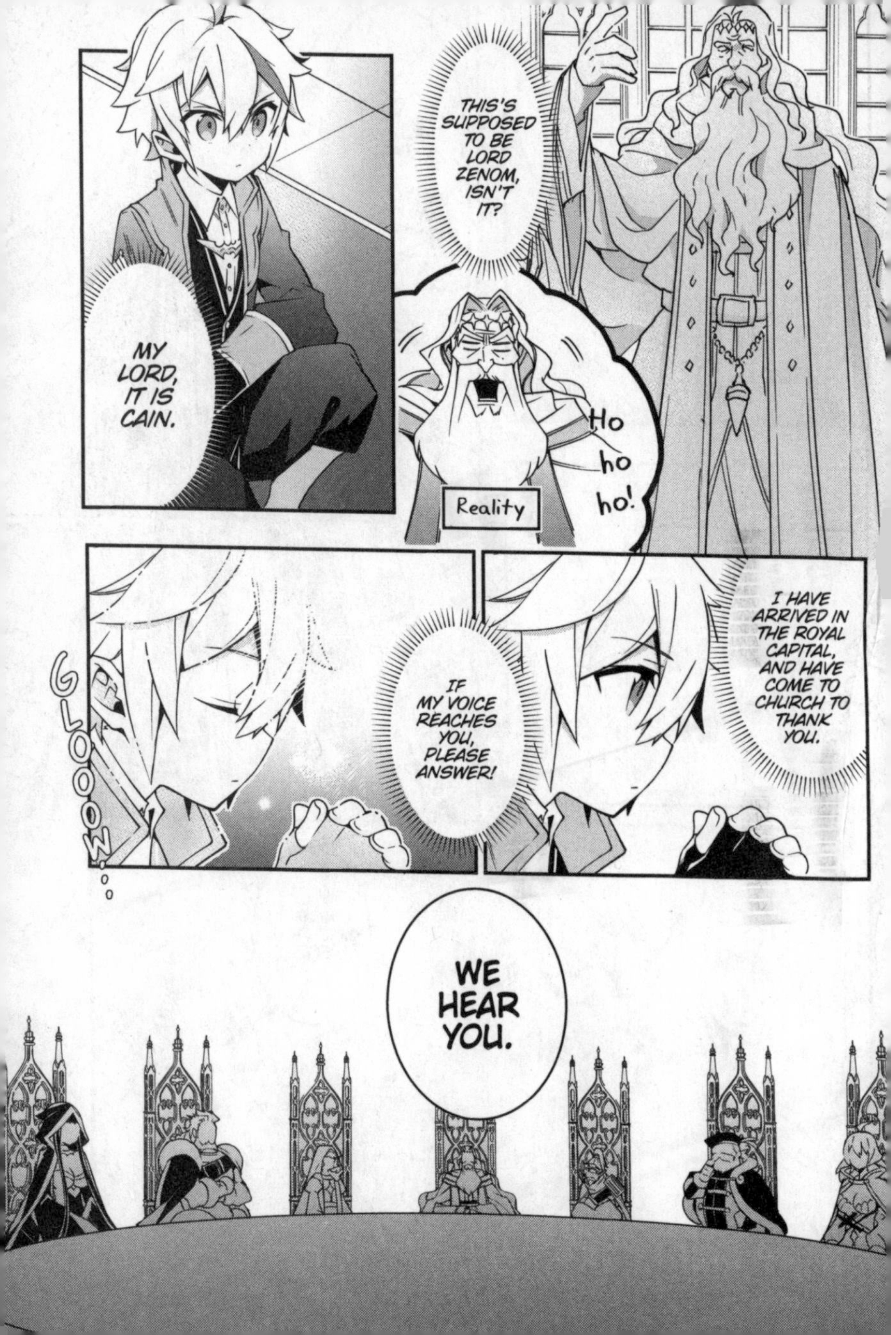
THIS'S SUPPOSED TO BE LORD ZENOM, ISN'T IT?
Ho ho ho!
Reality
MY LORD, IT IS CAIN.
I HAVE ARRIVED IN THE ROYAL CAPITAL, AND HAVE COME TO CHURCH TO THANK YOU.
IF MY VOICE REACHES YOU, PLEASE ANSWER!
GLOOOW...
WE HEAR YOU.

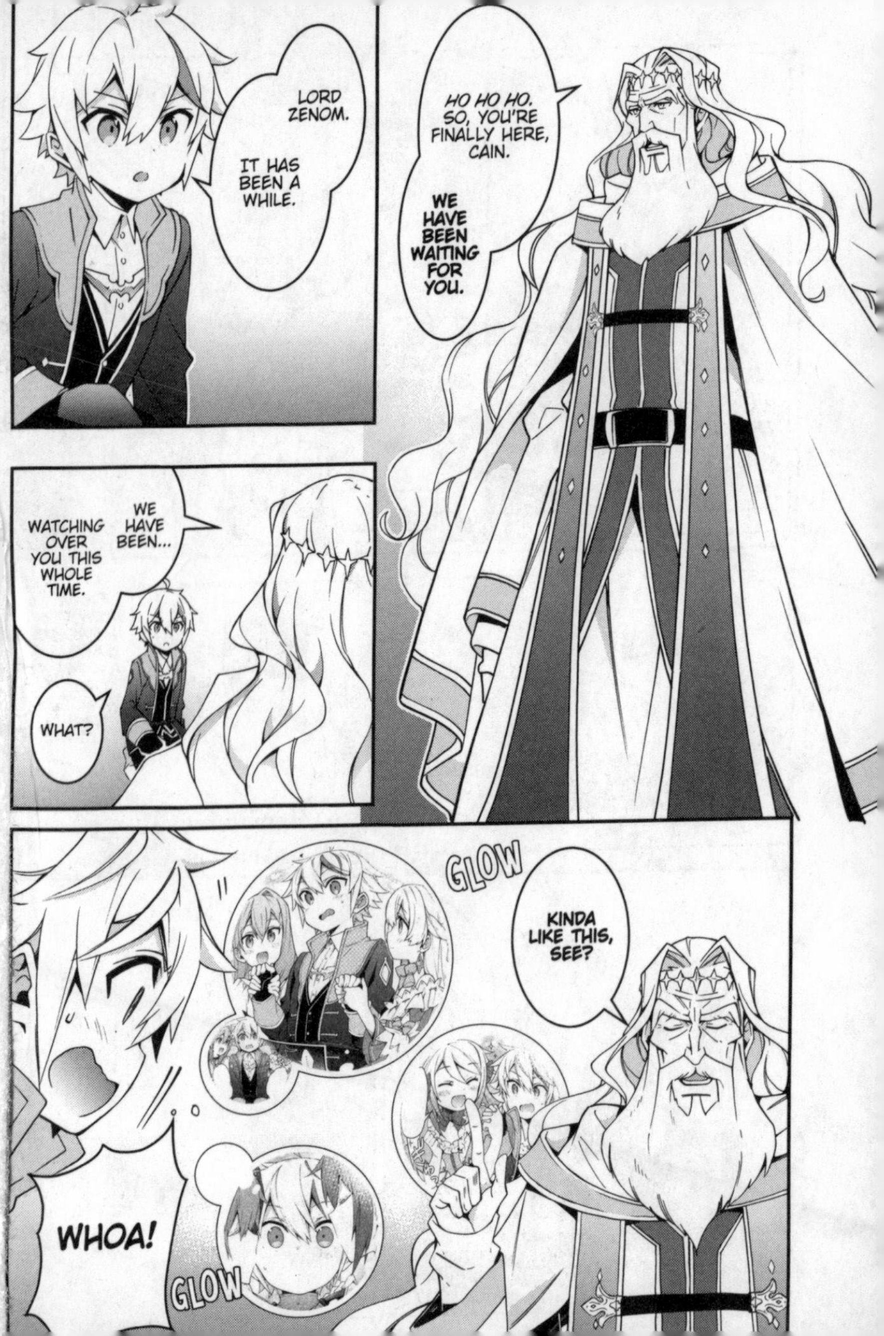
HO HO HO. SO, YOU'RE FINALLY HERE, CAIN.
WE HAVE BEEN WAITING FOR YOU.
LORD ZENOM.
IT HAS BEEN A WHILE.
WE HAVE BEEN...
WATCHING OVER YOU THIS WHOLE TIME.
WHAT?
GLOW
KINDA LIKE THIS, SEE?
GLOW
WHOA!

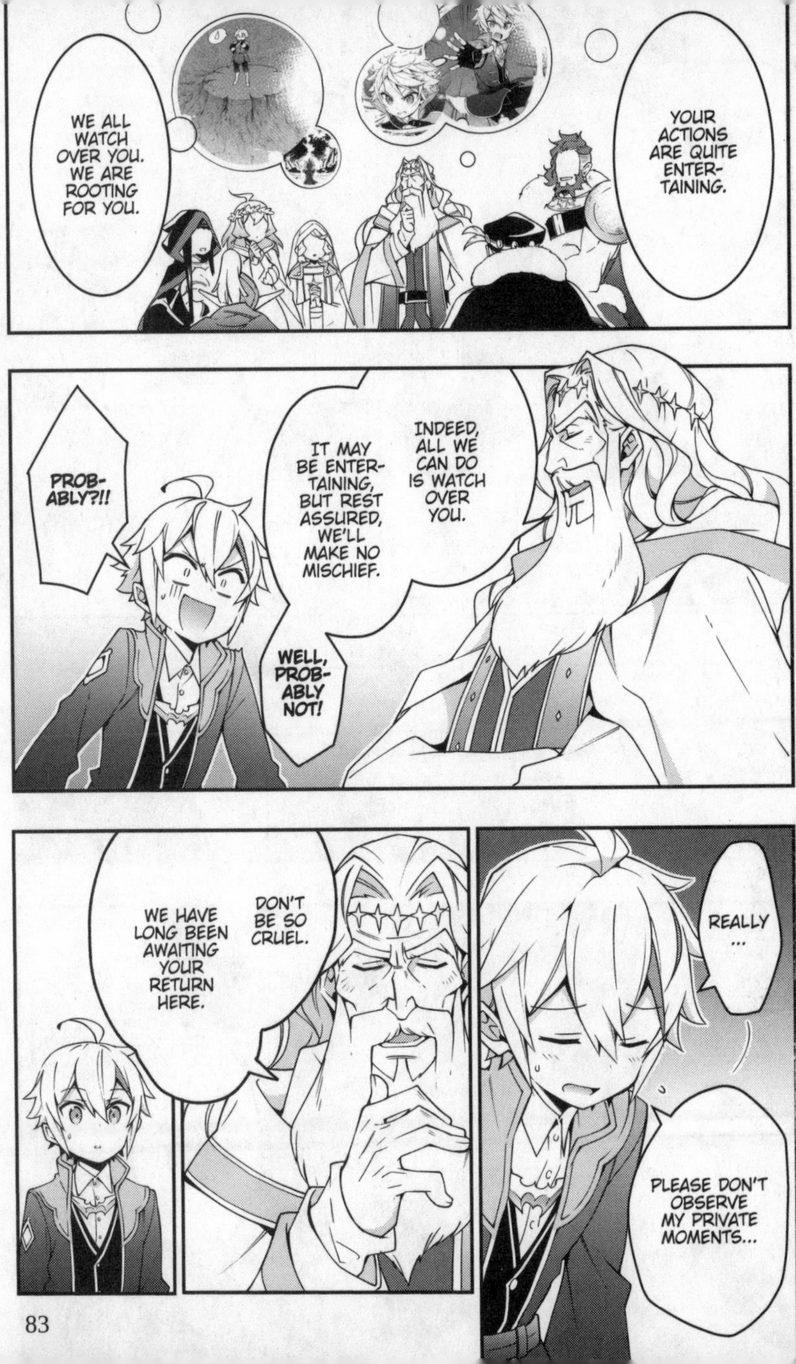
YOUR ACTIONS ARE QUITE ENTERTAINING.
WE ALL WATCH OVER YOU. WE ARE ROOTING FOR YOU.
INDEED, ALL WE CAN DO IS WATCH OVER YOU.
IT MAY BE ENTERTAINING, BUT REST ASSURED, WE'LL MAKE NO MISCHIEF.
WELL, PROBABLY NOT!
PROBABLY?!!
REALLY...
PLEASE DON'T OBSERVE MY PRIVATE MOMENTS...
DON'T BE SO CRUEL.
WE HAVE LONG BEEN AWAITING YOUR RETURN HERE.

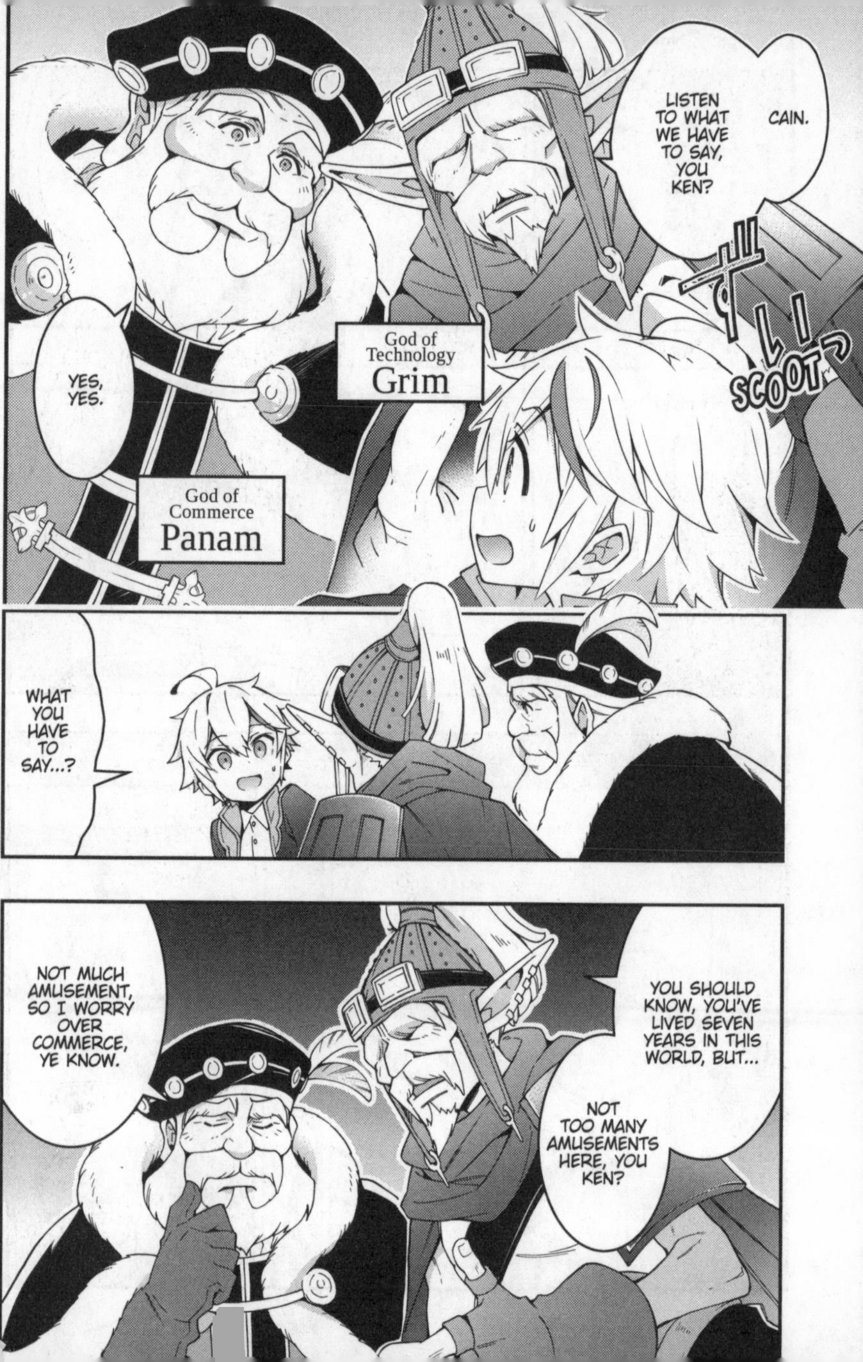
CAIN.
LISTEN TO WHAT WE HAVE TO SAY, YOU KEN?
SCOOT
God of Technology Grim
YES, YES.
God of Commerce Panam
WHAT YOU HAVE TO SAY...?
YOU SHOULD KNOW, YOU'VE LIVED SEVEN YEARS IN THIS WORLD, BUT...
NOT TOO MANY AMUSEMENTS HERE, YOU KEN?
NOT MUCH AMUSEMENT, SO I WORRY OVER COMMERCE, YE KNOW.

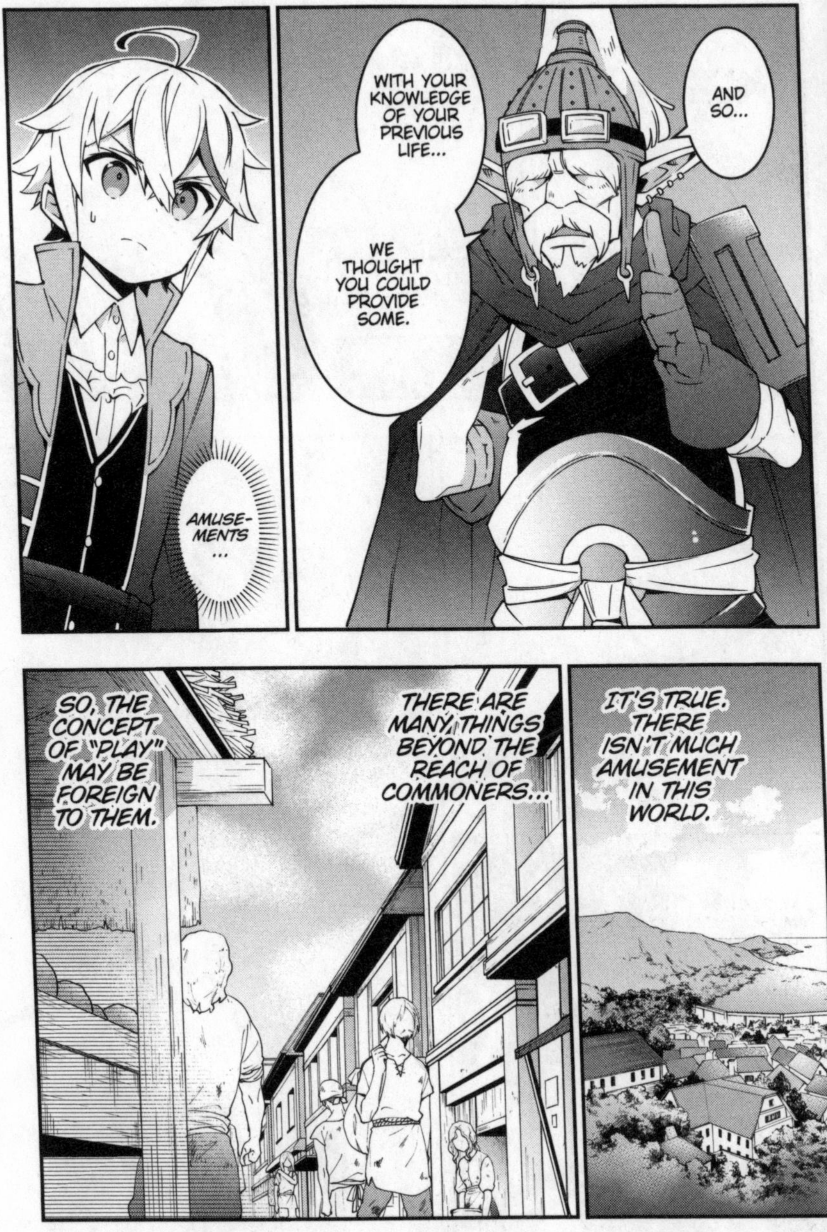
AND SO...
WITH YOUR KNOWLEDGE OF YOUR PREVIOUS LIFE...
WE THOUGHT YOU COULD PROVIDE SOME.
AMUSE-MENTS...
IT'S TRUE. THERE ISN'T MUCH AMUSEMENT IN THIS WORLD.
THERE ARE MANY THINGS BEYOND THE REACH OF COMMONERS...
SO, THE CONCEPT OF "PLAY" MAY BE FOREIGN TO THEM.

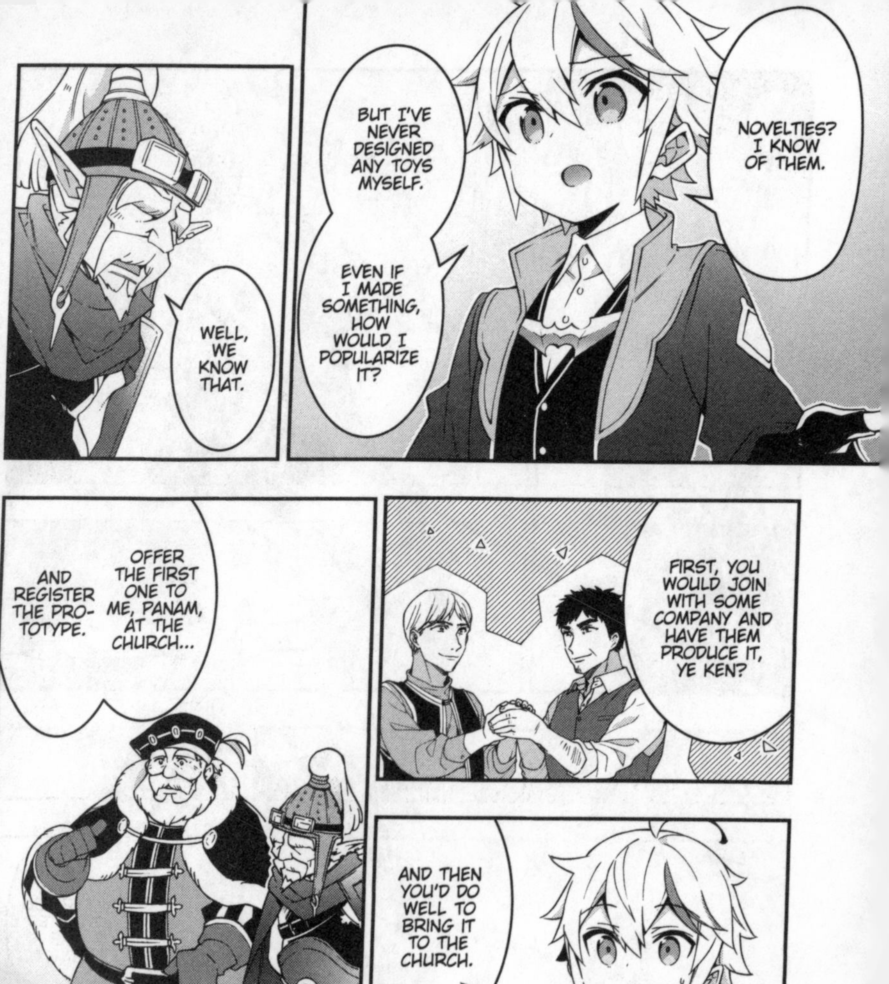
NOVELTIES? I KNOW OF THEM.
BUT I'VE NEVER DESIGNED ANY TOYS MYSELF.
EVEN IF I MADE SOMETHING, HOW WOULD I POPULARIZE IT?
WELL, WE KNOW THAT.
FIRST, YOU WOULD JOIN WITH SOME COMPANY AND HAVE THEM PRODUCE IT, YE KEN?
AND THEN YOU'D DO WELL TO BRING IT TO THE CHURCH.
TO THE CHURCH?
OFFER THE FIRST ONE TO ME, PANAM, AT THE CHURCH...
AND REGISTER THE PROTOTYPE.

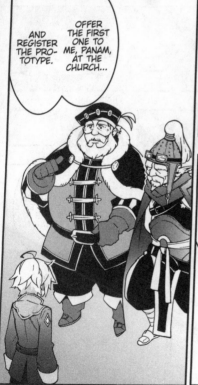

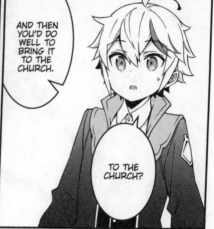

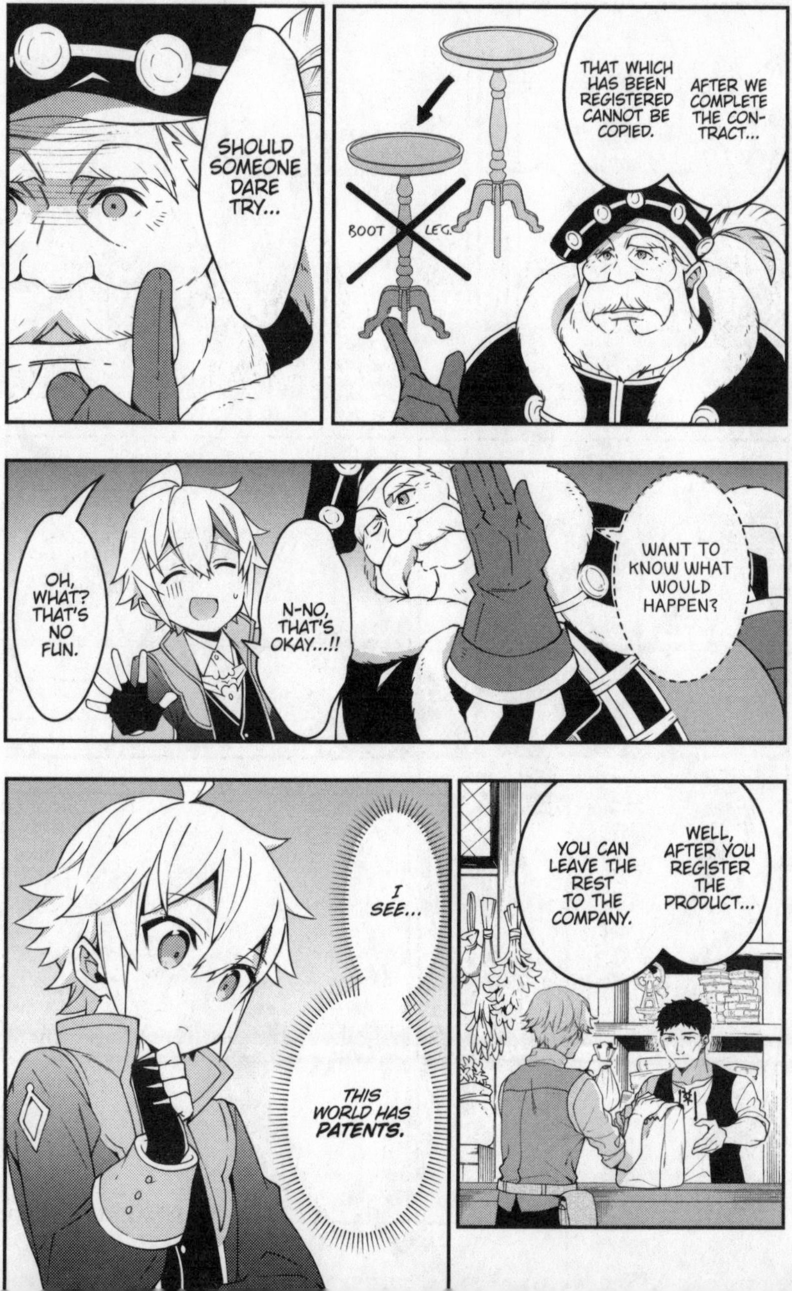
AFTER WE COMPLETE THE CON-TRACT...
THAT WHICH HAS BEEN REGISTERED CANNOT BE COPIED.
BOOT
LEG.
SHOULD SOMEONE DARE TRY...
WANT TO KNOW WHAT WOULD HAPPEN?
N-NO, THAT'S OKAY...!!
OH, WHAT? THAT'S NO FUN.
WELL, AFTER YOU REGISTER THE PRODUCT...
YOU CAN LEAVE THE REST TO THE COMPANY.
I SEE...
THIS WORLD HAS PATENTS.

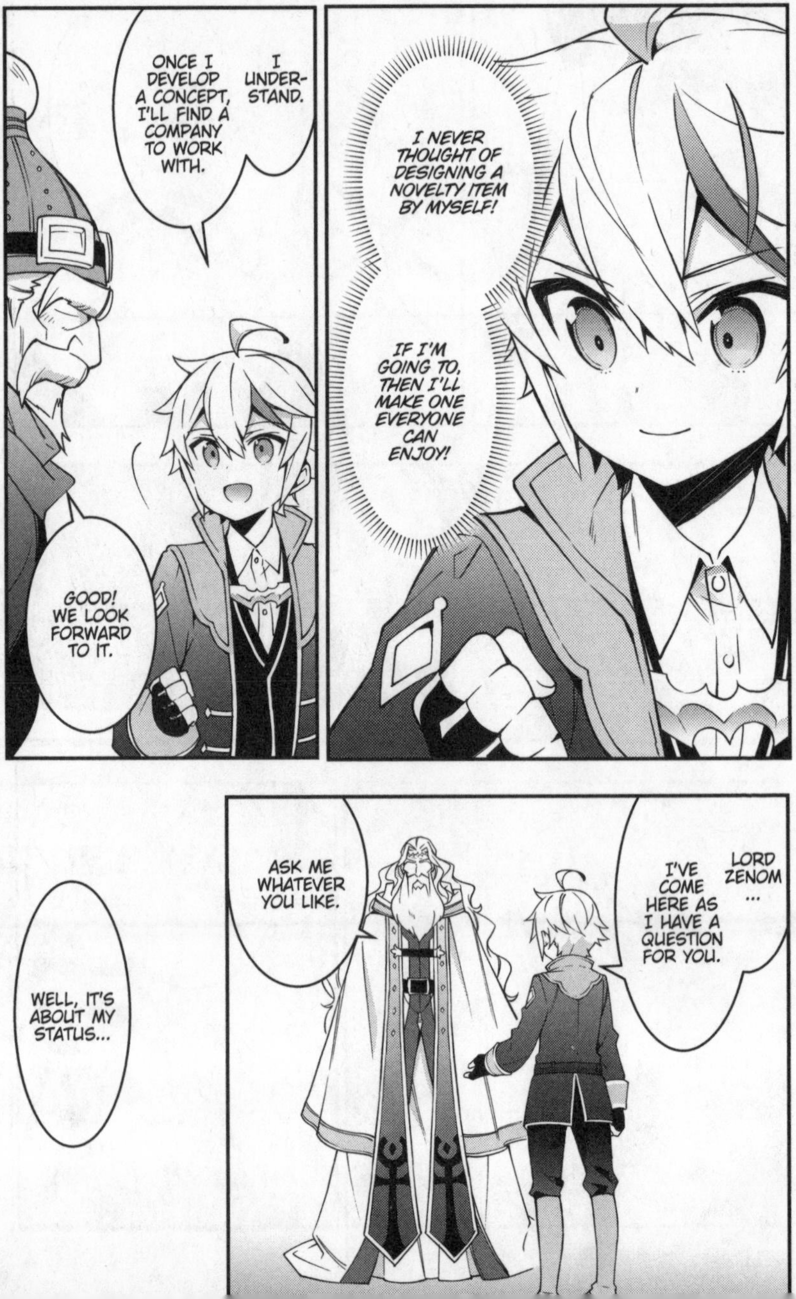
I NEVER THOUGHT OF DESIGNING A NOVELTY ITEM BY MYSELF!
IF I'M GOING TO, THEN I'LL MAKE ONE EVERYONE CAN ENJOY!
I UNDER-STAND.
ONCE I DEVELOP A CONCEPT, I'LL FIND A COMPANY TO WORK WITH.
GOOD! WE LOOK FORWARD TO IT.
LORD ZENOM ...
I'VE COME HERE AS I HAVE A QUESTION FOR YOU.
ASK ME WHATEVER YOU LIKE.
WELL, IT'S ABOUT MY STATUS...

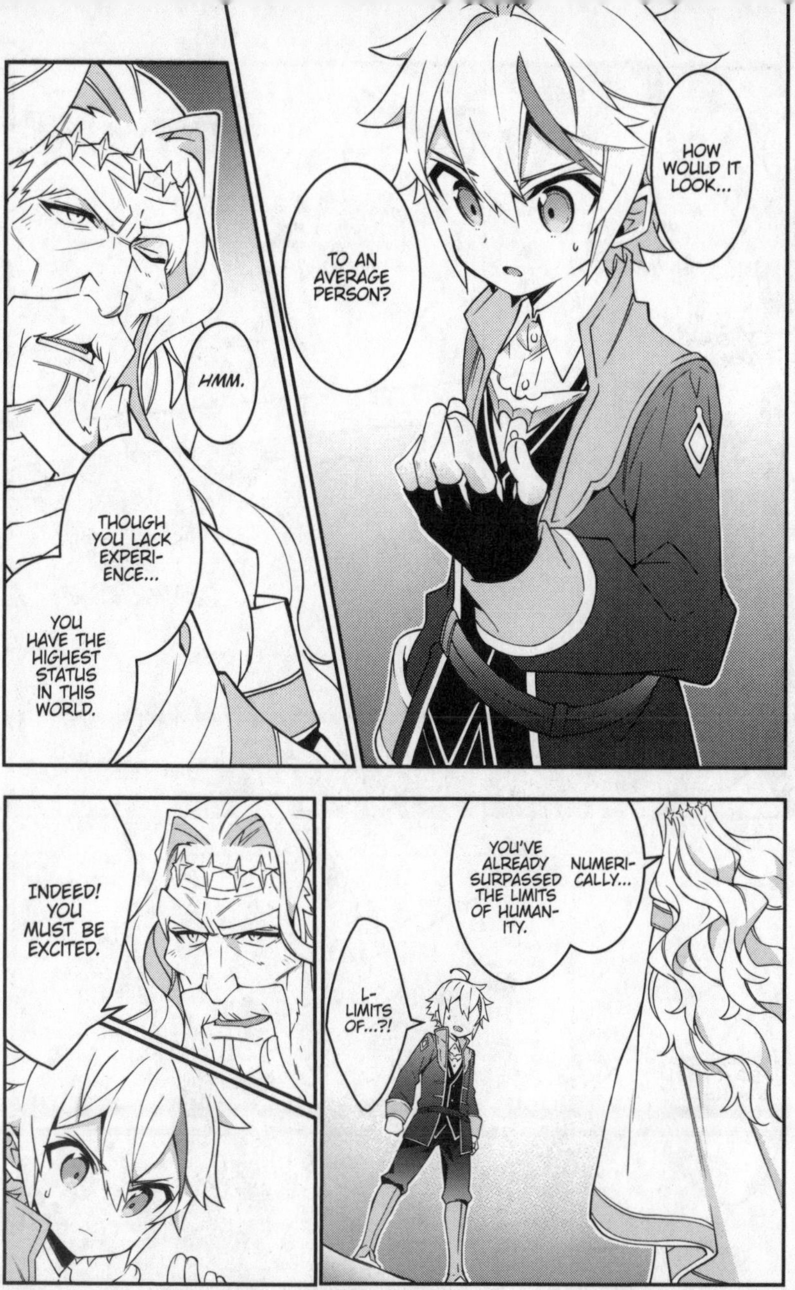
HOW WOULD IT LOOK...
TO AN AVERAGE PERSON?
HMM.
THOUGH YOU LACK EXPERIENCE...
YOU HAVE THE HIGHEST STATUS IN THIS WORLD.
NUMERICALLY...
YOU'VE ALREADY SURPASSED THE LIMITS OF HUMANITY.
L-LIMITS OF...?!
INDEED! YOU MUST BE EXCITED.

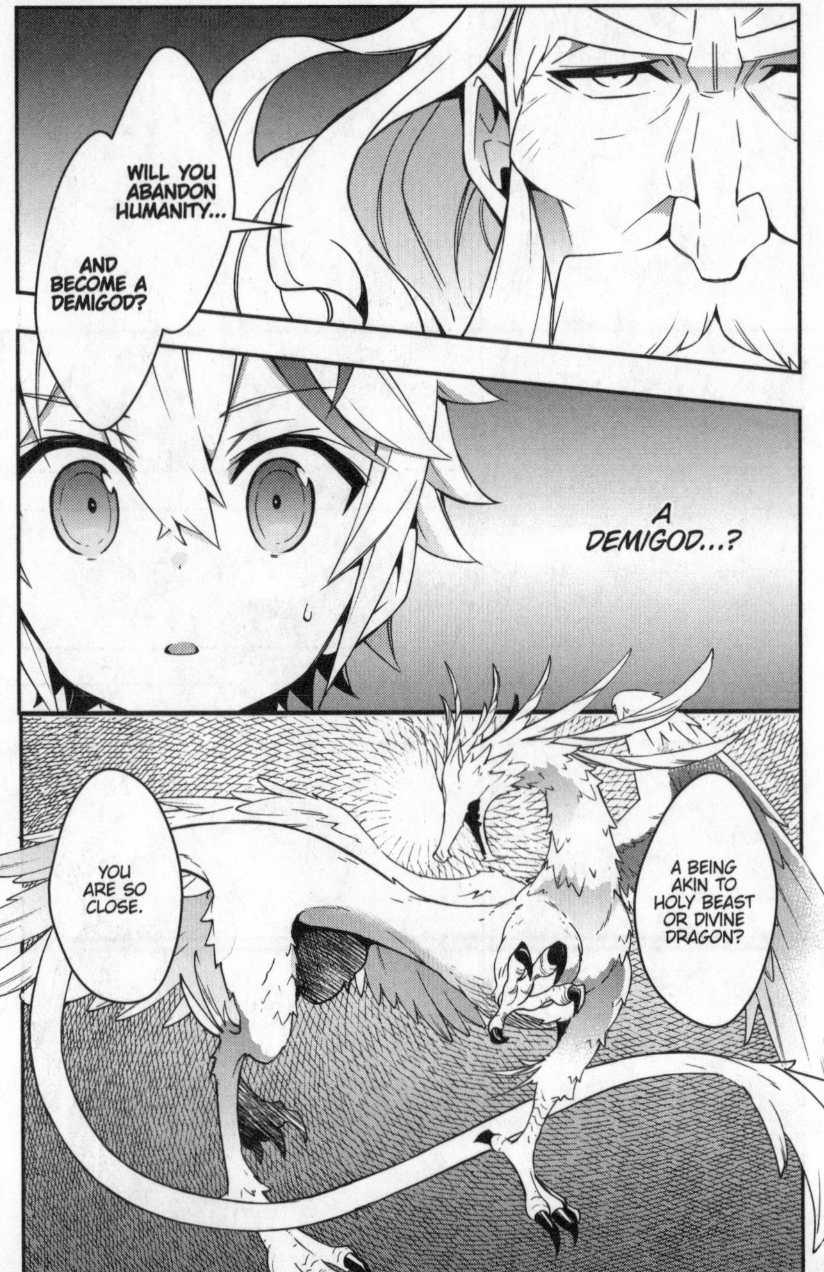
WILL YOU ABANDON HUMANITY...
AND BECOME A DEMIGOD?
A DEMIGOD...?
A BEING AKIN TO HOLY BEAST OR DIVINE DRAGON?
YOU ARE SO CLOSE.

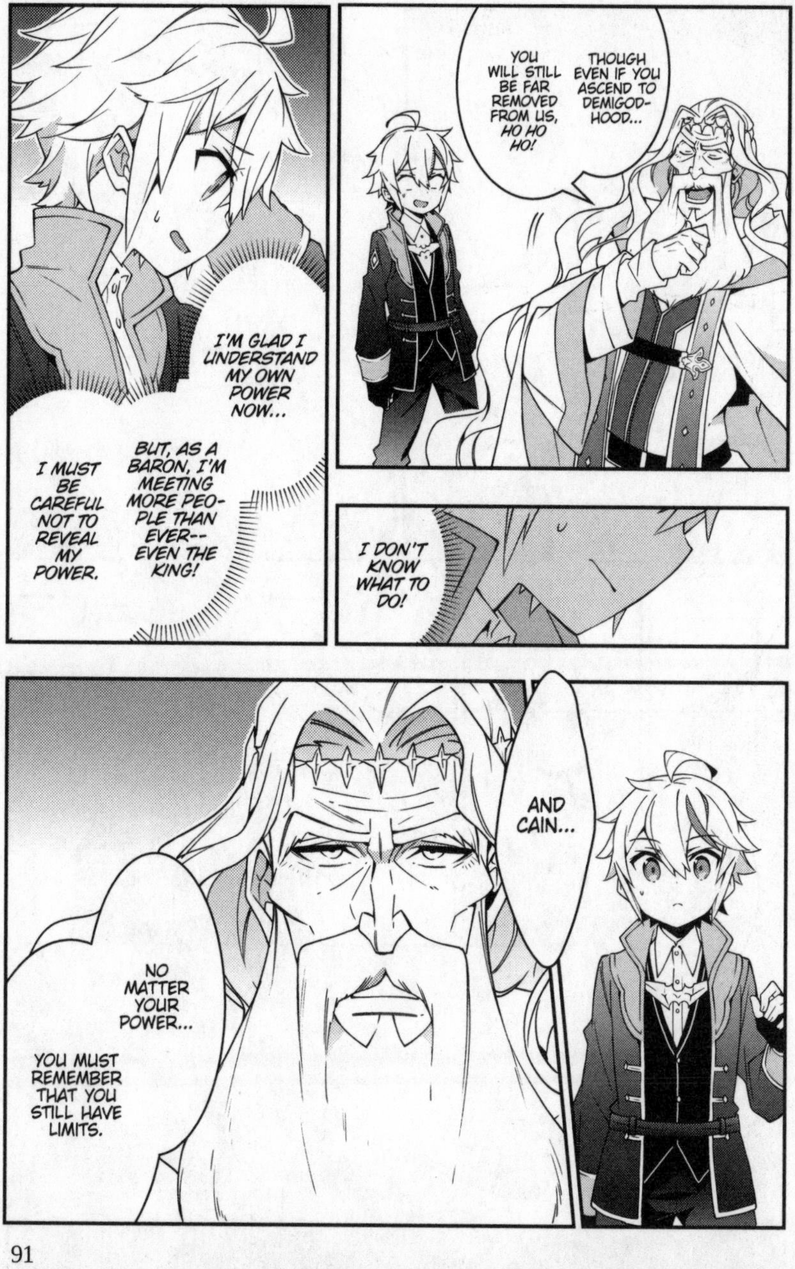
THOUGH EVEN IF YOU ASCEND TO DEMIGOD-HOOD...
YOU WILL STILL BE FAR REMOVED FROM US, HO HO HO!
I DON'T KNOW WHAT TO DO!
I'M GLAD I UNDERSTAND MY OWN POWER NOW...
BUT, AS A BARON, I'M MEETING MORE PEO-PLE THAN EVER--EVEN THE KING!
I MUST BE CAREFUL NOT TO REVEAL MY POWER.
AND CAIN...
NO MATTER YOUR POWER...
YOU MUST REMEMBER THAT YOU STILL HAVE LIMITS.

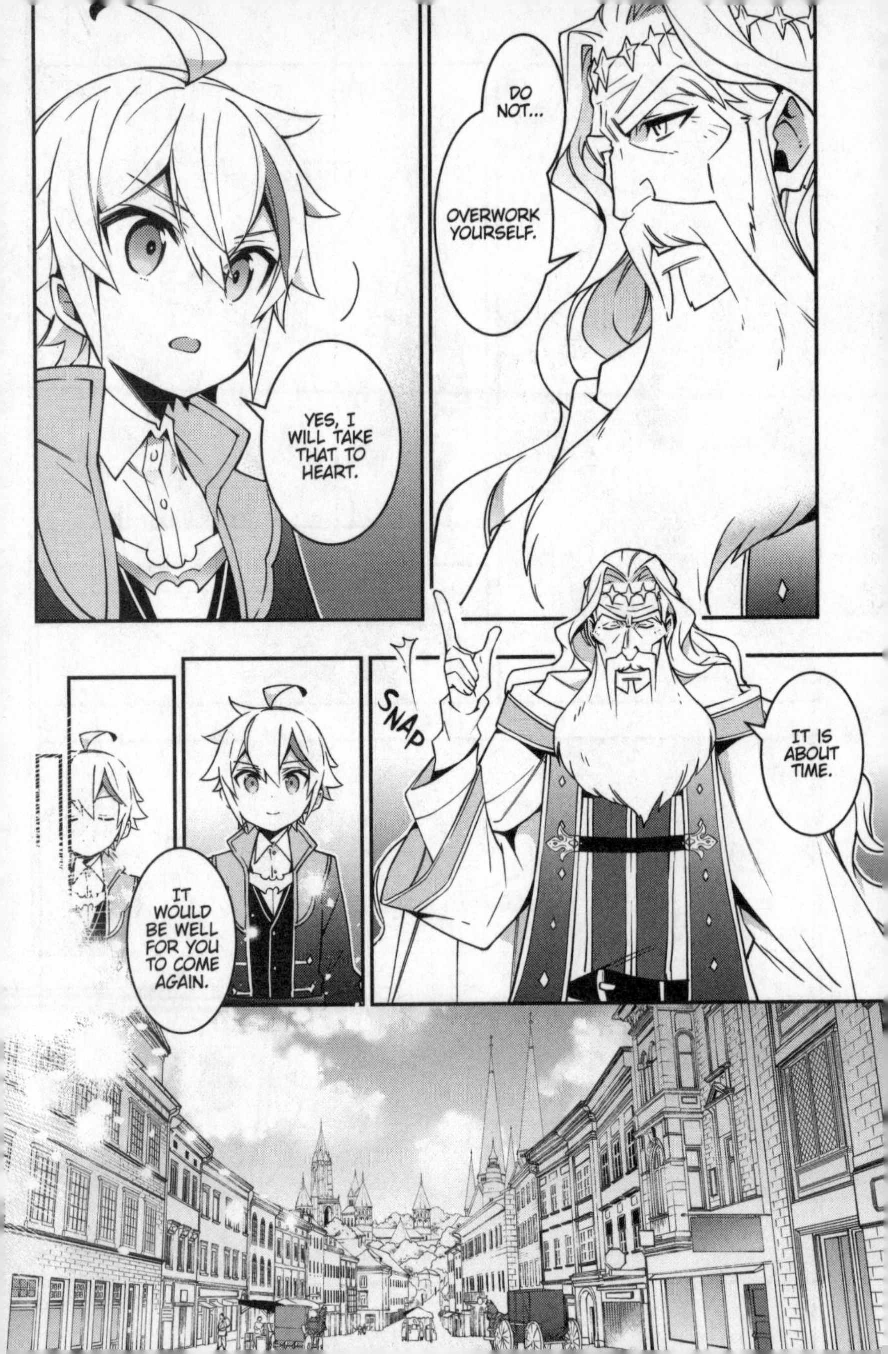
DO NOT...
OVERWORK YOURSELF.
YES, I WILL TAKE THAT TO HEART.
SNAP
IT IS ABOUT TIME.
IT WOULD BE WELL FOR YOU TO COME AGAIN.

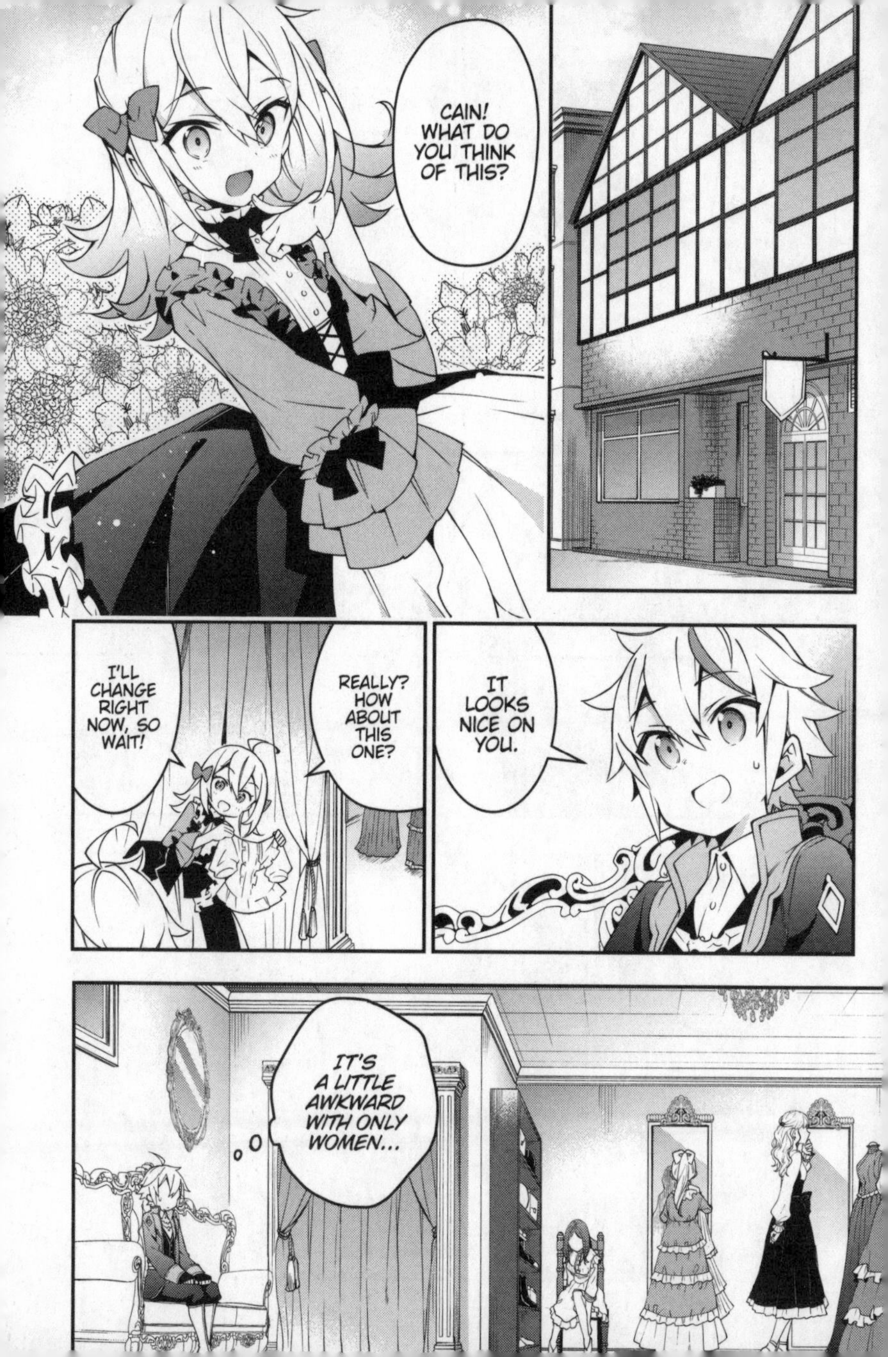
CAIN! WHAT DO YOU THINK OF THIS?
IT LOOKS NICE ON YOU.
REALLY? HOW ABOUT THIS ONE?
I'LL CHANGE RIGHT NOW, SO WAIT!
IT'S A LITTLE AWKWARD WITH ONLY WOMEN...

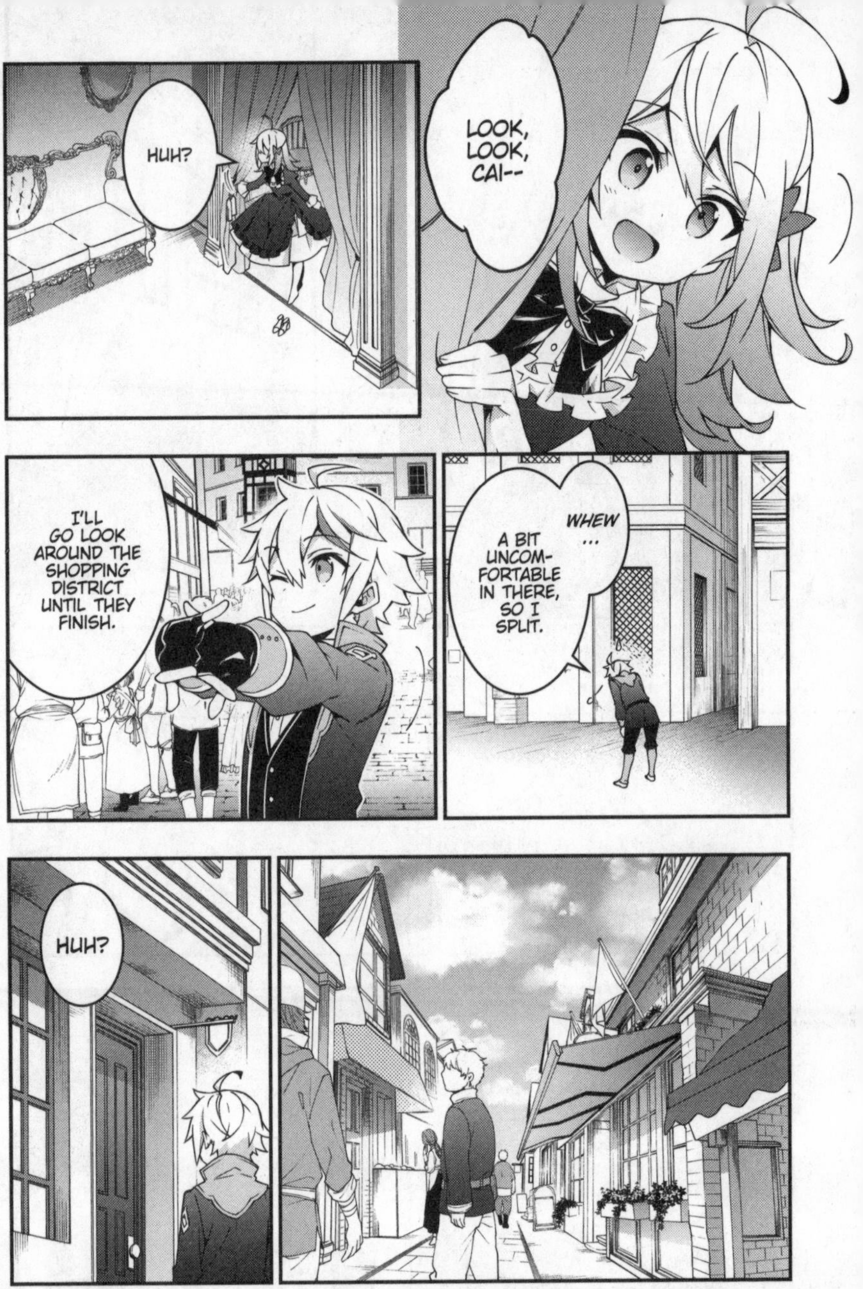
LOOK, LOOK, CAI--
HUH?
WHEW ...
A BIT UNCOM-FORTABLE IN THERE, SO I SPLIT.
I'LL GO LOOK AROUND THE SHOPPING DISTRICT UNTIL THEY FINISH.
HUH?

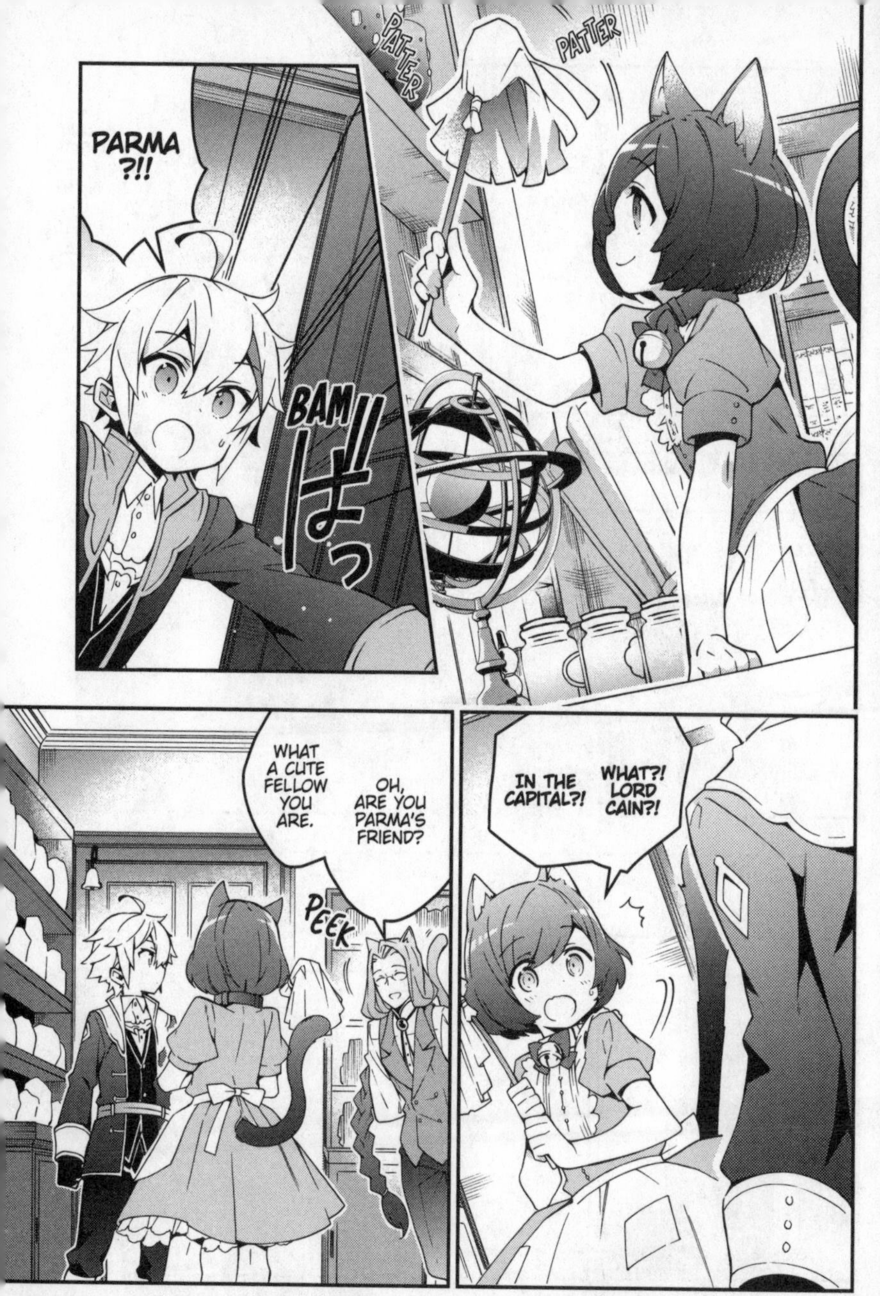
PATTER
PATTER
PARMA ?!!
BAM
WHAT?! LORD CAIN?!
IN THE CAPITAL?!
OH, ARE YOU PARMA'S FRIEND?
WHAT A CUTE FELLOW YOU ARE.
PEEK

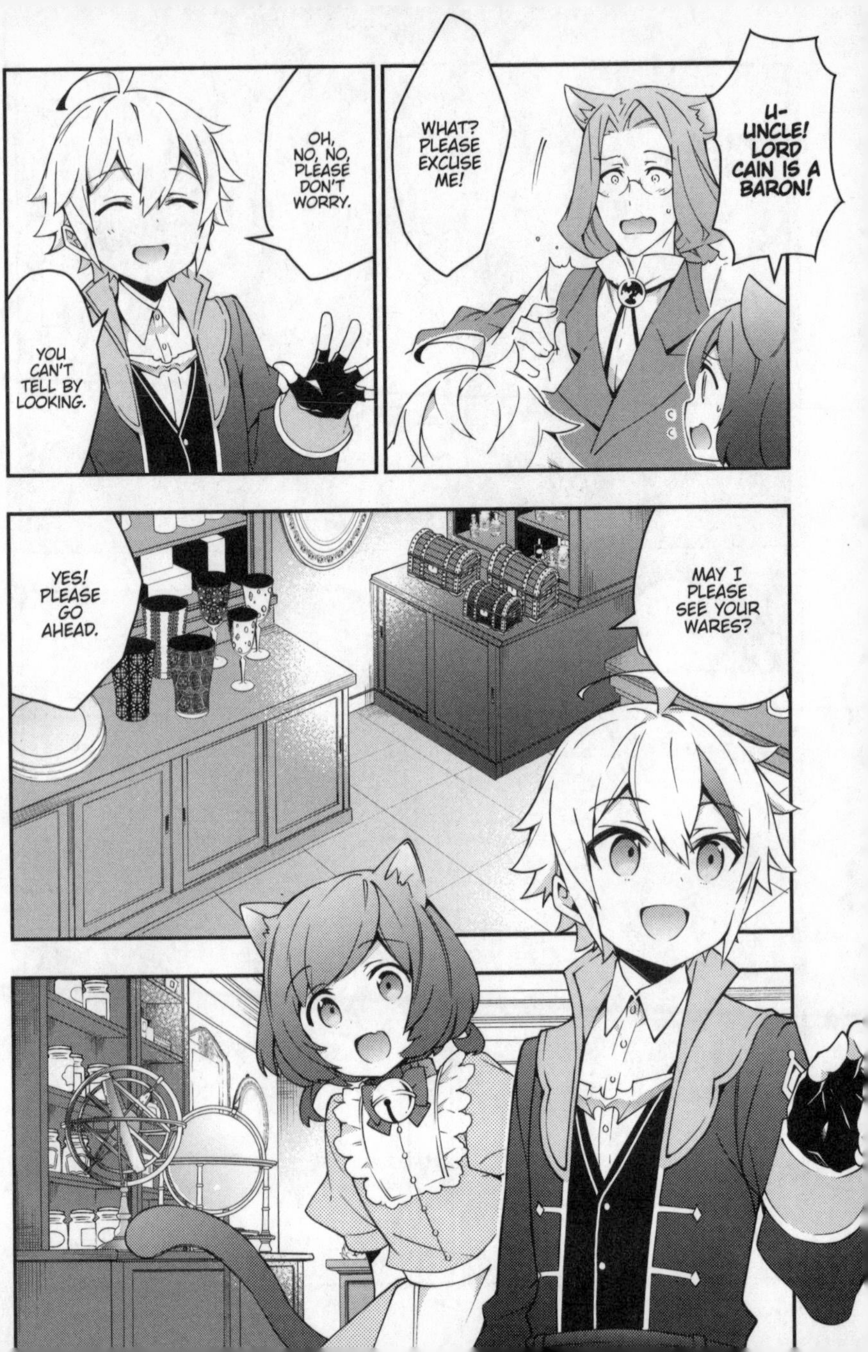
U-UNCLE! LORD CAIN IS A BARON!
WHAT? PLEASE EXCUSE ME!
OH, NO, NO, PLEASE DON'T WORRY.
YOU CAN'T TELL BY LOOKING.
MAY I PLEASE SEE YOUR WARES?
YES! PLEASE GO AHEAD.

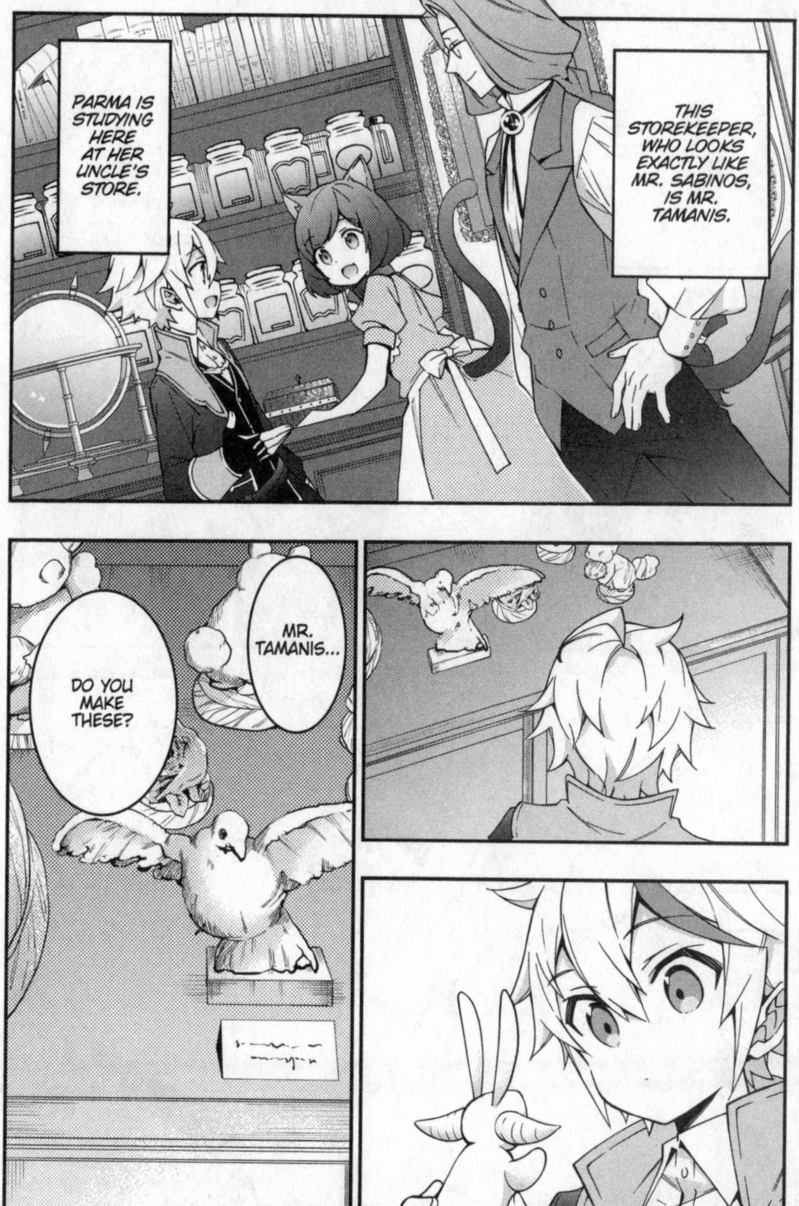
THIS STOREKEEPER, WHO LOOKS EXACTLY LIKE MR. SABINOS, IS MR. TAMANIS.
PARMA IS STUDYING HERE AT HER UNCLE'S STORE.
MR. TAMANIS...
DO YOU MAKE THESE?

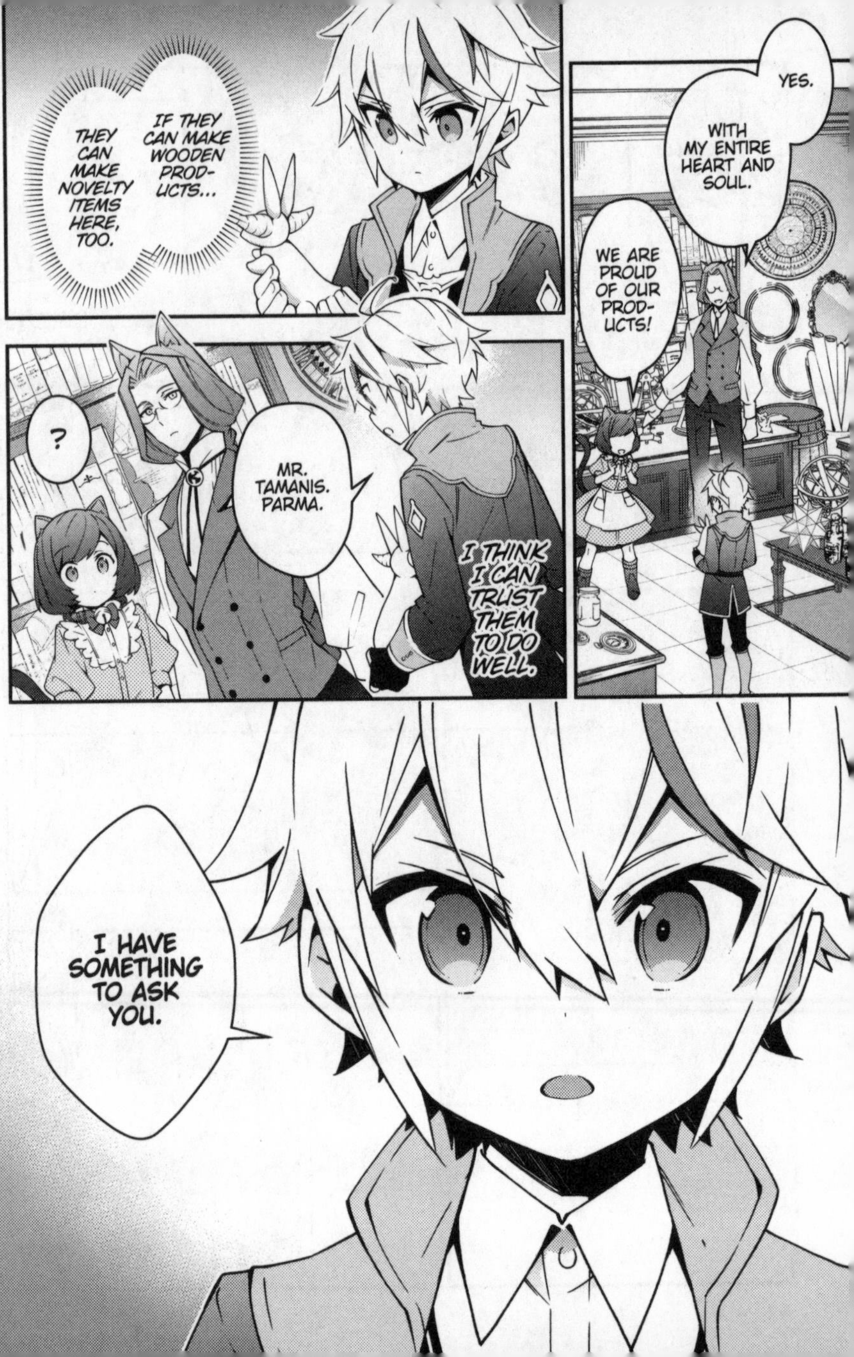
YES.
WITH MY ENTIRE HEART AND SOUL.
WE ARE PROUD OF OUR PROD-UCTS!
IF THEY CAN MAKE WOODEN PROD-UCTS...
THEY CAN MAKE NOVELTY ITEMS HERE, TOO.
I THINK I CAN TRUST THEM TO DO WELL.
MR. TAMANIS. PARMA.
?
I HAVE SOMETHING TO ASK YOU.

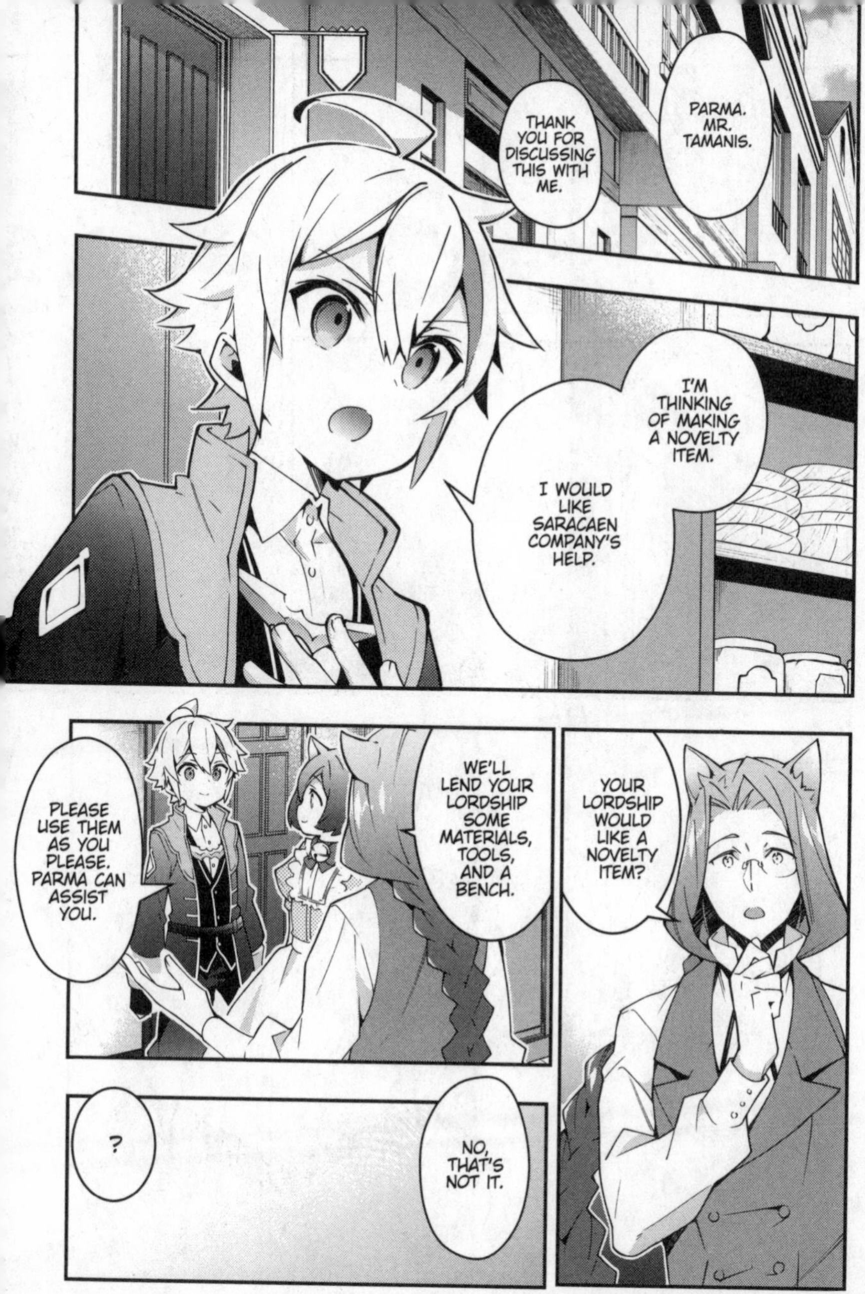
PARMA. MR. TAMANIS.
THANK YOU FOR DISCUSSING THIS WITH ME.
I'M THINKING OF MAKING A NOVELTY ITEM.
I WOULD LIKE SARACAEN COMPANY'S HELP.
YOUR LORDSHIP WOULD LIKE A NOVELTY ITEM?
WE'LL LEND YOUR LORDSHIP SOME MATERIALS, TOOLS, AND A BENCH.
PLEASE USE THEM AS YOU PLEASE. PARMA CAN ASSIST YOU.
NO, THAT'S NOT IT.
?

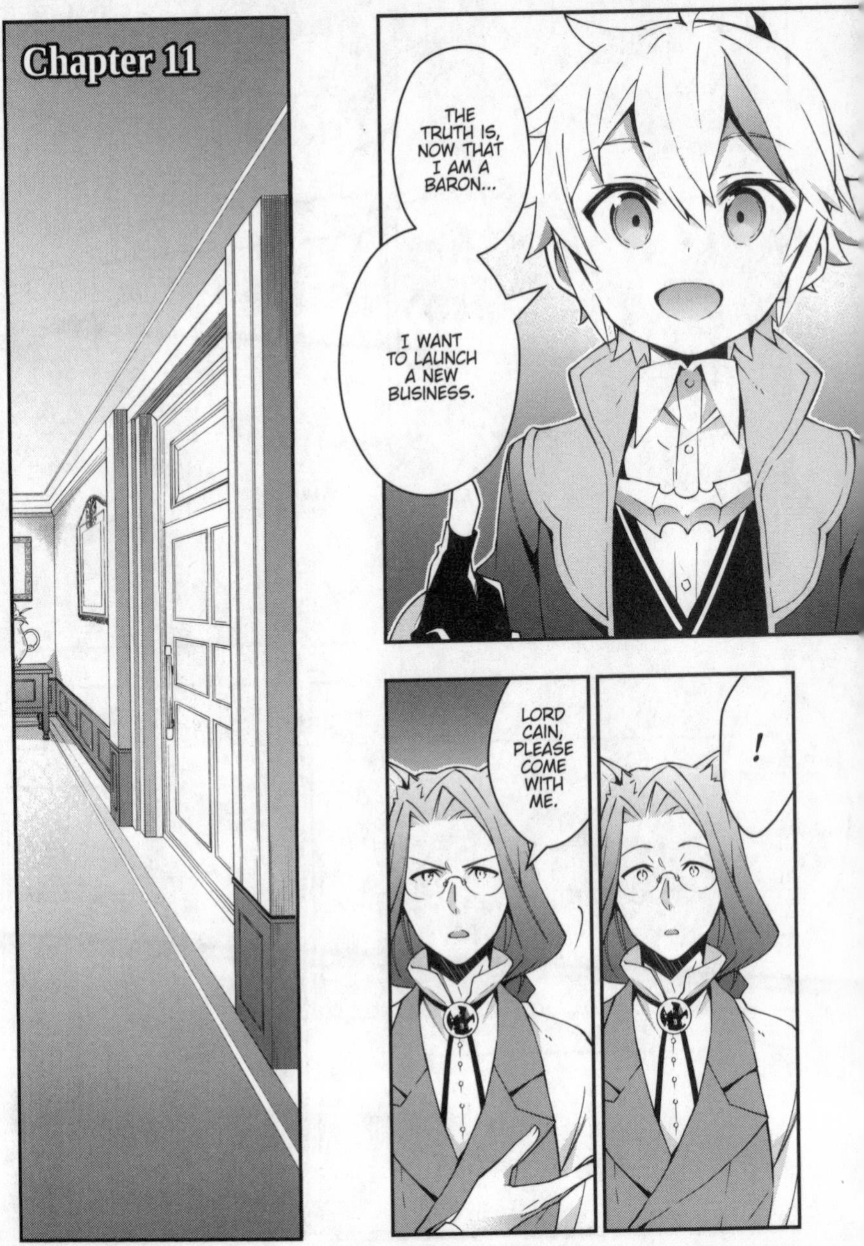
THE TRUTH IS, NOW THAT I AM A BARON...
I WANT TO LAUNCH A NEW BUSINESS.
!
LORD CAIN, PLEASE COME WITH ME.
Chapter 11

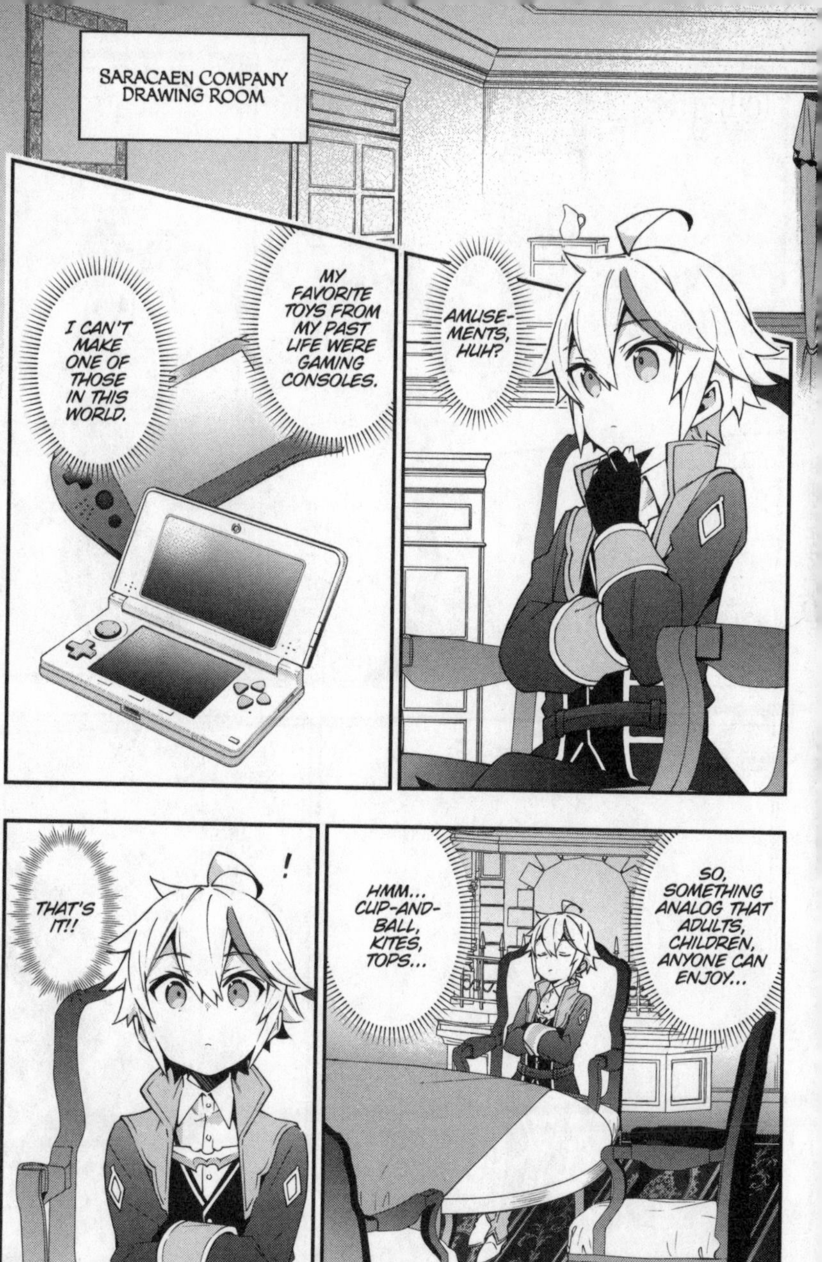
SARACAEN COMPANY DRAWING ROOM
AMUSE-MENTS, HUH?
MY FAVORITE TOYS FROM MY PAST LIFE WERE GAMING CONSOLES.
I CAN'T MAKE ONE OF THOSE IN THIS WORLD.
SO, SOMETHING ANALOG THAT ADULTS, CHILDREN, ANYONE CAN ENJOY...
HMM... CUP-AND-BALL, KITES, TOPS...
!
THAT'S IT!!

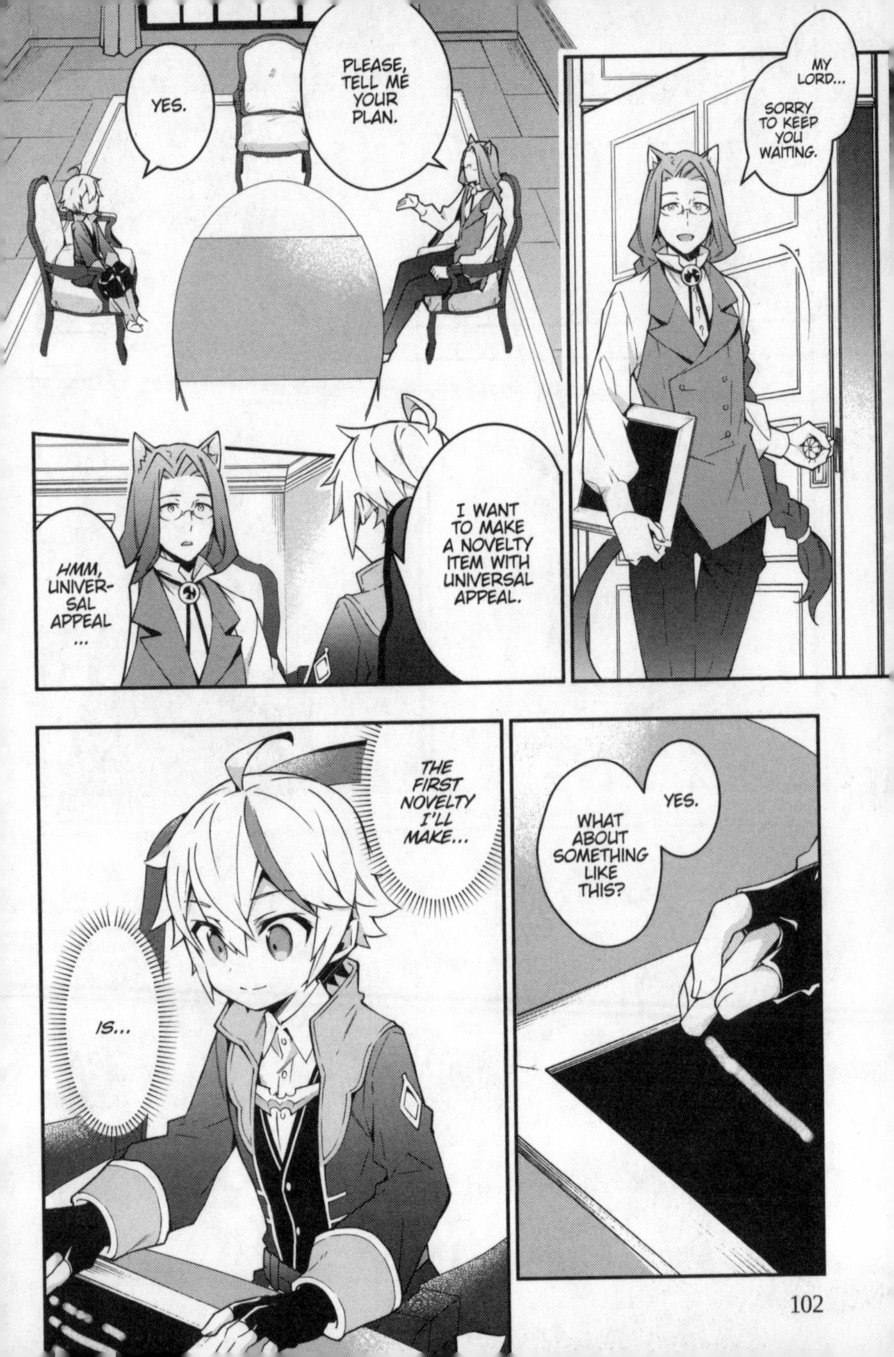
MY LORD...
SORRY TO KEEP YOU WAITING.
PLEASE, TELL ME YOUR PLAN.
YES.
I WANT TO MAKE A NOVELTY ITEM WITH UNIVERSAL APPEAL.
HMM, UNIVER-SAL APPEAL...
YES.
WHAT ABOUT SOMETHING LIKE THIS?
THE FIRST NOVELTY I'LL MAKE...
IS...

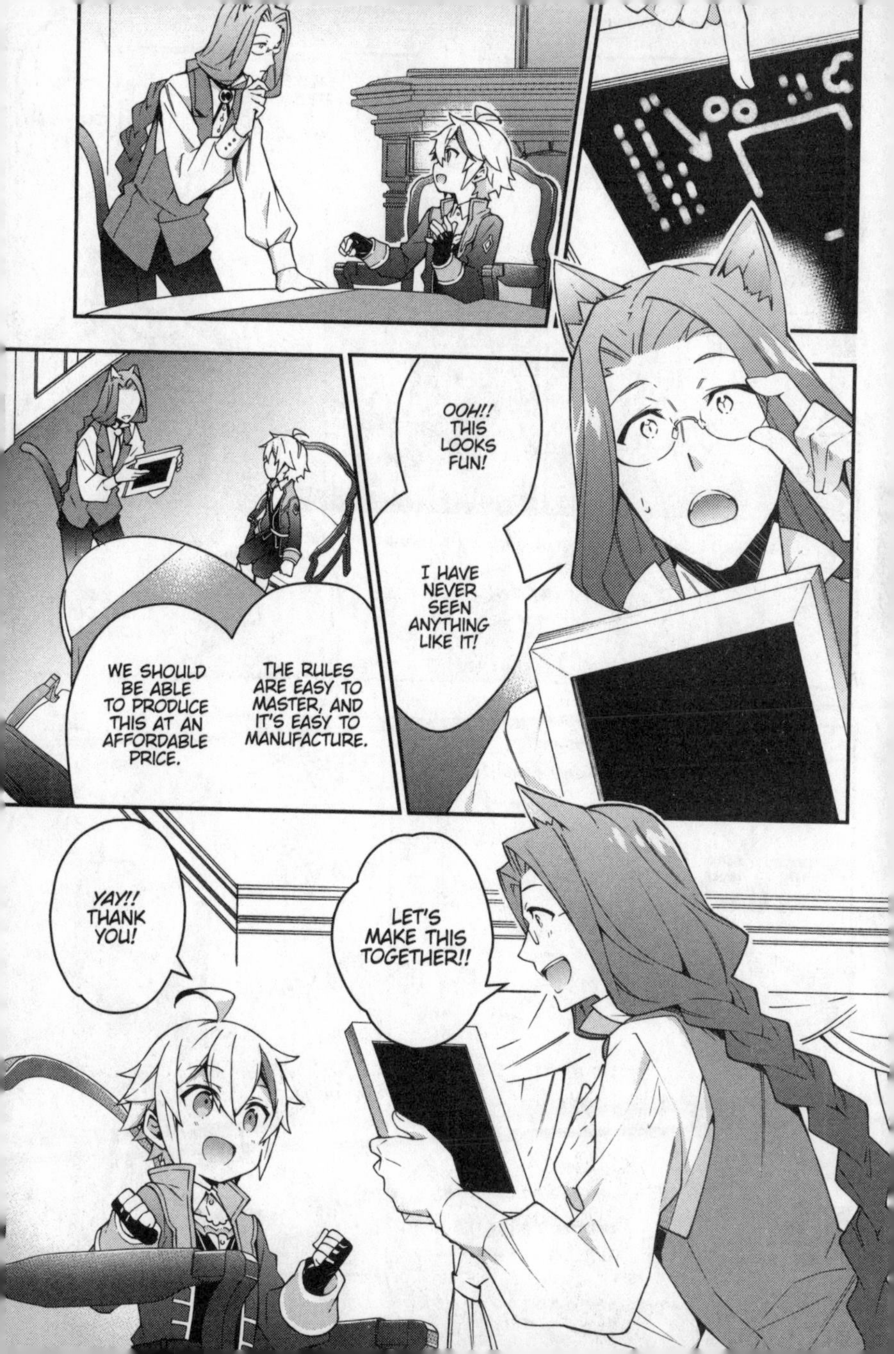
OOH!! THIS LOOKS FUN!
I HAVE NEVER SEEN ANYTHING LIKE IT!
THE RULES ARE EASY TO MASTER, AND IT'S EASY TO MANUFACTURE.
WE SHOULD BE ABLE TO PRODUCE THIS AT AN AFFORDABLE PRICE.
LET'S MAKE THIS TOGETHER!!
YAY!! THANK YOU!

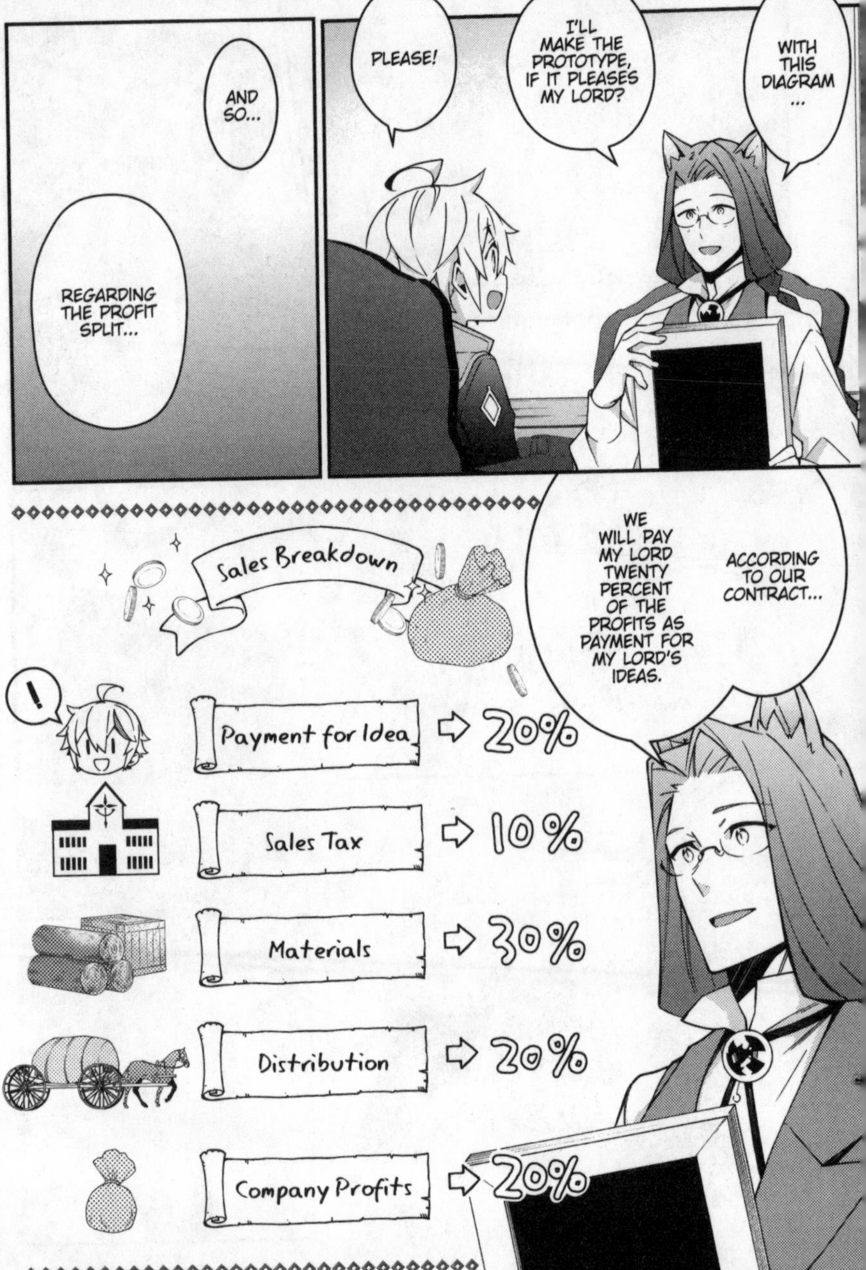
WITH THIS DIAGRAM...
I'LL MAKE THE PROTOTYPE, IF IT PLEASES MY LORD?
PLEASE!
AND SO...
REGARDING THE PROFIT SPLIT...
ACCORDING TO OUR CONTRACT...
WE WILL PAY MY LORD TWENTY PERCENT OF THE PROFITS AS PAYMENT FOR MY LORD'S IDEAS.
Sales Breakdown
!
Payment for Idea → 20%
Sales Tax → 10%
Materials → 30%
Distribution → 20%
Company Profits → 20%

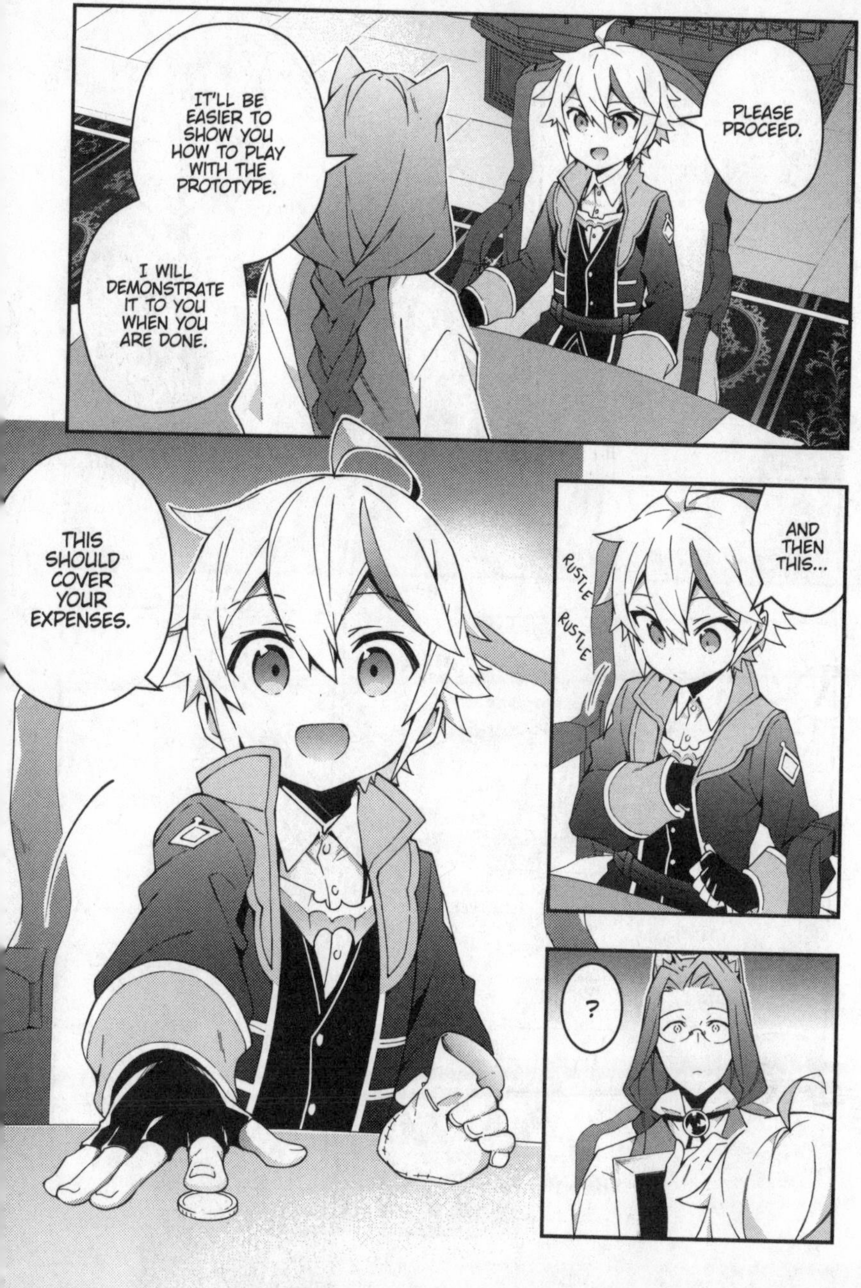
PLEASE PROCEED.
IT'LL BE EASIER TO SHOW YOU HOW TO PLAY WITH THE PROTOTYPE.
I WILL DEMONSTRATE IT TO YOU WHEN YOU ARE DONE.
AND THEN THIS...
RUSTLE
RUSTLE
?
THIS SHOULD COVER YOUR EXPENSES.

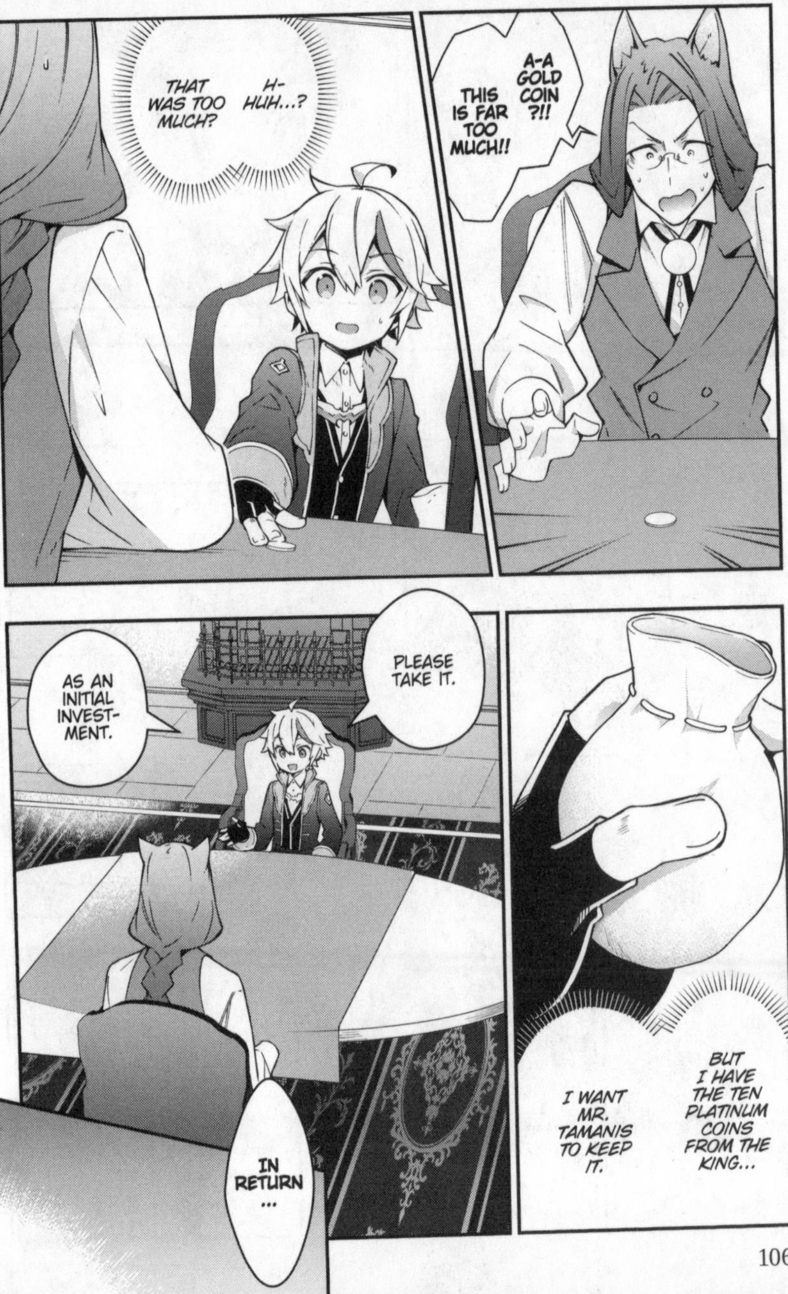
A-A GOLD COIN ?!!
THIS IS FAR TOO MUCH!!
H-HUH...?
THAT WAS TOO MUCH?
BUT I HAVE THE TEN PLATINUM COINS FROM THE KING...
I WANT MR. TAMANIS TO KEEP IT.
PLEASE TAKE IT.
AS AN INITIAL INVEST-MENT.
IN RETURN ...

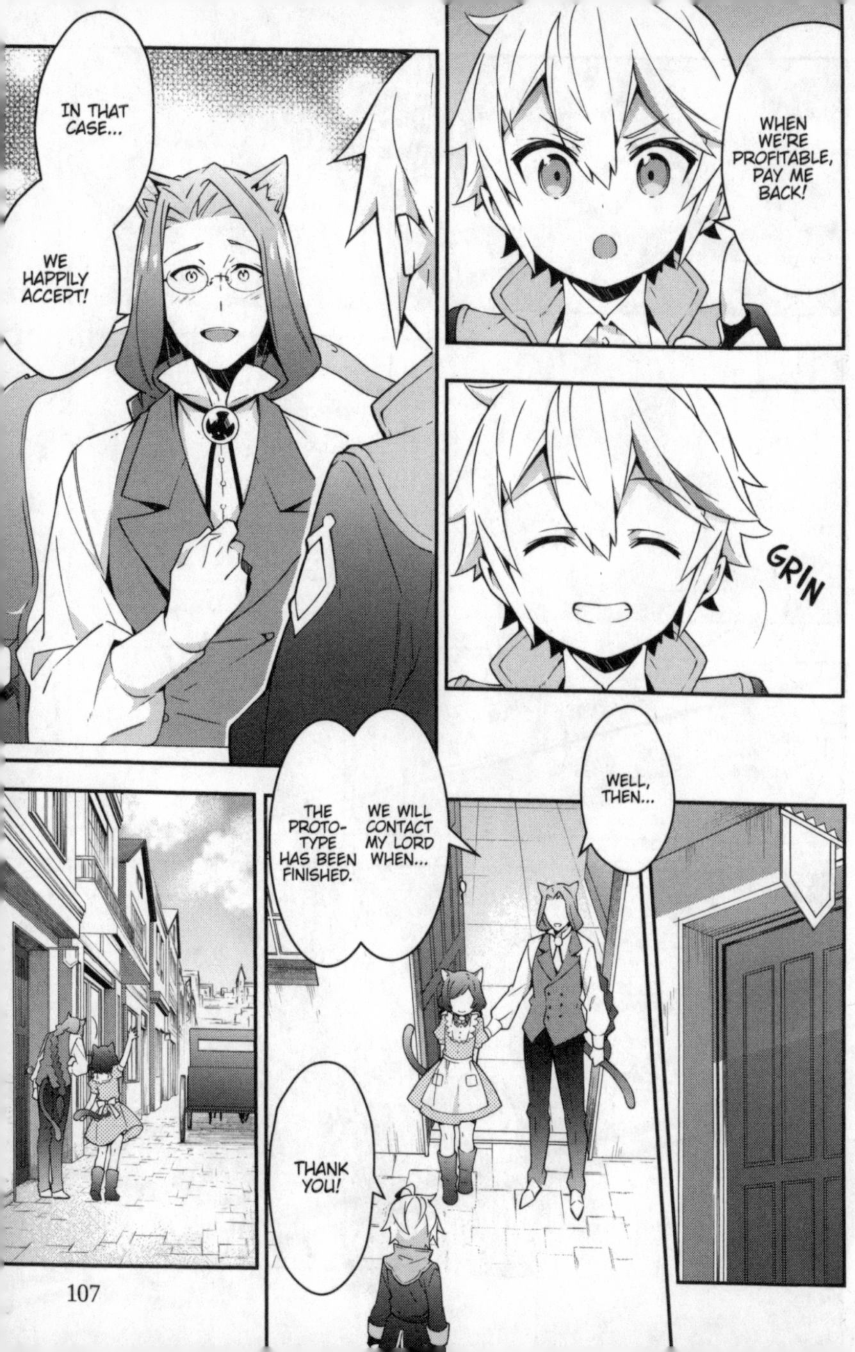
WHEN WE'RE PROFITABLE, PAY ME BACK!
GRIN
IN THAT CASE...
WE HAPPILY ACCEPT!
WELL, THEN...
WE WILL CONTACT MY LORD WHEN...
THE PROTOTYPE HAS BEEN FINISHED.
THANK YOU!

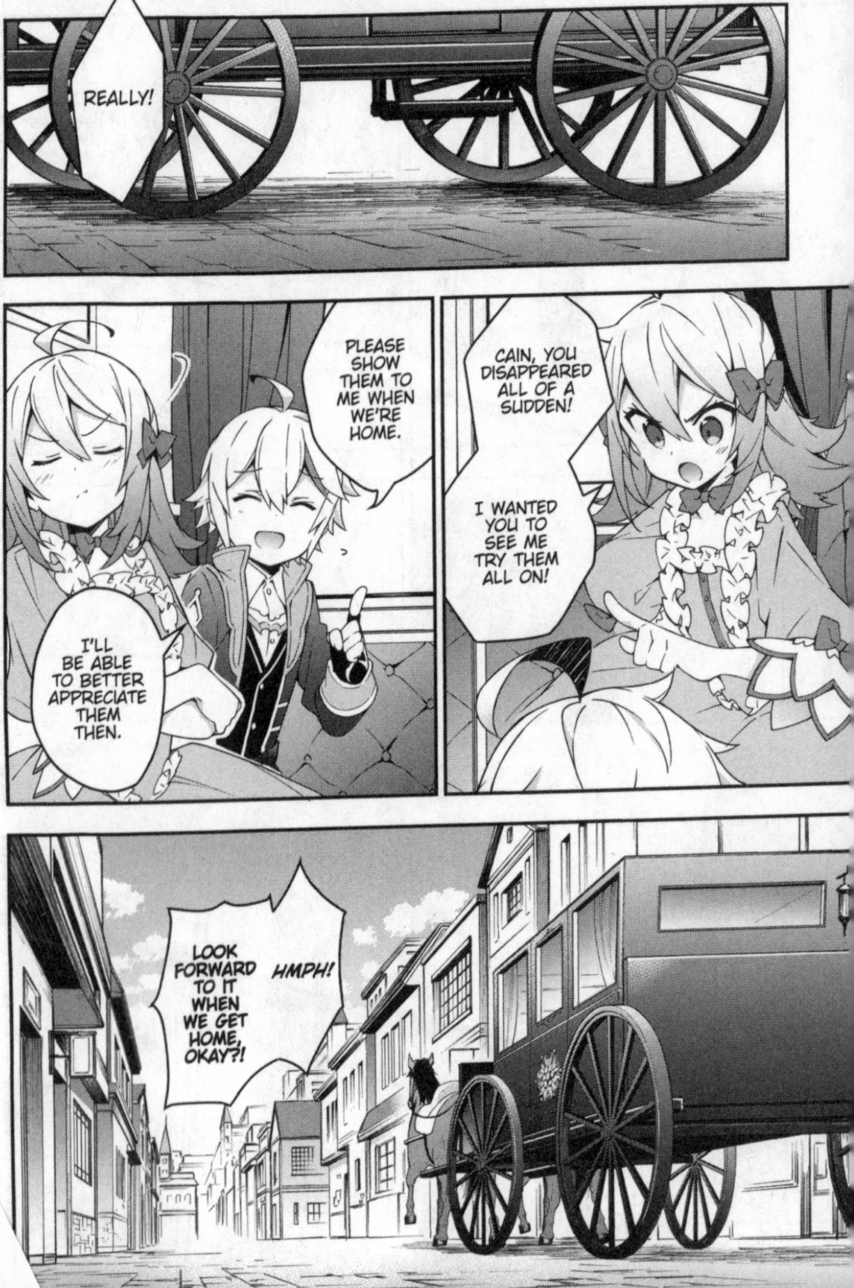
REALLY!
CAIN, YOU DISAPPEARED ALL OF A SUDDEN!
I WANTED YOU TO SEE ME TRY THEM ALL ON!
PLEASE SHOW THEM TO ME WHEN WE'RE HOME.
I'LL BE ABLE TO BETTER APPRECIATE THEM THEN.
HMPH!
LOOK FORWARD TO IT WHEN WE GET HOME, OKAY?!

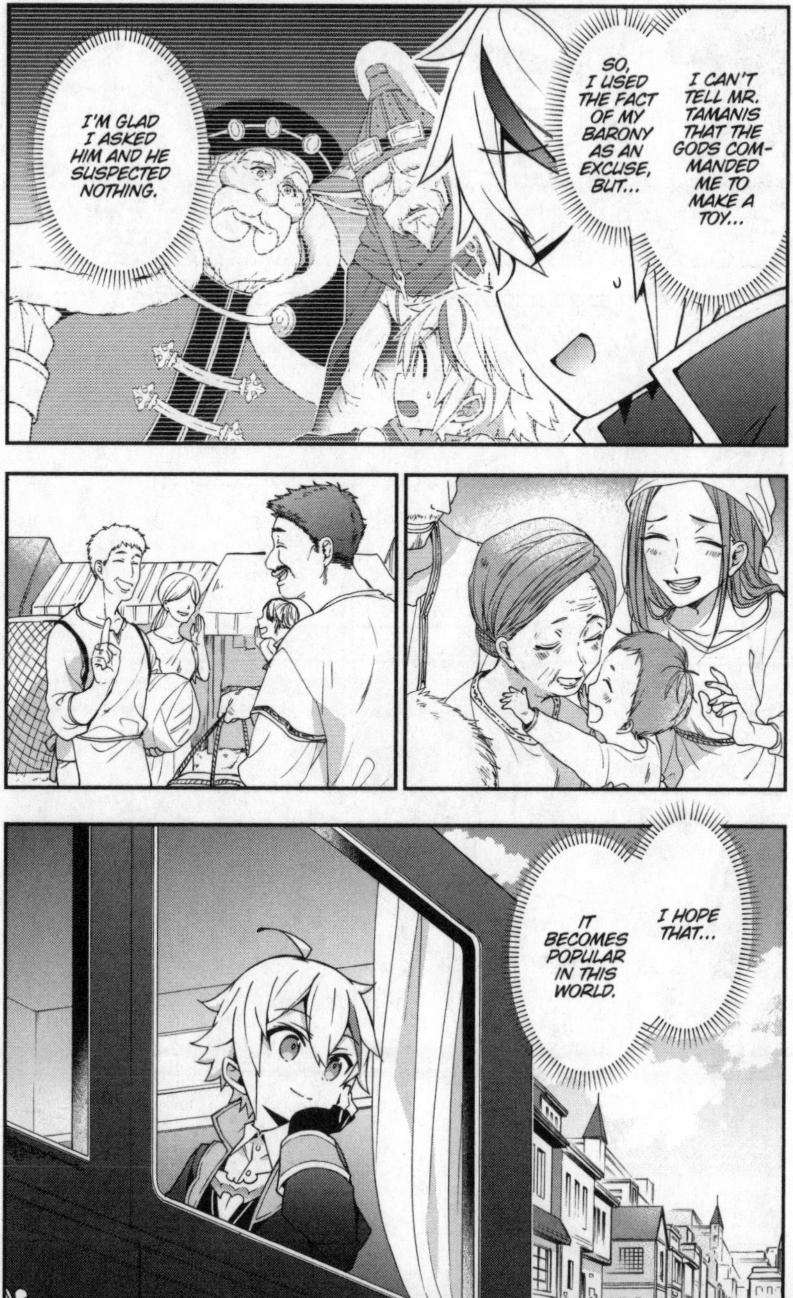
I CAN'T TELL MR. TAMANIS THAT THE GODS COM-MANDED ME TO MAKE A TOY...
SO, I USED THE FACT OF MY BARONY AS AN EXCUSE, BUT...
I'M GLAD I ASKED HIM AND HE SUSPECTED NOTHING.
I HOPE THAT...
IT BECOMES POPULAR IN THIS WORLD.

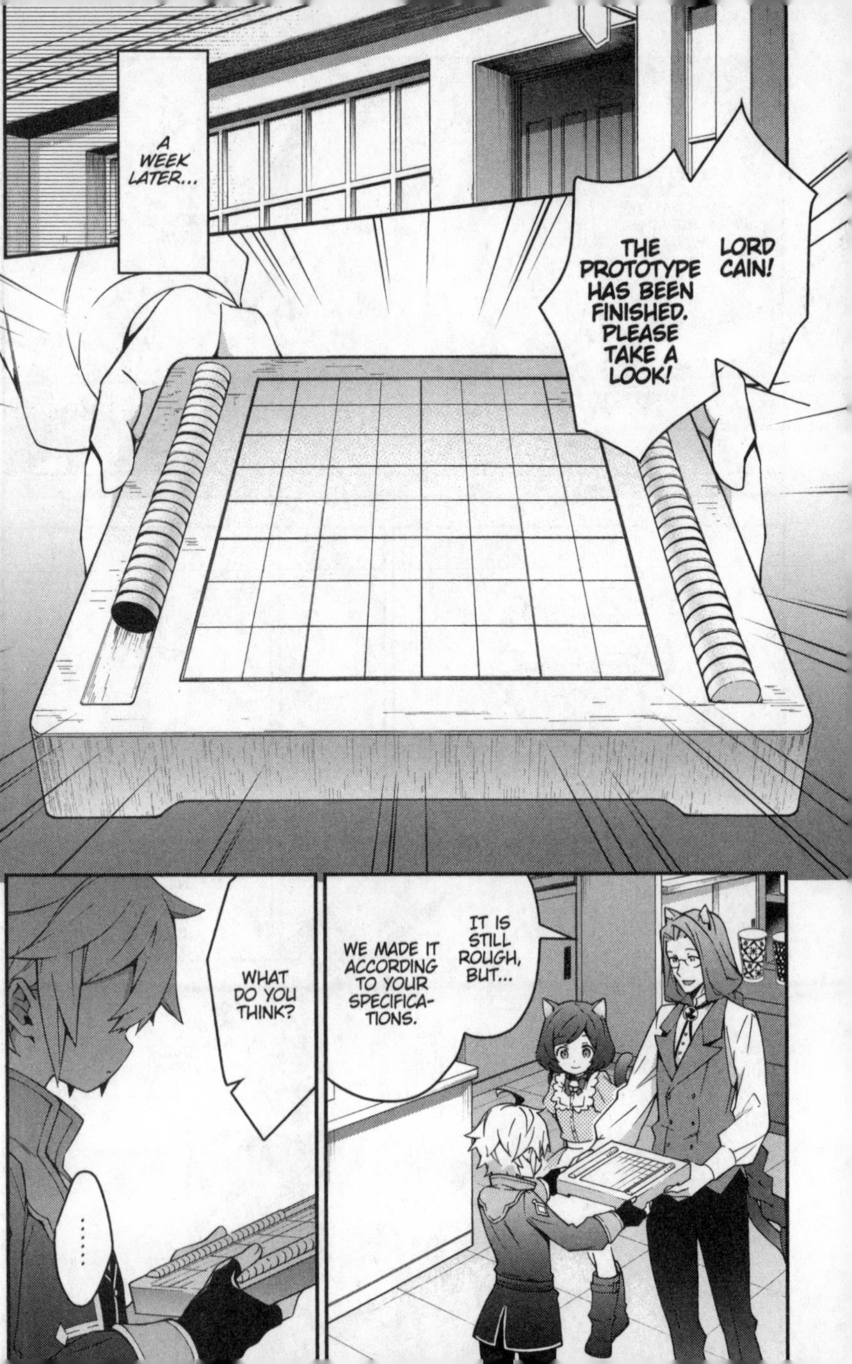
A WEEK LATER...
LORD CAIN! THE PROTOTYPE HAS BEEN FINISHED. PLEASE TAKE A LOOK!
IT IS STILL ROUGH, BUT...
WE MADE IT ACCORDING TO YOUR SPECIFICATIONS.
WHAT DO YOU THINK?
......

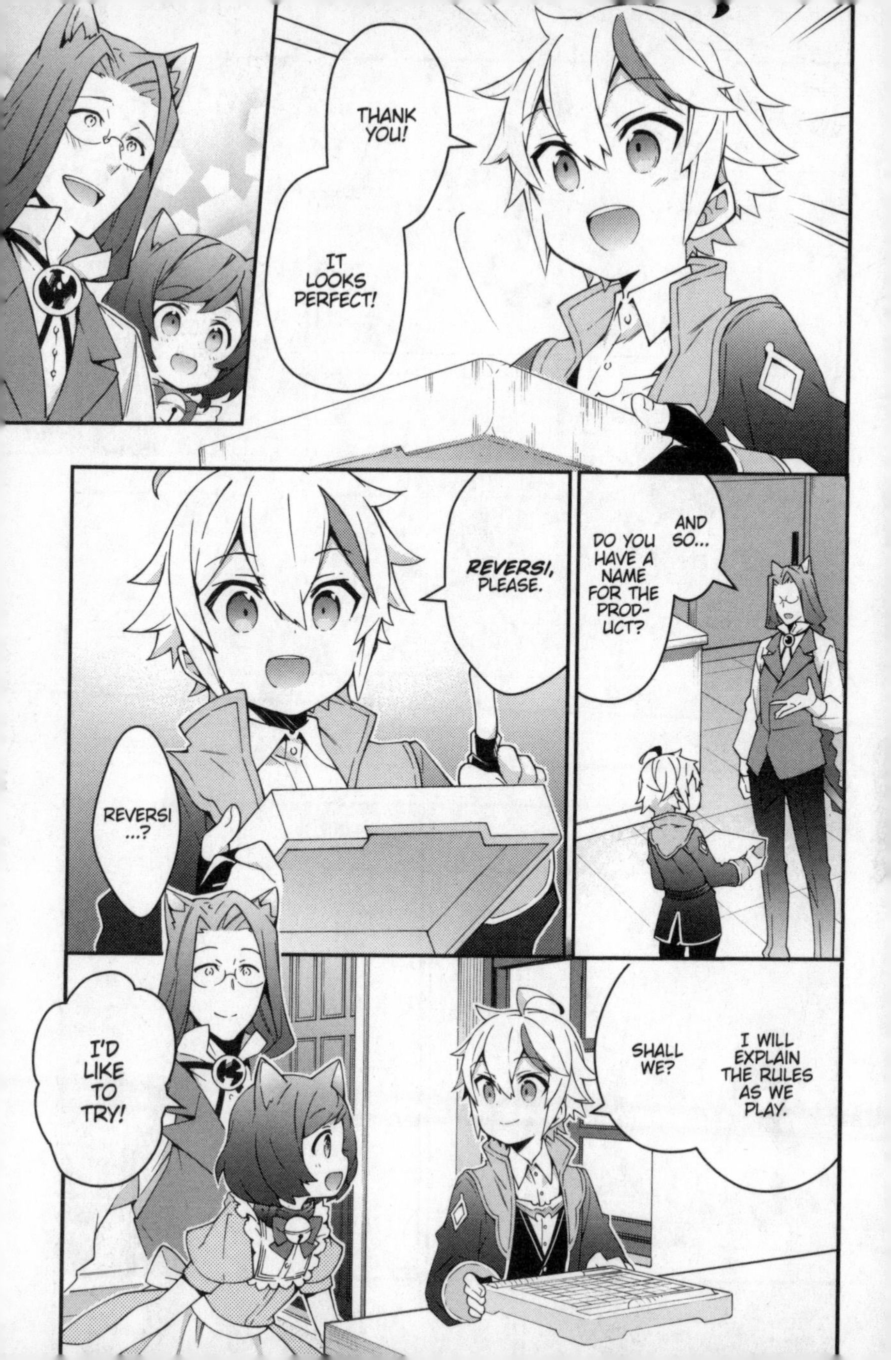
THANK YOU!
IT LOOKS PERFECT!
AND SO...
DO YOU HAVE A NAME FOR THE PROD-UCT?
REVERSI, PLEASE.
REVERSI ...?
I WILL EXPLAIN THE RULES AS WE PLAY.
SHALL WE?
I'D LIKE TO TRY!

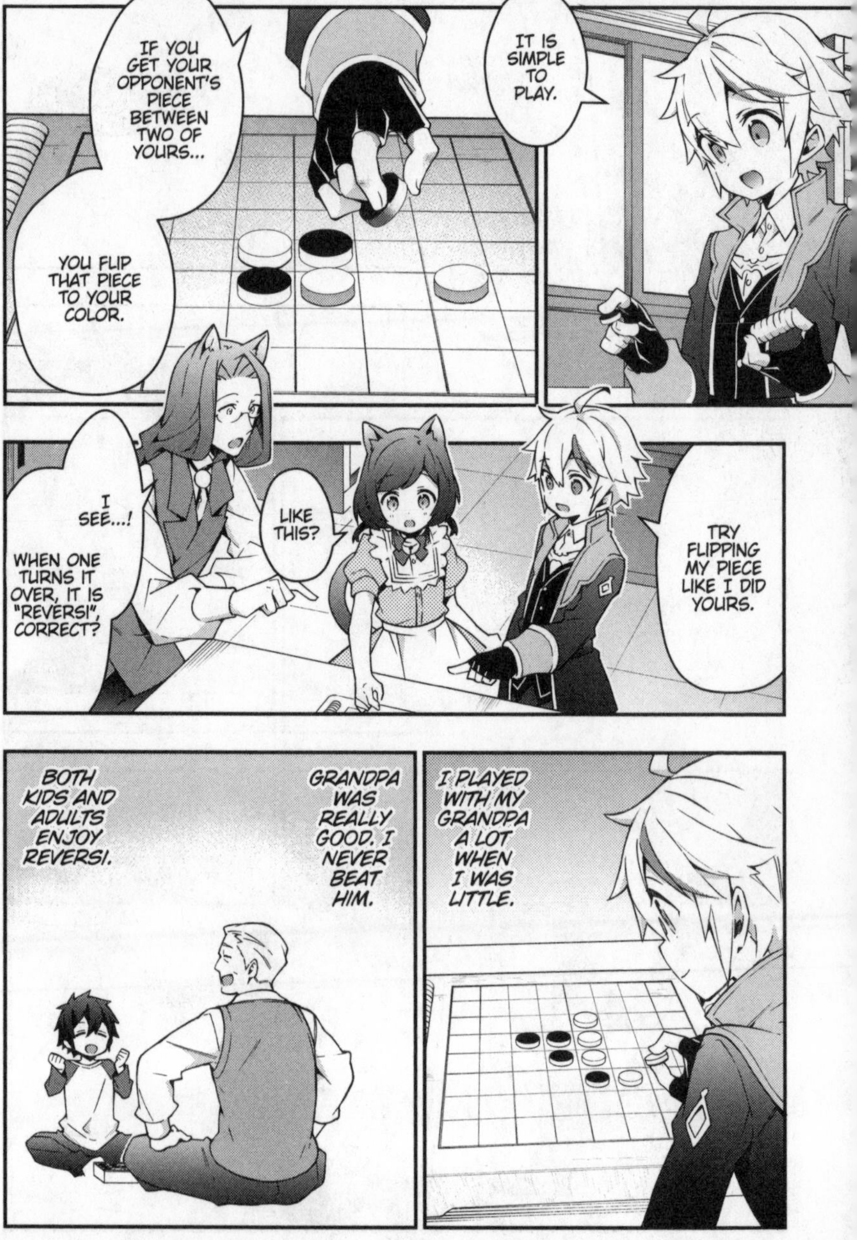
IT IS SIMPLE TO PLAY.
IF YOU GET YOUR OPPONENT'S PIECE BETWEEN TWO OF YOURS...
YOU FLIP THAT PIECE TO YOUR COLOR.
TRY FLIPPING MY PIECE LIKE I DID YOURS.
LIKE THIS?
I SEE...!
WHEN ONE TURNS IT OVER, IT IS "REVERSI", CORRECT?
I PLAYED WITH MY GRANDPA A LOT WHEN I WAS LITTLE.
GRANDPA WAS REALLY GOOD. I NEVER BEAT HIM.
BOTH KIDS AND ADULTS ENJOY REVERSI.

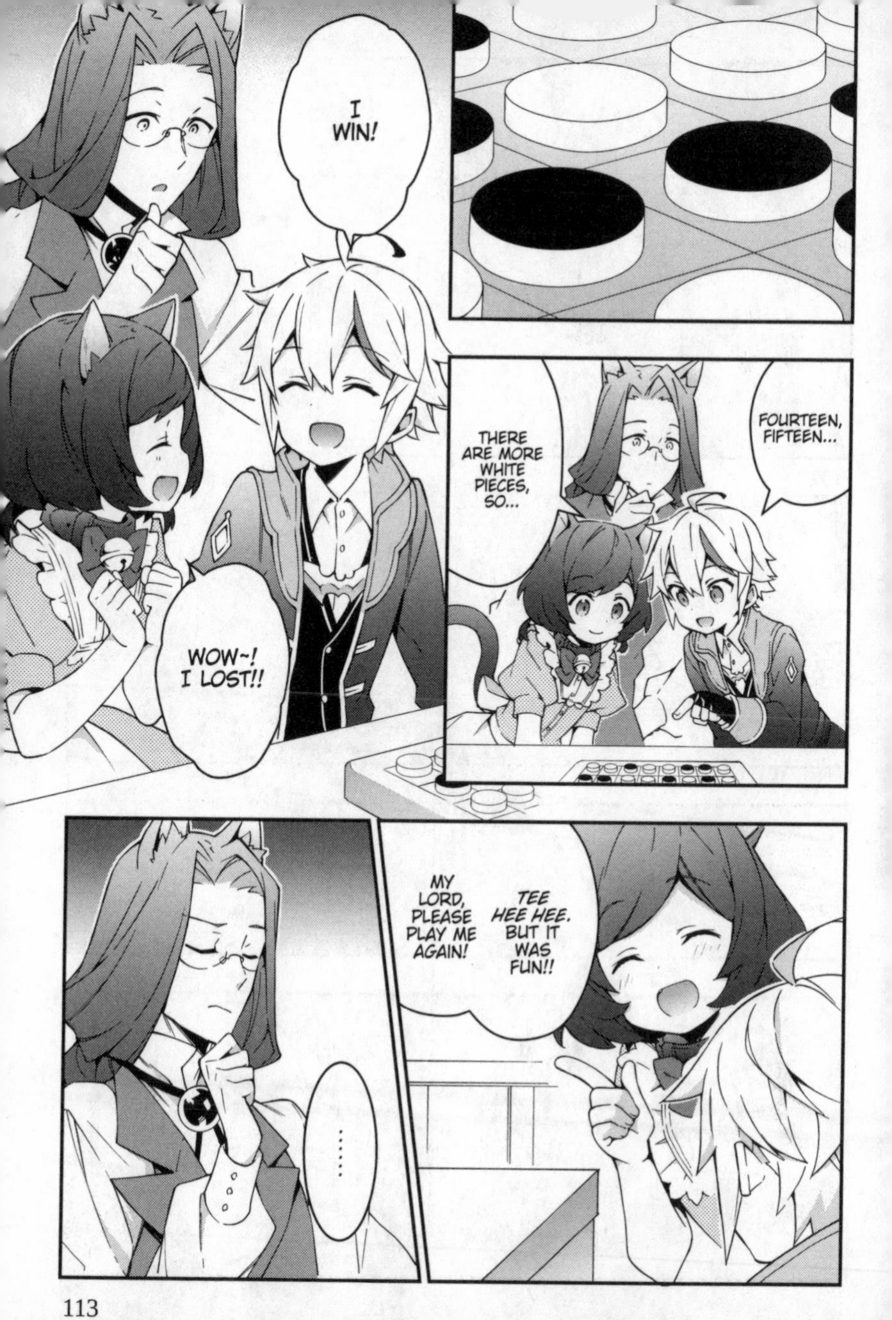
FOURTEEN, FIFTEEN...
THERE ARE MORE WHITE PIECES, SO...
I WIN!
WOW~! I LOST!!
TEE HEE HEE. BUT IT WAS FUN!!
MY LORD, PLEASE PLAY ME AGAIN!
......

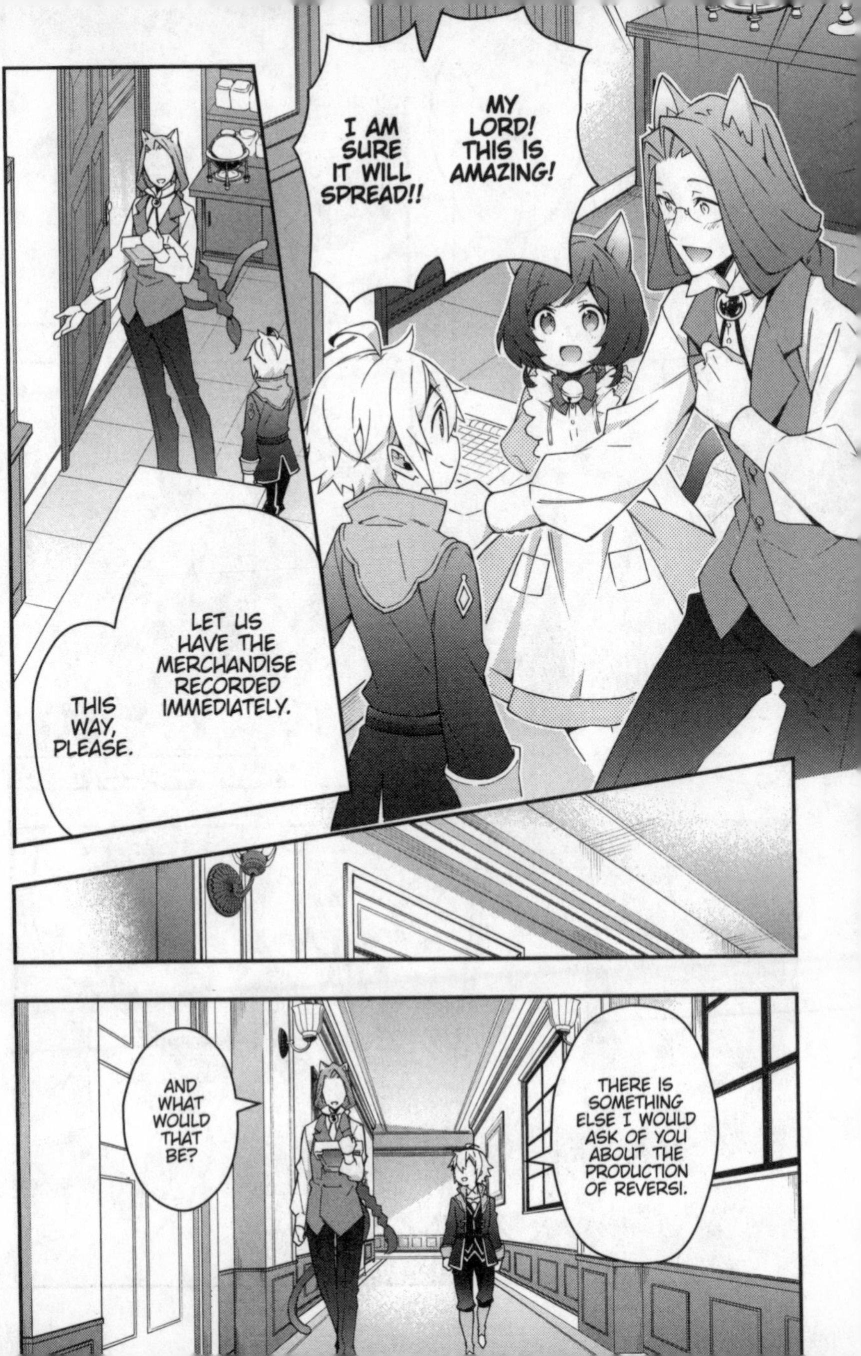
MY LORD! THIS IS AMAZING!
I AM SURE IT WILL SPREAD!!
LET US HAVE THE MERCHANDISE RECORDED IMMEDIATELY.
THIS WAY, PLEASE.
THERE IS SOMETHING ELSE I WOULD ASK OF YOU ABOUT THE PRODUCTION OF REVERSI.
AND WHAT WOULD THAT BE?

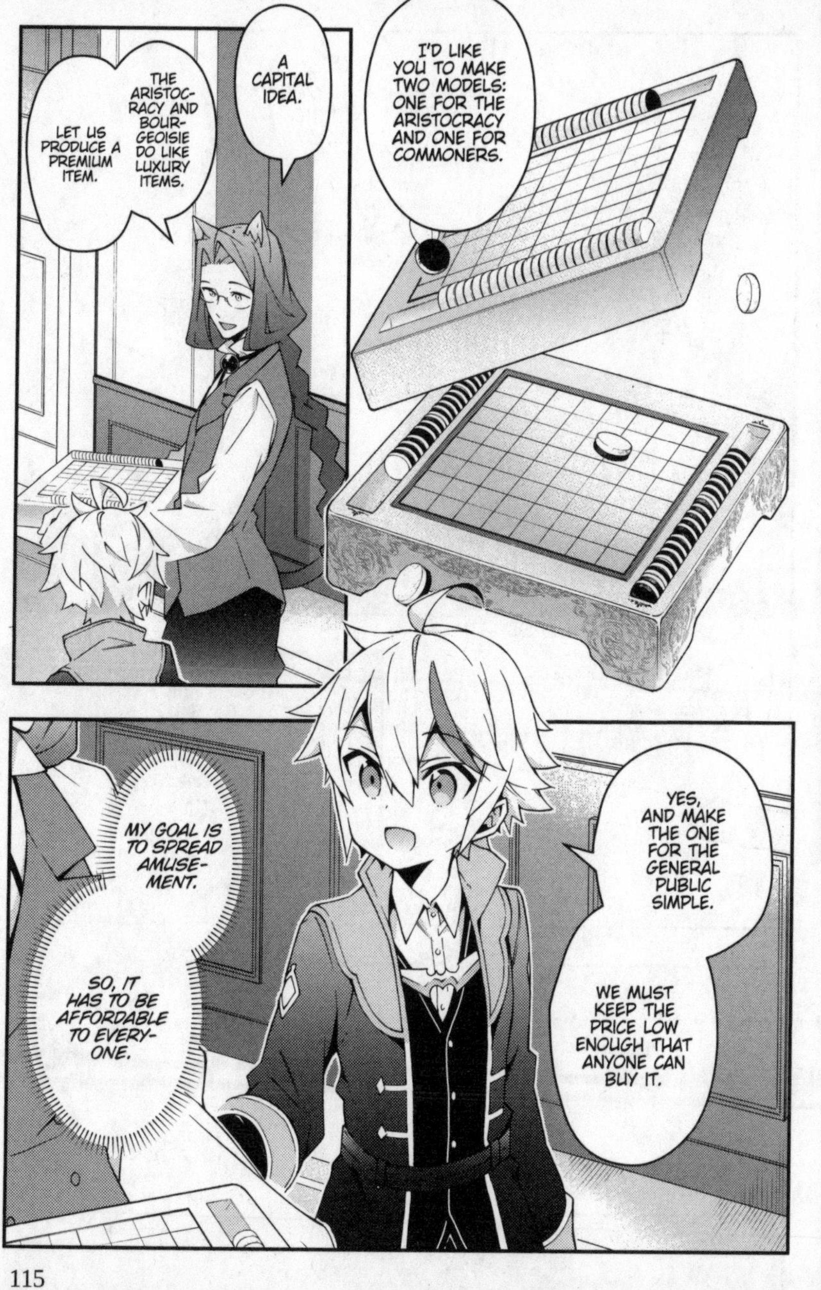
I'D LIKE YOU TO MAKE TWO MODELS: ONE FOR THE ARISTOCRACY AND ONE FOR COMMONERS.
A CAPITAL IDEA.
THE ARISTOCRACY AND BOURGEOISIE DO LIKE LUXURY ITEMS.
LET US PRODUCE A PREMIUM ITEM.
YES, AND MAKE THE ONE FOR THE GENERAL PUBLIC SIMPLE.
WE MUST KEEP THE PRICE LOW ENOUGH THAT ANYONE CAN BUY IT.
MY GOAL IS TO SPREAD AMUSEMENT.
SO, IT HAS TO BE AFFORDABLE TO EVERYONE.

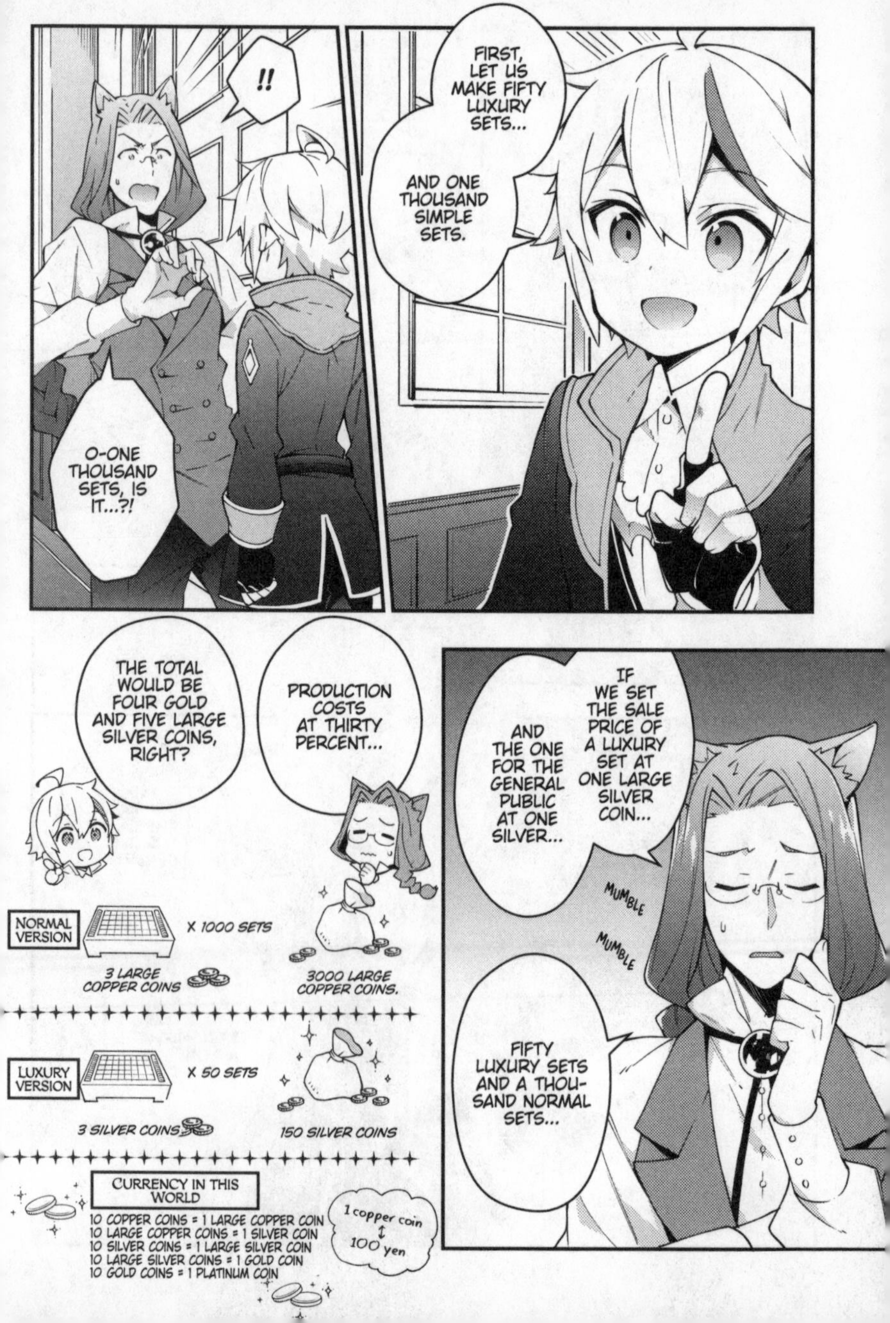
FIRST, LET US MAKE FIFTY LUXURY SETS...
AND ONE THOUSAND SIMPLE SETS.
!!
O-ONE THOUSAND SETS, IS IT...?!
IF WE SET THE SALE PRICE OF A LUXURY SET AT ONE LARGE SILVER COIN...
AND THE ONE FOR THE GENERAL PUBLIC AT ONE SILVER...
MUMBLE
MUMBLE
FIFTY LUXURY SETS AND A THOUSAND NORMAL SETS...
PRODUCTION COSTS AT THIRTY PERCENT...
THE TOTAL WOULD BE FOUR GOLD AND FIVE LARGE SILVER COINS, RIGHT?
NORMAL VERSION
X 1000 SETS
3 LARGE COPPER COINS
3000 LARGE COPPER COINS.
LUXURY VERSION
X 50 SETS
3 SILVER COINS
150 SILVER COINS
CURRENCY IN THIS WORLD
10 COPPER COINS = 1 LARGE COPPER COIN
10 LARGE COPPER COINS = 1 SILVER COIN
10 SILVER COINS = 1 LARGE SILVER COIN
10 LARGE SILVER COINS = 1 GOLD COIN
10 GOLD COINS = 1 PLATINUM COIN
1 copper coin ↕ 100 yen

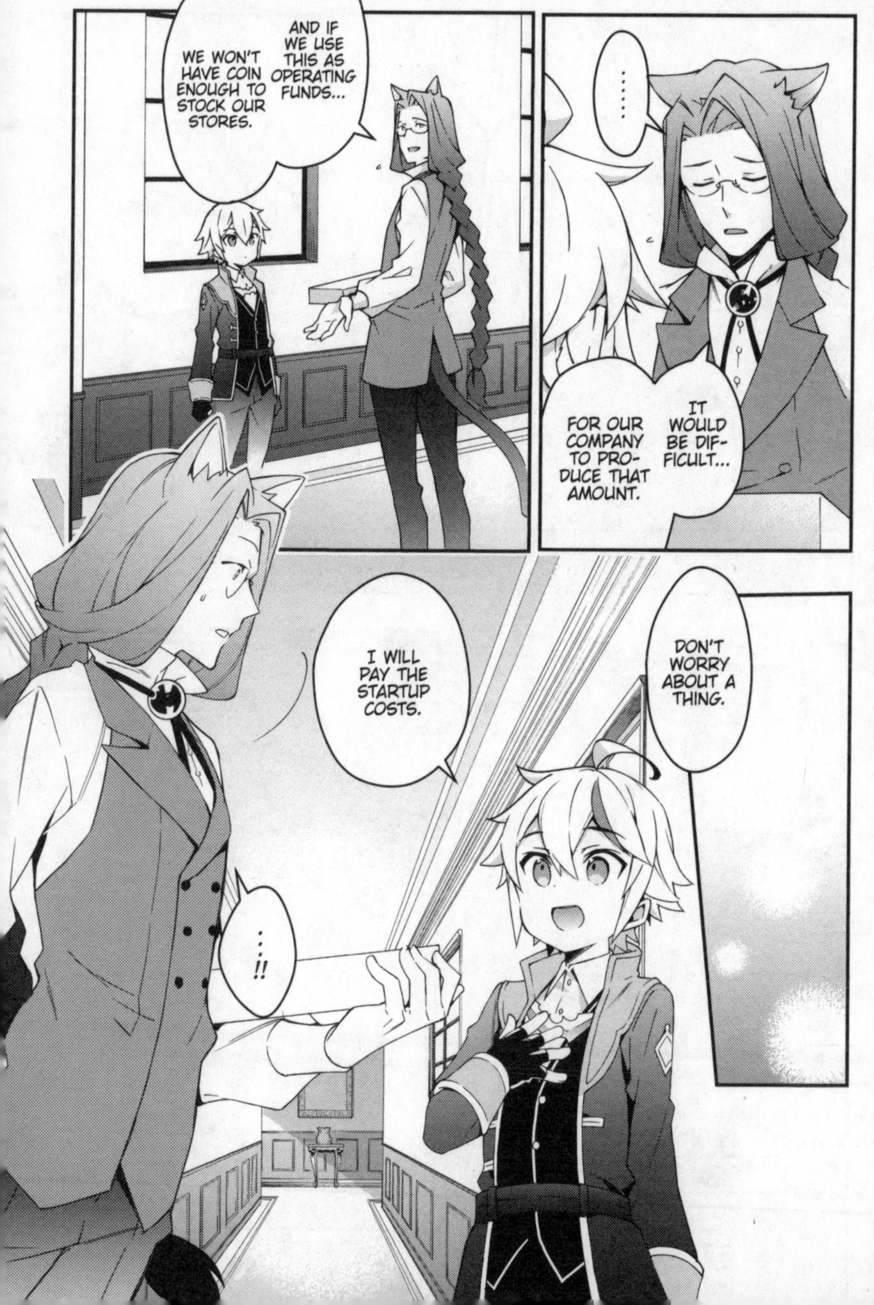
......
IT WOULD BE DIFFICULT...
FOR OUR COMPANY TO PRODUCE THAT AMOUNT.
AND IF WE USE THIS AS OPERATING FUNDS...
WE WON'T HAVE COIN ENOUGH TO STOCK OUR STORES.
DON'T WORRY ABOUT A THING.
I WILL PAY THE STARTUP COSTS.
...!!

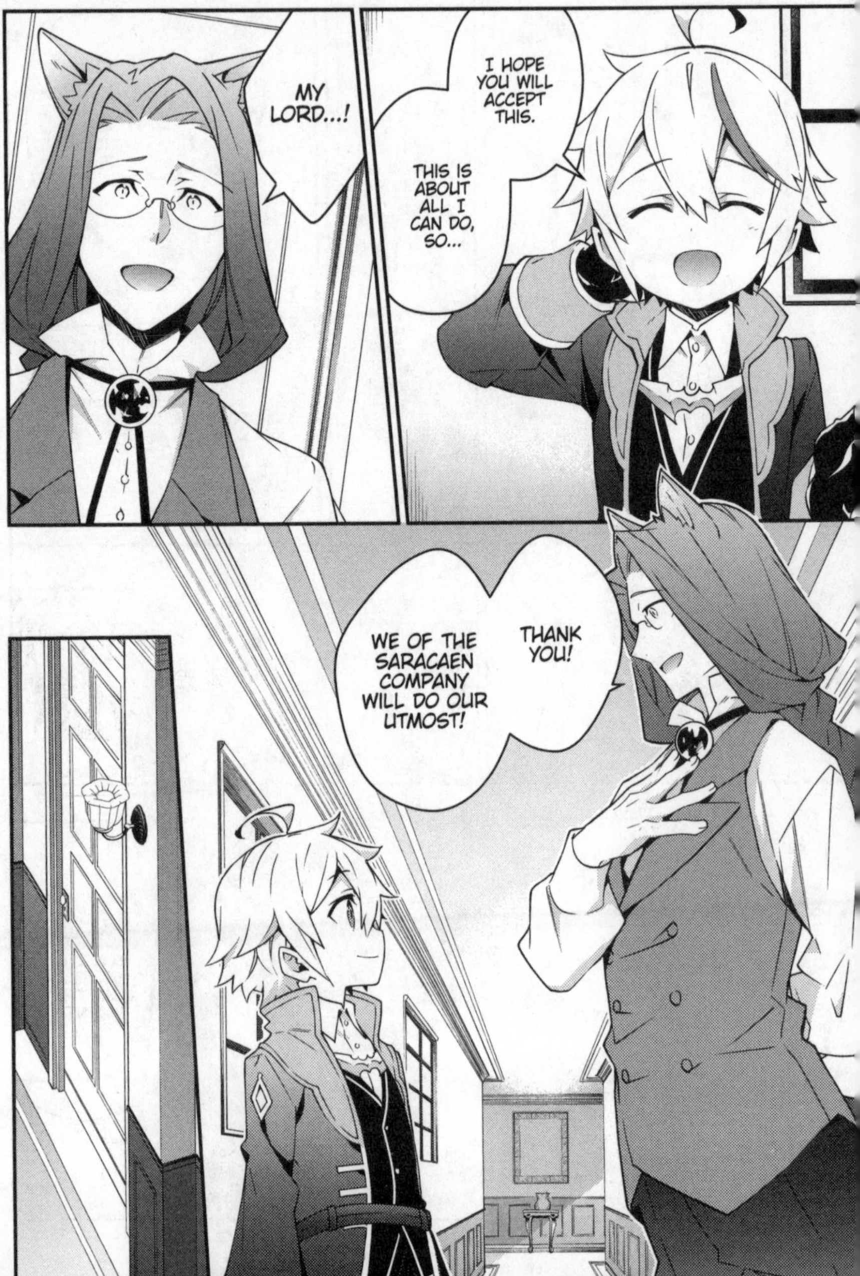
I HOPE YOU WILL ACCEPT THIS.
THIS IS ABOUT ALL I CAN DO, SO...
MY LORD...!
THANK YOU!
WE OF THE SARACAEN COMPANY WILL DO OUR UTMOST!

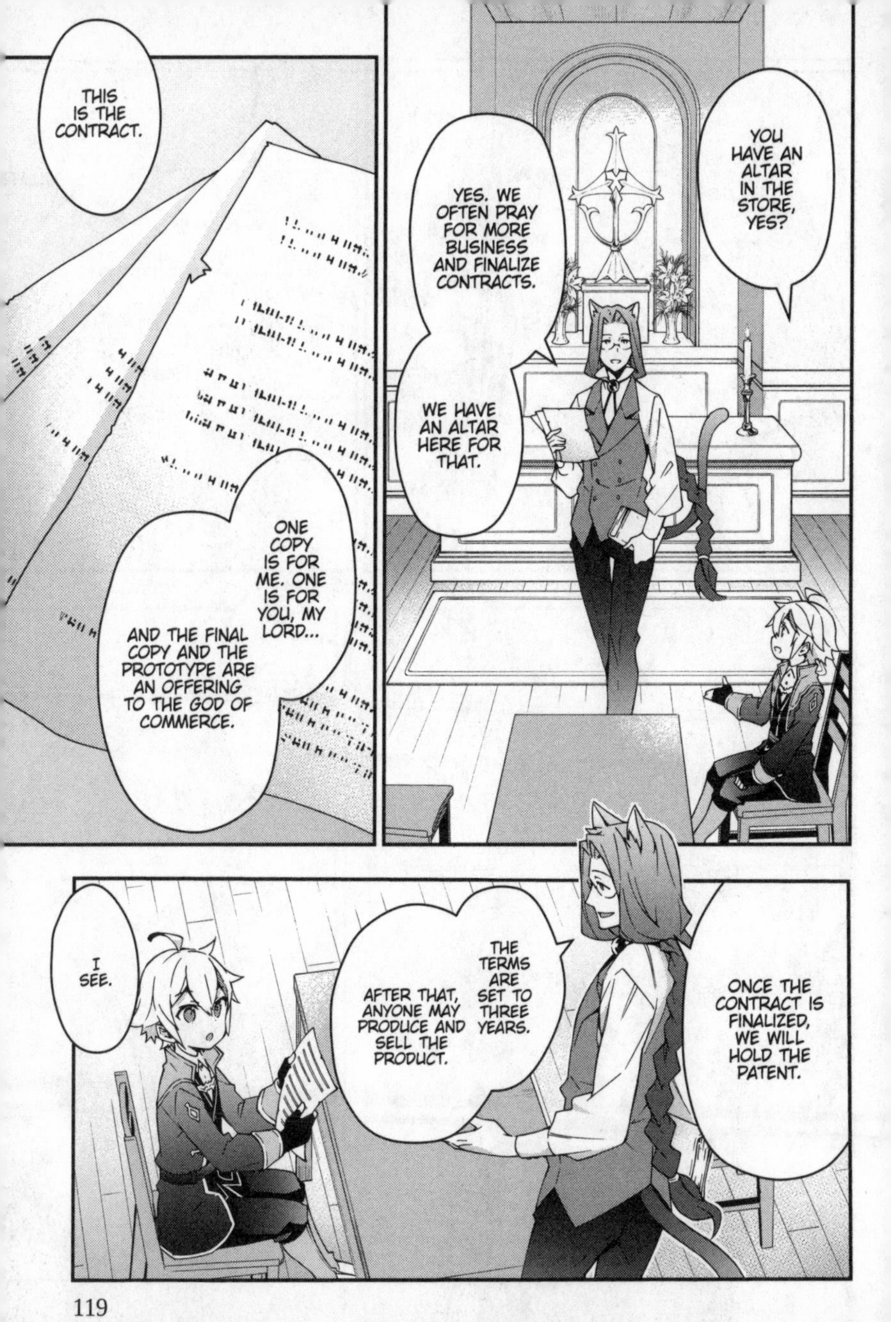
YOU HAVE AN ALTAR IN THE STORE, YES?
YES. WE OFTEN PRAY FOR MORE BUSINESS AND FINALIZE CONTRACTS.
WE HAVE AN ALTAR HERE FOR THAT.
THIS IS THE CONTRACT.
ONE COPY IS FOR ME. ONE IS FOR YOU, MY LORD...
AND THE FINAL COPY AND THE PROTOTYPE ARE AN OFFERING TO THE GOD OF COMMERCE.
ONCE THE CONTRACT IS FINALIZED, WE WILL HOLD THE PATENT.
THE TERMS ARE SET TO THREE YEARS.
AFTER THAT, ANYONE MAY PRODUCE AND SELL THE PRODUCT.
I SEE.

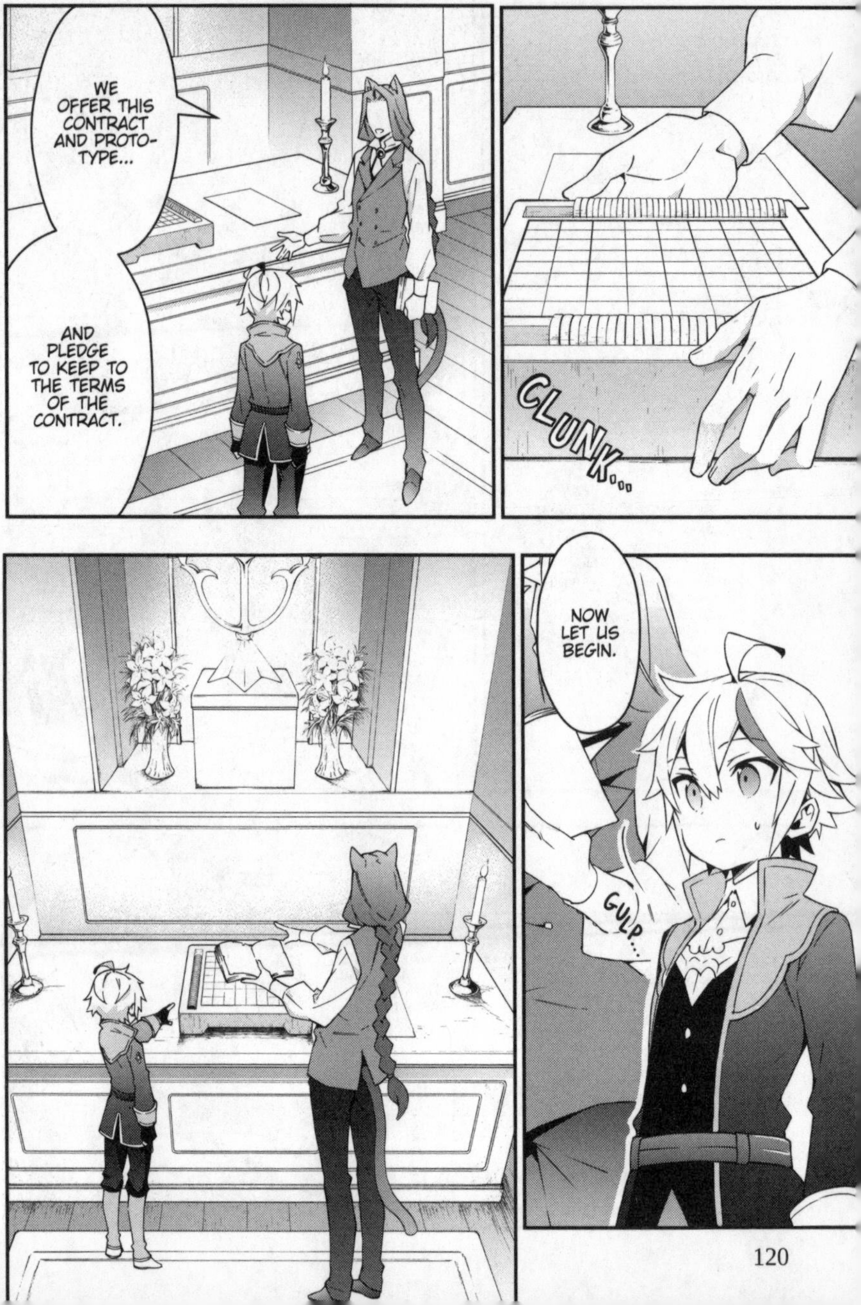
CLUNK...
WE OFFER THIS CONTRACT AND PROTO-TYPE...
AND PLEDGE TO KEEP TO THE TERMS OF THE CONTRACT.
NOW LET US BEGIN.
GULP...

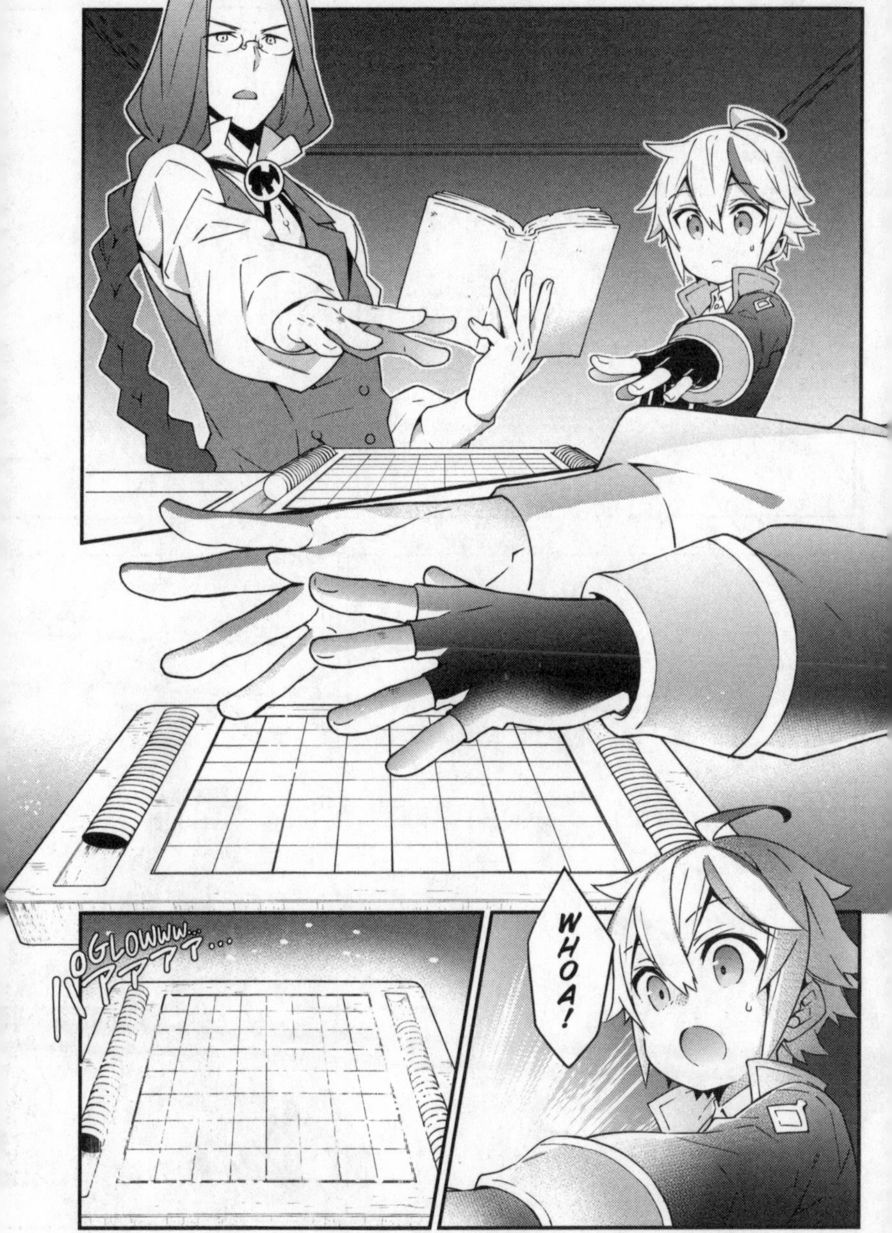
WHOA!
GLOWWW...

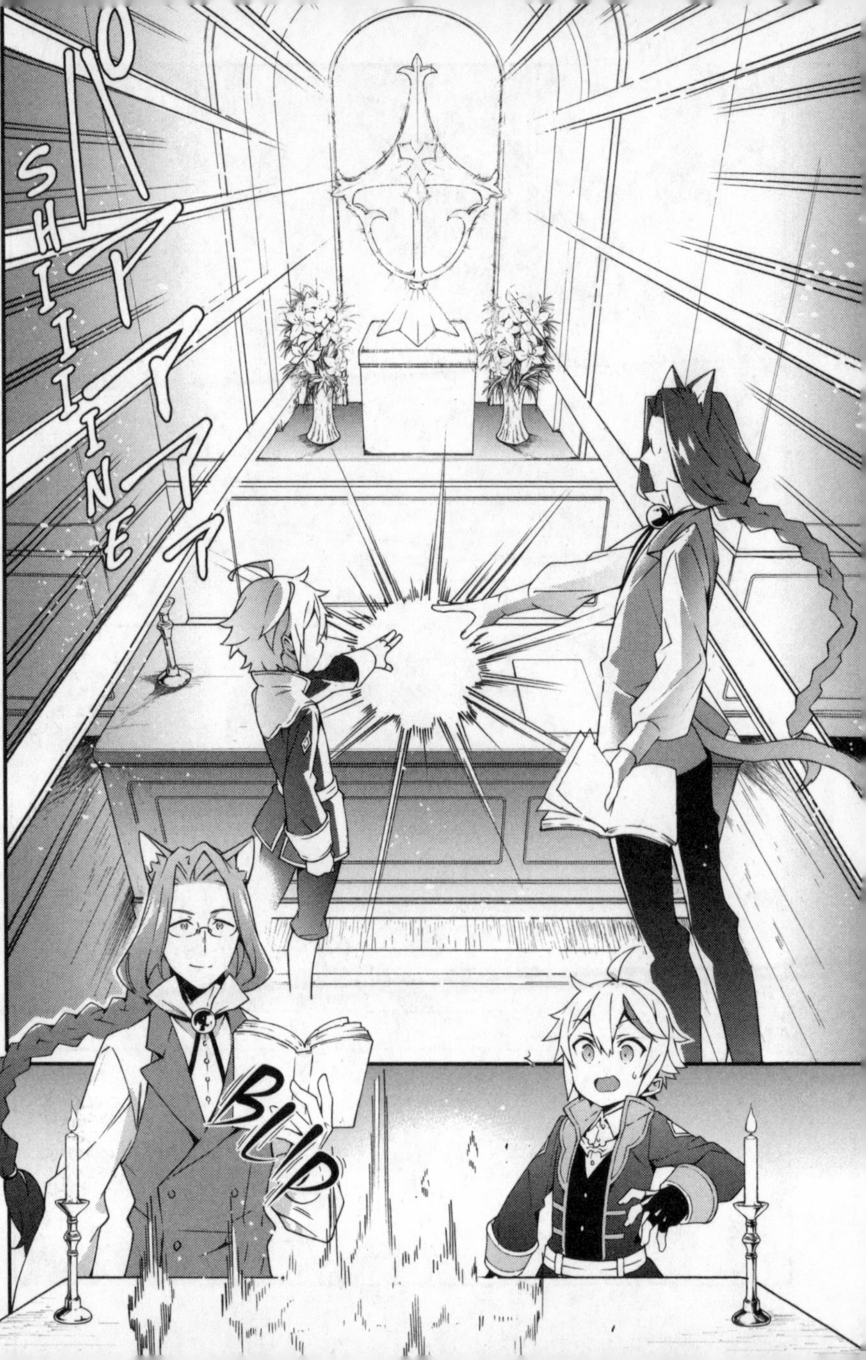
パァァァア
SHIIINE
BLIP

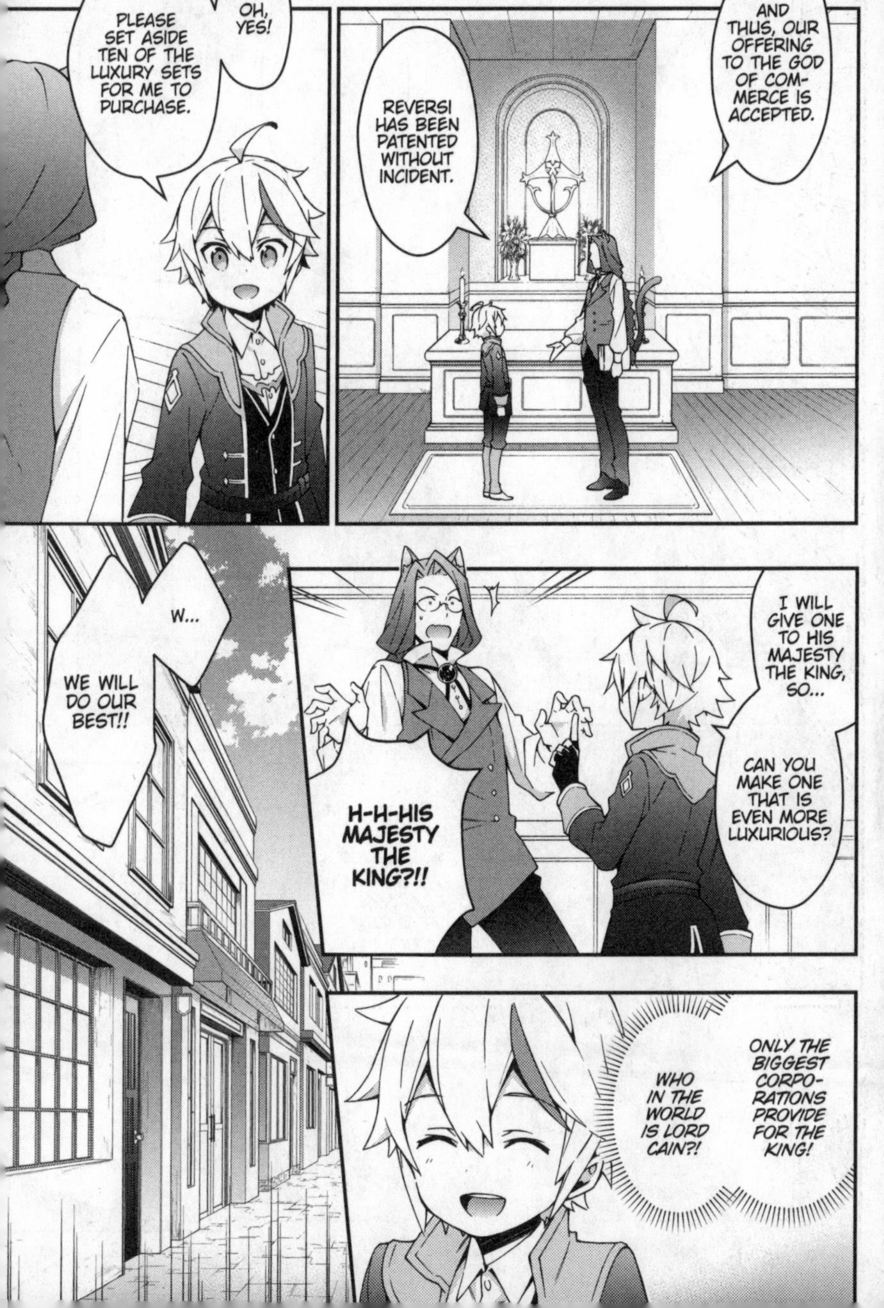
AND THUS, OUR OFFERING TO THE GOD OF COM- MERCE IS ACCEPTED.
REVERSI HAS BEEN PATENTED WITHOUT INCIDENT.
PLEASE SET ASIDE TEN OF THE LUXURY SETS FOR ME TO PURCHASE.
OH, YES!
I WILL GIVE ONE TO HIS MAJESTY THE KING, SO...
CAN YOU MAKE ONE THAT IS EVEN MORE LUXURIOUS?
H-H-HIS MAJESTY THE KING?!!
ONLY THE BIGGEST CORPO- RATIONS PROVIDE FOR THE KING!
WHO IN THE WORLD IS LORD CAIN?!
W...
WE WILL DO OUR BEST!!

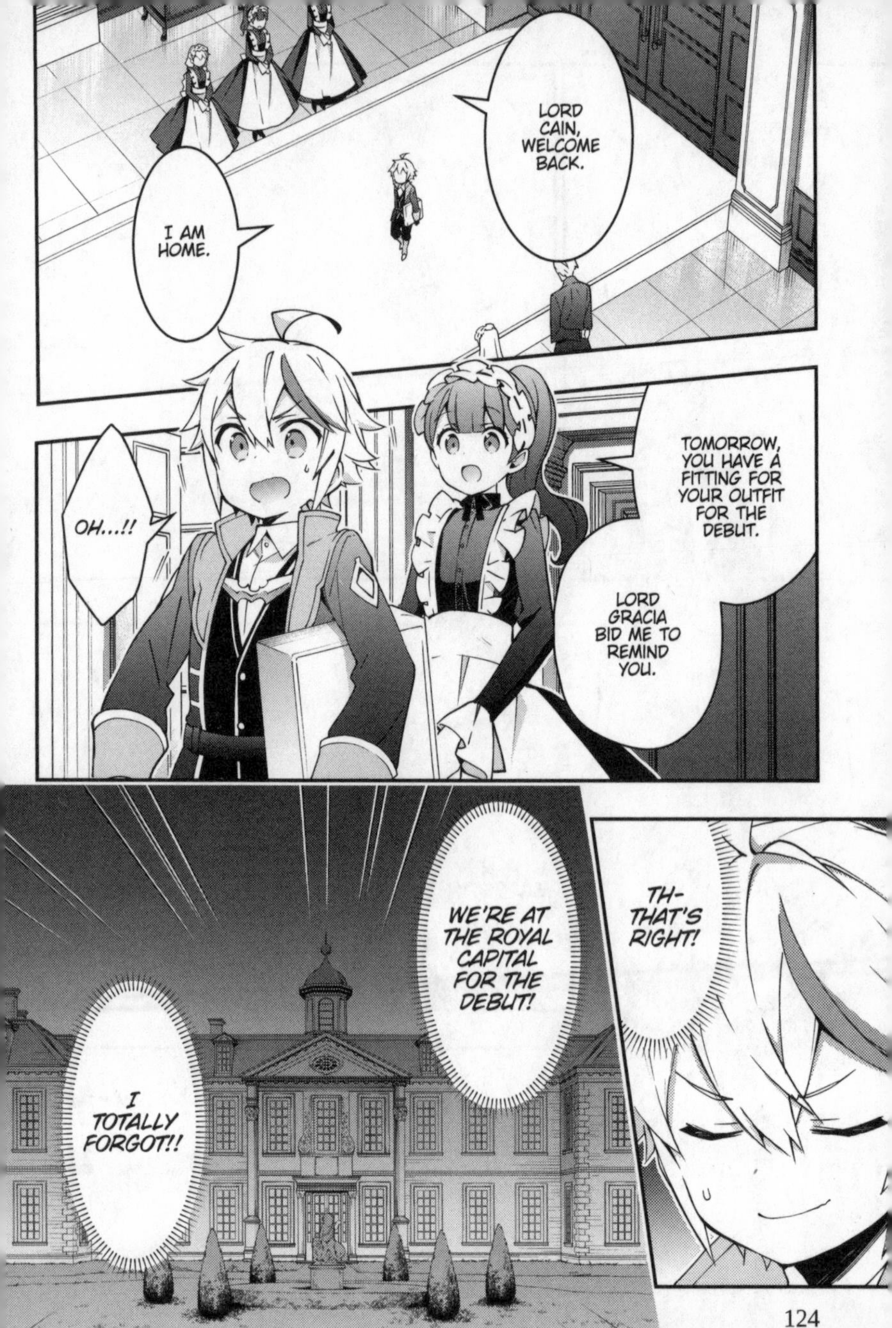
LORD CAIN, WELCOME BACK.
I AM HOME.
TOMORROW, YOU HAVE A FITTING FOR YOUR OUTFIT FOR THE DEBUT.
LORD GRACIA BID ME TO REMIND YOU.
OH...!!
TH- THAT'S RIGHT!
WE'RE AT THE ROYAL CAPITAL FOR THE DEBUT!
I TOTALLY FORGOT!!

CHRONICLES OF AN ARISTOCRAT REBORN IN ANOTHER WORLD

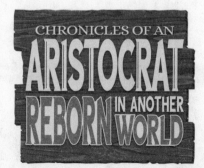

Regarding Reversi, of course the luxury board's materials and design differ from the normal version.

But the pieces differ, too.

The pieces of the luxury item are made by pressing two expensive materials.

The pieces of the normal version are painted on one side.

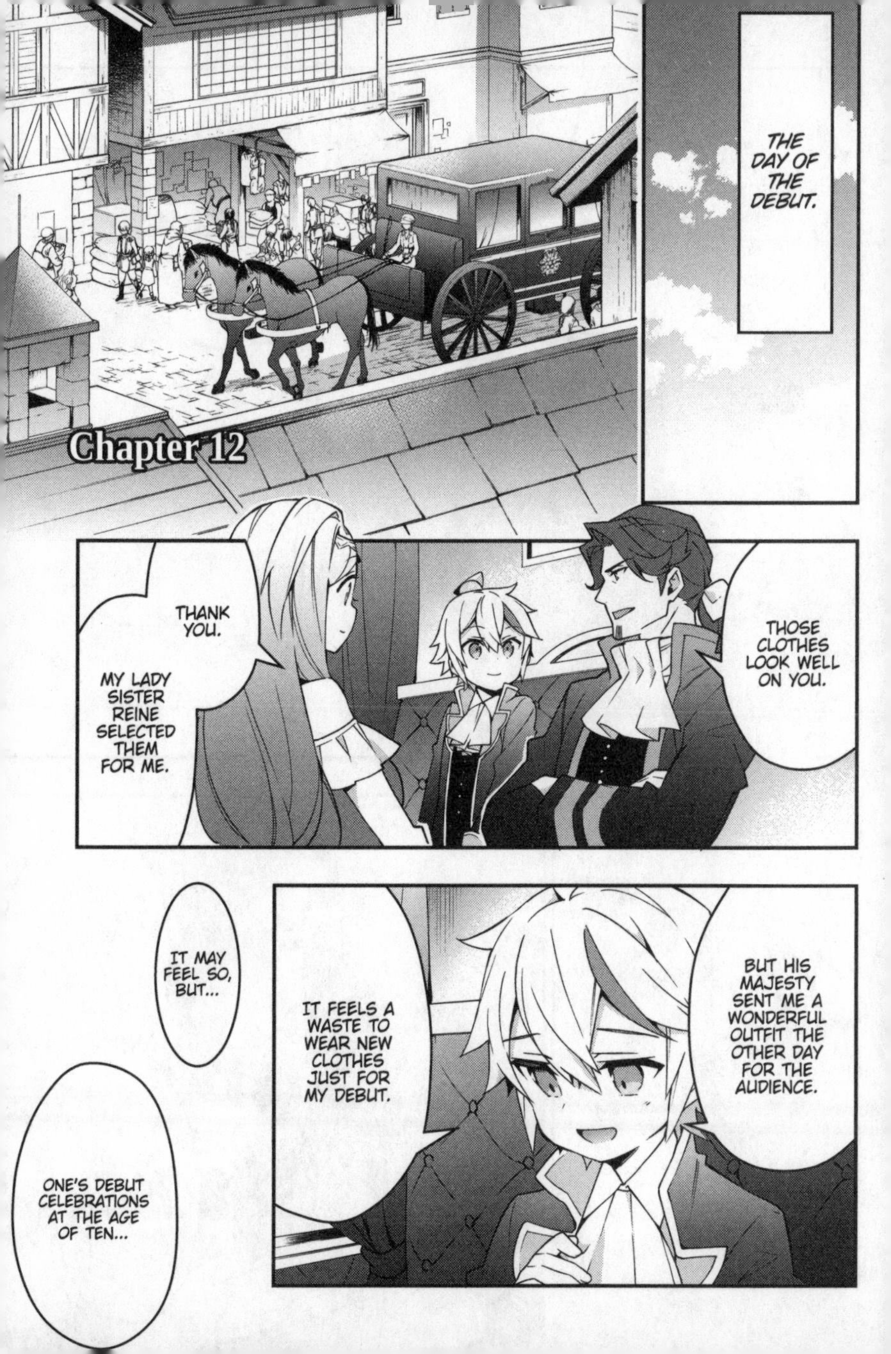
THE DAY OF THE DEBUT.
Chapter 12
THOSE CLOTHES LOOK WELL ON YOU.
THANK YOU.
MY LADY SISTER REINE SELECTED THEM FOR ME.
BUT HIS MAJESTY SENT ME A WONDERFUL OUTFIT THE OTHER DAY FOR THE AUDIENCE.
IT FEELS A WASTE TO WEAR NEW CLOTHES JUST FOR MY DEBUT.
IT MAY FEEL SO, BUT...
ONE'S DEBUT CELEBRATIONS AT THE AGE OF TEN...

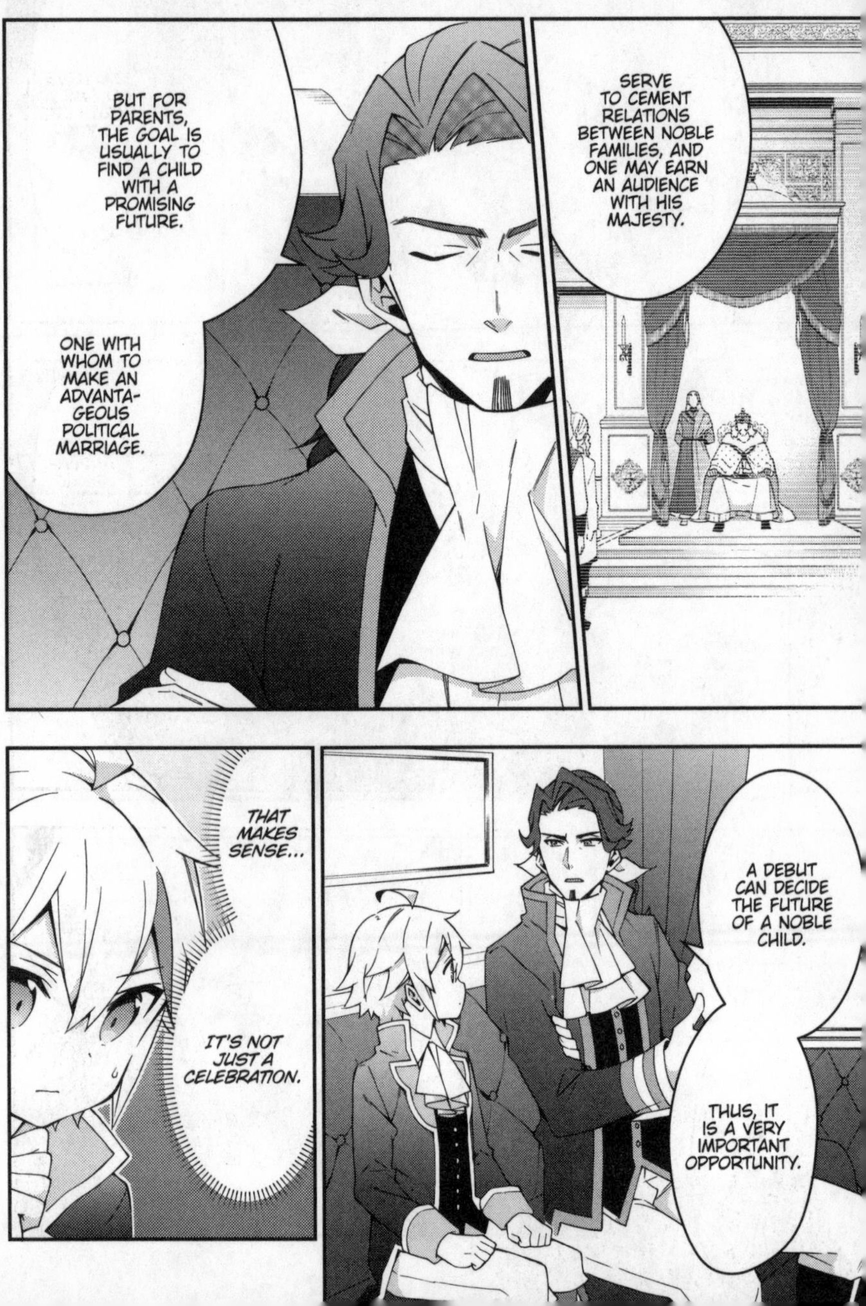
SERVE TO CEMENT RELATIONS BETWEEN NOBLE FAMILIES, AND ONE MAY EARN AN AUDIENCE WITH HIS MAJESTY.
BUT FOR PARENTS, THE GOAL IS USUALLY TO FIND A CHILD WITH A PROMISING FUTURE.
ONE WITH WHOM TO MAKE AN ADVANTA-GEOUS POLITICAL MARRIAGE.
A DEBUT CAN DECIDE THE FUTURE OF A NOBLE CHILD.
THUS, IT IS A VERY IMPORTANT OPPORTUNITY.
THAT MAKES SENSE...
IT'S NOT JUST A CELEBRATION.

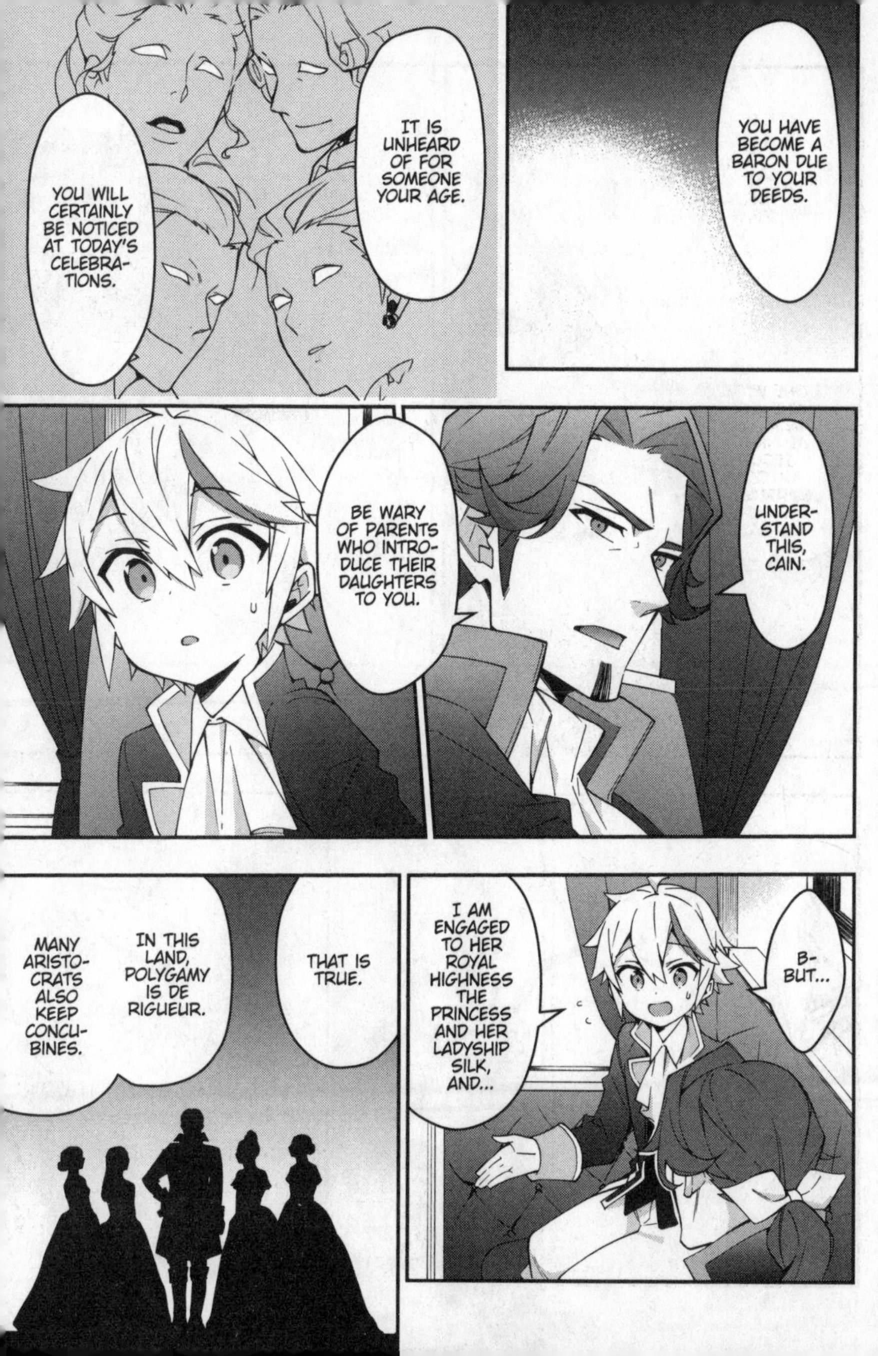
YOU HAVE BECOME A BARON DUE TO YOUR DEEDS.
IT IS UNHEARD OF FOR SOMEONE YOUR AGE.
YOU WILL CERTAINLY BE NOTICED AT TODAY'S CELEBRATIONS.
UNDERSTAND THIS, CAIN.
BE WARY OF PARENTS WHO INTRODUCE THEIR DAUGHTERS TO YOU.
B-BUT...
I AM ENGAGED TO HER ROYAL HIGHNESS THE PRINCESS AND HER LADYSHIP SILK, AND...
THAT IS TRUE.
IN THIS LAND, POLYGAMY IS DE RIGUEUR.
MANY ARISTOCRATS ALSO KEEP CONCUBINES.

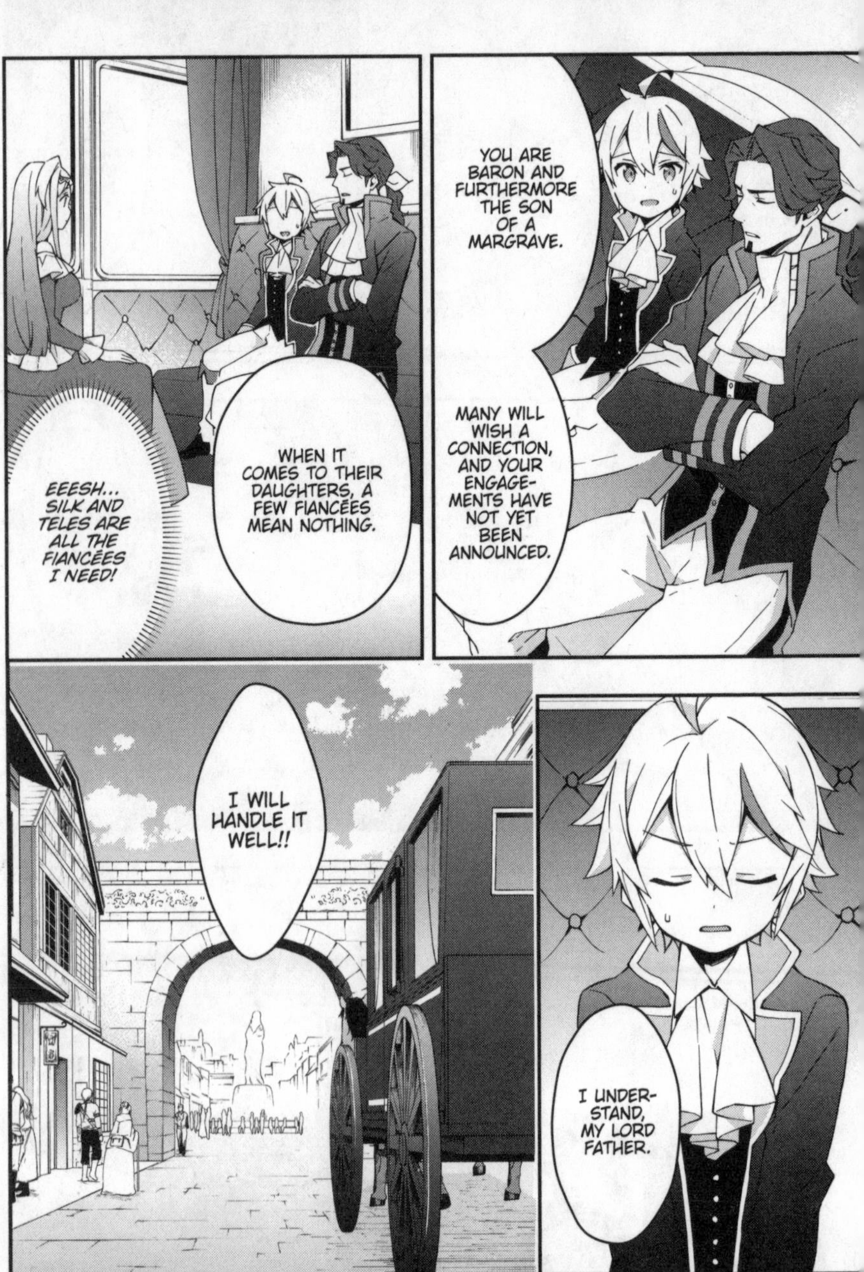
YOU ARE BARON AND FURTHERMORE THE SON OF A MARGRAVE.
MANY WILL WISH A CONNECTION, AND YOUR ENGAGE-MENTS HAVE NOT YET BEEN ANNOUNCED.
WHEN IT COMES TO THEIR DAUGHTERS, A FEW FIANCÉES MEAN NOTHING.
EEESH... SILK AND TELES ARE ALL THE FIANCÉES I NEED!
I UNDER-STAND, MY LORD FATHER.
I WILL HANDLE IT WELL!!

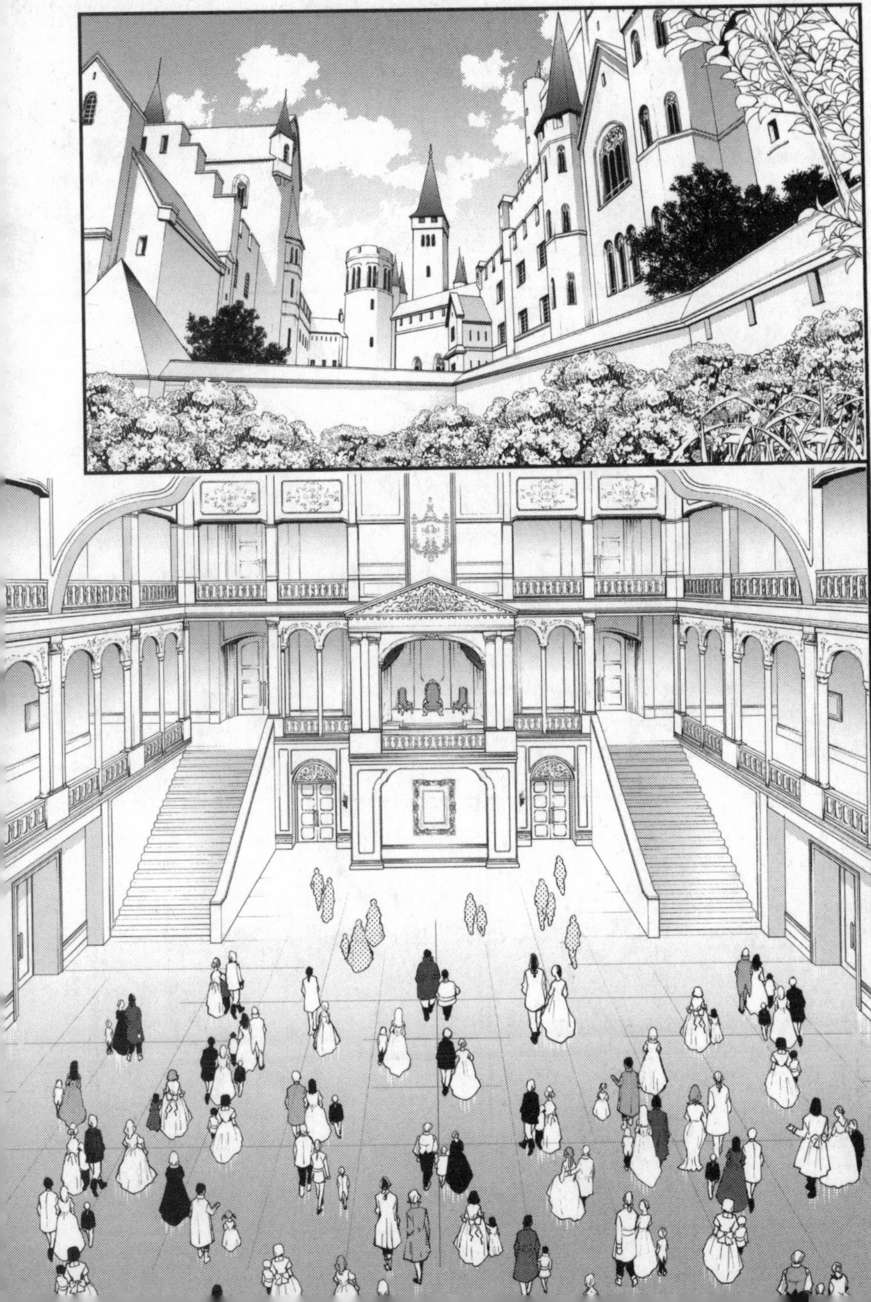

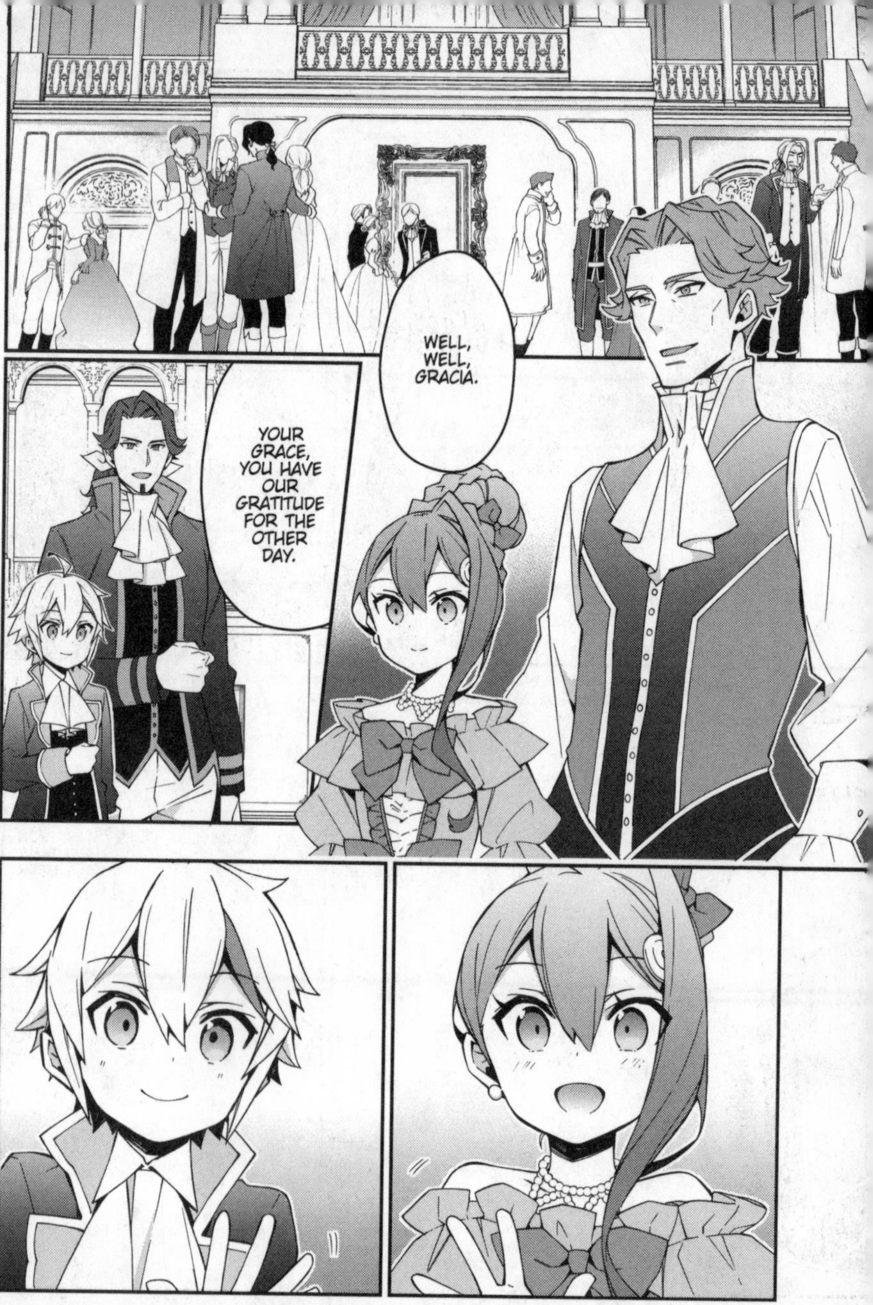
WELL, WELL, GRACIA.
YOUR GRACE, YOU HAVE OUR GRATITUDE FOR THE OTHER DAY.

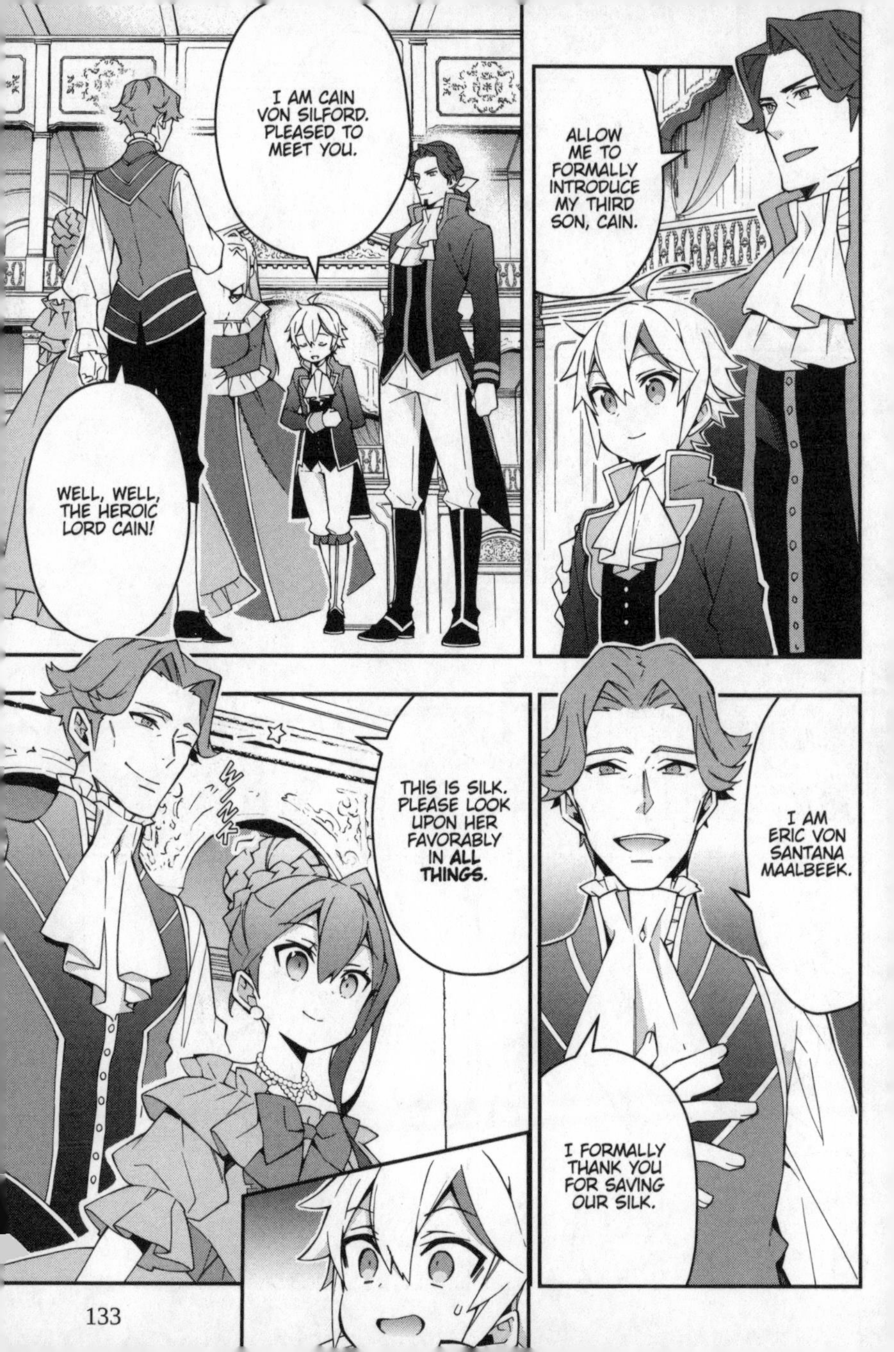
ALLOW ME TO FORMALLY INTRODUCE MY THIRD SON, CAIN.
I AM CAIN VON SILFORD. PLEASED TO MEET YOU.
WELL, WELL, THE HEROIC LORD CAIN!
I AM ERIC VON SANTANA MAALBEEK.
I FORMALLY THANK YOU FOR SAVING OUR SILK.
THIS IS SILK. PLEASE LOOK UPON HER FAVORABLY IN **ALL THINGS.**
WINK

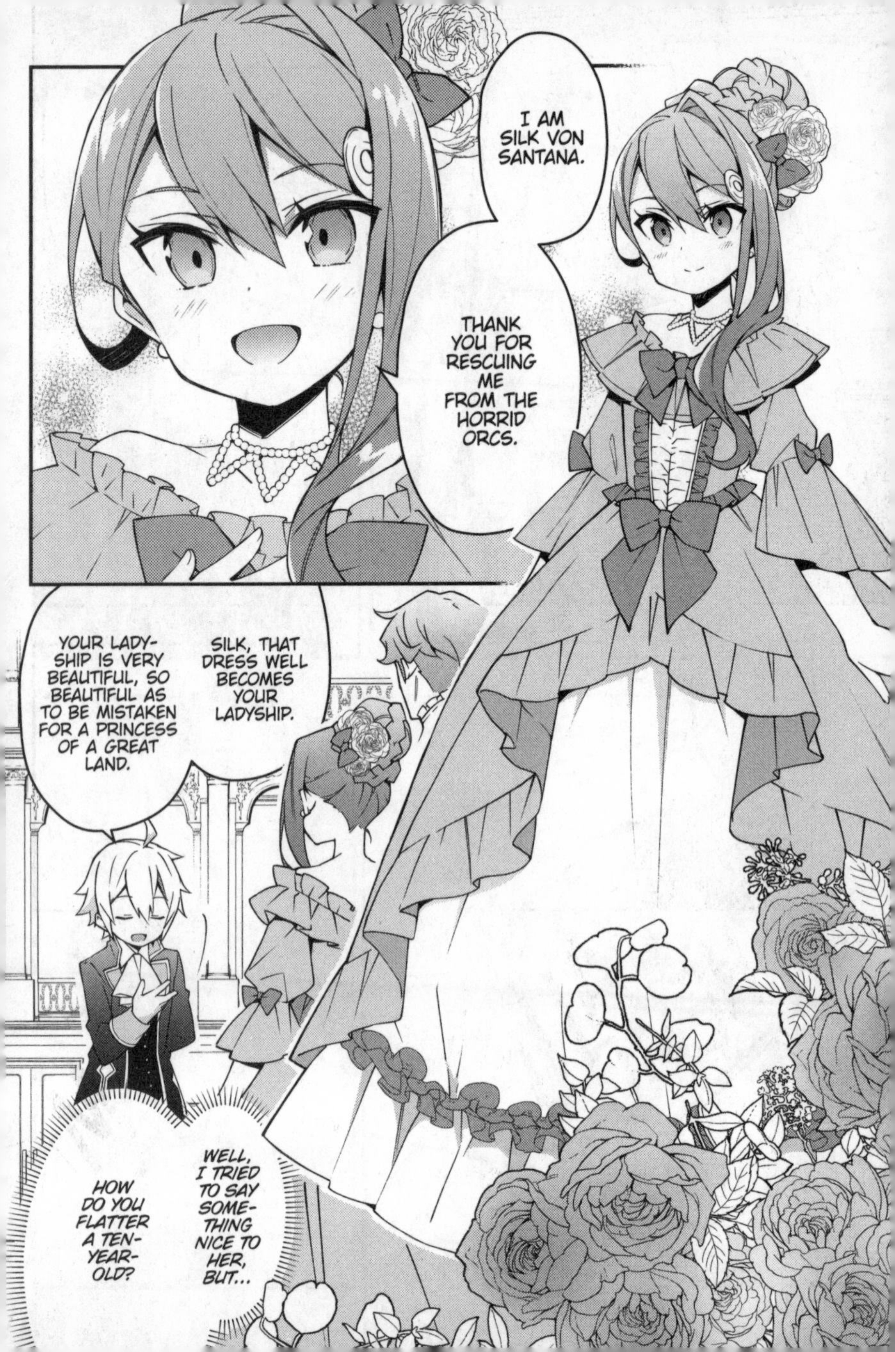
I AM SILK VON SANTANA.
THANK YOU FOR RESCUING ME FROM THE HORRID ORCS.
SILK, THAT DRESS WELL BECOMES YOUR LADYSHIP.
YOUR LADYSHIP IS VERY BEAUTIFUL, SO BEAUTIFUL AS TO BE MISTAKEN FOR A PRINCESS OF A GREAT LAND.
WELL, I TRIED TO SAY SOMETHING NICE TO HER, BUT...
HOW DO YOU FLATTER A TEN-YEAR-OLD?

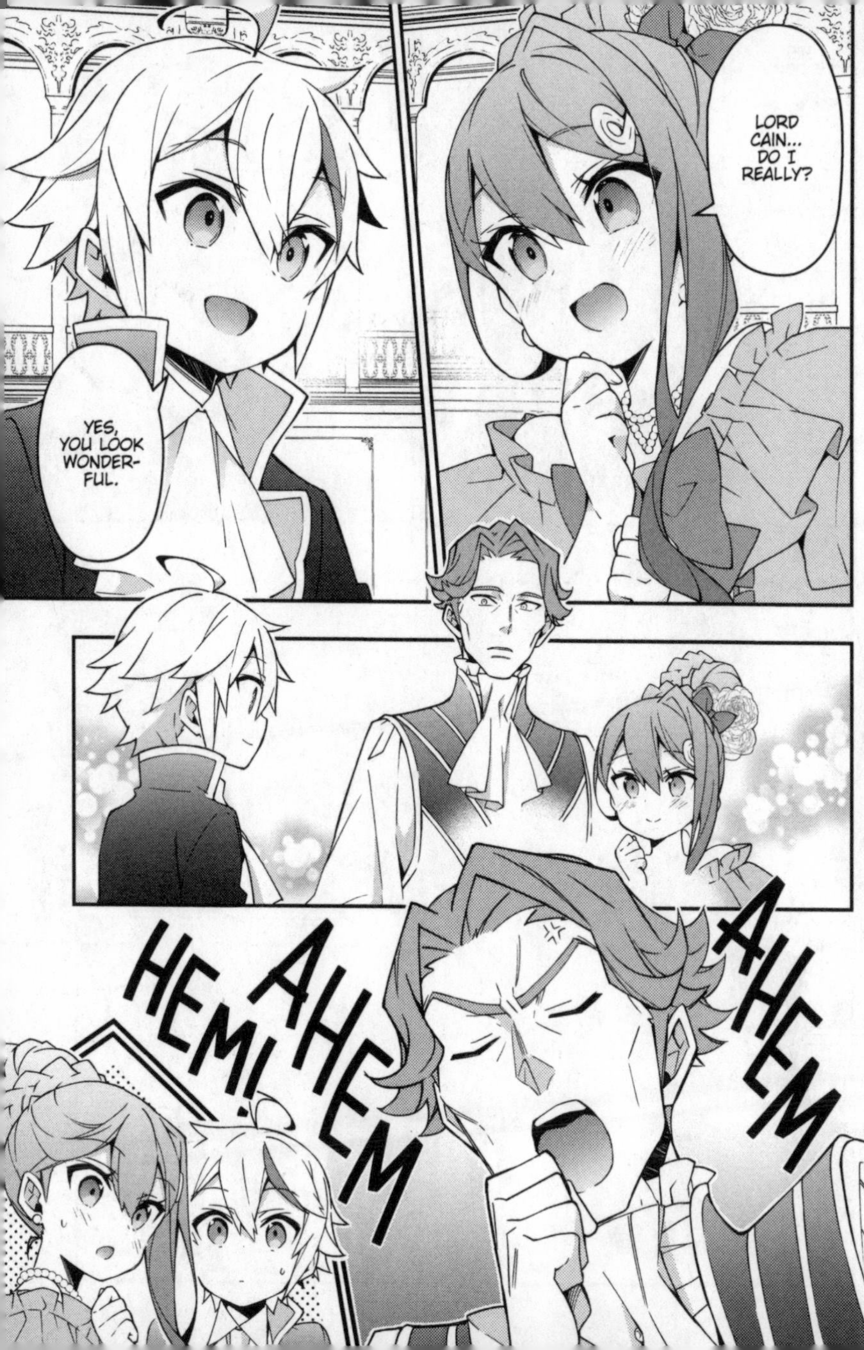
LORD CAIN... DO I REALLY?
YES, YOU LOOK WONDER-FUL.
AHEM
HEM!
AHEM

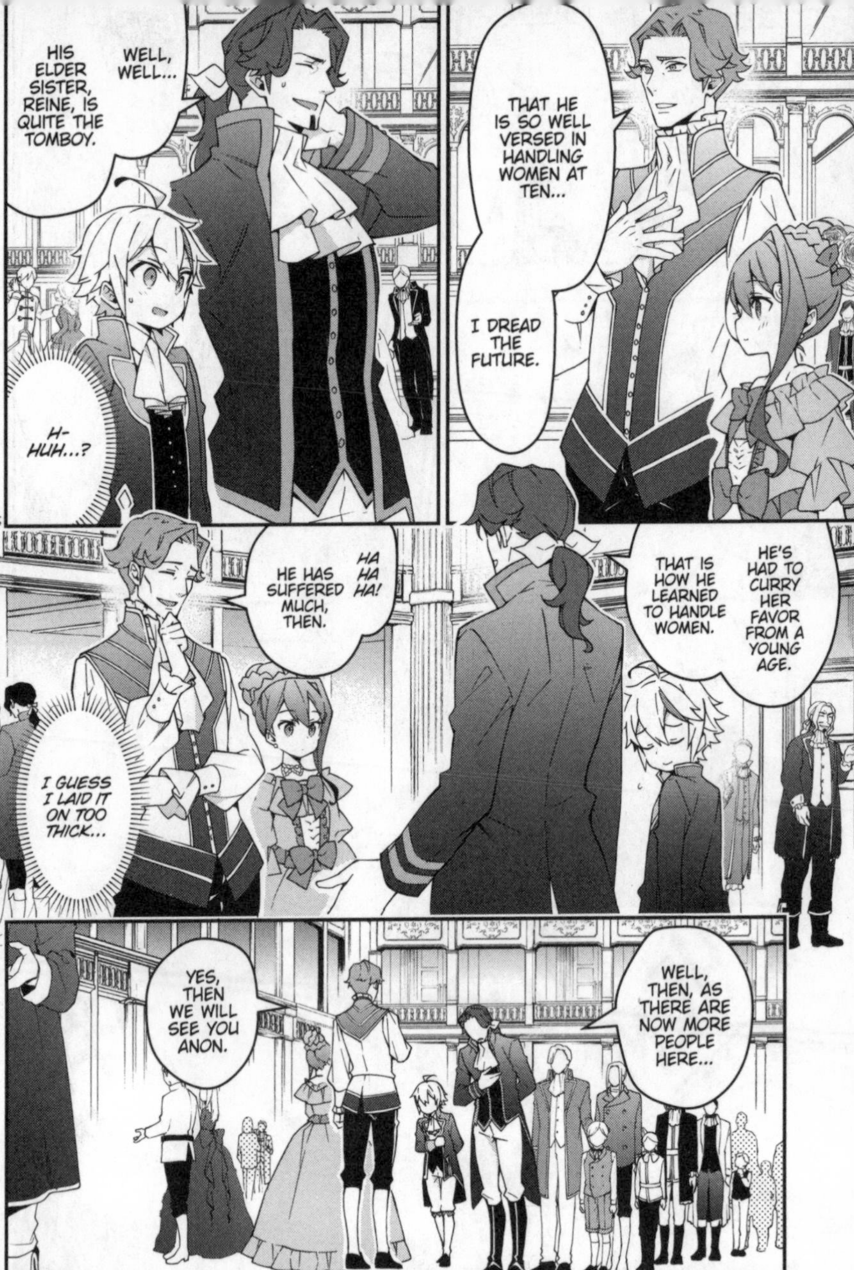
THAT HE IS SO WELL VERSED IN HANDLING WOMEN AT TEN...
I DREAD THE FUTURE.
WELL, WELL...
HIS ELDER SISTER, REINE, IS QUITE THE TOMBOY.
H-HUH...?
HE'S HAD TO CURRY HER FAVOR FROM A YOUNG AGE.
THAT IS HOW HE LEARNED TO HANDLE WOMEN.
HA HA HA!
HE HAS SUFFERED MUCH, THEN.
I GUESS I LAID IT ON TOO THICK...
WELL, THEN, AS THERE ARE NOW MORE PEOPLE HERE...
YES, THEN WE WILL SEE YOU ANON.

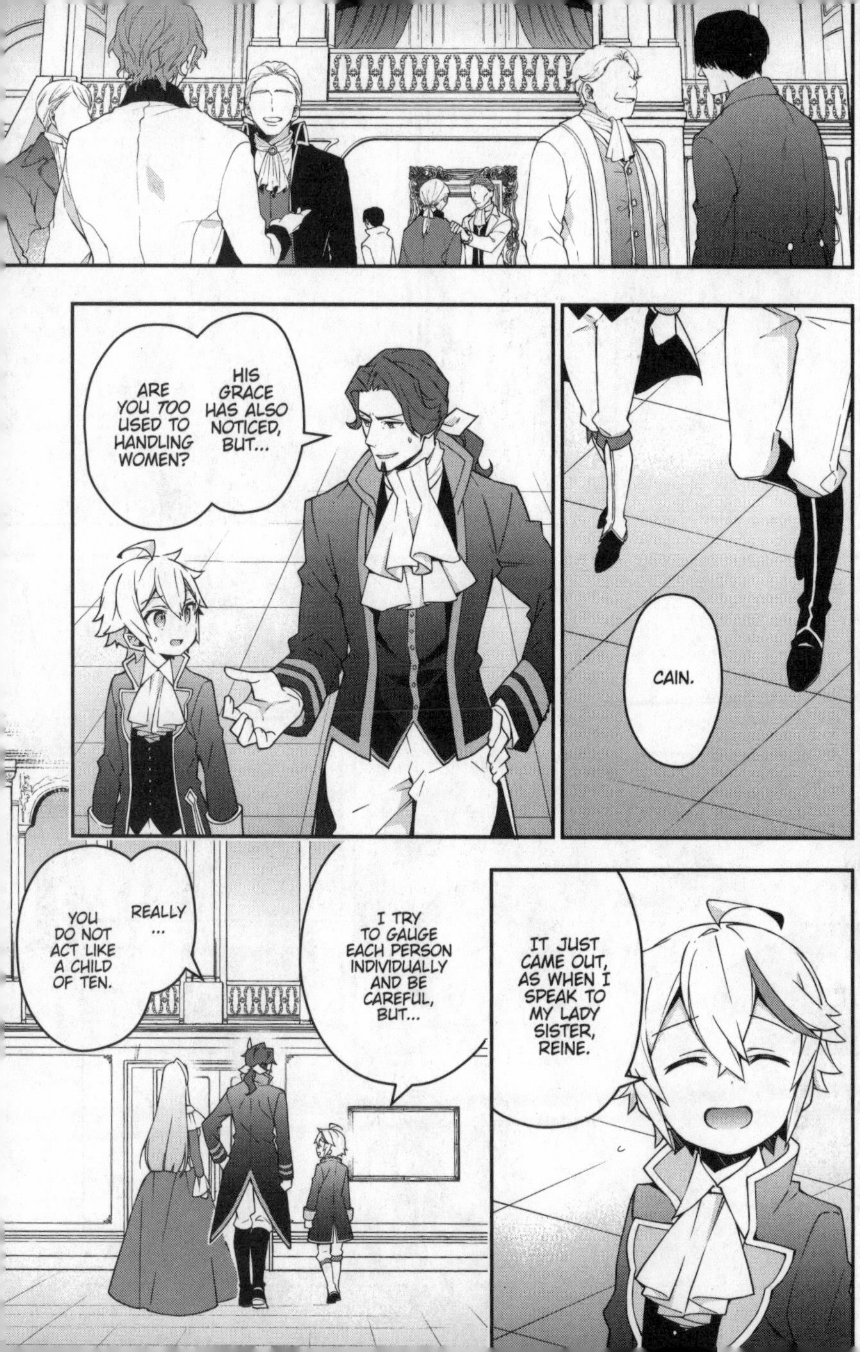
CAIN.
HIS GRACE HAS ALSO NOTICED, BUT...
ARE YOU *TOO* USED TO HANDLING WOMEN?
IT JUST CAME OUT, AS WHEN I SPEAK TO MY LADY SISTER, REINE.
I TRY TO GAUGE EACH PERSON INDIVIDUALLY AND BE CAREFUL, BUT...
REALLY...
YOU DO NOT ACT LIKE A CHILD OF TEN.

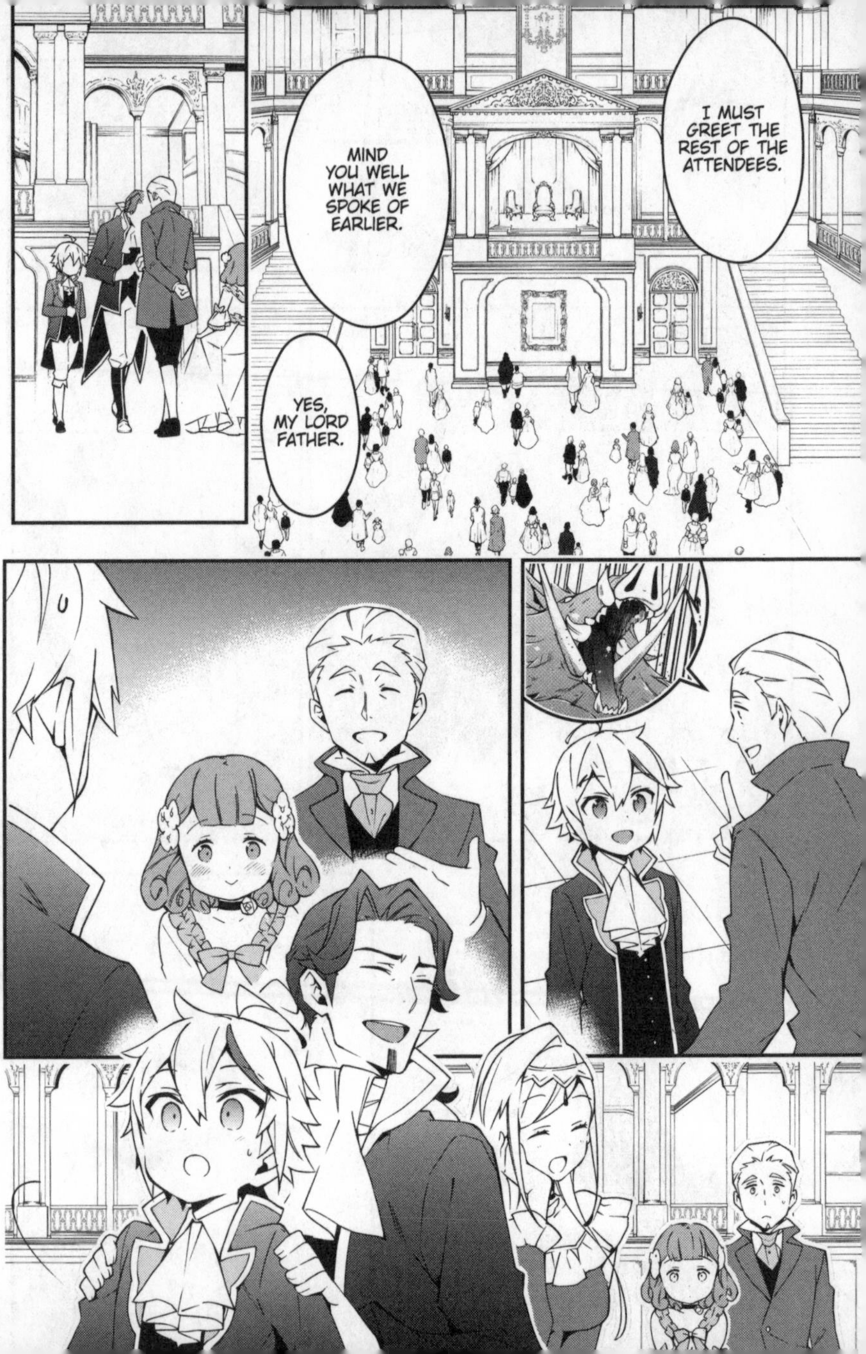
I MUST GREET THE REST OF THE ATTENDEES.
MIND YOU WELL WHAT WE SPOKE OF EARLIER.
YES, MY LORD FATHER.

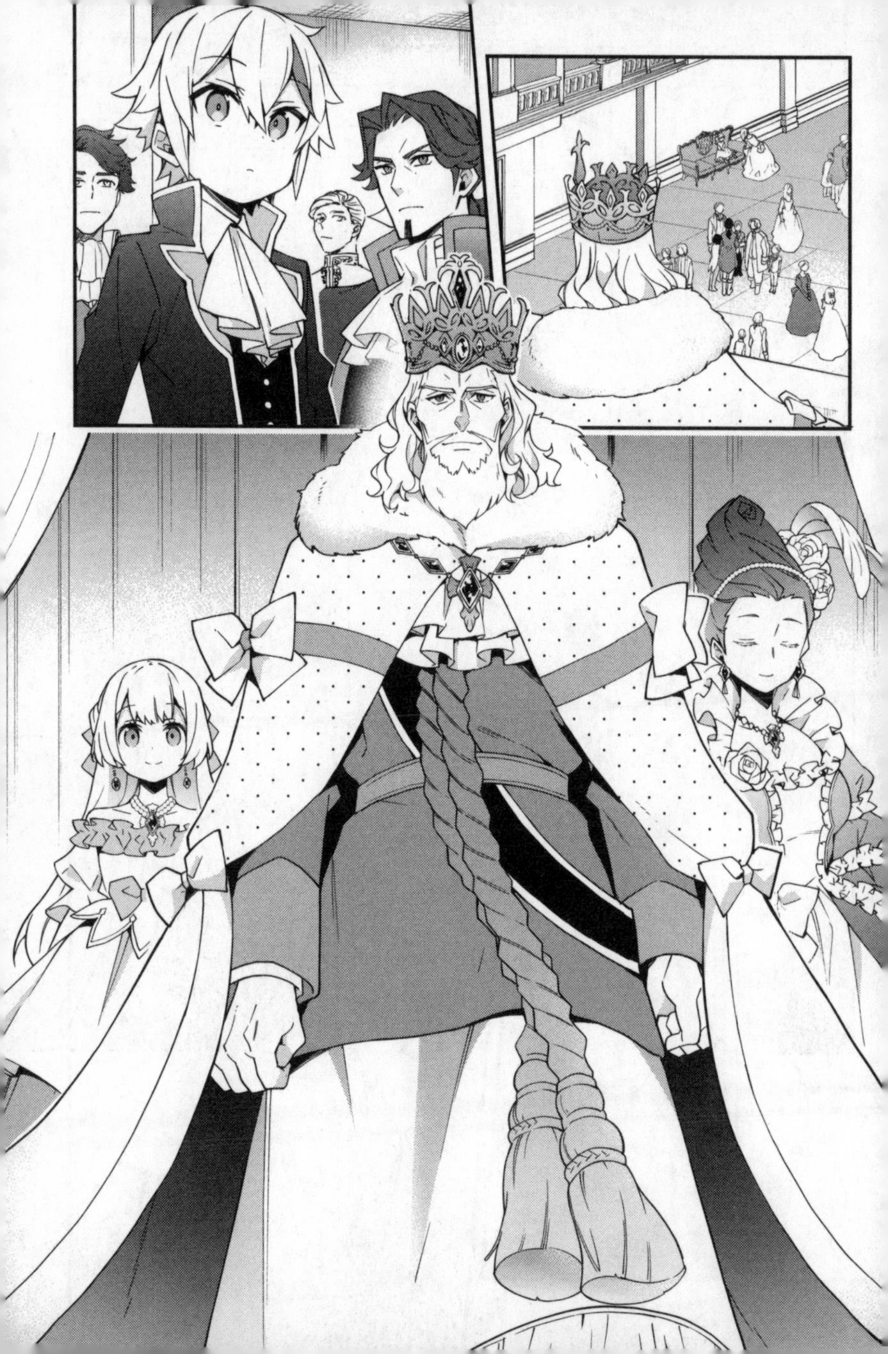

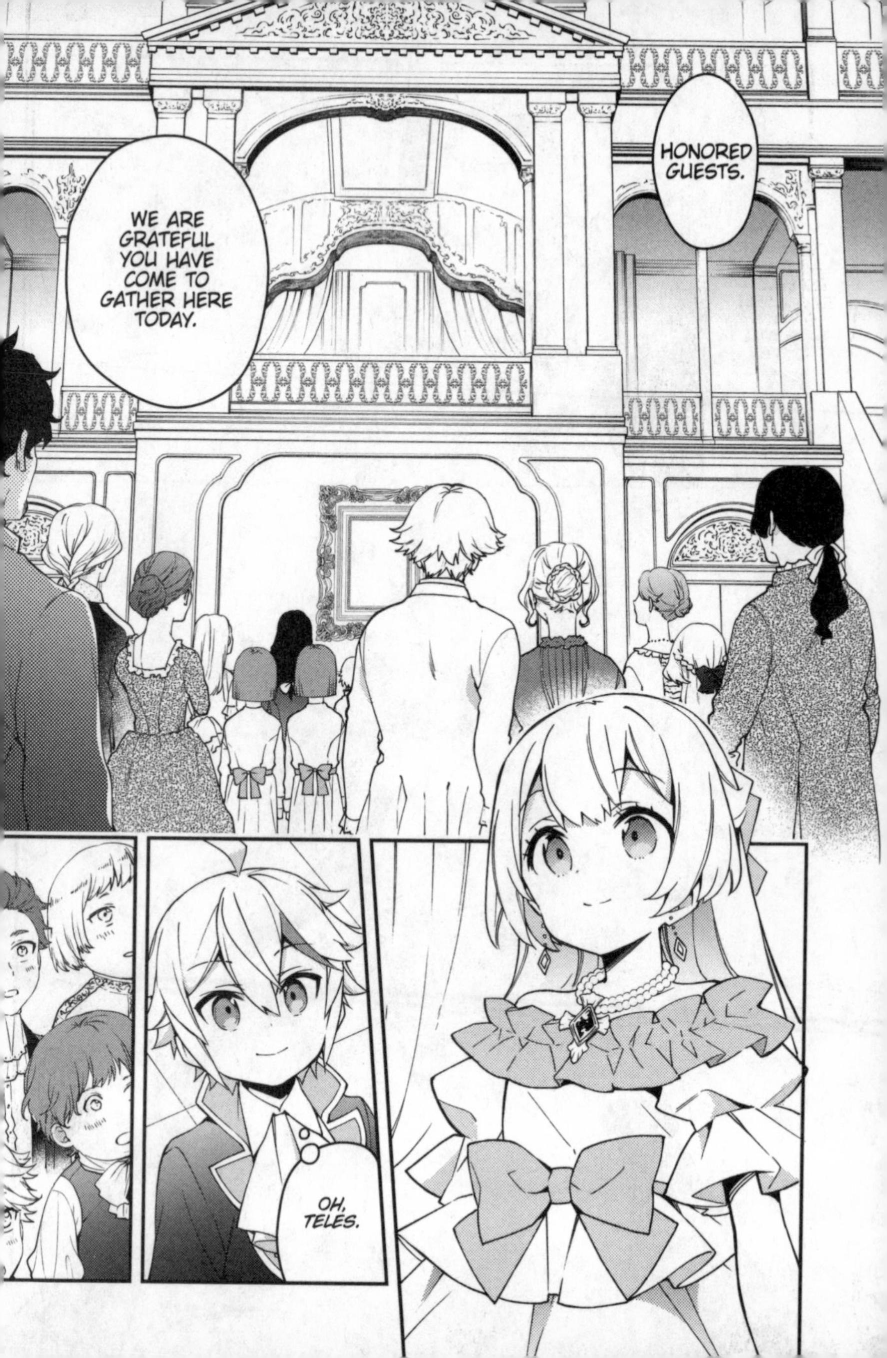
HONORED GUESTS.
WE ARE GRATEFUL YOU HAVE COME TO GATHER HERE TODAY.
OH, TELES.

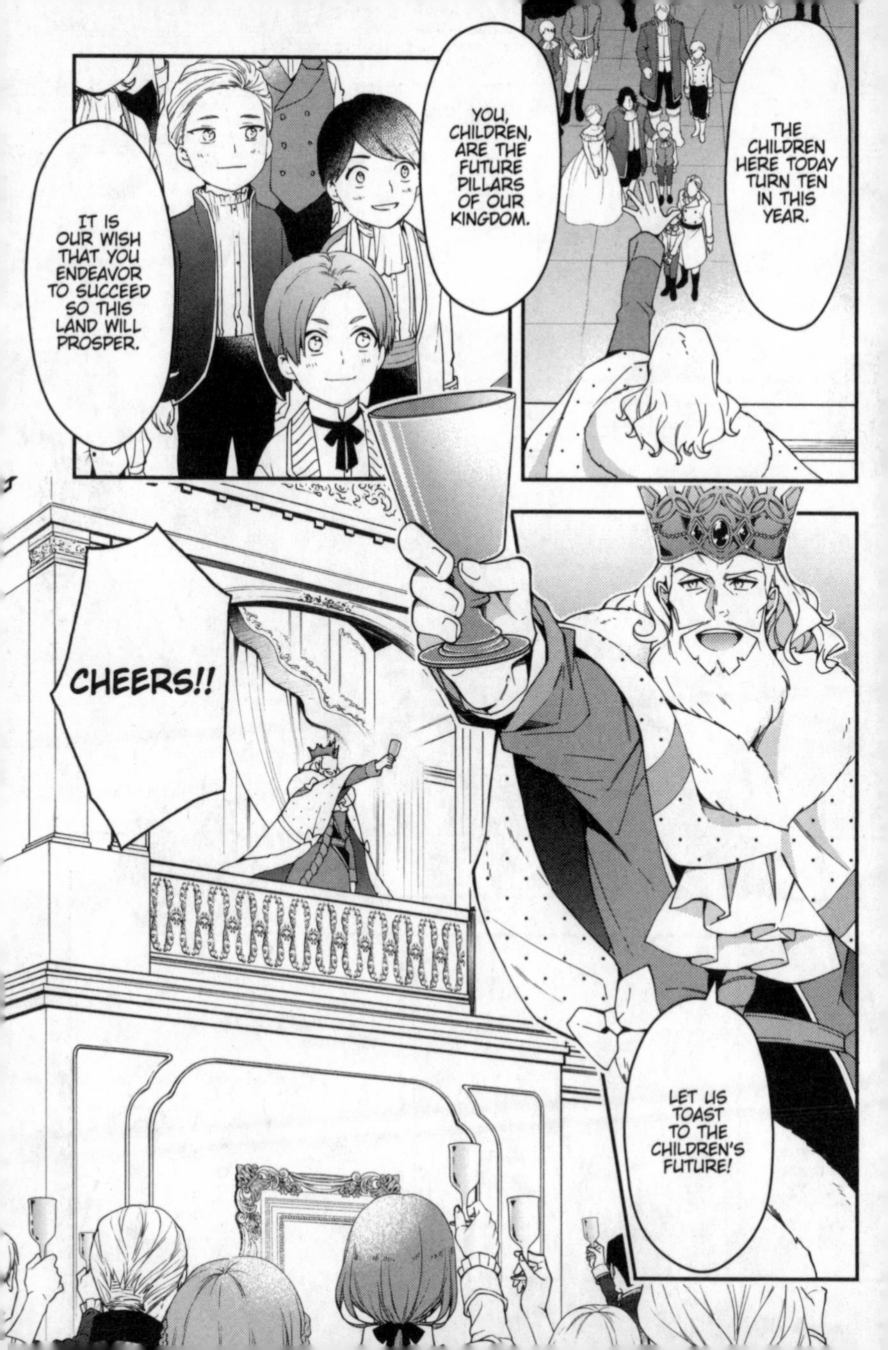
THE CHILDREN HERE TODAY TURN TEN IN THIS YEAR.
YOU, CHILDREN, ARE THE FUTURE PILLARS OF OUR KINGDOM.
IT IS OUR WISH THAT YOU ENDEAVOR TO SUCCEED SO THIS LAND WILL PROSPER.
LET US TOAST TO THE CHILDREN'S FUTURE!
CHEERS!!

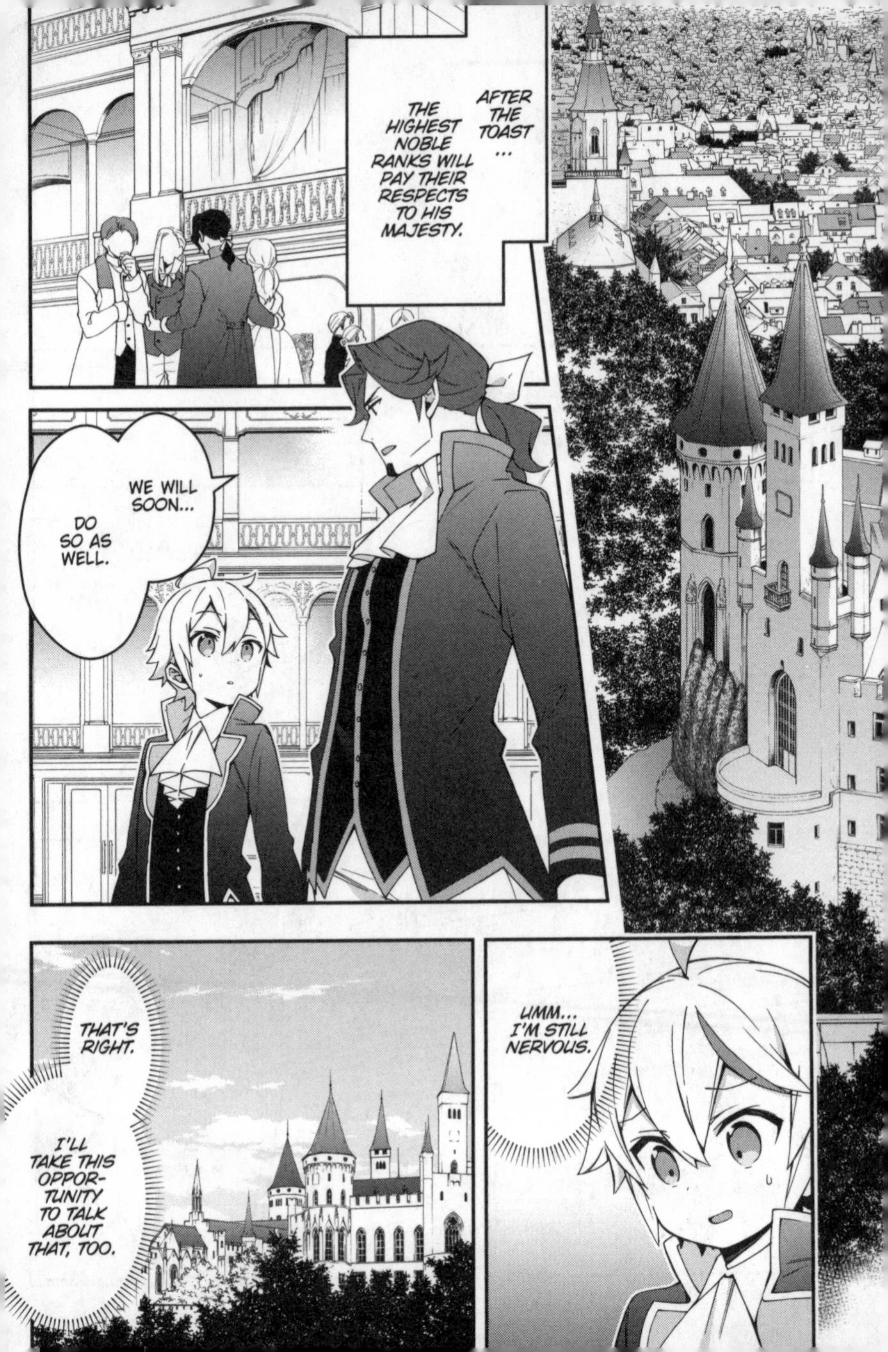
AFTER THE TOAST...
THE HIGHEST NOBLE RANKS WILL PAY THEIR RESPECTS TO HIS MAJESTY.
WE WILL SOON...
DO SO AS WELL.
UMM... I'M STILL NERVOUS.
THAT'S RIGHT.
I'LL TAKE THIS OPPOR-TUNITY TO TALK ABOUT THAT, TOO.

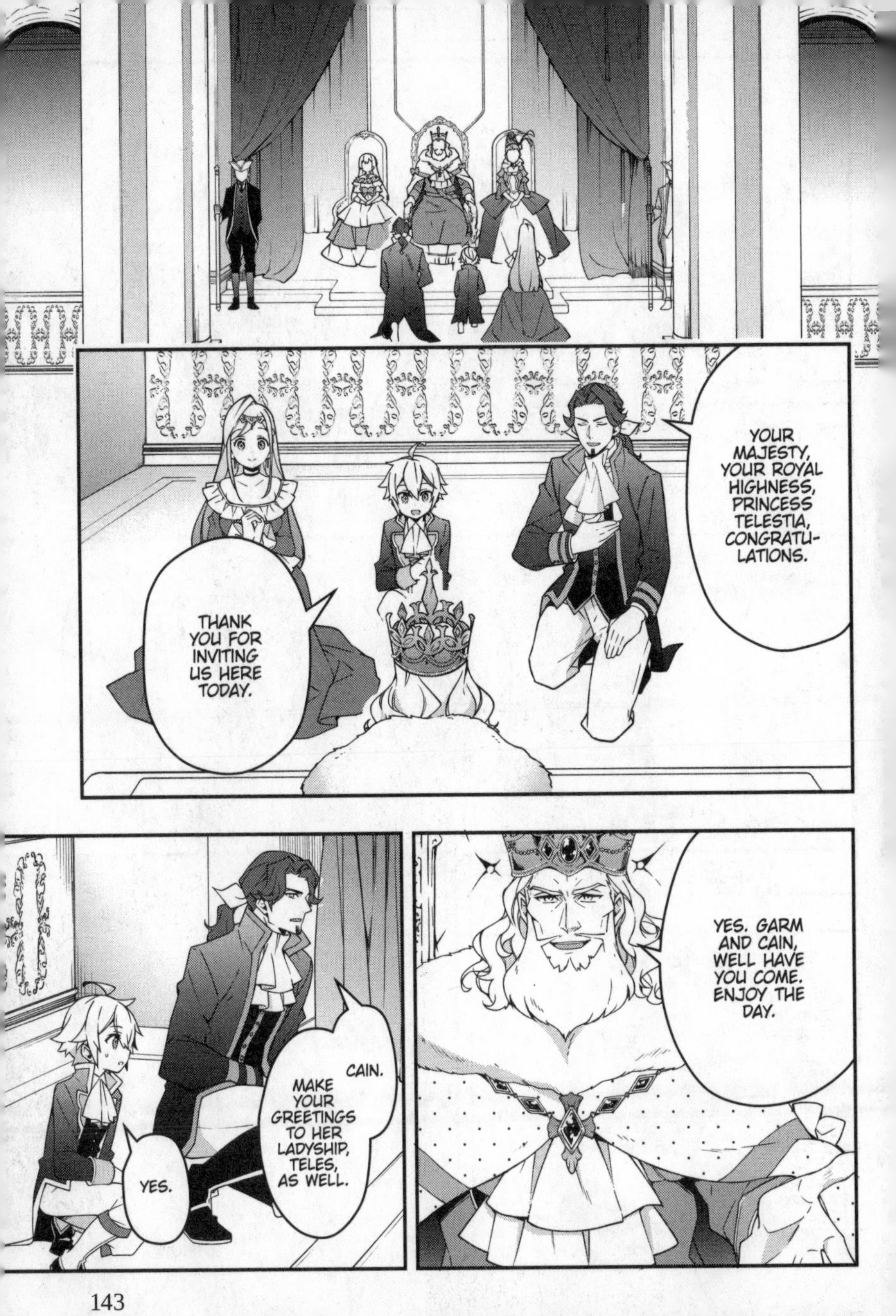
YOUR MAJESTY, YOUR ROYAL HIGHNESS, PRINCESS TELESTIA, CONGRATULATIONS.
THANK YOU FOR INVITING US HERE TODAY.
YES. GARM AND CAIN, WELL HAVE YOU COME. ENJOY THE DAY.
CAIN. MAKE YOUR GREETINGS TO HER LADYSHIP, TELES, AS WELL.
YES.

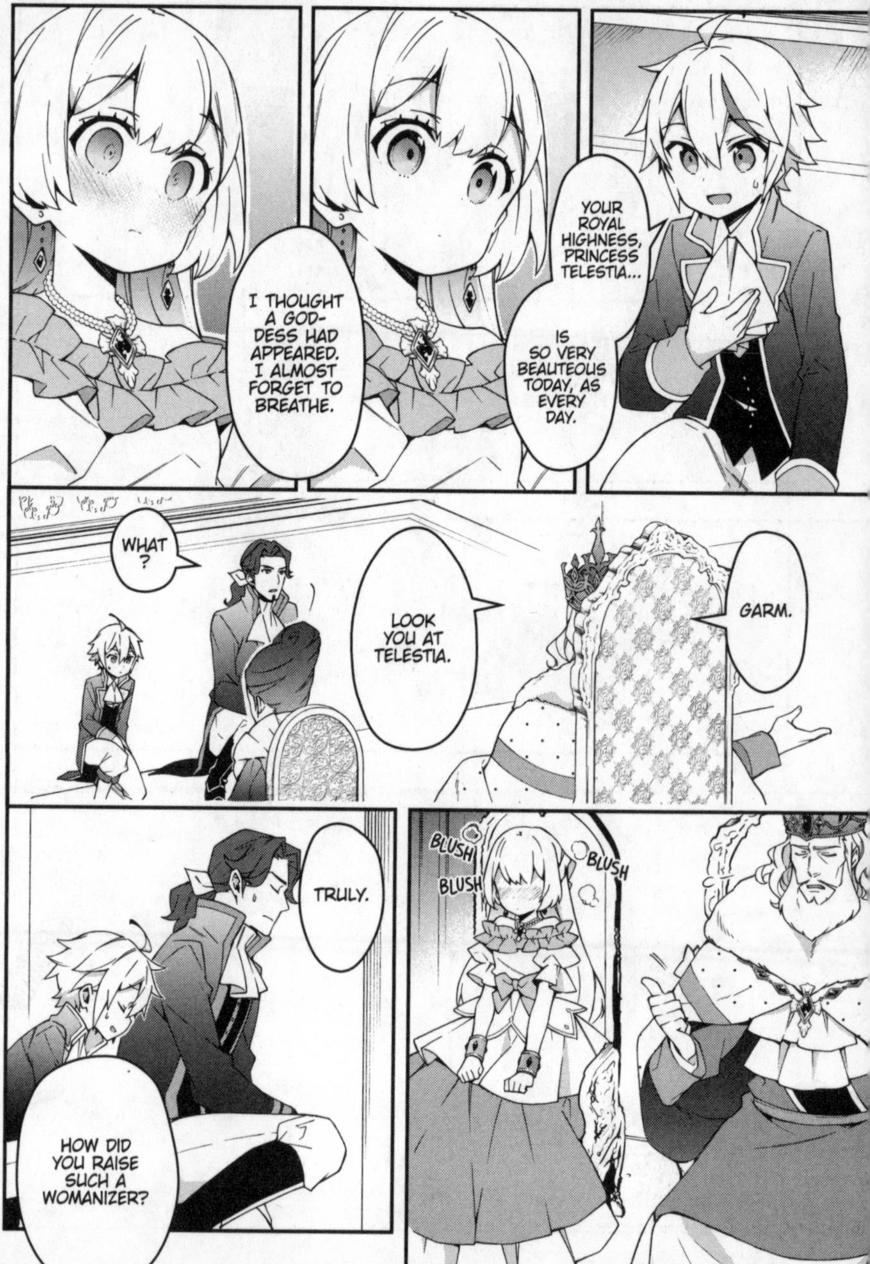
YOUR ROYAL HIGHNESS, PRINCESS TELESTIA...
IS SO VERY BEAUTEOUS TODAY, AS EVERY DAY.
I THOUGHT A GOD-DESS HAD APPEARED. I ALMOST FORGET TO BREATHE.
GARM.
LOOK YOU AT TELESTIA.
WHAT?
BLUSH
BLUSH
BLUSH
TRULY.
HOW DID YOU RAISE SUCH A WOMANIZER?

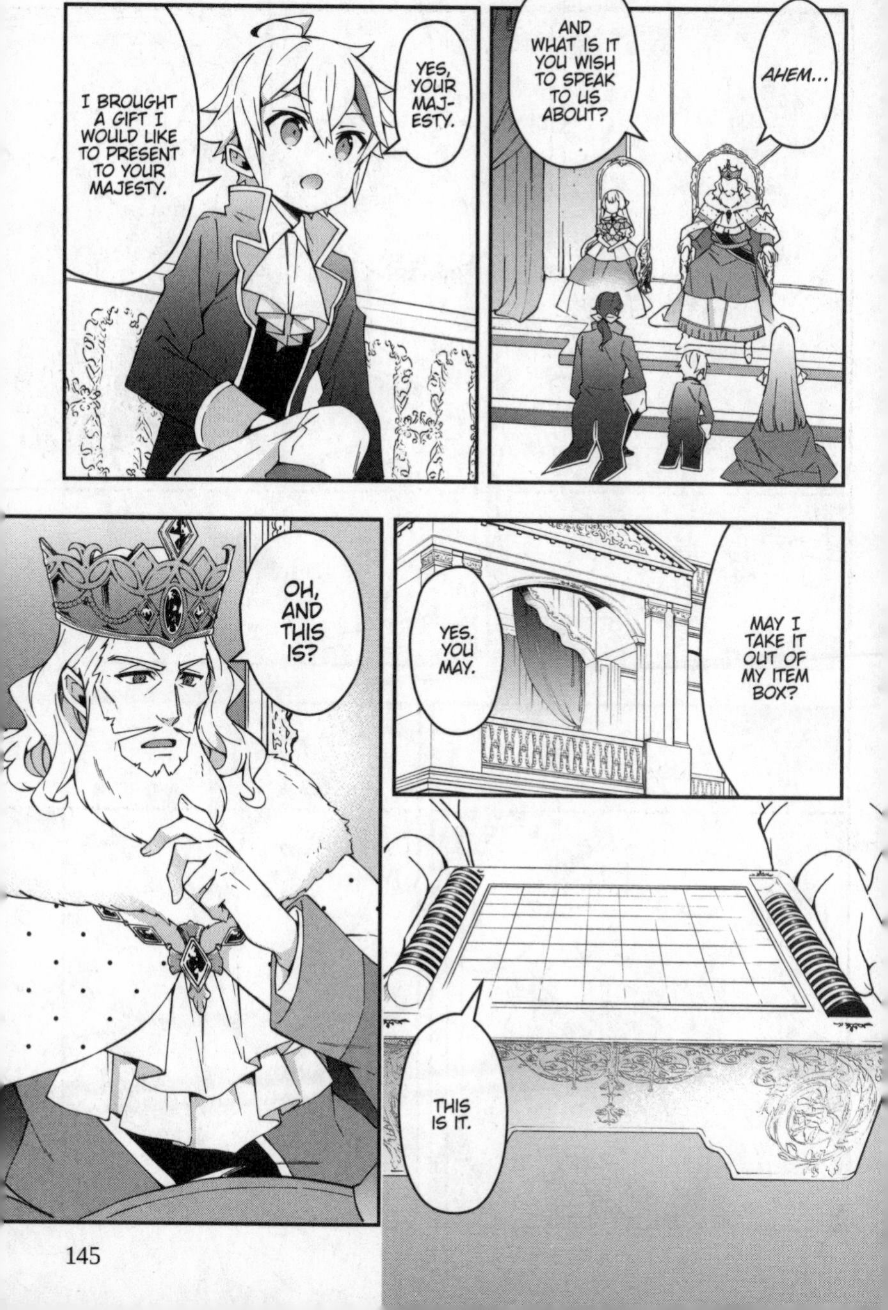

AHEM...
AND WHAT IS IT YOU WISH TO SPEAK TO US ABOUT?
YES, YOUR MAJESTY.
I BROUGHT A GIFT I WOULD LIKE TO PRESENT TO YOUR MAJESTY.
MAY I TAKE IT OUT OF MY ITEM BOX?
YES. YOU MAY.
THIS IS IT.
OH, AND THIS IS?

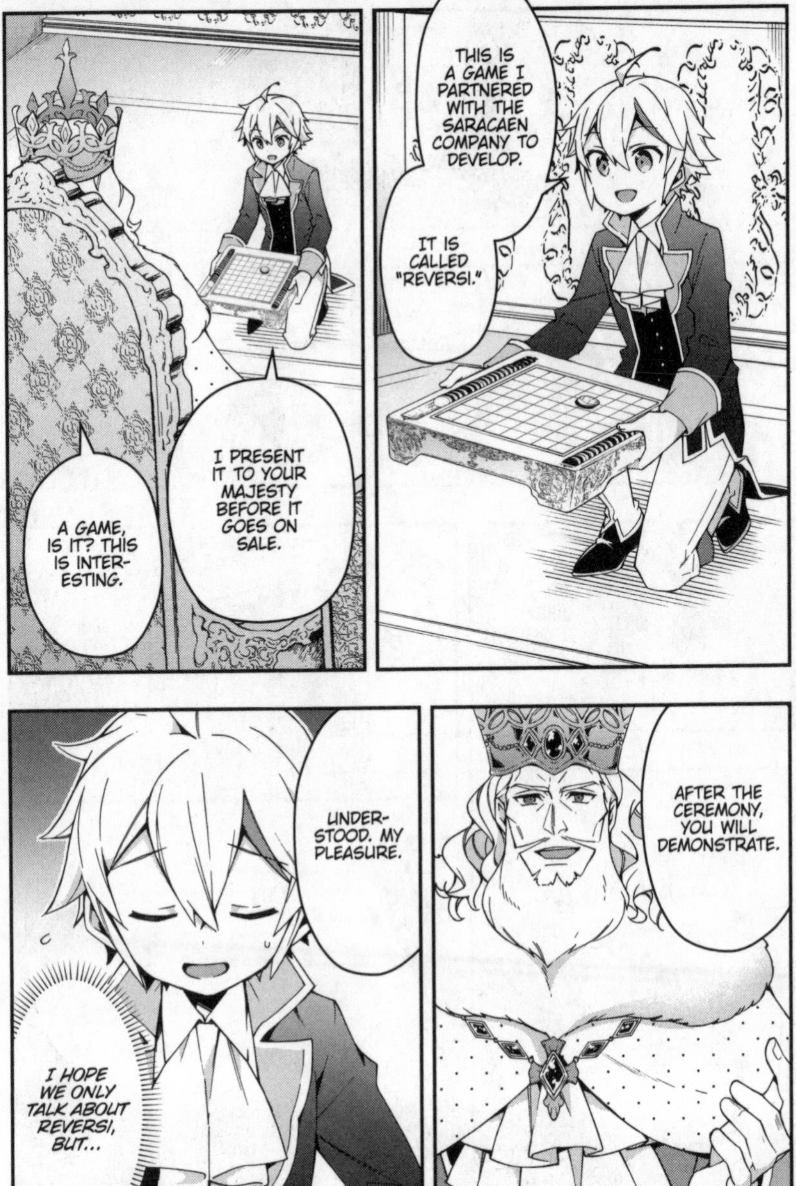
THIS IS A GAME I PARTNERED WITH THE SARACAEN COMPANY TO DEVELOP.
IT IS CALLED "REVERSI."
I PRESENT IT TO YOUR MAJESTY BEFORE IT GOES ON SALE.
A GAME, IS IT? THIS IS INTER-ESTING.
AFTER THE CEREMONY, YOU WILL DEMONSTRATE.
UNDER-STOOD. MY PLEASURE.
I HOPE WE ONLY TALK ABOUT REVERSI, BUT...

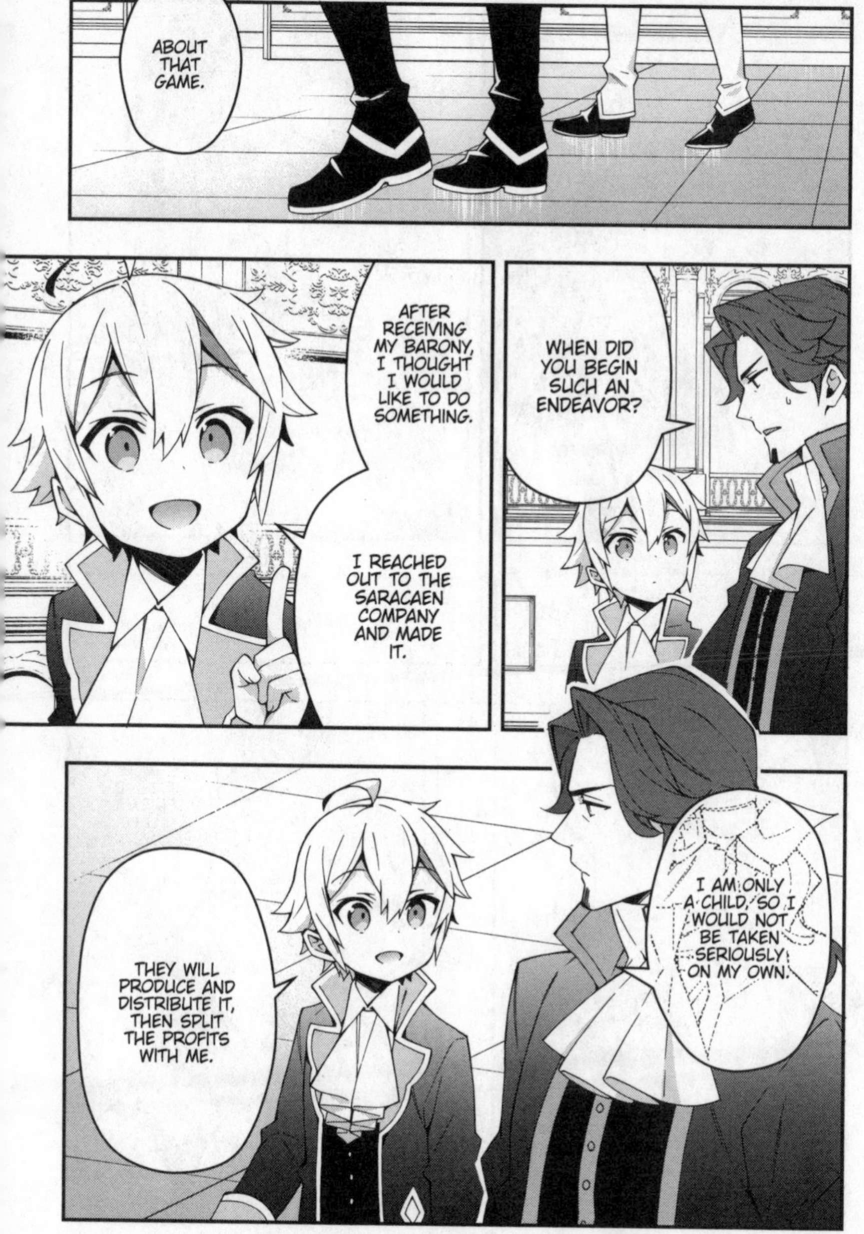
ABOUT THAT GAME.
WHEN DID YOU BEGIN SUCH AN ENDEAVOR?
AFTER RECEIVING MY BARONY, I THOUGHT I WOULD LIKE TO DO SOMETHING.
I REACHED OUT TO THE SARACAEN COMPANY AND MADE IT.
I AM ONLY A CHILD, SO I WOULD NOT BE TAKEN SERIOUSLY ON MY OWN.
THEY WILL PRODUCE AND DISTRIBUTE IT, THEN SPLIT THE PROFITS WITH ME.

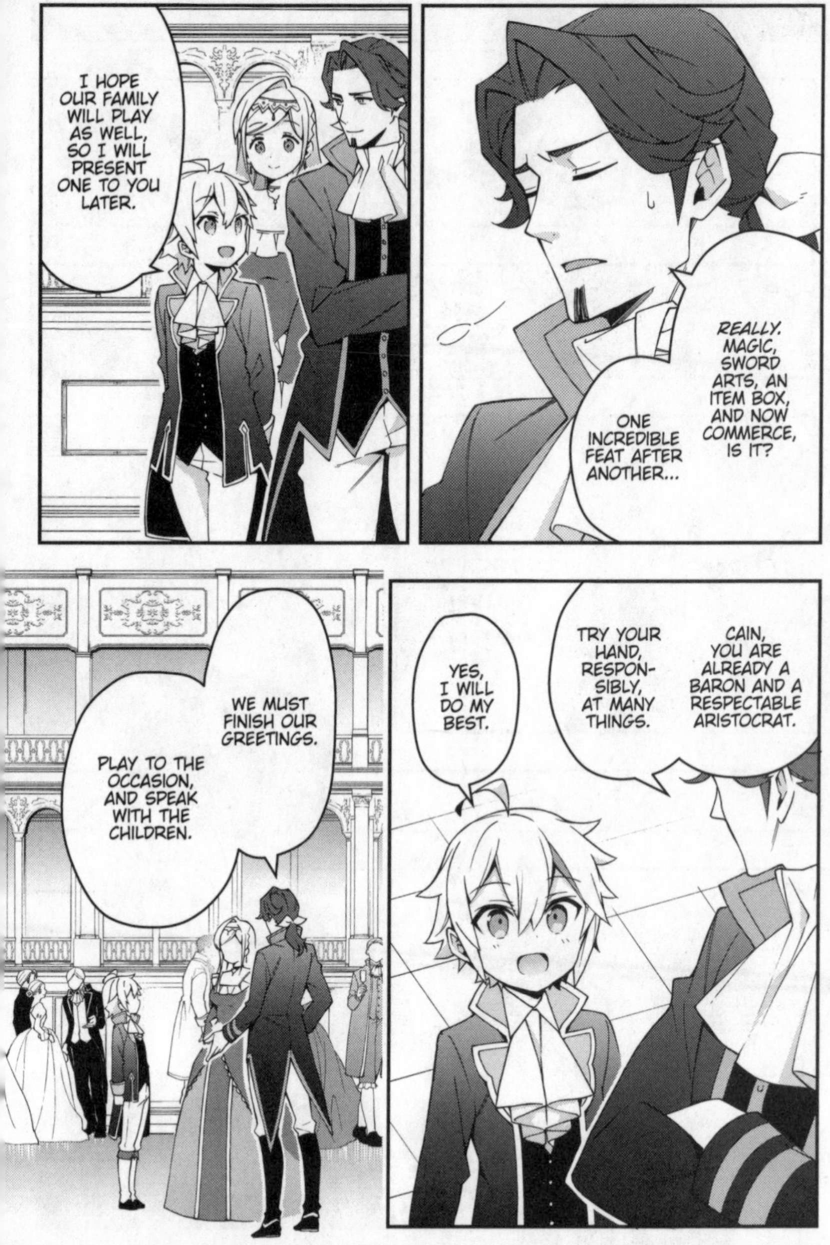
REALLY. MAGIC, SWORD ARTS, AN ITEM BOX, AND NOW COMMERCE, IS IT?
ONE INCREDIBLE FEAT AFTER ANOTHER...
I HOPE OUR FAMILY WILL PLAY AS WELL, SO I WILL PRESENT ONE TO YOU LATER.
CAIN, YOU ARE ALREADY A BARON AND A RESPECTABLE ARISTOCRAT.
TRY YOUR HAND, RESPON-SIBLY, AT MANY THINGS.
YES, I WILL DO MY BEST.
WE MUST FINISH OUR GREETINGS.
PLAY TO THE OCCASION, AND SPEAK WITH THE CHILDREN.

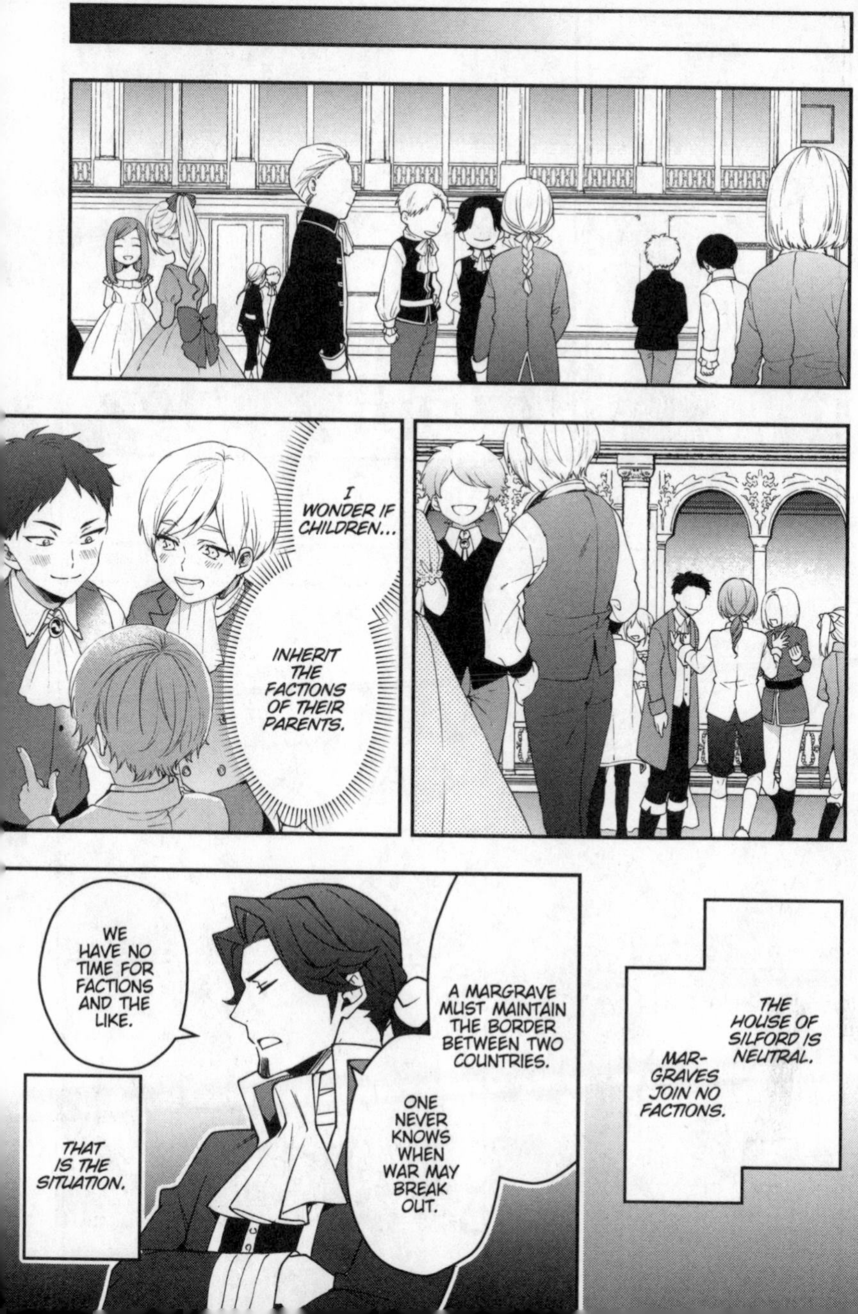
I WONDER IF CHILDREN...
INHERIT THE FACTIONS OF THEIR PARENTS.
THE HOUSE OF SILFORD IS NEUTRAL.
MAR-GRAVES JOIN NO FACTIONS.
A MARGRAVE MUST MAINTAIN THE BORDER BETWEEN TWO COUNTRIES.
ONE NEVER KNOWS WHEN WAR MAY BREAK OUT.
WE HAVE NO TIME FOR FACTIONS AND THE LIKE.
THAT IS THE SITUATION.

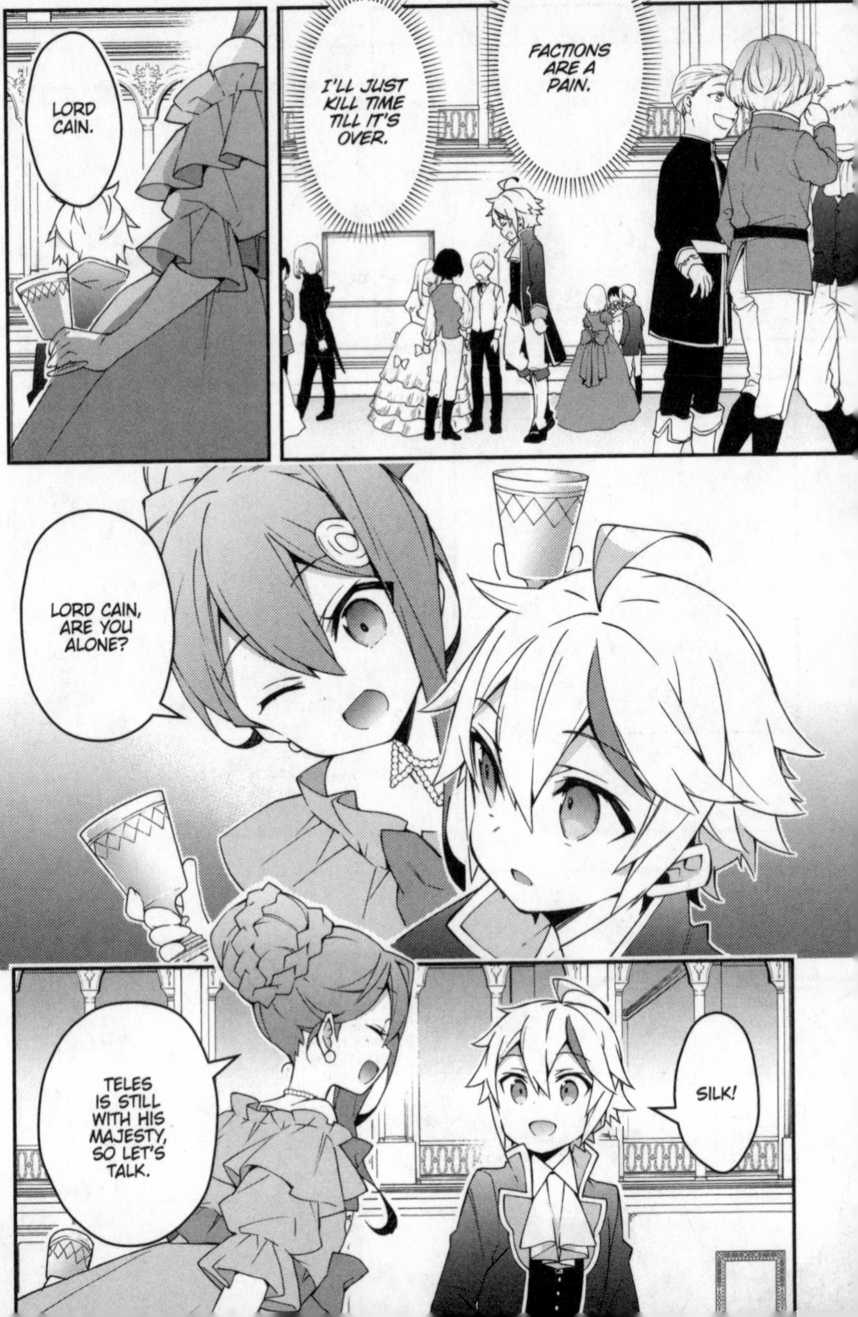
FACTIONS ARE A PAIN.
I'LL JUST KILL TIME TILL IT'S OVER.
LORD CAIN.
LORD CAIN, ARE YOU ALONE?
SILK!
TELES IS STILL WITH HIS MAJESTY, SO LET'S TALK.

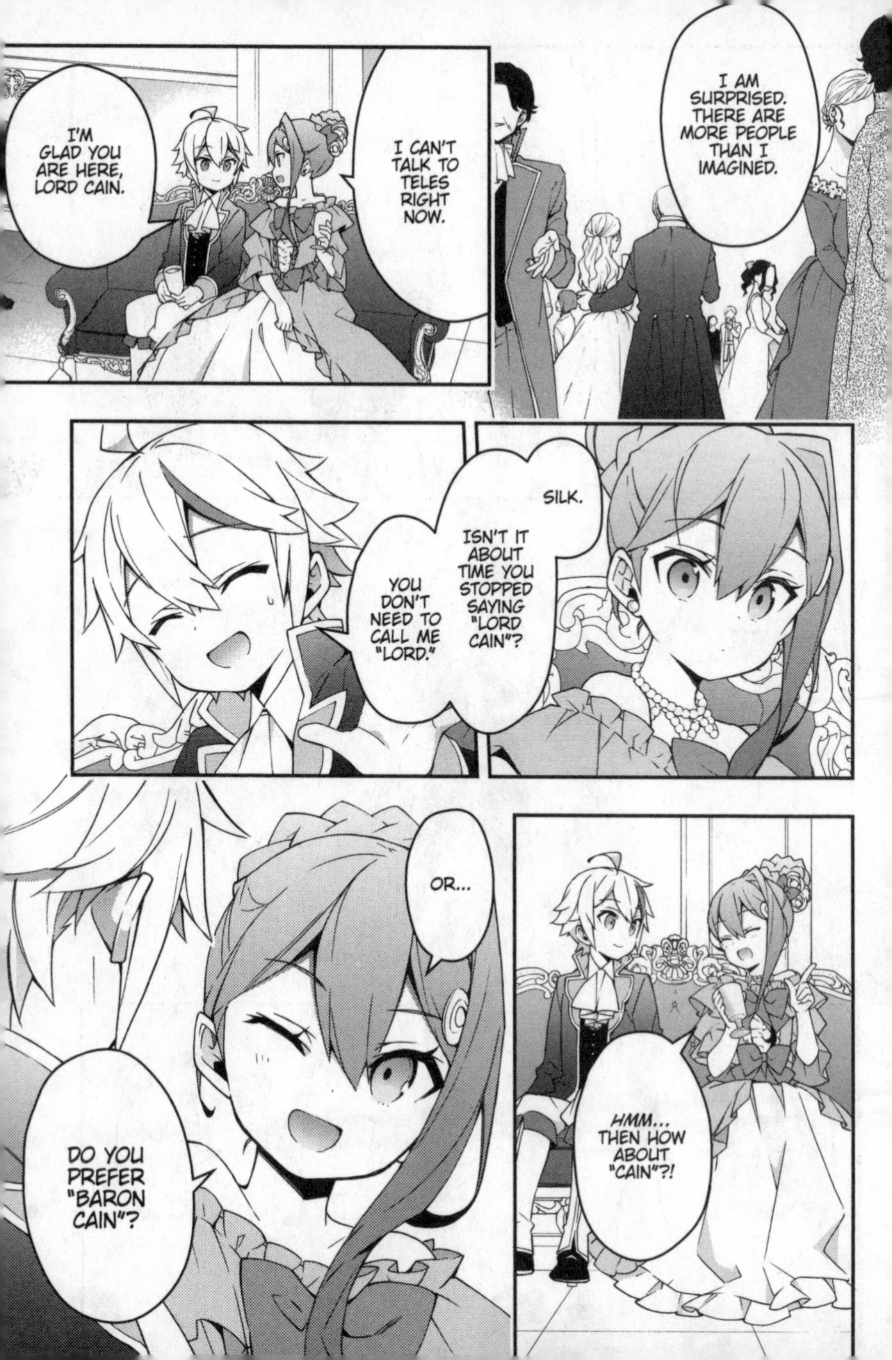
I AM SURPRISED. THERE ARE MORE PEOPLE THAN I IMAGINED.
I CAN'T TALK TO TELES RIGHT NOW.
I'M GLAD YOU ARE HERE, LORD CAIN.
SILK.
ISN'T IT ABOUT TIME YOU STOPPED SAYING "LORD CAIN"?
YOU DON'T NEED TO CALL ME "LORD."
HMM... THEN HOW ABOUT "CAIN"?!
OR...
DO YOU PREFER "BARON CAIN"?

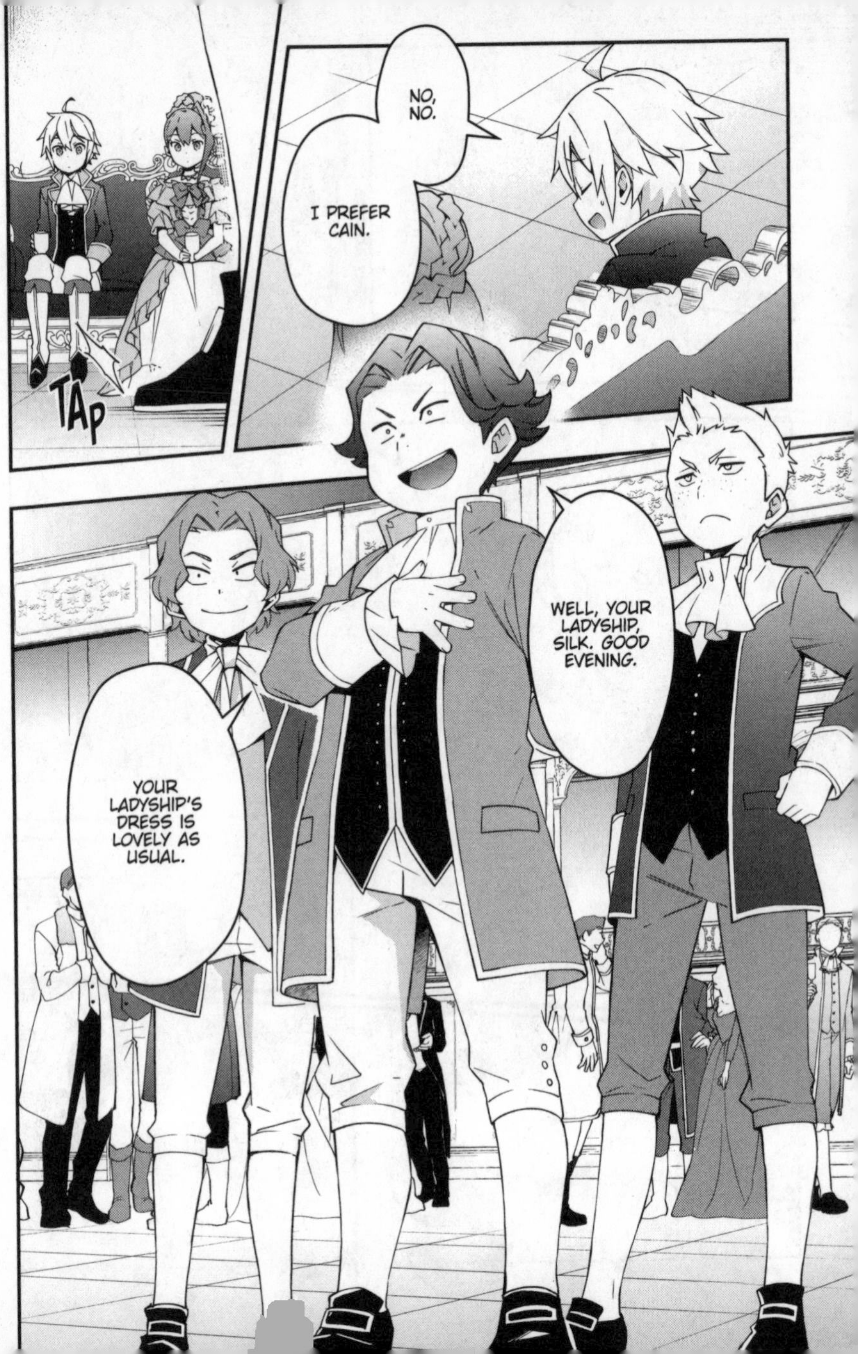
NO, NO.
I PREFER CAIN.
TAP
WELL, YOUR LADYSHIP, SILK. GOOD EVENING.
YOUR LADYSHIP'S DRESS IS LOVELY AS USUAL.

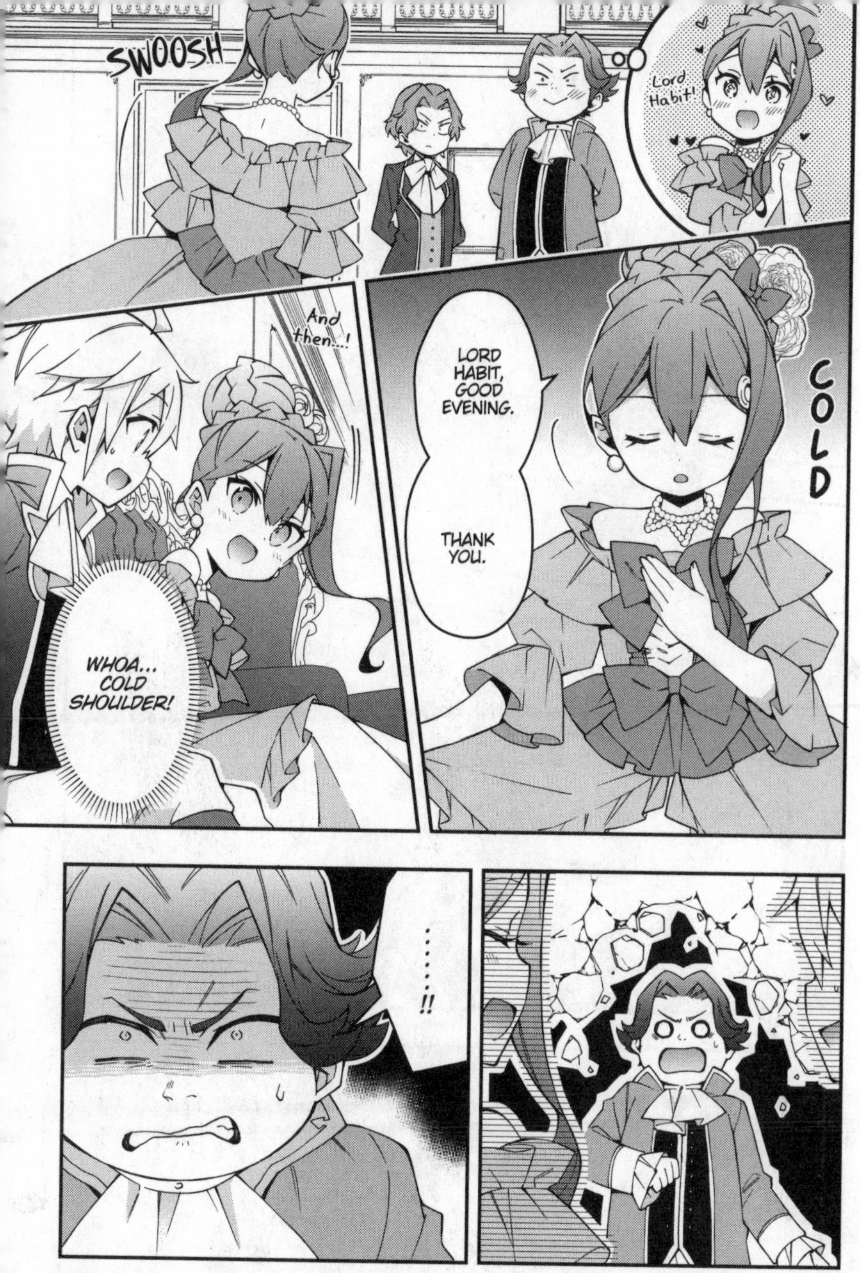

Lord Habit!
SWOOSH
COLD
LORD HABIT, GOOD EVENING.
THANK YOU.
And then...!
WHOA... COLD SHOULDER!
......!!

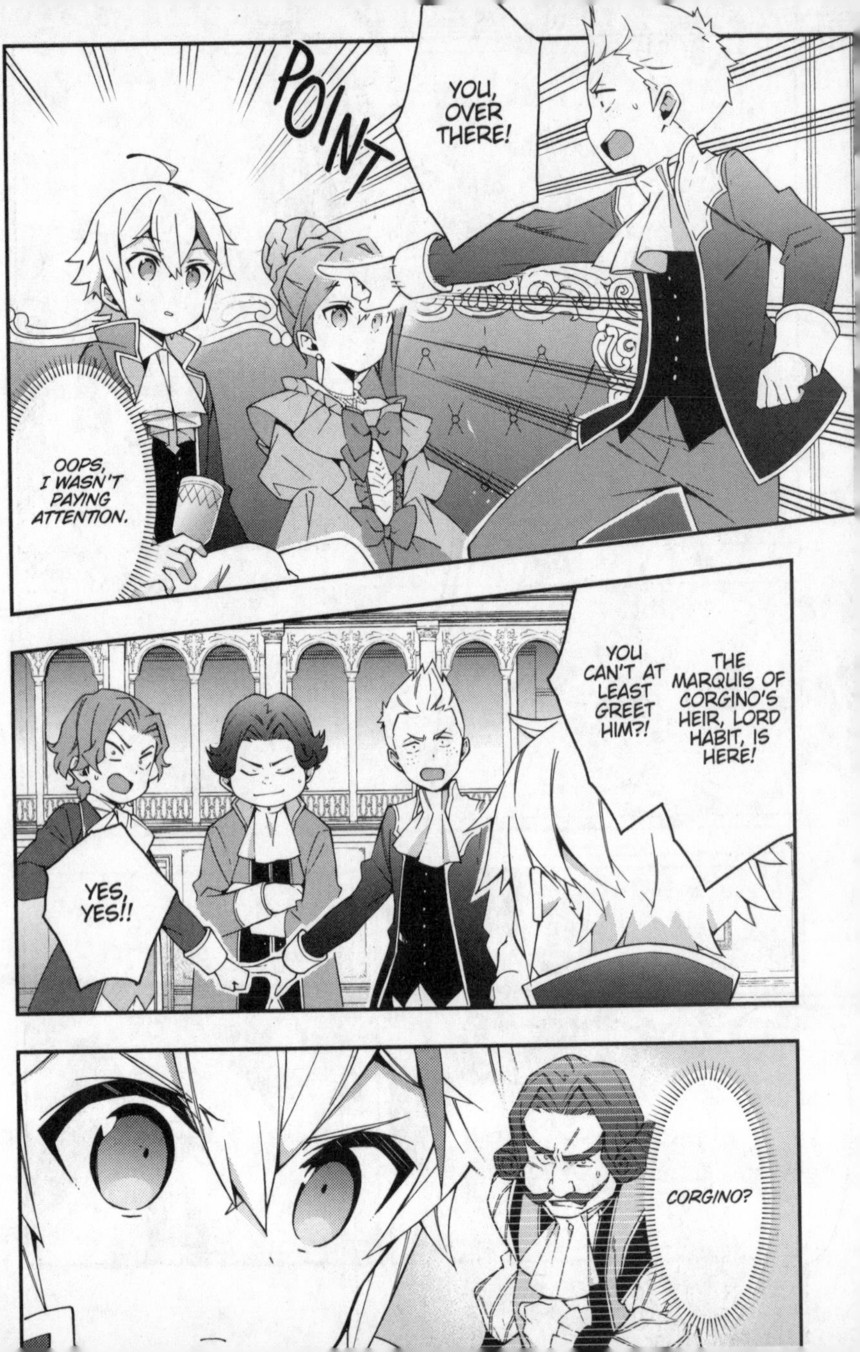
YOU, OVER THERE!
POINT
OOPS, I WASN'T PAYING ATTENTION.
THE MARQUIS OF CORGINO'S HEIR, LORD HABIT, IS HERE!
YOU CAN'T AT LEAST GREET HIM?!
YES, YES!!
CORGINO?

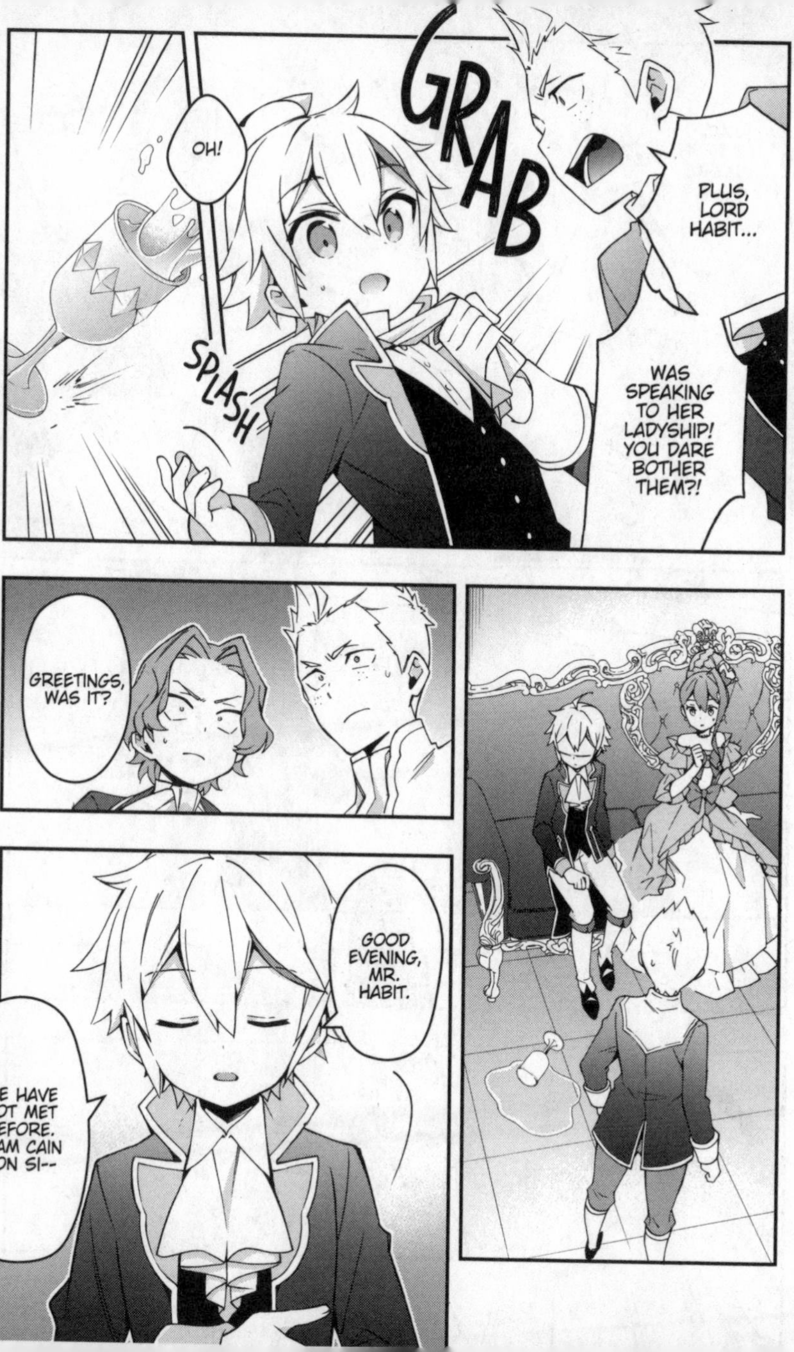
GRAB
PLUS, LORD HABIT...
WAS SPEAKING TO HER LADYSHIP! YOU DARE BOTHER THEM?!
OH!
SPLASH
GREETINGS, WAS IT?
GOOD EVENING, MR. HABIT.
WE HAVE NOT MET BEFORE. I AM CAIN VON SI--

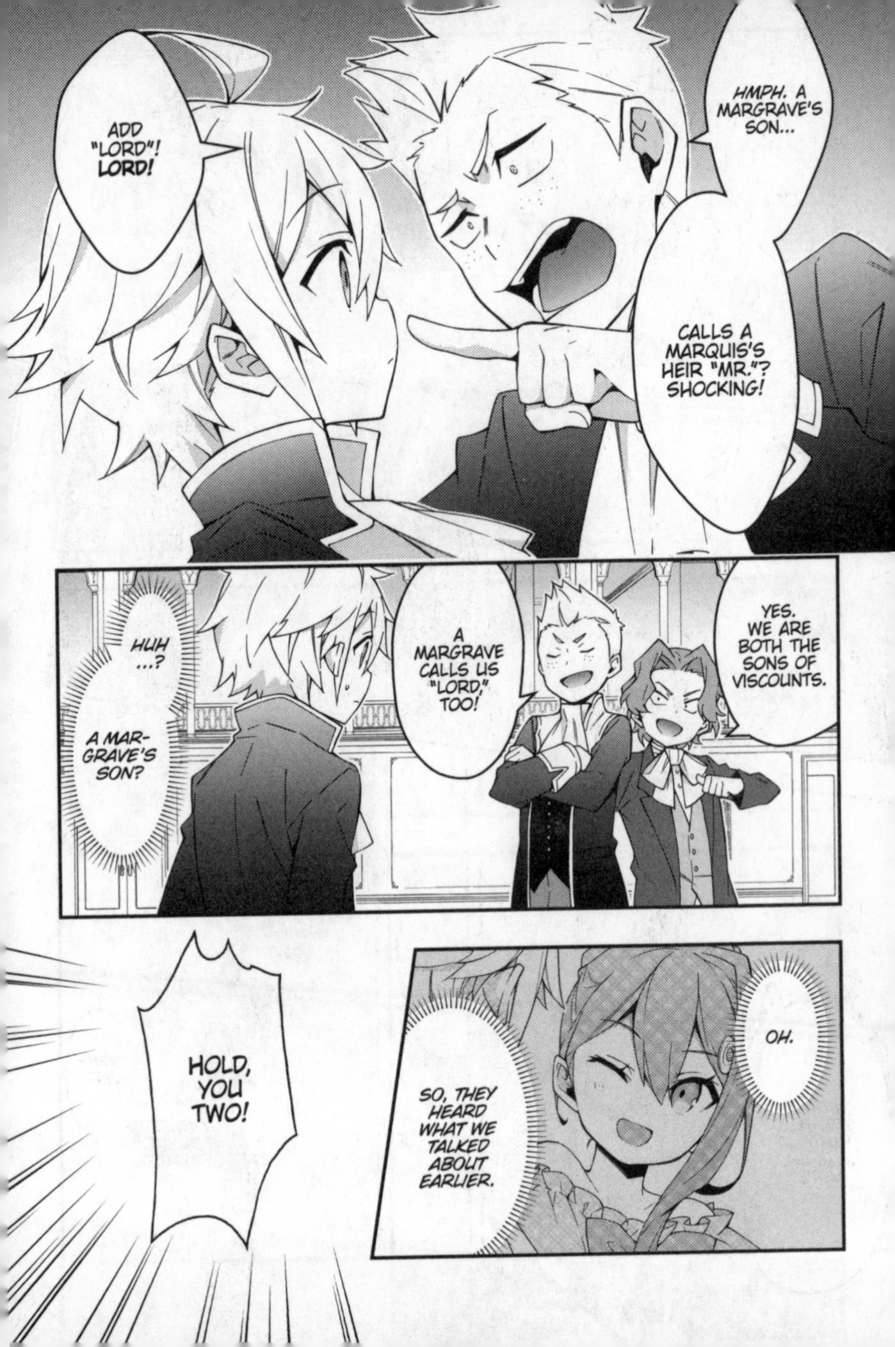
HMPH. A MARGRAVE'S SON...
CALLS A MARQUIS'S HEIR "MR."? SHOCKING!
ADD "LORD"! LORD!
YES. WE ARE BOTH THE SONS OF VISCOUNTS.
A MARGRAVE CALLS US "LORD," TOO!
HUH ...?
A MAR-GRAVE'S SON?
OH.
SO, THEY HEARD WHAT WE TALKED ABOUT EARLIER.
HOLD, YOU TWO!

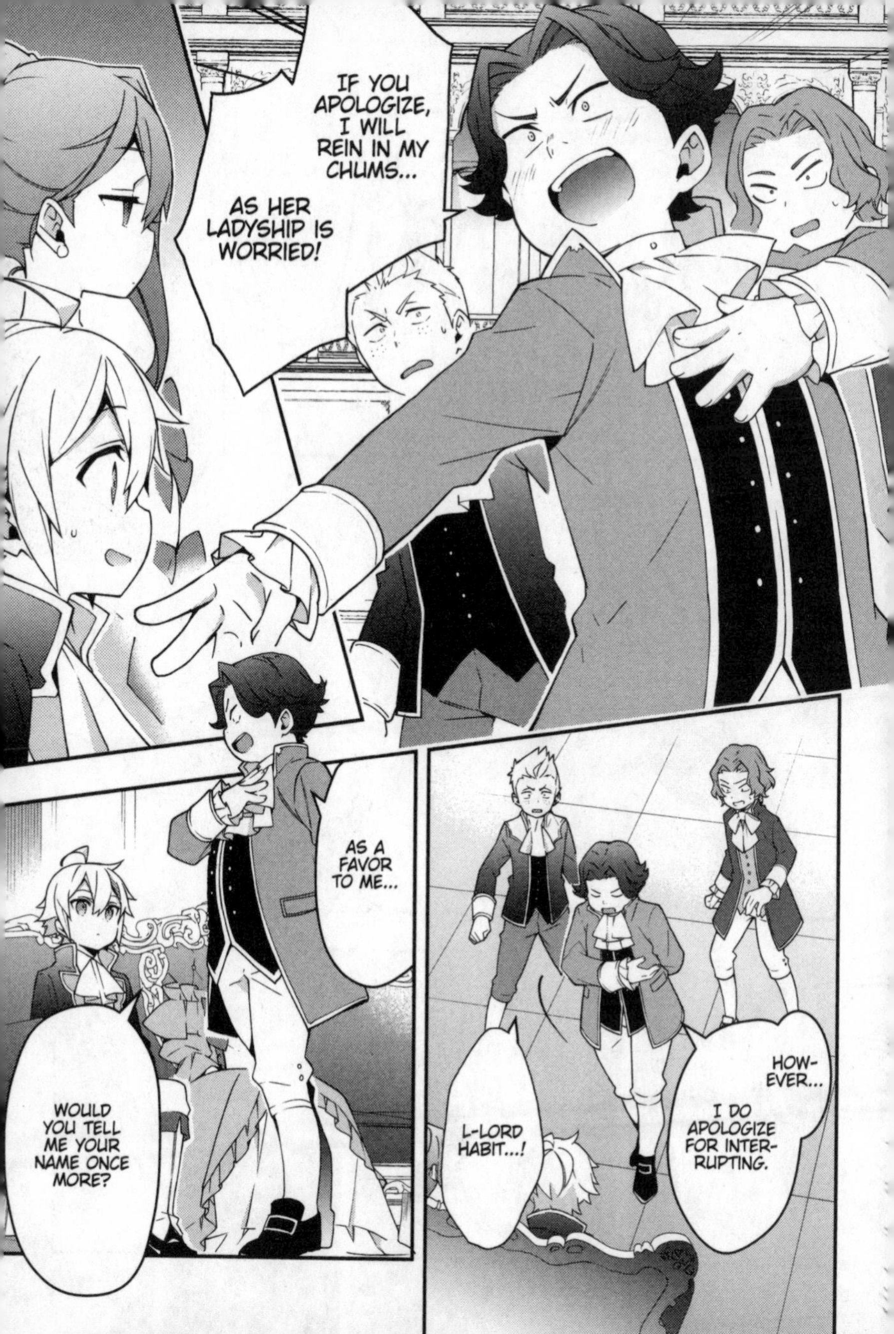
IF YOU APOLOGIZE, I WILL REIN IN MY CHUMS...
AS HER LADYSHIP IS WORRIED!
HOW-EVER... I DO APOLOGIZE FOR INTER-RUPTING.
L-LORD HABIT...!
AS A FAVOR TO ME...
WOULD YOU TELL ME YOUR NAME ONCE MORE?

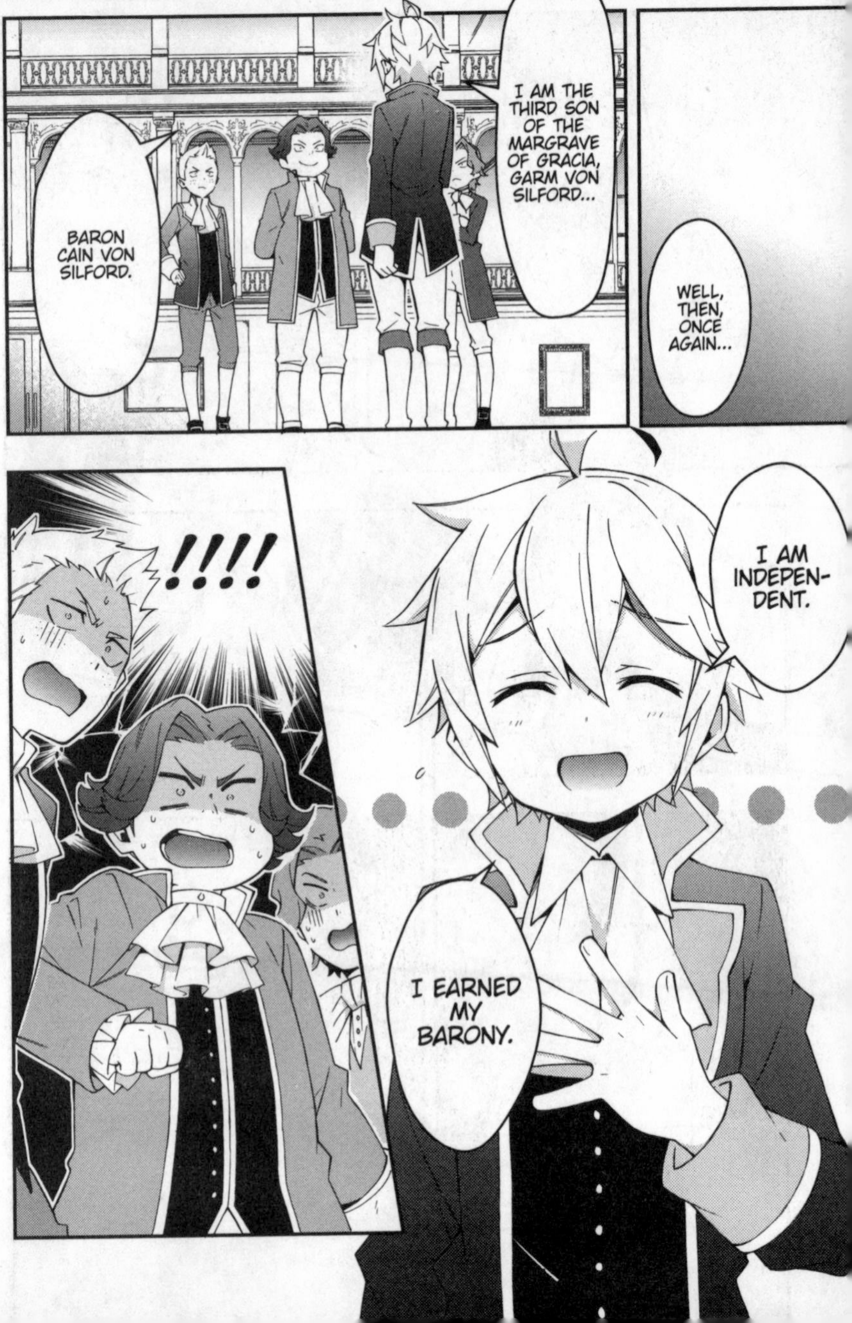
WELL, THEN, ONCE AGAIN...
I AM THE THIRD SON OF THE MARGRAVE OF GRACIA, GARM VON SILFORD...
BARON CAIN VON SILFORD.
I AM INDEPEN-DENT.
I EARNED MY BARONY.
!!!!

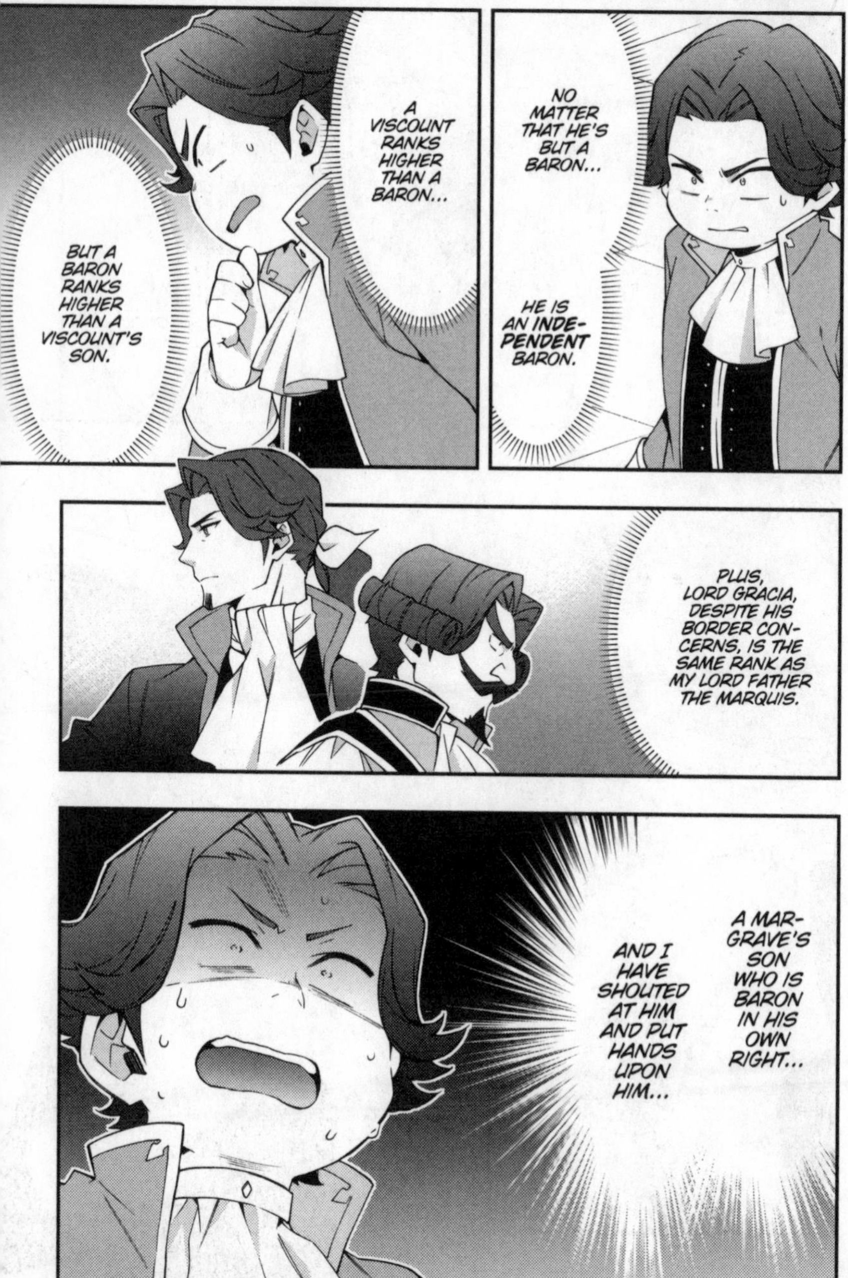
NO MATTER THAT HE'S BUT A BARON...
HE IS AN INDEPENDENT BARON.
A VISCOUNT RANKS HIGHER THAN A BARON...
BUT A BARON RANKS HIGHER THAN A VISCOUNT'S SON.
PLUS, LORD GRACIA, DESPITE HIS BORDER CONCERNS, IS THE SAME RANK AS MY LORD FATHER THE MARQUIS.
A MARGRAVE'S SON WHO IS BARON IN HIS OWN RIGHT...
AND I HAVE SHOUTED AT HIM AND PUT HANDS UPON HIM...

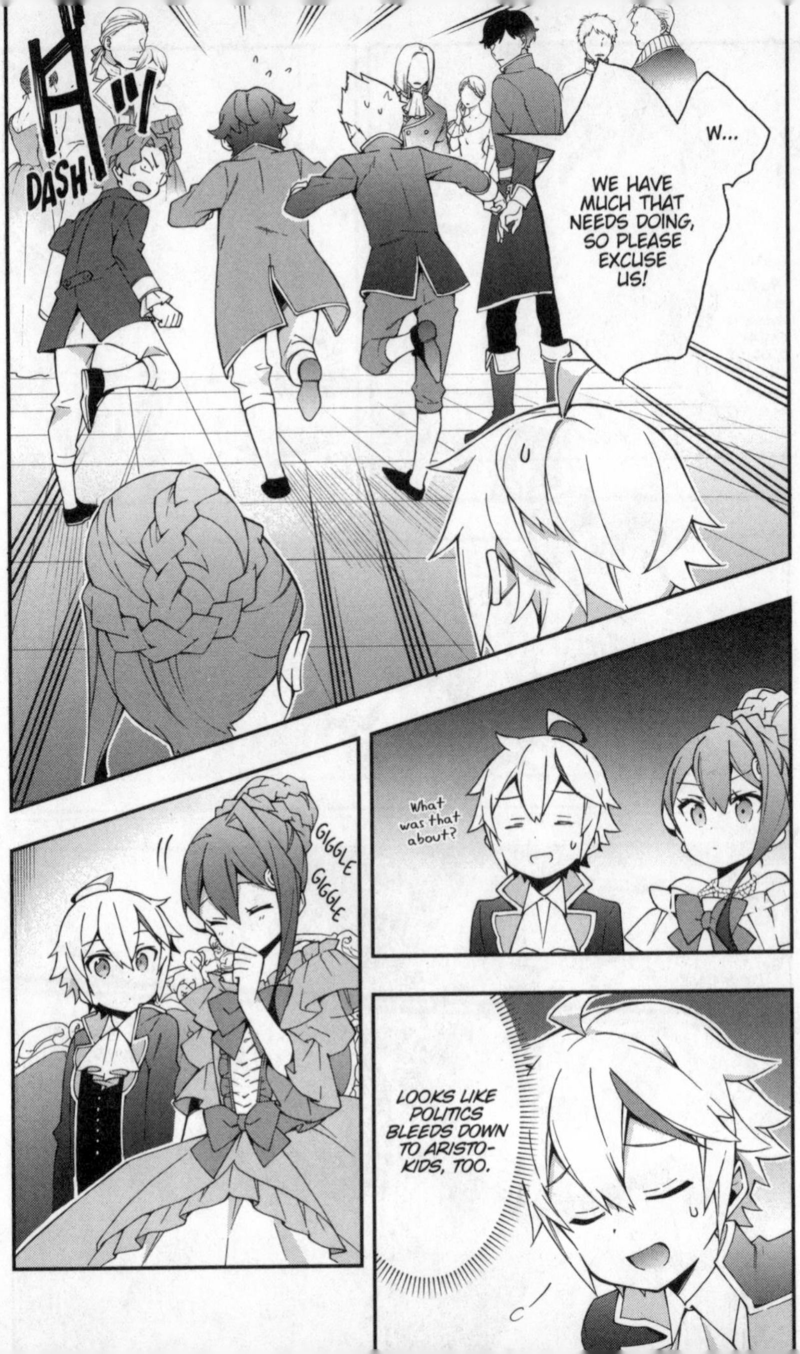
W...
WE HAVE MUCH THAT NEEDS DOING, SO PLEASE EXCUSE US!
DASH
What was that about?
GIGGLE GIGGLE
LOOKS LIKE POLITICS BLEEDS DOWN TO ARISTO-KIDS, TOO.

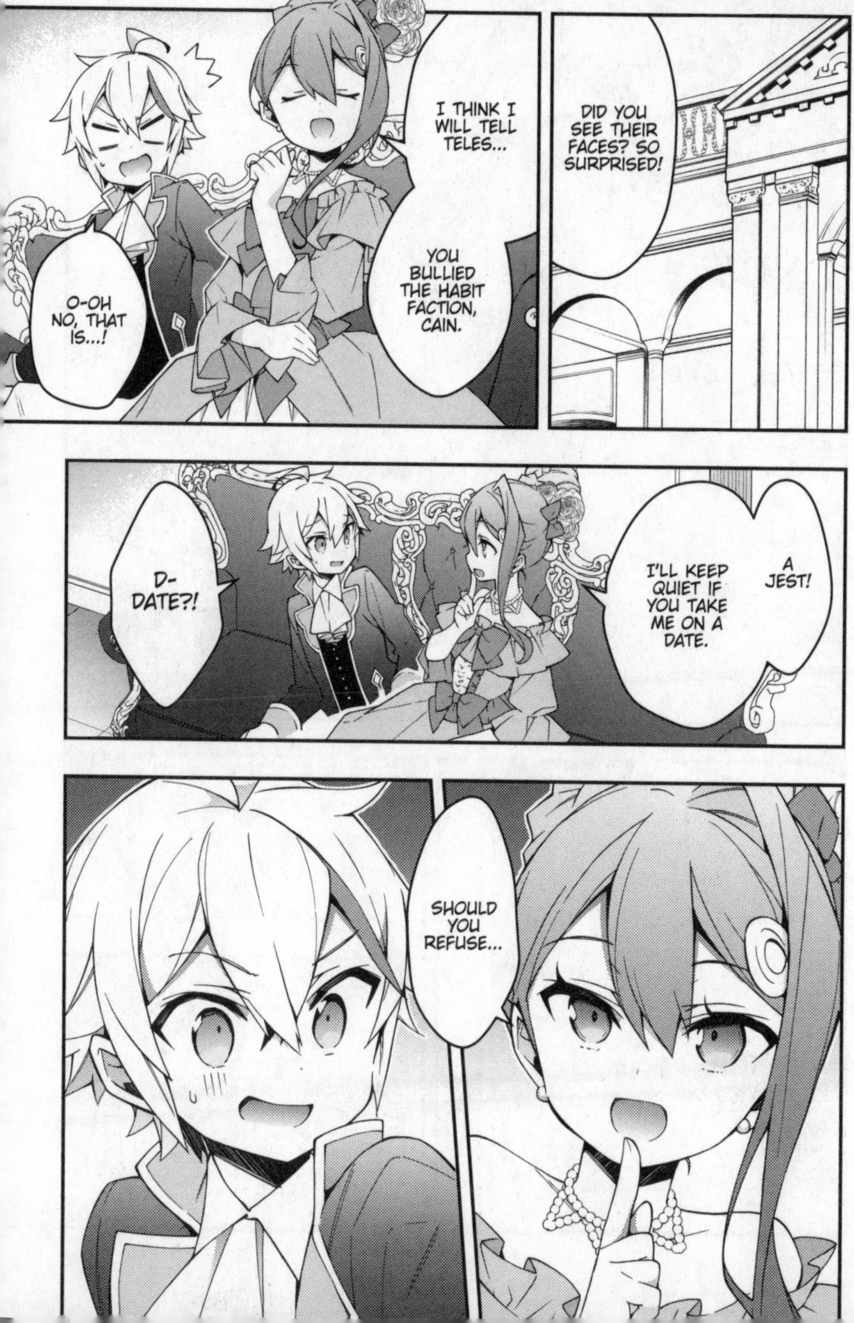
DID YOU SEE THEIR FACES? SO SURPRISED!
I THINK I WILL TELL TELES...
YOU BULLIED THE HABIT FACTION, CAIN.
O-OH NO, THAT IS...!
A JEST!
I'LL KEEP QUIET IF YOU TAKE ME ON A DATE.
D-DATE?!
SHOULD YOU REFUSE...

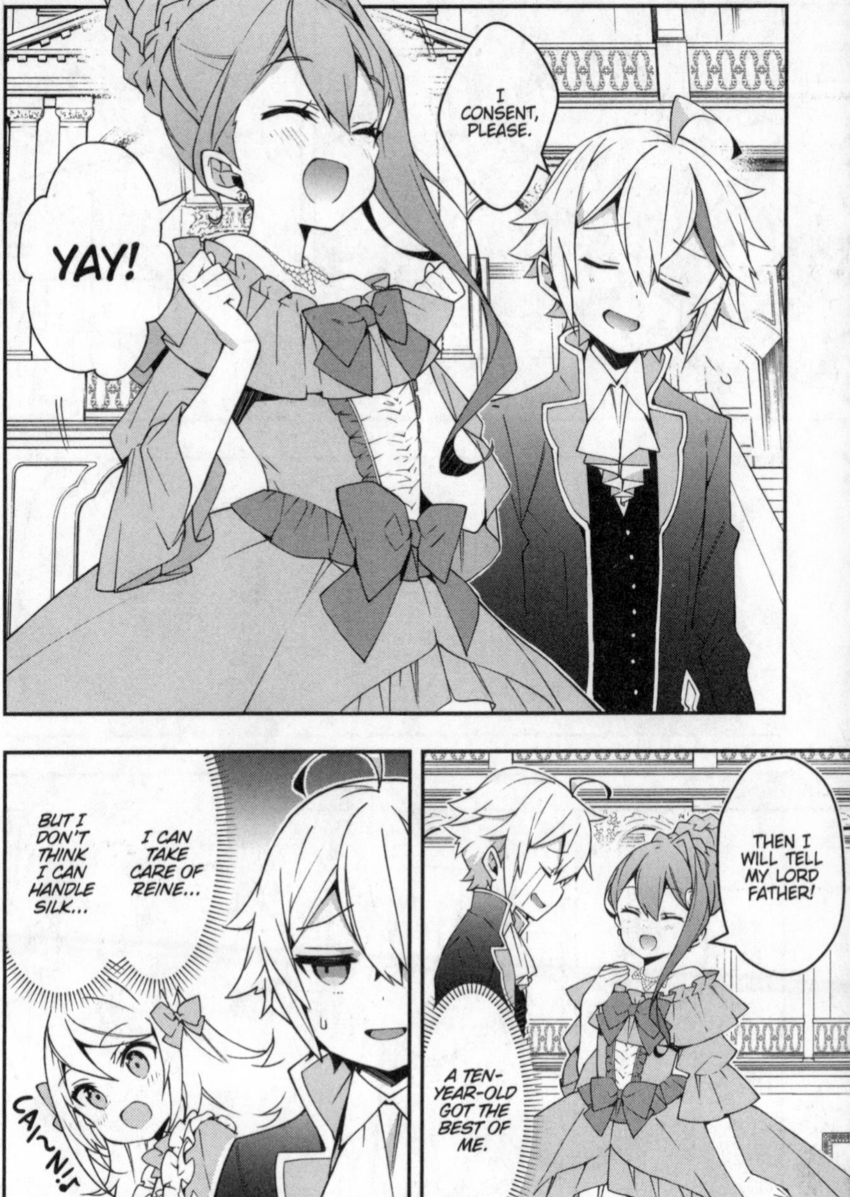
I CONSENT, PLEASE.
YAY!
THEN I WILL TELL MY LORD FATHER!
A TEN-YEAR-OLD GOT THE BEST OF ME.
I CAN TAKE CARE OF REINE...
BUT I DON'T THINK I CAN HANDLE SILK...
CAI~N!?

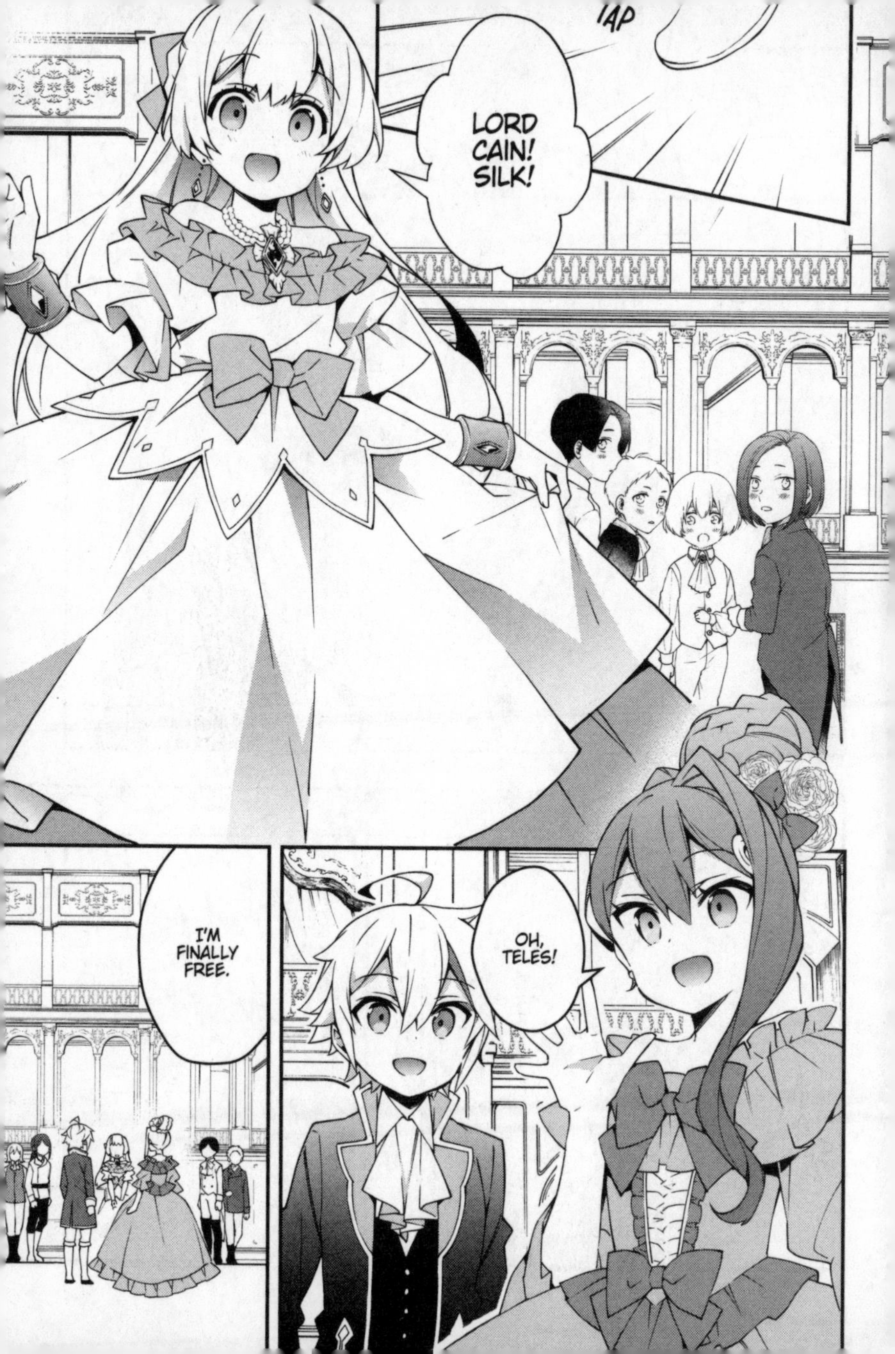
IAP
LORD CAIN! SILK!
OH, TELES!
I'M FINALLY FREE.

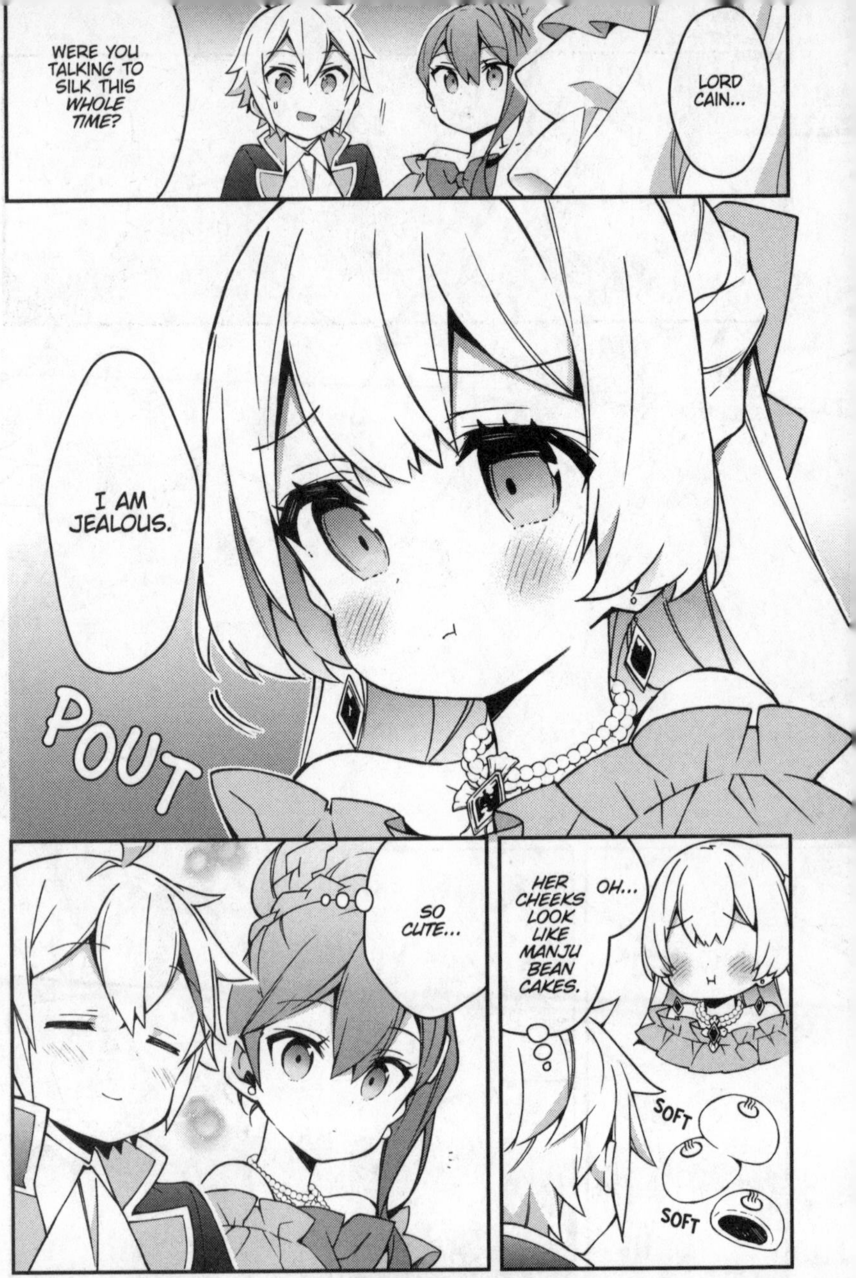
LORD CAIN...
WERE YOU TALKING TO SILK THIS *WHOLE TIME?*
I AM JEALOUS.
POUT
OH...
HER CHEEKS LOOK LIKE MANJU BEAN CAKES.
SOFT
SOFT
SO CUTE...

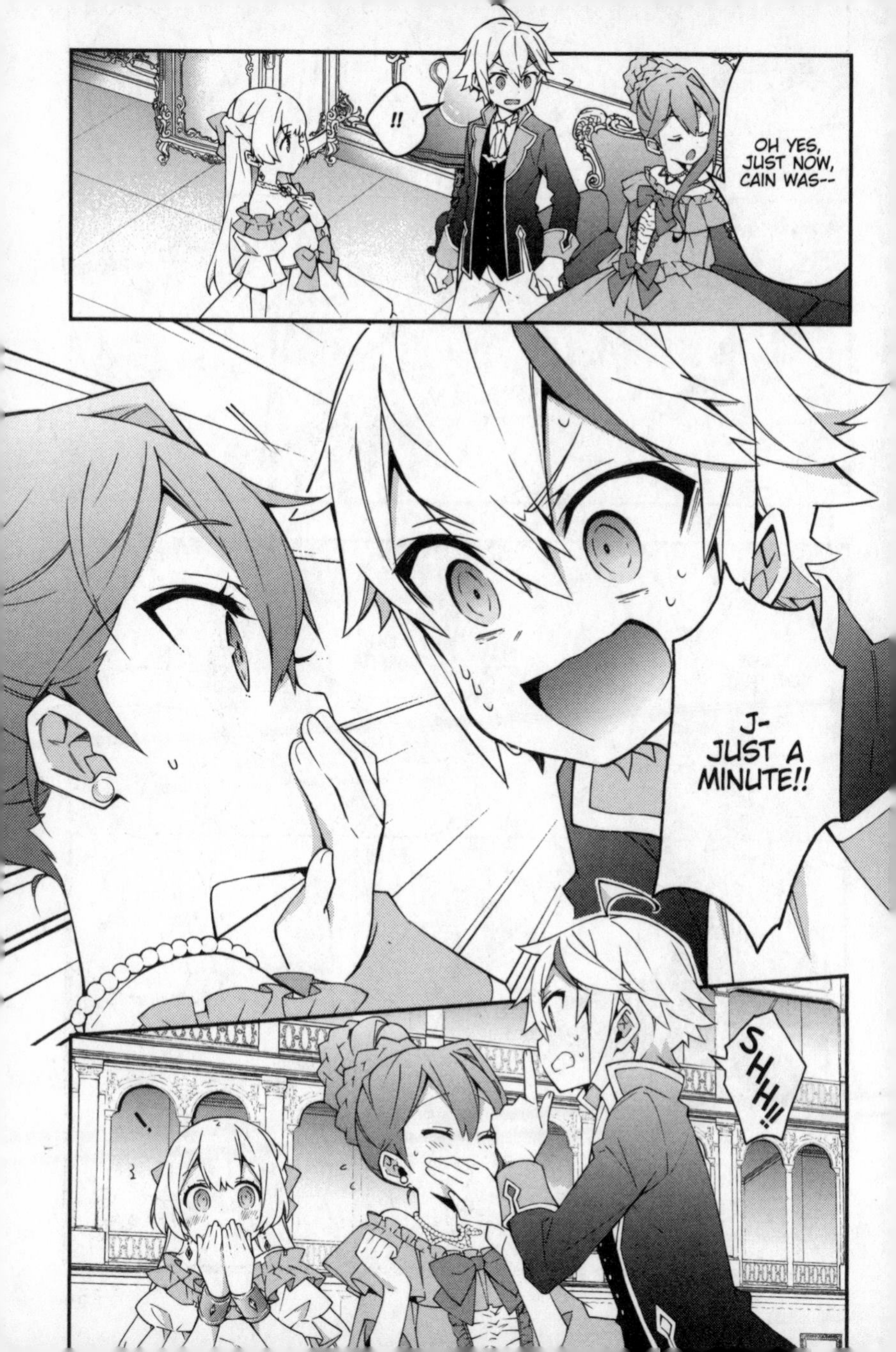
OH YES, JUST NOW, CAIN WAS--
!!
J- JUST A MINUTE!!
SHH!!
!

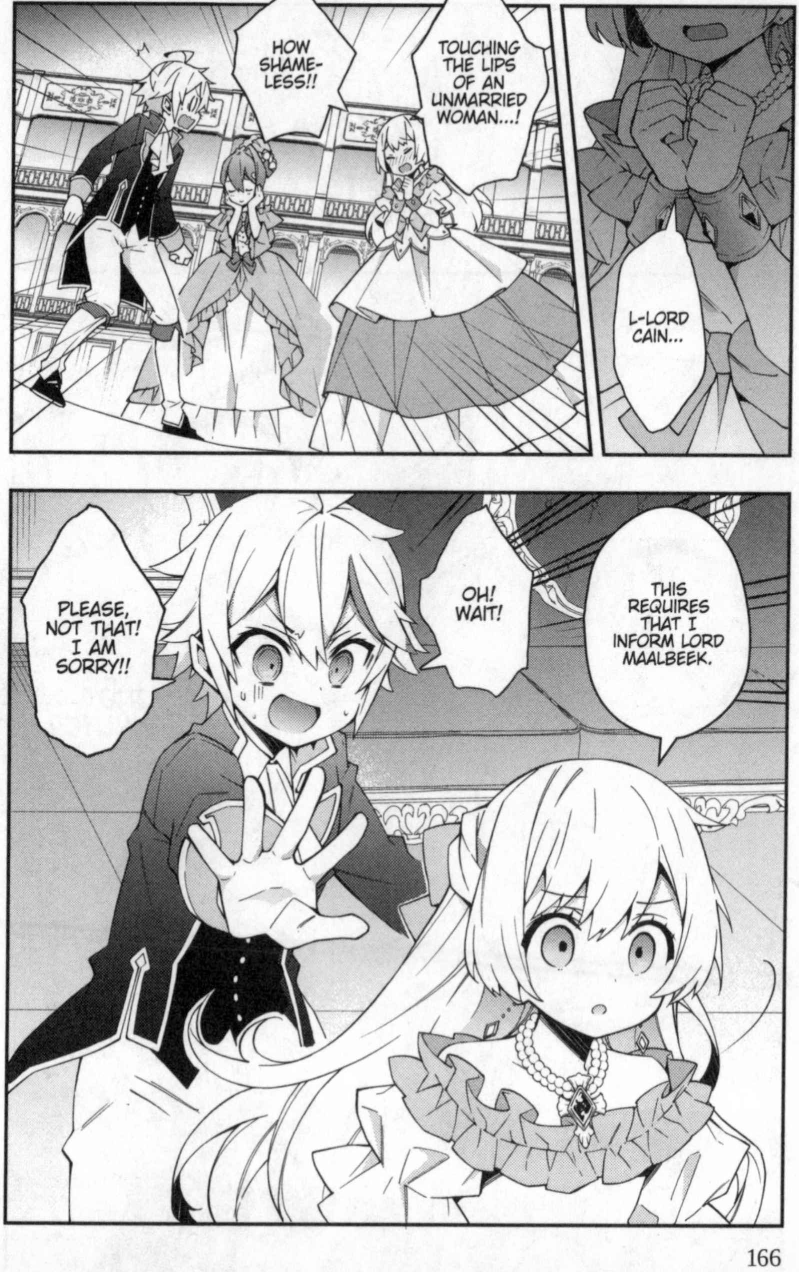
L-LORD CAIN...
TOUCHING THE LIPS OF AN UNMARRIED WOMAN...!
HOW SHAME-LESS!!
THIS REQUIRES THAT I INFORM LORD MAALBEEK.
OH! WAIT!
PLEASE, NOT THAT! I AM SORRY!!

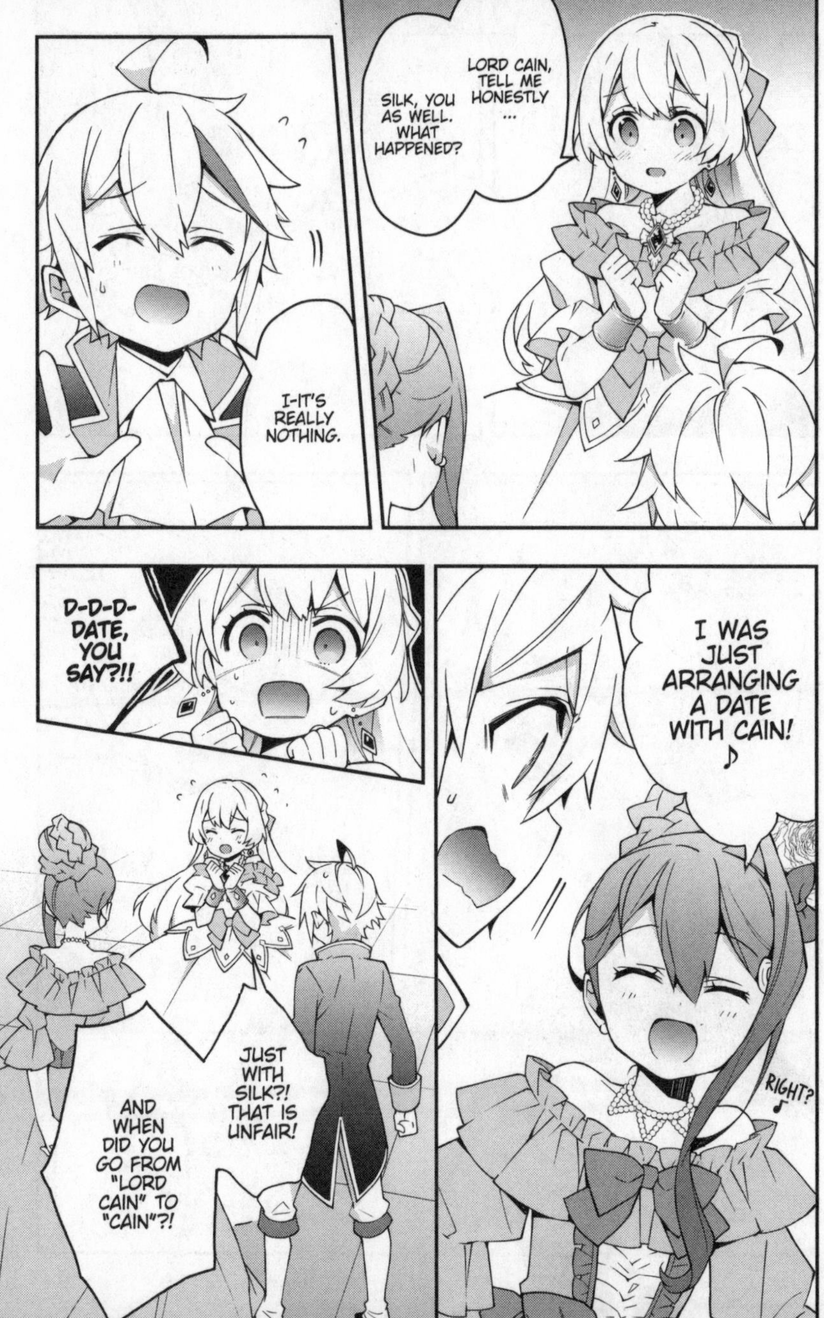
LORD CAIN, TELL ME HONESTLY ...
SILK, YOU AS WELL. WHAT HAPPENED?
I-IT'S REALLY NOTHING.
I WAS JUST ARRANGING A DATE WITH CAIN! ♪
RIGHT? ♪
D-D-D-DATE, YOU SAY?!!
JUST WITH SILK?! THAT IS UNFAIR!
AND WHEN DID YOU GO FROM "LORD CAIN" TO "CAIN"?!

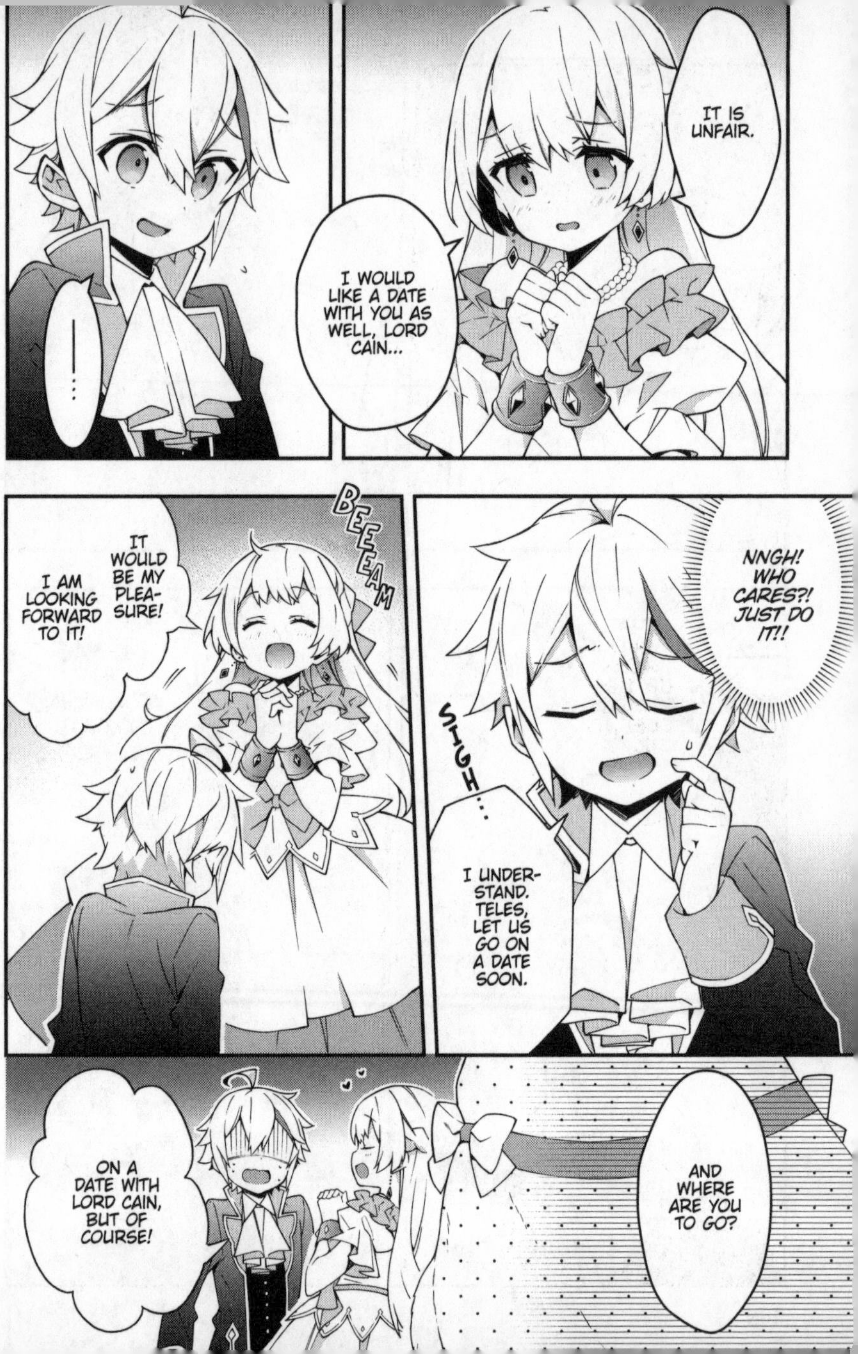
IT IS UNFAIR.
I WOULD LIKE A DATE WITH YOU AS WELL, LORD CAIN...
—......
NNGH! WHO CARES?! JUST DO IT!!
SIGH...
I UNDERSTAND. TELES, LET US GO ON A DATE SOON.
BEEEAM
IT WOULD BE MY PLEASURE!
I AM LOOKING FORWARD TO IT!
AND WHERE ARE YOU TO GO?
ON A DATE WITH LORD CAIN, BUT OF COURSE!

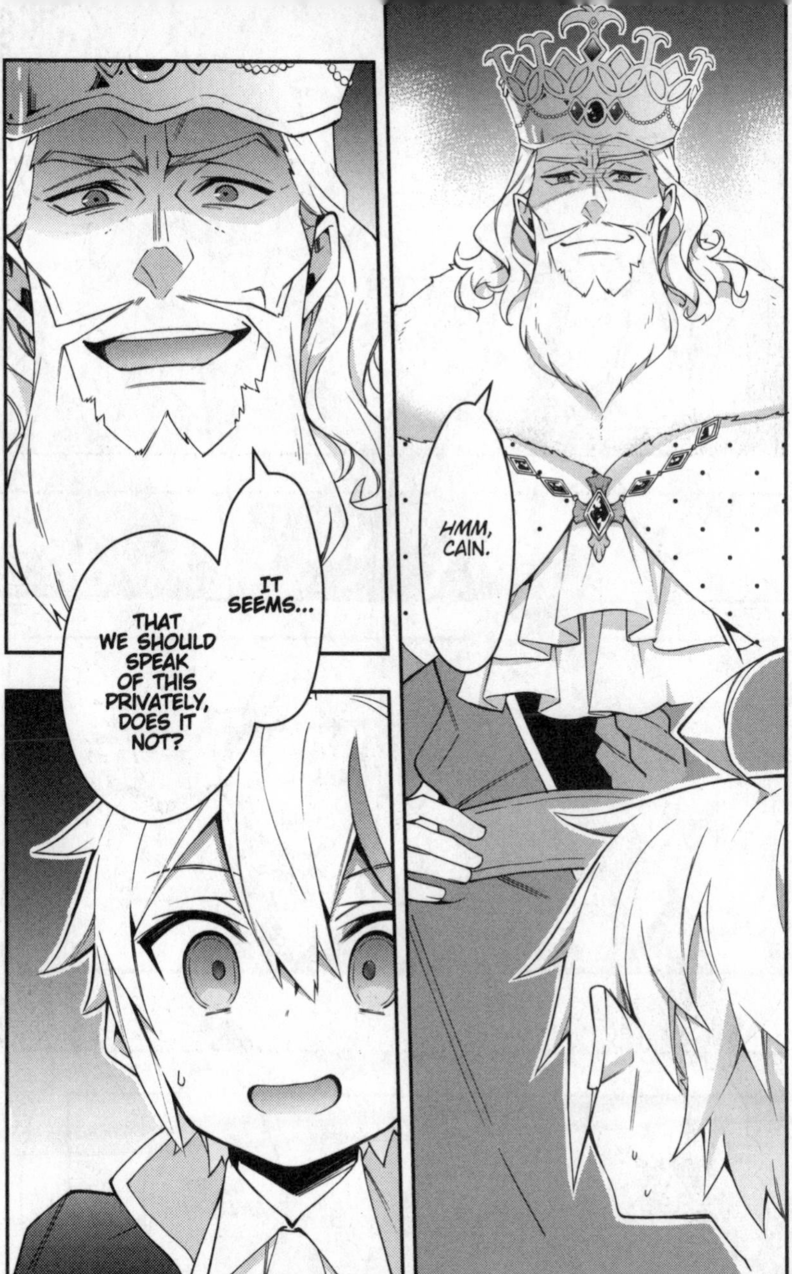
HMM, CAIN.
IT SEEMS...
THAT WE SHOULD SPEAK OF THIS PRIVATELY, DOES IT NOT?

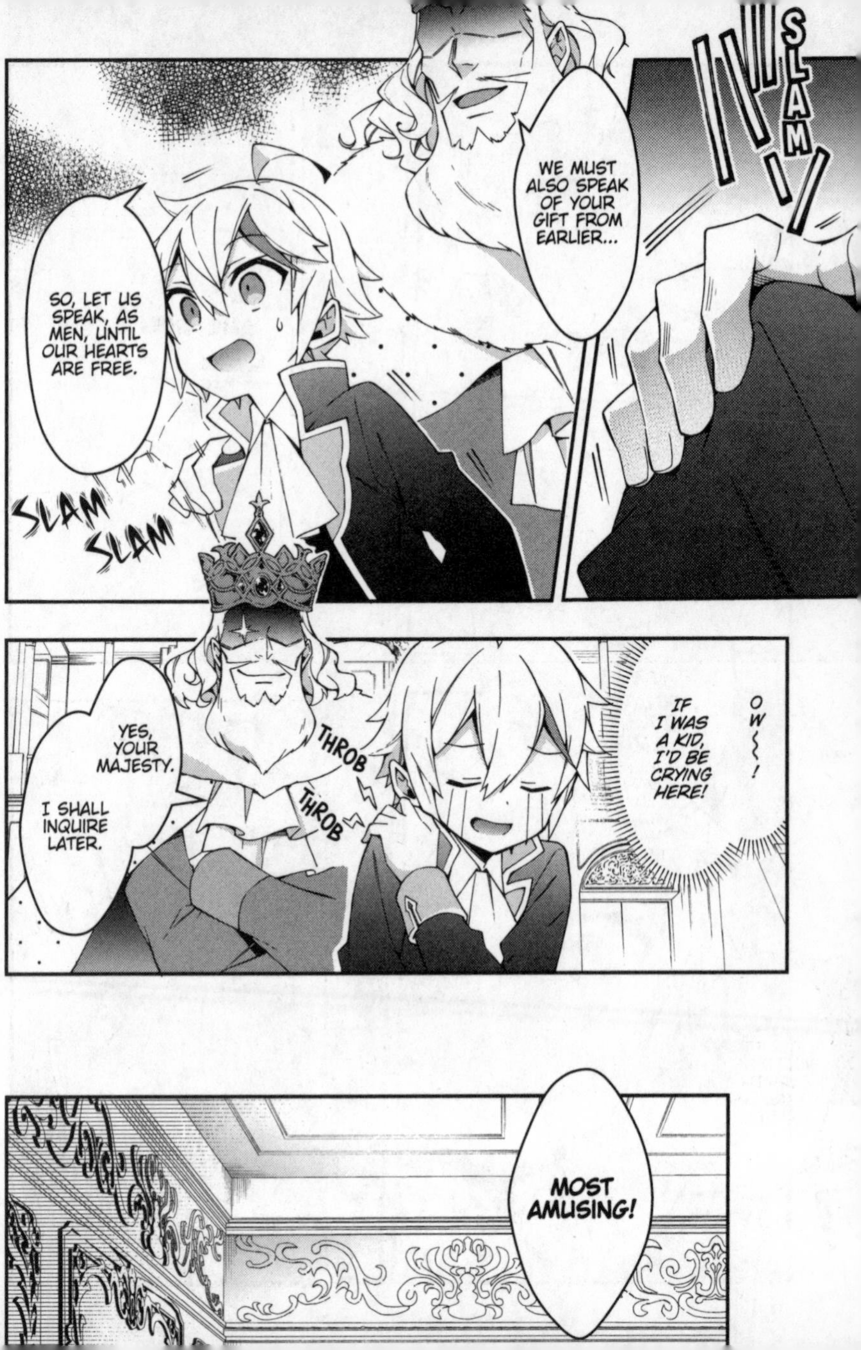
SLAM
WE MUST ALSO SPEAK OF YOUR GIFT FROM EARLIER...
SO, LET US SPEAK, AS MEN, UNTIL OUR HEARTS ARE FREE.
SLAM SLAM
OW~!
IF I WAS A KID, I'D BE CRYING HERE!
THROB THROB
YES, YOUR MAJESTY.
I SHALL INQUIRE LATER.
MOST AMUSING!

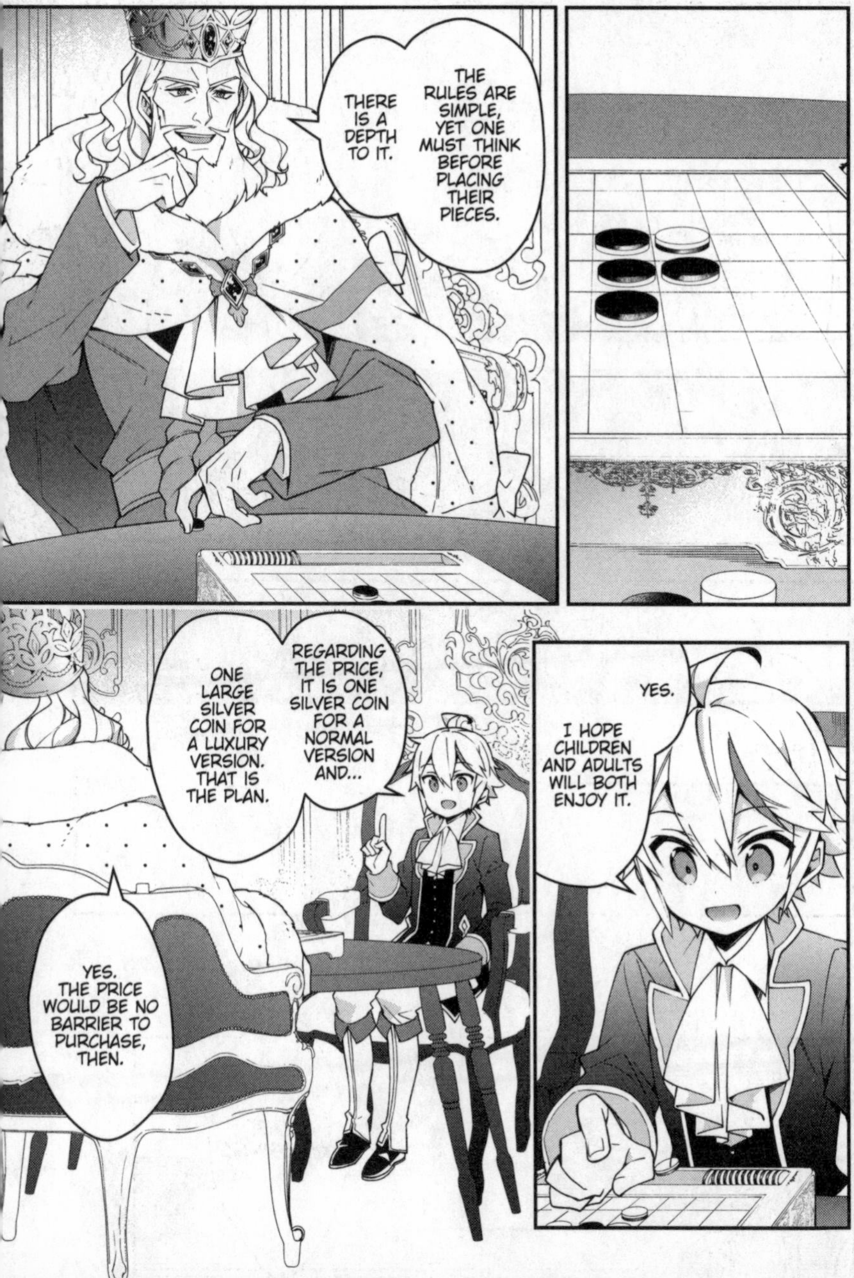
THE RULES ARE SIMPLE, YET ONE MUST THINK BEFORE PLACING THEIR PIECES.
THERE IS A DEPTH TO IT.
YES.
I HOPE CHILDREN AND ADULTS WILL BOTH ENJOY IT.
REGARDING THE PRICE, IT IS ONE SILVER COIN FOR A NORMAL VERSION AND...
ONE LARGE SILVER COIN FOR A LUXURY VERSION. THAT IS THE PLAN.
YES. THE PRICE WOULD BE NO BARRIER TO PURCHASE, THEN.

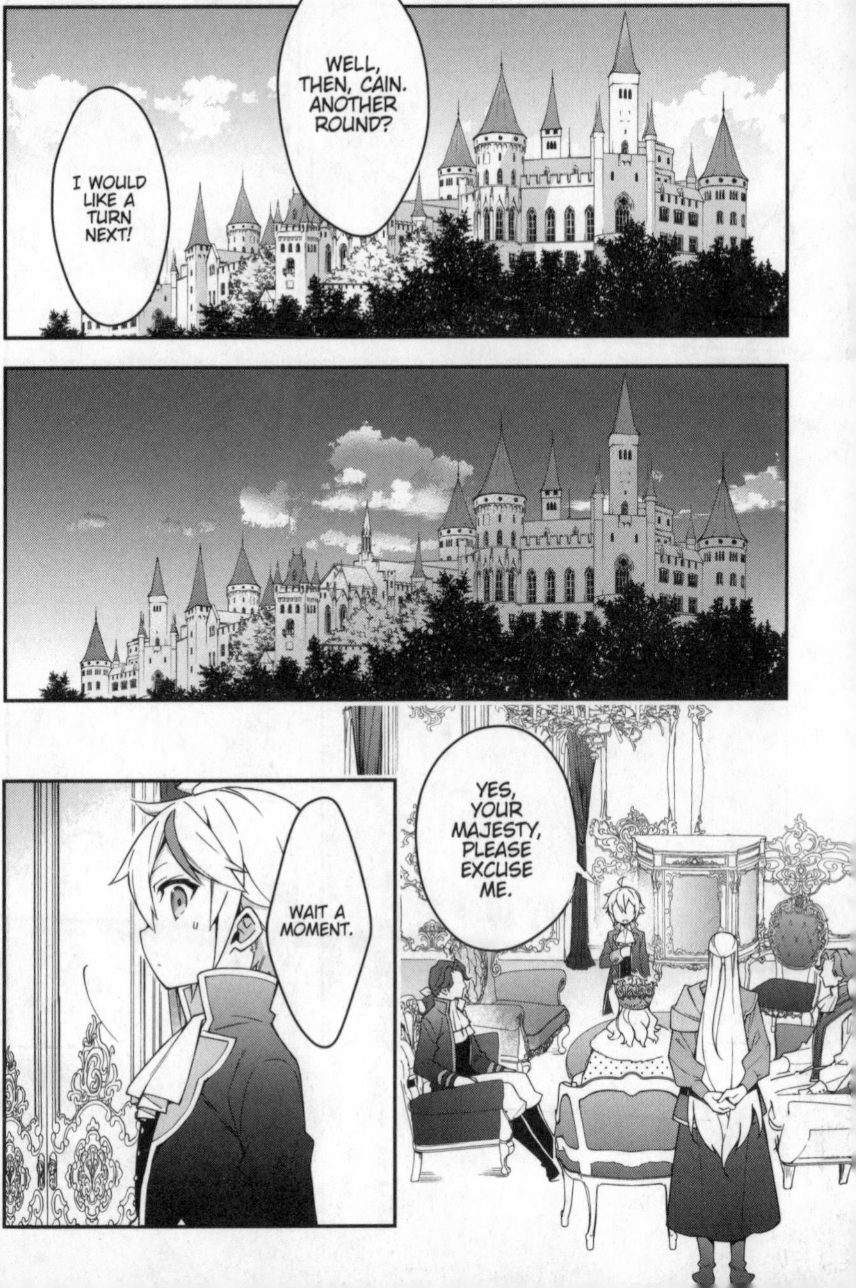
WELL, THEN, CAIN. ANOTHER ROUND?
I WOULD LIKE A TURN NEXT!
YES, YOUR MAJESTY, PLEASE EXCUSE ME.
WAIT A MOMENT.

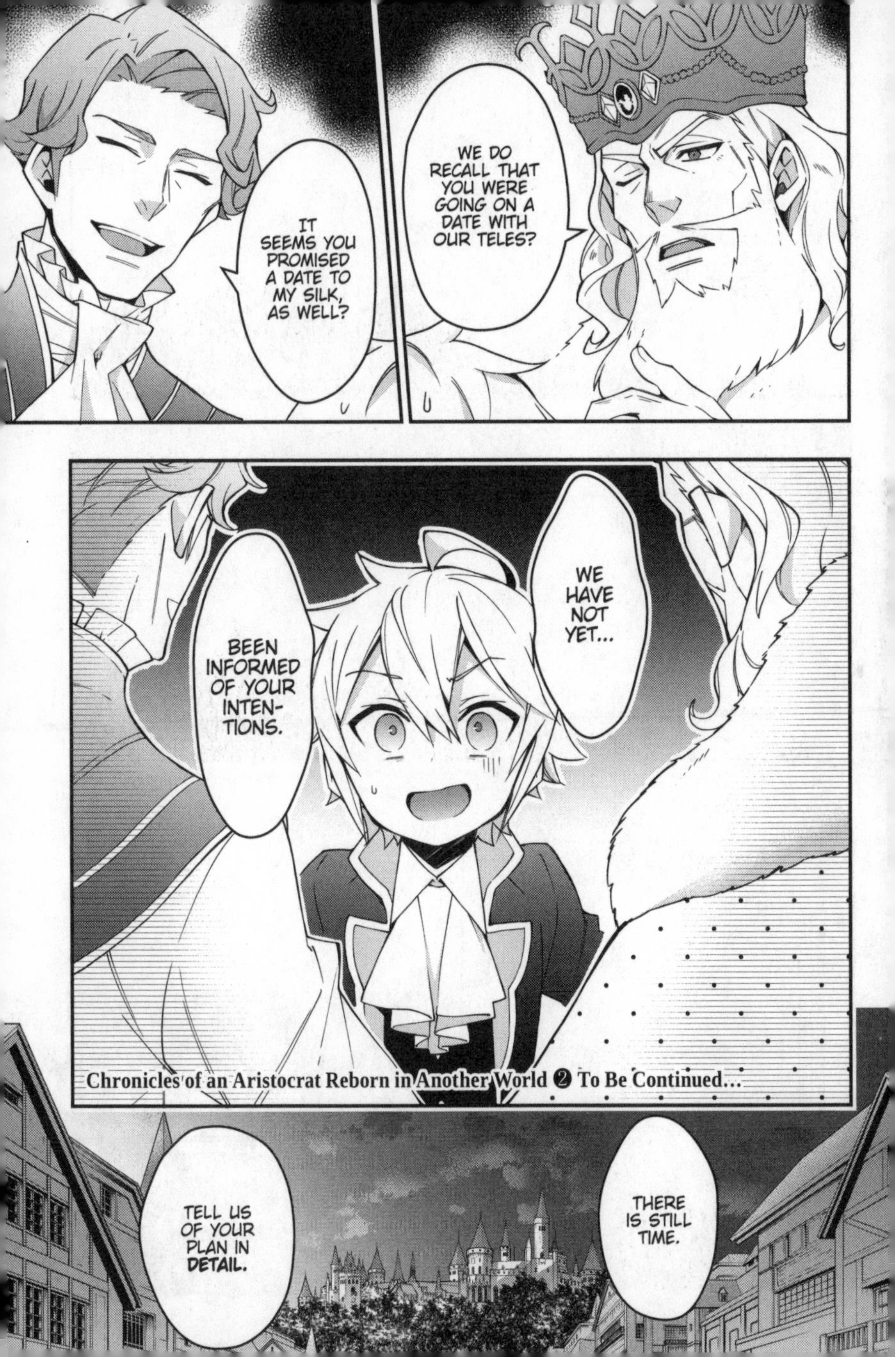
WE DO RECALL THAT YOU WERE GOING ON A DATE WITH OUR TELES?
IT SEEMS YOU PROMISED A DATE TO MY SILK, AS WELL?
WE HAVE NOT YET...
BEEN INFORMED OF YOUR INTENTIONS.
Chronicles of an Aristocrat Reborn in Another World ❷ To Be Continued...
THERE IS STILL TIME.
TELL US OF YOUR PLAN IN DETAIL.

CHRONICLES OF AN ARISTOCRAT REBORN IN ANOTHER WORLD

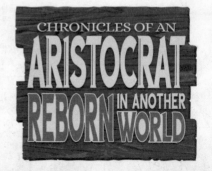

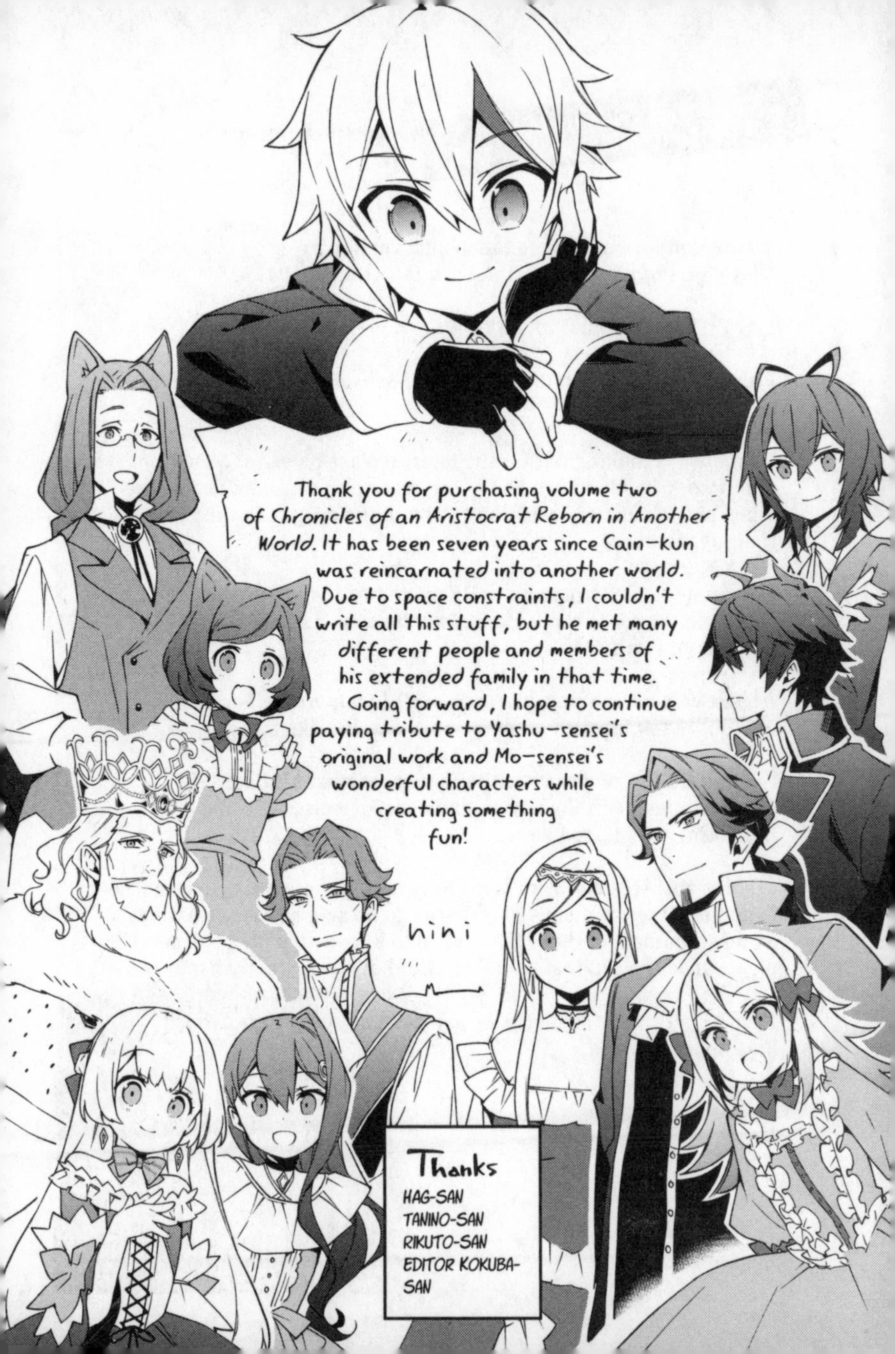
Thank you for purchasing volume two of Chronicles of an Aristocrat Reborn in Another World. It has been seven years since Cain-kun was reincarnated into another world. Due to space constraints, I couldn't write all this stuff, but he met many different people and members of his extended family in that time.
Going forward, I hope to continue paying tribute to Yashu-sensei's original work and Mo-sensei's wonderful characters while creating something fun!
nini
Thanks
HAG-SAN
TANINO-SAN
RIKUTO-SAN
EDITOR KOKUBA-SAN

Comments from the Author of the Original Story: Yashu

Thank you for purchasing the manga version of *Chronicles of an Aristocrat Reborn into Another World.*

I'm Yashu, the author of the original novels.

I also look forward to the manga nini-sensei creates every month, as a fan.

I am always looking out for the latest release dates for *MAGComi* and *Niko Niko Manga* and have fun rereading different parts, like when new characters who don't exist in the original works make their appearance.

In volume two, Garm and family moved from the Territory of Gracia to the royal capital, and Cain became a baron and head of his own family.

Also, two new heroines just appeared! I want to see Parma grown up, too. I look forward to more fun scenarios like these.

I would like to cooperate with the manga artist nini-sensei, character designer Mo-sensei, and everyone else involved in making this a good work.

Finally, this will end with some advertising, but volume five of the original novel from Saga Forest will go on sale at the same time as this volume. For those who "have to know what happens next!" please read the original novel. It would make me really happy.

Please continue to support *Chronicles of an Aristocrat Reborn into Another World.*

Comments from the Character Designer, Mo-Sensei

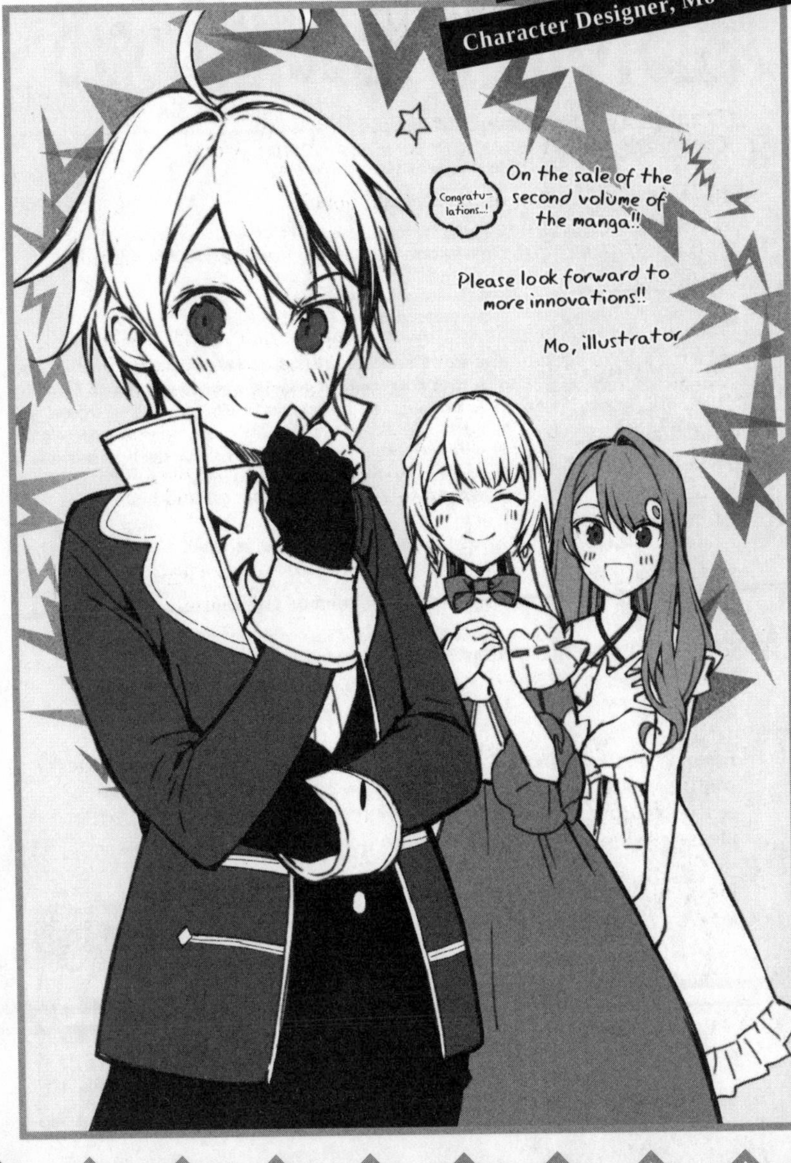
Congratu-lations...!
On the sale of the second volume of the manga!!
Please look forward to more innovations!!
Mo, illustrator

SEVEN SEAS ENTERTAINMENT PRESENTS

CHRONICLES OF AN
ARISTOCRAT REBORN IN ANOTHER WORLD

story: Yashu   art: nini   character design: Mo   Vol. 2

TRANSLATION
Beni Axia Conrad

LETTERING
Phil Christie

COVER DESIGN
Hanase Qi

LOGO DESIGN
George Panella

PROOFREADER
Rebecca Schneidereit

COPY EDITOR
Dawn Davis

EDITOR
Nick Mamatas

PREPRESS TECHNICIAN
Rhiannon Rasmussen-Silverstein

PRODUCTION ASSOCIATE
Christa Miesner

PRODUCTION MANAGER
Lissa Pattillo

MANAGING EDITOR
Julie Davis

ASSOCIATE PUBLISHER
Adam Arnold

PUBLISHER
Jason DeAngelis

Tenseikizoku no Isekaiboukenroku Vol. 2
©nini 2019
©Yashu 2019／HIFUMI SHOBO
Originally published in Japan in 2019 by MAG Garden Corporation, TOKYO.
English translation rights arranged through TOHAN CORPORATION, Tokyo.

Yashu Tenseikizoku no Isekaiboukenroku
Original Japanese edition published by HIFUMISHOBO Co., LTD.

Seven Seas press and purchase enquiries can be sent to Marketing Manager Lianne Sentar at press@gomanga.com. Information regarding the distribution and purchase of digital editions is available from Digital Manager CK Russell at digital@gomanga.com.

Seven Seas and the Seven Seas logo are trademarks of Seven Seas Entertainment. All rights reserved.

ISBN: 978-1-64827-562-3
Printed in Canada
First Printing: November 2021
10 9 8 7 6 5 4 3 2 1

////// READING DIRECTIONS //////

This book reads from *right to left*, Japanese style. If this is your first time reading manga, you start reading from the top right panel on each page and take it from there. If you get lost, just follow the numbered diagram here. It may seem backwards at first, but you'll get the hang of it! Have fun!!

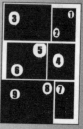

Follow us online: www.SevenSeasEntertainment.com